FARMERS AND WEAVERS

ARCHAEOLOGICAL INVESTIGATIONS AT KINGSWAY BUSINESS PARK AND CUTACRE COUNTRY PARK, GREATER MANCHESTER

Richard A Gregory, Peter Arrowsmith, Ian Miller, and Michael Nevell

With Contributions by
Jeremy Bradley, Caroline Bulcock, Chris Cumberpatch, Denise Druce, Chris Healey, Christine Howard-Davis, Andy Phelps, Rebekah Pressler, Mairead Rutherford, Chris Wild, and Tim Young

Illustrations by
Adam Parsons and Marie Rowland

2021

LANCASTER IMPRINTS

Published by
Oxford Archaeology North
Mill 3
Moor Lane Mills
Moor Lane
Lancaster
LA1 1QD
(*Phone:* 01524 541000)
(*website:* www.oxfordarchaeology.com)

Distributed by
Oxbow Books Ltd
10 Hythe Bridge Street
Oxford
OX1 2EW
(*Phone:* 01865 241249; *Fax:* 01865 794449)

Printed by
Print2Demand, 17 Burgess Road, Hastings, East Sussex, TN35 4NR

The appendices are available on the Oxford Archaeology (OA) Library at:
https://library.oxfordarchaeology.com/5834/

ISBN 978-1-907686-36-8
ISSN 345-5205

Series editor
Rachel Newman
Indexer
Marie Rowland
Design, layout, and formatting
Adam Parsons

Front cover: *top, excavating the farmhouse at Ashes (Cutacre); bottom, recording the archaeological remains at Near Moor (Kingsway)*

Rear Cover: *top left, Wharton Hall following excavation (Cutacre); middle left, the excavated cellars at Higher Moss Side Farm (Kingsway); bottom left, recording a seventeenth-century cellar at Ashes; right, the weaver's cottage at Castle Farm (Kingsway)*

L ANCASTER
 IMPRINTS   Lancaster Imprints is the publication series of Oxford Archaeology North. The series covers work on major excavations and surveys of all periods undertaken by the organisation and associated bodies.

Contents

List of Illustrations

Figures

Plates

Tables

Contributors

Peter Arrowsmith
Marple, Stockport

Jeremy Bradley
formerly Oxford Archaeology North

Caroline Bulcock
formerly Oxford Archaeology North

Chris Cumberpatch
22 Tennyson Road, Sheffield S6 2WE

Denise Druce
Oxford Archaeology North, Mill 3, Moor Lane Mills, Moor Lane, Lancaster LA1 1QD

Richard A Gregory
Oxford Archaeology North, Mill 3, Moor Lane Mills, Moor Lane, Lancaster LA1 1QD

Chris Healey
formerly Oxford Archaeology North

Chris Howard-Davis
formerly Oxford Archaeology North

Ian Miller
Centre for Applied Archaeology, University of Salford, School of Environment and Life Sciences, Peel Building, Salford M5 4WT

Michael Nevell
Industrial Heritage Support Officer for England, Ironbridge Gorge Museum Trust, Coalbrookdale, Telford, Shropshire TF8 7DQ

Andy Phelps
Oxford Archaeology North, Mill 3, Moor Lane Mills, Moor Lane, Lancaster LA1 1QD

Rebekah Pressler
formerly Oxford Archaeology North

Mairead Rutherford
Oxford Archaeology North, Mill 3, Moor Lane Mills, Moor Lane, Lancaster LA1 1QD

Chris Wild
Centre for Applied Archaeology, University of Salford, School of Environment and Life Sciences, Peel Building, Salford M5 4WT

Tim Young
Unit 6, Western Industrial Estate, Caerphilly, Wales CF83 1BQ

Abbreviations

aOD	Above Ordnance Datum
AMS	Accelerator mass spectrometry
BA	Bolton Archives
CfAA	Centre for Applied Archaeology
CL	Chetham's Library
CNDR	Carlisle Northern Development Route
CPR	Charred plant remains
GMAU	Greater Manchester Archaeological Unit
GMAAS	Greater Manchester Archaeological Advisory Service
HER	Historic Environment Record
LA	Lancashire Archives
L&YR	Lancashire and Yorkshire Railway
MA	Manchester Archives
NHLE	National Heritage List for England
NML: MAL	National Museums Liverpool: Maritime Archives and Library
NRO	Northamptonshire Record Office
OA	Oxford Archaeology
OS	Ordnance Survey
RCHME	Royal Commission on the Historical Monuments of England
RLSL	Rochdale Local Studies Library
SCA	Salford City Archives
SEM	Scanning electron microscope
SUERC	Scottish Universities Environmental Research Centre
UMAU	University of Manchester Archaeological Unit
WSI	Written Scheme of Investigation

Foreword

The redevelopment sites at Cutacre and Kingsway gave archaeologists a rare opportunity to investigate and record two large-scale post-medieval farming landscapes in the northern half of Greater Manchester. At Cutacre, south of Bolton, extensive historical open-cast coal mining had denuded much of the site of archaeological potential, whilst also leaving a massive and unsightly spoil heap. Yet, remarkably, archaeologists found significant remains from several periods including some dating to the prehistoric and medieval eras. Of particular note was the discovery of Greater Manchester's first example of a Middle Bronze Age roundhouse; medieval iron smelting, together with a seventeenth-century hall and farm site, were also of great importance.

Kingsway, near Rochdale, differed in that the landscape had remained pretty much intact, with a mixture of extant farm complexes as well as sites of demolished buildings. Building surveys and excavations combined to allow archaeologists to chart this farming landscape's evolution over the last 400 years. This saw the emergence of a prosperous farming and weaving community in the seventeenth century that continued to develop across the eighteenth and earlier part of the nineteenth centuries, before entering into a period of decline. It is also worth noting that the Kingsway Business Park saw one of the most extensive archaeological surveys in Greater Manchester of post-medieval/industrial-period rural buildings.

Oxford Archaeology, supported by a range of specialists and consultants, has done an amazing job of maximising archaeological information from sometimes unpromising physical remains. One of the most rewarding aspects of the archaeological investigations has been the successful appliance of a variety of modern scientific techniques to maximise understanding of the excavated evidence. The work has been secured through the planning system via archaeological conditions attached to planning consent, and the developers are to be thanked for funding this wide-ranging suite of archaeological works. Dissemination of the impressive results of these two major landscape studies is a crucial element for advancing research and providing public benefit. The Greater Manchester Archaeological Advisory Service is pleased to note that this academic monograph is part of suite of dissemination measures that also include heritage information boards and two popular publications.

Norman Redhead

Heritage Management Director,
Greater Manchester Archaeological Advisory Service

Summary

During the first years of the twenty-first century, two areas in Greater Manchester were subjected to extensive schemes of redevelopment, which provided an important opportunity to investigate the archaeology in two distinctive landscapes. One of these now forms the site of the Kingsway Business Park (centred on SD 918 120), some 3 km to the south-east of Rochdale, whilst the other is at the Cutacre Country Park (centred on SD 698 040), approximately 4.75 km to the south-west of Bolton. Historically, both landscapes were within Lancashire and, significantly, they allow the historical trajectories of the region's rural landscapes to be examined in some depth.

Within each of these landscapes, a combination of non-intrusive and intrusive archaeological techniques was employed to explore the archaeology. These techniques included desk-based assessment, geophysical, topographical, and standing-building survey, trial trenching, and open-area excavation. Importantly, in a number of instances, archaeological excavation followed on from standing-building survey, and this integrated approach allowed for a more nuanced understanding of the history and development of the respective site. In addition, palaeoenvironmental coring was undertaken in both areas as a means of examining the form and character of the early environment.

The work was undertaken by Oxford Archaeology North and the former University of Manchester Archaeological Unit, and at the Kingsway Business Park it resulted in the detailed archaeological examination, in the form of building survey and/or open-area excavation, of 12 sites, whilst five sites were subjected to open-area excavation and/or building survey at Cutacre. The majority of the sites produced good evidence for post-medieval and later rural occupation, though important evidence for prehistoric and medieval activity was also found in both landscapes.

At Kingsway, pollen analysis provided insights into the prehistoric environment, with evidence of episodes of human clearance dating to the late Mesolithic and Neolithic periods, whilst at Cutacre, more direct evidence for late Mesolithic activity was represented by a small collection of worked-stone tools. In this latter landscape, a Bronze Age settlement was also excavated at Cinder Hill, dating to the latter half of the second millennium cal BC. This comprised a post-built roundhouse, and two sequential four-post structures that may have functioned as malting houses, the first to be recorded in Greater Manchester.

At Kingsway, the evidence for medieval activity was slim, but it is possible that two early routeways may date to this period. Cutacre produced more substantive evidence for medieval activity. This included pollen signatures, suggestive of woodland clearance, cereal cultivation, and pastoral farming, dating to the early medieval period, along with evidence for the changing farming regimes that were in operation in the late medieval period. A late medieval iron bloomery was also excavated, which was associated with furnace bases, and other features associated with the production and working of iron.

Open-area excavation, building survey, and documentary research in both of the landscapes produced valuable evidence relating to the different types of post-medieval rural houses and farm buildings that existed across a wide swathe of northern Greater Manchester. The investigated buildings dated to the early seventeenth- to mid-eighteenth century, and included a gentry house at Wharton Hall, Cutacre, and a selection of smaller rural houses that were occupied by freehold yeoman farmers at Kingsway, and tenant farmers at Cutacre. These latter house types included several two-cell houses and double-pile houses, along with a three-cell house, and a T-shaped house. Several associated barns/shippons were also investigated. Some of these were detached structures, whilst others adjoined the dwellings and, in some instances, the linear layout of dwelling and barn/shippon mimicked that found in a Pennine laithe house.

Both areas also revealed important evidence for late eighteenth- and nineteenth-century activity. Whilst in many instances this entailed the modification and rebuilding of the post-medieval properties, at Kingsway evidence of several distinctive types of semi-domestic buildings was recorded, intimately linked to the production of textiles. These were weavers' cottages, and comprised both dwelling and workshop, where handloom weaving of woollen cloth was undertaken.

Acknowledgements

The archaeological investigations undertaken at the Kingsway Business Park and Cutacre Country Park owe their success to many individuals, and the close co-operation of the different companies involved in the two respective projects. With regard to work at the Kingsway Business Park, Oxford Archaeology North would like to thank Forbes Marsden and Paul Gajos, then of John Samuels Archaeological Consultants, for commissioning and supporting the various stages of archaeological fieldwork, on behalf of Wilson Bowden Developments Ltd. The archaeological evaluations were completed by Paul Gajos, David Tonks, and Pip Kok, whilst the open-area excavations were directed by Chris Healey, Paul Clark, and Jeremy Bradley, who were assisted by Emily Betts, Caroline Bulcock, Mark Chesterman, Jason Clarke, Pip Howarth, Philip Jefferson, Andy Lane, David Tonks, Caroline Raynor, and Alastair Vannan. All surveys were undertaken by Chris Wild, Chris Ridings, and Peter Schofield, and the palaeoenvironmental work was completed by Elizabeth Huckerby, Denise Druce, and Sandra Bonsall. Ian Miller was responsible for project management. The Kingsway archaeological building surveys were undertaken by Michael Nevell, Ivan Hradil, Brian Grimsditch, and Carolanne King of the former University of Manchester Archaeological Unit. This element of the project was managed by Michael Nevell, who would like to thank DLA Landscape & Urban Design for commissioning and supporting the work. The post-excavation analysis and publication of the Kingsway dataset was commissioned by CgMs, on behalf of Wilson Bowden Developments Ltd, and thanks are extended to Paul Clark, who acted as the CgMs archaeological consultant on the latter stages of the project. The post-excavation work was managed by Ian Miller, when at Oxford Archaeology North, and thanks are extended to the numerous staff from Oxford Archaeology North who completed the stratigraphic, artefactual, and palaeoenvironmental analyses and reporting.

The archaeological work at Cutacre Country Park was undertaken by Oxford Archaeology North, and thanks are offered to Brian Worsley of UK Coal Mining Ltd for commissioning the work, and Mick Rawlings, of RPS Planning and Development, who acted as UK Coal Mining Ltd's Archaeological Project Manager. The excavations were directed by Andrew Bates, Paul Clark, Vix Hughes, Sean McPhillips, and Alastair Vannan, who were assisted by Alex Beben, Ralph Brown, Caroline Bulcock, Ged Callaghan, Tim Christian, Kelly Clapperton, Steve Clarke, Liz Collinson, Pascal Eloy, Mark Gibson, Pip Howarth, Kathryn Levey, Tom Mace, Janice McLeish, Mark Oldham, Des O'Leary, Hugo Pinto, Steve Tamberello, Stuart Thomas, Toni Walford, and Lindsay Winter. Survey work was undertaken by Karl Taylor, whilst the fieldwork was managed by Emily Mercer and Fraser Brown. The building surveys at Mills Brow and Spout Fold were managed by Karl Taylor, and were completed by Andy Phelps and Chris Wild, whilst the archaeological evaluation at Hulton Heys was managed by Ian Miller, when at Oxford Archaeology North, and directed by Graham Mottershead.

Post-excavation analysis and publication of the archaeological data from the Cutacre Country Park was funded by the Harworth Group, and Oxford Archaeology North would like to express thanks to Chris Davidson for commissioning this work. This phase of the project benefited from the work of many individuals, which included numerous members of staff from Oxford Archaeology North, who undertook the analysis of the structural remains, artefacts, and plant remains. Thanks are also extended to Peter Arrowsmith, who collated and analysed the documentary evidence, and Tim Young, who undertook analysis of the industrial residues from the medieval bloomery. As part of this latter analysis, electron microscopy was undertaken on the Zeiss Sigma HD Analytical Field Emission Gun scanning electronic microscope (ASEM) in the School of Earth and Ocean Sciences, Cardiff University, and the assistance of Matthew Locke with the operation of the new microscope and subsequent data processing is gratefully acknowledged.

Some of the historical maps and images used in this volume are held by Manchester Libraries and Archives (Plates 57 and 77) and the Salford Local Library History Collection (Plates 75 and 76), and the assistance of Jane Hodkinson, Archives and Local History, Manchester Central Library, and Duncan McCormick, Salford Local History Library, is gratefully acknowledged. In addition, thanks are also extended to Alexandra Mitchell, the Peel Group Archivist, for supplying a digital version of a late eighteenth-century Bridgewater estate map (Fig 44; Pl 59), and Norman Redhead, of the Greater Manchester Archaeological Advisory Service, for supplying numerous images of the Kingsway building surveys and excavations (Plates 25-33; 41-8; 50; 82-4; 86-91; 108-15; 117-19; 122-5; 127; 128; 130-7; 139-40; 144; 145; 165; 169-71; and 174). Other images in the volume have been supplied courtesy of Bolton Archives (Pl 74), Rochdale Local Studies Library (Pl 92), the Royal Commission on the Ancient and Historical Monuments of Wales (Pl 163), and the Pitt Rivers Museum, University of Oxford (Pl 176).

More generally, the post-excavation process has been greatly assisted by Rachel Newman (Oxford Archaeology North's Senior Executive Officer: Research and Publication), who edited individual reports and also this volume. Rachel also edited the content on two information boards that have been erected at the Kingsway Business Park, outlining the archaeological remains there, along with two popular publications, in the *Greater Manchester's Past Revealed* series, respectively detailing the archaeology at Cutacre Country Park and Kingsway Business Park. These latter publications were produced by staff from Oxford Archaeology North and are available from the Greater Manchester Archaeological Advisory Service.

A debt of gratitude must be extended to Norman Redhead, first in his role as Assistant County Archaeologist for Greater Manchester, and latterly as Heritage Management Director (Archaeology), Greater Manchester Archaeological Advisory Service. Norman has overseen all of the archaeological elements connected with both of the projects, from their inception in the early 1990s through to their completion, and has provided invaluable help and support throughout all of the archaeological work.

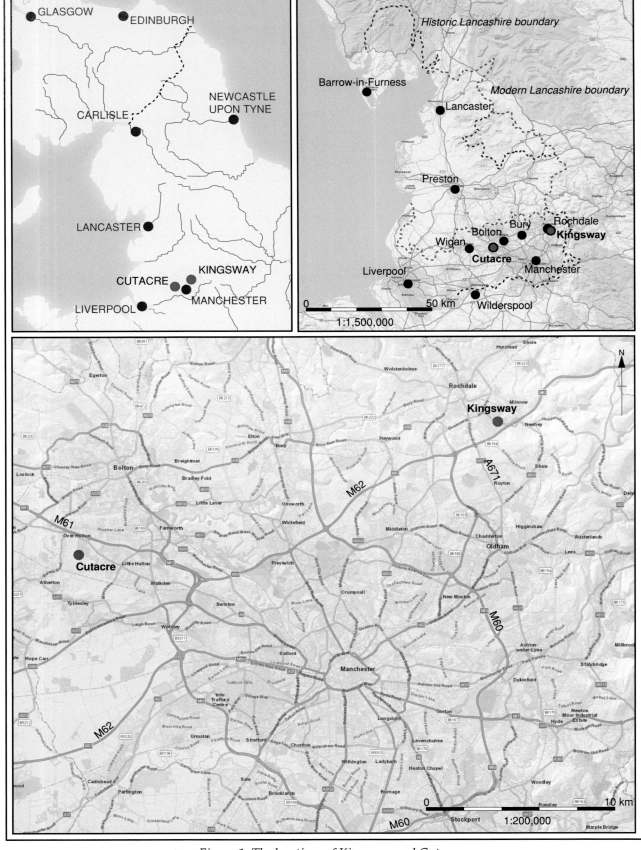

Figure 1: The locations of Kingsway and Cutacre

1

INTRODUCTION

Richard A Gregory

This volume presents the results of a series of archaeological investigations undertaken by Oxford Archaeology (OA) North and the former University of Manchester Archaeological Unit (UMAU) in two tracts of contrasting landscape in Greater Manchester (Fig 1), both of which have now been extensively redeveloped. Historically, both landscapes were within rural Lancashire, forming areas which throughout their histories were to have some input into farming and industry in the wider region; as such, they allow the historical trajectories of Greater Manchester's rural landscapes to be examined in some depth. Significantly, the archaeological investigations provide important insights into the use of these areas through prehistory to the post-medieval period, particularly with regard to settlement, farming, and rural industry.

One of the landscapes (centred on SD 918 120), now the site of the Kingsway Business Park, lies some 3 km to the south-east of Rochdale and *c* 2.5 km south-west of Milnrow; it presently forms an 170 ha mixed-use commercial site in the metropolitan borough of Rochdale, constructed by Wilson Bowden Developments Ltd. It is sandwiched between several major routes of communication (Fig 2): the M62, forming its southern boundary; the Kingsway (A664); Rochdale Canal; and the Rochdale to Oldham railway (formerly part of the Lancashire and Yorkshire Railway (L&YR)) that together bound its northern side. Its eastern edge is delimited by the built-up area of Lady House, and similarly, its western side is partly bounded by areas of modern housing, to the east of Buersill, and also by two small historic routeways. These are known as Lower Lane and Broad Lane, both of which existed by the post-medieval period.

The other landscape lies *c* 20 km to the south-west, at Cutacre (centred on SD 698 040; Fig 1), approximately 4.75 km to the south-west of Bolton. It is larger in size, covering some 314 ha, and straddles the three metropolitan boroughs of Bolton, Salford, and Wigan (Fig 3). Cutacre lies between the modern settlements of Little Hulton, in Walkden; Shakerley, in Atherton; and Over Hulton, in West Houghton, and, as with the

Kingsway Business Park (above), it is surrounded by several major communication routes. These are the A6 and M61 to its north, and the A579 to its west, whilst to the south is a section of railway between Salford and Wigan. This landscape has been redeveloped by the Harworth Group and, in a similar vein to the Kingsway Business Park, now forms a mixed-use commercial site and public open-space. However, prior to this development, the area was used as a surface mining and tip-reclamation facility, which was operated by UK Coal Mining Ltd.

Landscape Character

Of the two landscapes, topographically, that in the Kingsway Business Park is within the Manchester Pennine fringe, and thus occupies the transitional zone between the open moorlands of the Southern Pennines and the densely populated urban conurbation of Manchester (Countryside Commission 1998, 121). Prior to the construction of the business park, this area formed a tract of agricultural land, typical of other Pennine-fringe landscapes, close to the borders of Lancashire and Yorkshire. Historically, the main economic pursuits were focused on stock rearing and rough grazing, and also small-scale textile manufacture. This latter activity became fairly widespread during the late eighteenth and early nineteenth centuries, and was normally undertaken within a domestic or semi-domestic context (*cf* Timmins 1977).

This gently undulating landscape, rising from a height of *c* 145 m above Ordnance Datum (aOD) in the north-west, to *c* 175 m aOD in the south-east, was characterised by areas of post-medieval enclosure and settlement, in the form of isolated farms and hamlets, many of which were of some antiquity, and also by areas of moorland and mossland. In addition, the Stanney Brook, a small tributary of the River Roch, flows through this landscape in a north-westerly direction, parallel with the River Beal, and Buckley Hill Lane (Fig 2). This latter route

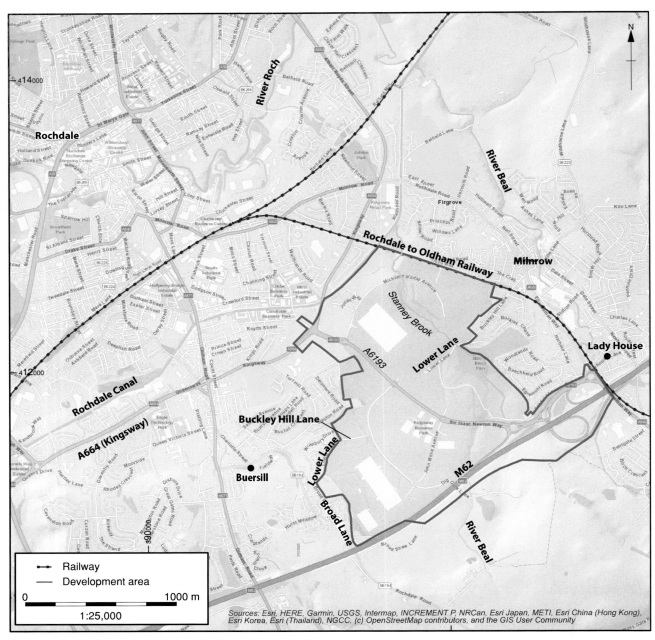

Figure 2: Kingsway Business Park and the area covered by the archaeological investigation

was present by the post-medieval period and was a continuation of Lower Lane, forming a significant route that now crosses the business park in a north-east/south-west direction. A more recently constructed road, the A6193 (Sir Isaac Newton Way), crosses the park in the opposite direction, and partly follows the route of Moor Bank Lane, another historic routeway, which was also extant by the post-medieval period.

The geology of this area is typical of that found in other parts of the Southern Pennines, in that it largely consists of the Pennine Lower Coal Measures Formation, laid down between 313 and 304 million years ago (the Westphalian epoch), along with a contemporary band of Milnrow Sandstone (Crofts *et*

al 2010), which runs from the centre of the business park in a westerly direction (Fig 4). Similarly, the superficial geology of this area is comparable to that in other parts of the Pennine fringe, in that it largely consists of glaciofluvial deposits and till, deposited between two million and 11,000 years ago, during the Pleistocene epoch. Since the end of Pleistocene, in more recent geological times (the Holocene), pockets of alluvium were laid down within the area now occupied by the business park (*ibid*). Areas of peat also developed from the Mesolithic period onwards and it appears that these may once have been fairly extensive in the central and northern parts (*p 12*).

In contrast, Cutacre is a lower-lying landscape, on the north-western edge of the Manchester and

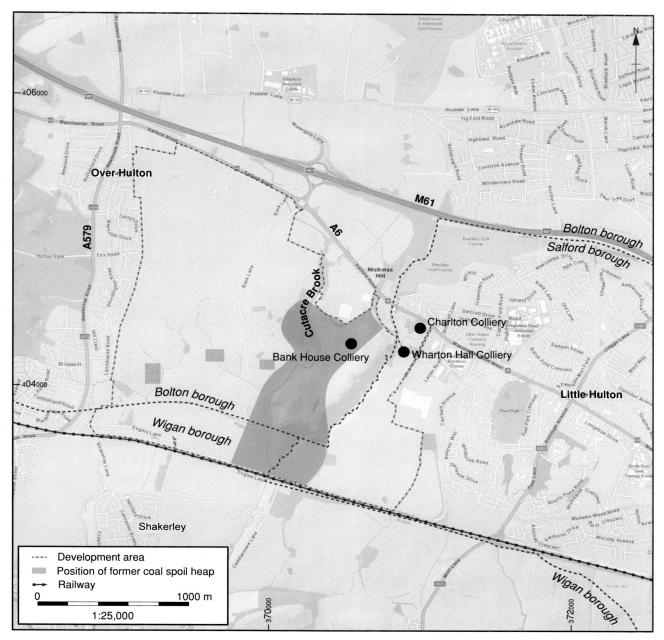

Figure 3: Cutacre and the area covered by the archaeological investigation

Salford urban conurbation (Fig 1), situated within a wider topographical zone that has been classified as the Lancashire Coal Measures character area (Countryside Commission 1998; Fig 5). Prior to the current phase of redevelopment, it contained a substantial disued coal tip, which covered a fairly large portion of this landscape, and formed the largest spoil heap in Europe (Miller and Plummer 2016). This tip lay in the eastern half of the area, and had been partly created through mining activity associated with the former Charlton Colliery (Fig 3), the pit-head of which was adjacent to the north-eastern boundary of the site, and also through the dumping of spoil, which had been transported from Brackley Colliery, immediately to the north, Mosley Common Colliery, c 2.5 km to the south-west, and

Sandhole (or the Bridgewater) Colliery, c 5 km to the west (Hayes 2004, 163). Another smaller coal tip was also present in the south-eastern part of the site, which was associated with another former colliery, once within the development area, known as Wharton Hall Colliery. Coal mining in this and also the wider area formed a significant industry from the fifteenth century onwards, with large collieries appearing in the nineteenth century, of which Charlton and Wharton Hall collieries formed two such examples (Atkinson 1998, 4).

Topographically, beyond these colliery spoil tips, the land slopes in a southerly direction, falling from c 130 m aOD, at the northern edge of the site, to c 70 m aOD, at the site's southern margin, and, prior

3

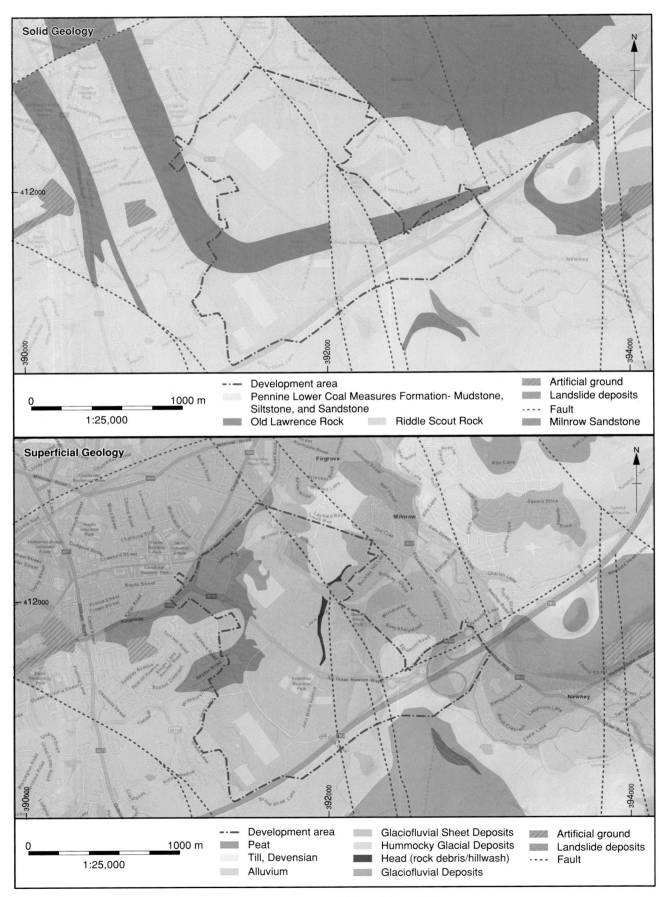

Figure 4: Solid and superficial geology at Kingsway

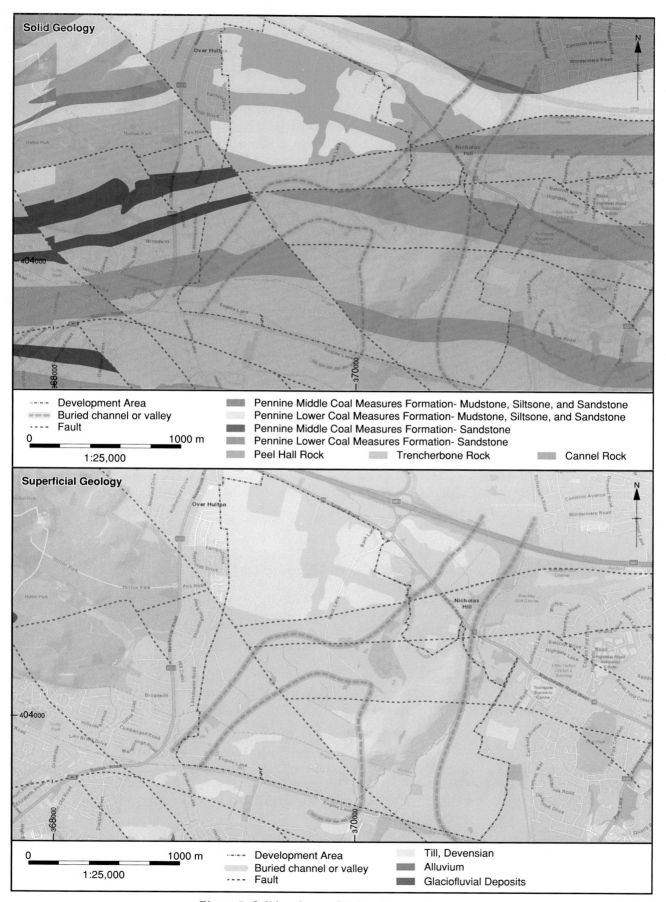

Figure 5: Solid and superficial geology at Cutacre

to redevelopment, formed low-grade agricultural land that was divided by degraded hedgerows, reflecting post-medieval enclosure and farming. Further evidence for post-medieval farming consisted of several extant farmhouses, which are depicted on historical mapping (*eg* Ordnance Survey (OS) 1849). Other topographical features of note comprise several small watercourses, such as Cutacre Brook, which traverse the area, flowing southwards. In addition, the western portion of the site was peppered with small ponds (*ibid*), which may have been water-filled coal pits, clay-extraction pits connected with local brick-making, or marl pits, whereby lime-rich clay was extracted and spread over the fields as a fertiliser.

Given the importance of coal mining to the area, unsurprisingly, the geology of Cutacre is typical of that associated with other parts of the former South Lancashire Coal Field, in that it comprises Pennine Middle Coal Measures Formation, interspersed with bands of sandstone, classified as Peel Hall Rock. These that were laid down between 313 and 304 million years ago (the Westphalian epoch; Crofts *et al* 2012; Fig 5). The superficial geology comprises glacial till of Devensian age (*c* 115,000-12,000 BC; *ibid*).

Archaeological Investigation

Although the two landscapes are different in terms of topography and setting, both have been subjected to similar schemes of archaeological investigation over the last three decades. In all instances, this work has resulted from planning conditions attached to the consent for the redevelopment of these two landscapes, and all phases of work were guided by advice from the Archaeological Advisory Service (Norman Redhead, initially the Assistant County Archaeologist for Greater Manchester, and latterly the Heritage Management Director (Archaeology), Greater Manchester Archaeological Advisory Service (GMAAS)). This archaeological work has comprised assessment, survey, evaluation, and open-area excavation, along with post-excavation assessment and analysis.

Assessment
The first stage of archaeological work completed for both landscapes consisted of desk-based assessments. These were designed to identify the known archaeological sites, and the potential for other sites that had not, as yet, been recognised, assess their significance, and formulate a series of recommendations, which would mitigate the impact of the proposed development on the archaeological resource contained within the respective landscapes.

These studies collated evidence derived from cartographic and documentary sources, as well examining aerial photographs and information now contained within the Historic Environment Record (HER). They were supplemented by rapid walkover surveys in order to confirm, and add to, the results obtained from the desk-based sources.

At Cutacre, this assessment work was initially undertaken in 1991 (GMAU 1991) and was designed to examine the Lomax opencast coal site. However, this initial assessment was revised and updated in 1996, when a slightly smaller area was considered, as part of the Cutacre reclamation and opencast coal project (UMAU 1996).

This latter work indicated that this landscape had considerable archaeological potential, identifying 117 sites of varying archaeological significance. These included post-medieval farmhouses, ponds, coal-working and colliery sites, and associated features, and also several potential small-scale post-medieval industrial sites, which were identified on the basis of field-name evidence. However, following on from this work, and some ten years later, a further stage of desk-based assessment work was undertaken.

This additional research focused explicitly on three former colliery sites, known as Bank House Colliery, Wharton/Charlton Colliery, and Wharton Hall Colliery (Fig 3), and considered a range of primary and secondary documentary sources. It was principally designed to provide additional information on the development and form of these sites and identify any associated remains that might be present within the Cutacre site (OA North 2006a).

In 2013, a fourth desk-based assessment was completed, which examined an area that fell within the boundaries of the study area considered by the earlier assessments (Arrowsmith 2013). Importantly, this study provided additional information on 20 of the previously identified sites, as well as identifying two additional sites.

At the Kingsway Business Park, an archaeological assessment was completed in 1998 (Arrowsmith and Wilson 1998), which was later updated in 2004 (Wilson and Nevell 2004), identifying 58 sites, which had varying levels of archaeological significance. Around half of these sites were post-medieval farmhouses, farm buildings, and cottages, which were either extant at the time of the assessment, or had been identified from historical mapping. The remaining sites formed historic routeways, structures such as gateposts, stray archaeological finds, and former field boundaries, and areas of ridge and furrow.

Non-intrusive survey

Following on from the desk-based assessments, a further programme of non-intrusive archaeological investigation was instigated at both Cutacre and Kingsway. At Cutacre, this comprised both geophysical and building surveys, whilst at Kingsway Business Park, a fairly extensive programme of building survey was completed, along with a topographical survey of several landscape features.

Building survey at Kingsway and Cutacre

At Kingsway, the scheme of building survey focused on eight extant farmhouses/cottages (cf Hradil and Nevell 2004), which were to be demolished during the construction of the business park (Fig 6). This survey was initiated in 2004 and was completed over a three-year period by UMAU, during which time Near Moor Bank Farm (Hradil and Nevell 2004), Mayfields Farm and Cottage (King and Nevell 2005a), Wychenley Cottage (Hradil and Nevell 2005), Lower Moss Side Farm (King and Nevell 2005b), Lower Lane Farm (King and Nevell 2006), and

Castle Farm (Hradil *et al* 2007) were subjected to a Royal Commission on the Historical Monuments England (RCHME) Level II-style survey (RCHME 1996). This entailed completing limited historical research, a photographic survey of the exterior and interior elements of the respective buildings, written building descriptions, as well as measured surveys of the ground- and first-floor plans of the buildings (at a scale of 1:50 or 1:100), together with cross-section drawings, to assist in the interpretation of their development.

Of the two remaining farms, Castle House (Hradil and Nevell 2007) was subjected to a RCHME Level I-style survey (RCHME 1996), which comprised limited historical research and a photographic survey of the exterior and interior elements of the building, whilst Moss Side Farm (King and Nevell 2005c) was subjected to a Level I/II survey. Again, this latter survey entailed the completion of limited historical research and a photographic survey of the exterior and interior elements of the building, together with the creation of sketch plans of these areas.

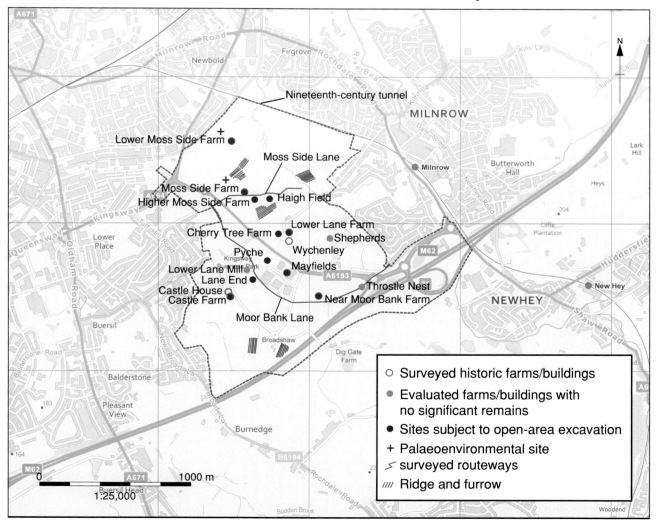

Figure 6: Archaeological sites, standing buildings, and other historical features at Kingsway surveyed and excavated

7

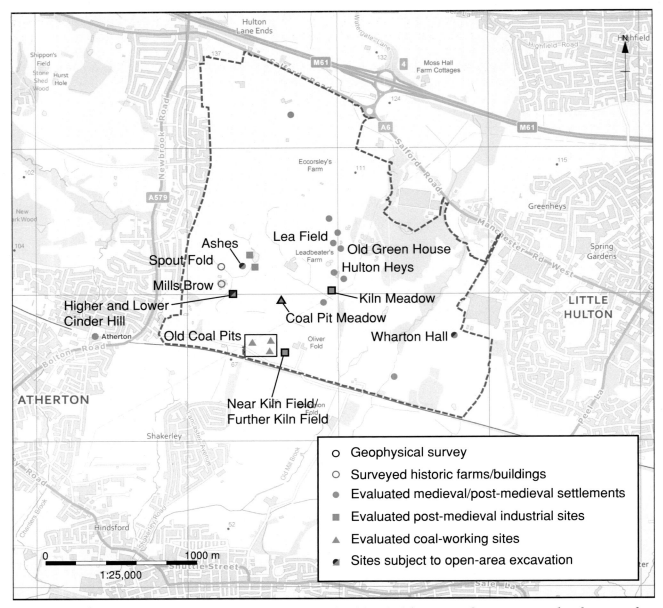

Figure 7: Archaeological sites, standing buildings, and other historical features at Cutacre surveyed and excavated

The building survey at Cutacre was undertaken in 2016, again as a means of recording the remains of two farms which were scheduled for redevelopment and partial demolition (OA North 2016; Fig 7). This survey focused on Spout Fold and Mills Brow farms and comprised a Level II/III-style survey, which involved undertaking detailed historical research, a photographic survey, along with the production of written descriptions, and measured plans and cross-sections, to produce evidence for the date and development of these farm complexes.

Geophysical survey at Cutacre
The geophysical survey at Cutacre was completed in 2005, in line with a Written Scheme of Investigation (WSI) issued by RPS (Archaeological Surveys 2005; 2006; RPS 2005), and its principal aim was to identify any potential buried archaeological remains at seven of

the sites identified by the initial desk-based assessment (*p 6*). This geophysical survey comprised a detailed magnetometer survey, using a Bartington Grad601-2 gradiometer, an instrument that is extremely sensitive and is able to measure magnetic variation to 0.1 nanoTesla (nT). Thus, depending on sub-surface conditions, it is used to detect buried archaeological features, such as walls, pits, ditches, surfaces, and also furnaces, ovens, kilns, and metalwork. Individual survey areas were divided into 30 m grids and, in line with recommended methodology (*cf* English Heritage 1995), data were collected at 0.25 m centres along traverses 1 m apart. Once collected, the data were then processed using specialist software.

Of the seven sites selected for survey (Fig 7), one comprised two adjacent fields named 'Higher Cinder Hill' and 'Lower Cinder Hill' on a survey of landholdings (the Bridgewater survey) made in 1722 (NRO E(B) 916; *Ch 5, p 93*). These names implied that this area may have witnessed early industrial activity, associated with burning/heating, and might, in turn, suggest that kilns or furnaces had once been operated in these fields. An area measuring 180 x 60 m was surveyed and, significantly, this showed magnetic debris situated at the northern end of the field. This was interpreted as a possible spread of thermoremnant material, such as brick or clinker, thus suggesting that this area had indeed witnessed some form of industrial activity (Sabin and Donaldson 2005).

The second site was a field named 'Coale (*sic*) Pit Meadow' on the Bridgewater survey of 1722 (NRO E(B) 916). There, an area of 120 x 90 m was surveyed, to identify any evidence relating to early coal working. The survey identified a very low-magnitude positive anomaly, which corresponded to a visible depression in the north-west corner of the field. This feature was interpreted as the coal pit that gave rise to the name of this field (*ibid*).

The third site examined was a field named 'Kiln Meadow' on a *c* 1772 map (the Bagot Estate map; MA L5/4/1/1; *Ch 5, p 93*), the survey covering two separate 30 x 30 m grids. In one of these, several positive linear and area anomalies, and negative linear anomalies, were detected, suggestive of buried archaeological remains (*ibid*).

Three of the other sites were marked as 'Old Coal Pit' on the first edition Ordnance Survey (OS) maps (1849; 1850a) and, at each, a 50 x 50 m area was surveyed. All these areas contained linear anomalies, which were thought to relate to buried remains (*ibid*). The last site comprised two fields named as 'Near Kiln Field' and 'Further Kiln Field' on the 1847 tithe map for the township of Tyldesley cum Shakerley (LA DRM/1/100). At this site, a 90 x 60 m area was surveyed and several positive linear anomalies were detected that were thought to relate to buried archaeological features (*ibid*).

Topographical survey at Kingsway
At the Kingsway Business Park, eight sites identified by the assessment were subjected to topographical and photographic survey, along with an additional site that was identified following the assessment (OA North 2006b). Two of these sites formed portions of historic routeways, which traversed the area that would later form the business park (Fig 6). One of these routes was Moss Side Lane which, prior to the development, ran in an east/west direction and joined with Buckley Hill Lane (*p 1*). The other site formed part of Moor Bank Lane, the route of which is now partly defined by Sir Isaac Newton Way (*p 2*). At both

of these sites, the survey methodology was broadly consistent with an RCHME Level II-style survey (*cf* English Heritage 2006), in that it involved the detailed surveying of the topography, using a total station and differential Global Positioning System (GPS), along with a photographic survey.

The other six sites were areas of ridge and furrow, which had been identified on aerial photographs, examined as part of the assessment (*p 6*). These were subjected to an RCHME Level I-style photographic survey, with Level II-style outline descriptions (*ibid*). However, during the survey of four of them, despite the perfect ground conditions for the identification of ephemeral surface features, with short grass within the pasture fields and low winter sunlight, no physical evidence for ridge and furrow was identified. The remaining site selected for survey was a nineteenth-century tunnel carrying the Stanney Brook beneath the Lancashire and Yorkshire Railway (L&YR) embankment. This structure was subjected to an RCHME Level I-style photographic survey (*ibid*).

Archaeological excavation
Field evaluation
The various archaeological assessments undertaken at Kingsway and Cutacre also identified several sites which might contain below-ground remains. Therefore, to ascertain the presence of such remains, field evaluation was first undertaken as a means of establishing the presence or absence of archaeological remains and, if present, of determining their date, significance, and potential. This entailed the excavation of *c* 1.6 m-wide trenches of various lengths across the identified sites; the methodology adopted included mechanical excavation of the uppermost levels of the trenches, after which cleaning and excavation progressed by hand, with the recovery of all artefacts. This was followed by the written, illustrative, and photographic recording of any exposed/excavated below-ground remains.

At the Kingsway Business Park, several trenches were excavated across those post-medieval farmstead sites which had been demolished prior to the archaeological building survey (*p 7*). These were Cherry Tree Farm, Pyche, Shepherds, and Throstle Nest. In addition, an evaluation trench was excavated across the site of Lower Lane Mill, which dated from the late eighteenth century (Haynes and Tipper 1994, 46; Fig 6). In these instances, the evaluation trenches indicated that significant below-ground remains relating to Cherry Tree Farm and Pyche survived, though none were present in the area of the Shepherds and Throstle Nest farms, or Lower Lane Mill (OA North 2005). Other sites that were evaluated were the course of a putative Roman road, post-medieval building platforms and a possible assart enclosure, and a nineteenth-century tramway, though, in all cases, no buried remains relating to these sites were uncovered (*ibid*).

A final element of the evaluation comprised the excavation of four trenches over the recently demolished Moss Side Farm, which had been recorded as part of the building survey (*p 7*). Significantly, these trenches indicated that significant buried remains were present that had not been previously recorded by the survey, and which might aid in an understanding of the development of settlement at this locale, and also the wider use of the landscape (*ibid*). This therefore suggested that it would be a worthwhile exercise to subject some of the other post-medieval farms, recorded as part of the building survey, to open-area excavation following their demolition (*below*).

The sites selected for evaluation at Cutacre were several medieval/post-medieval settlements, and areas associated with potential small-scale post-medieval industry and coal working (Fig 7). This evaluation indicated that no features of archaeological significance were present at two of the settlement sites, nor at four of the putative industrial sites (OA North 2006a). The features at one of the coal-working sites were considered to have little archaeological significance, whilst two other coal-working sites produced some evidence for early coal pits and later drainage features (*ibid*). The remaining sites, however, were found to contain more significant archaeological remains. These included: structural remains associated with two of the settlement sites, relating to Ashes and Wharton Hall; and deposits of metalworking slag at one of the industrial sites (Cinder Hil; *ibid*).

In addition to the 2006 evaluation, two further schemes of archaeological evaluation were completed in 2014, following commissions by the Harworth Group. The first involved the excavation of evaluation trenches across two post-medieval settlement sites (OA North 2014a). One of these was the site of Old Green House, which appears to have been the site of an early post-medieval farmstead, and is known to have contained buildings in the nineteenth century (Arrowsmith 2013). The other archaeological evaluation targeted the site of a late eighteenth-century barn, either rebuilt or replaced by a row of workers' cottages in the early nineteenth century, which was named Lea Field. Although, at both sites, the evaluation trenches revealed some degraded structural remains, these were considered to have little archaeological significance, and no further work was undertaken (OA North 2014a).

The other scheme targeted the site of Hulton Heys, which appears to have been a medieval and post-medieval farmstead. The evaluation consisted of the excavation of three trial trenches, which revealed pre-eighteenth-century remains, possibly relating to the farmstead, and structural remains forming elements of a mid-nineteenth-century cartshed (OA North 2014b). Based on these results, this site was considered to be archaeologically significant and a fuller programme of archaeological investigation was recommended, should these remains be impacted on by development. To date, no further development is planned for this site.

Open-area excavation
Once the sites had been evaluated, a more detailed and expansive phase of open-area excavation was undertaken at several sites, to record those remains fully, which would be impacted on by the various schemes of redevelopment. This phase of excavation aimed to produce a full record of the below-ground remains, and also to discern the chronological sequence of development at the respective sites. The excavation methodology employed at all of the open-area excavation sites was comparable and, in many respects, it followed that employed during the evaluation (*p 9*), comprising mechanical excavation of the upper layers of overburden, to expose any *in situ* archaeological remains and/or the natural subsoil (Pl 1), which was then followed by manual cleaning of these levels (Pl 2). Any structural remains were fully excavated, to determine their extent and form, and if possible their date, whilst any 'negative' features, such as ditches, pits, and postholes, were partially excavated, again with a view to determining their extent, form, and date. During the excavation, all of the remains were stratigraphically and planimetrically recorded through a combination of techniques, and all artefacts were also retrieved. In addition, where applicable, soil samples were taken, which were then subjected to palaeoenvironmental assessment and, if appropriate, analysis.

At Cutacre, based on the results of the archaeological evaluations (OA North 2006a), three of the sites were subjected to more extensive archaeological excavation. These were Ashes farm and Cinder Hill, which were excavated in December 2006, and Wharton Hall, excavated in July 2008 (Fig 7). The excavation methodologies conformed to a WSI produced by RPS and followed recommendations made by the then Assistant County Archaeologist for Greater Manchester (RPS 2006).

At Ashes, a single 40 x 32 m trench was excavated, which exposed the footprint of a building, as well as associated structures and adjacent areas of cobbling and drainage. Similarly, at Wharton Hall, a single open-area trench was excavated, with maximum dimensions of 150 x 63 m, revealing the foundations of the hall and several contemporary ancillary

Plate 1: Mechanical stripping in progress at Wharton Hall

Plate 2: The manual cleaning of a furnace at Cinder Hill

buildings, surfaces, and features. In contrast, the Cinder Hill site was divided, by necessity, into two discrete areas, which would form the focus of separate excavations. Within the southern part of the site, two adjacent trenches were excavated, one with maximum dimensions of 53 x 52 m, and the other measuring *c* 40 x 31 m, which exposed significant prehistoric remains (OA North 2010). In the northern portion of the site, a single trench was excavated, measuring *c* 50 x 43 m, and this uncovered evidence for medieval iron-working.

In the Kingsway Business Park, 11 sites were selected for open-area excavation (OA North 2006b). Seven of these (Lower Moss Side Farm; Moss Side Farm; Lower Lane Farm; Mayfields; Lane End; Near Moor Bank Farm; and Castle Farm) were demolished farms/cottages that had been recorded during the building survey, whilst the remaining four (Higher Moss Side Farm; Haigh Field; Cherry Tree Farm; and Pyche) formed sites that had been identified and investigated by the earlier archaeological assessment and evaluation (Fig 6). All of the sites contained evidence of post-medieval remains, and the trenches ranged in scale to cover the footprints of each respective farm/cottage.

Palaeoenvironmental investigation

In addition to the excavation work, a scheme of palaeoenvironmental investigation was undertaken, as a means of reconstructing the former environment at both the Kingsway Business Park and Cutacre. At the former, during the archaeological assessment (*p 6*), an area of peat was identified to the north of Moss Side Lane that was suspected of holding palaeoenvironmental potential (Fig 6). This area was therefore subjected to a programme of coring, which entailed extracting 15 cores, using a gouge auger, at 10 m intervals, along two transects (OA North 2005). However, laboratory-based assessment of these cores indicated that the peat in this area had been largely removed by cutting in the past, and consequently the palaeoenvironmental potential of this area was extremely limited.

Although the area to the north of Moss Side Lane proved unproductive, a later walkover survey, coupled with the observation of topsoil stripping, undertaken during the early stages of construction of the business park, successfully identified an area of peat, which was considered to hold significant palaeoenvironmental potential (OA North 2006b). This area lay to the north of Lower Moss Side Farm and contained peat with depths of over 1 m, which contained pollen that might allow insights into the prehistoric environment and land-use regimes. Therefore, a column monolith was extracted from this area, later analysis and radiocarbon dating indicating that the peat began to form in the Mesolithic period and contained valuable information relevant to the prehistoric environment (*Ch 2, p 19*; *Appendix 1*).

Similarly, at Cutacre, a monolith was extracted from a palaeochannel at Wharton Hall (Fig 7), which contained a sequence of pollen-bearing organic silty clays (*Appendix 1*). However, in contrast to the monoliths from the Kingsway Business Park, analysis and radiocarbon dating indicated that the Cutacre monolith contained evidence relevant to the medieval environment (*Ch 3, p 38*).

Post-excavation assessment

Following the completion of the intrusive investigations, the site archives were ordered and assessments were made of the data generated by the open-area excavations undertaken at the Kingsway Business Park and Cutacre. This resulted in the production of three reports, which considered, both quantitatively and qualitatively, the recorded stratigraphy, artefacts, and palaeoenvironmental samples derived from the excavations within these areas.

One of these detailed the results of the excavations at Kingsway (OA North 2006b), and made recommendations for additional analysis and publication, whilst two post-excavation assessment reports were compiled for the Cutace datasets, one explicitly relating to the remains from Cinder Hill and Ashes (OA North 2008a), the other presenting the excavated evidence from Wharton Hall (OA North 2010). Both of the Cutacre post-excavation assessment reports contained a statement of the potential for analysis of the data, and they also contained a series of updated aims and objectives, which could be addressed by the analysis, the scope of which was outlined. In both reports, these aims and objectives were formulated in the light of regional research priorities defined for the prehistoric (Hodgson and Brennand 2007), medieval (Newman and Newman 2007), post-medieval (Newman and McNeil 2007a), and industrial/modern periods (Newman and McNeil 2007b).

In terms of the Kingsway Business Park, it was anticipated that the data might specifically contribute to an understanding of:

- prehistoric vegetation change in relation to anthropogenic activity;

- the sequence of the archaeological structures and deposits revealed during the course of the investigation;

- and the development of a rural area on the fringe of the expanding conurbation of Manchester during the eighteenth and nineteenth centuries, based on the integration of information provided by documentary research, building surveys, archaeological excavation, and artefact analysis.

With regard to Cutacre, it was felt that the data might specifically contribute to an understanding of:

- the nature of earlier prehistoric occupation within the area;

- the nature of later prehistoric occupation and its continuity into the Roman period;

- the medieval organisation and settlement of the landscape and the activities undertaken within it, specifically the date and nature of metalworking activity, and the bloomery technology used;

- the nature and form of post-medieval settlement and occupation within the area and the impact of the industrialisation of the North West;

- the effects of topography and geomorphology on former settlements over time and on the survival of archaeological and palaeoenvironmental remains.

Analysis

The aims and objectives formulated during the post-excavation assessments acted as a framework for analysis, which focused on the documentary evidence, stratigraphical and palaeoenvironmental data, a selection of the artefactual remains, and the integration of the excavated remains with the evidence recorded during the standing building surveys. A programme of radiocarbon dating was also completed (*Appendix 2*), to assist interpretation of the palaeoenvironmental data from both Cutacre and the Kingsway Business Park, and the excavated prehistoric and medieval remains derived from one of the Cutacre sites (Cinder Hill).

Documentary evidence
As part of the analysis, a full and comprehensive review was made of the documentary evidence relevant to both the Kingsway and Cutacre sites, to situate the surveyed and excavated medieval and post-medieval remains within their local historical setting. For Kingsway, the documentary evidence was reviewed, printed and manuscript maps being examined, together with published and unpublished documentary sources, including trade directories, censuses, rate books, probate records, and parish registers. The collections consulted included those in the Rochdale Local Studies Library, Touchstones, Rochdale (RLSL), the Lancashire Archives (LA), and the National Archives (NA). These included: the Poor Rate Books for Castleton, dating to the mid- and late eighteenth century (RLSL LA/Z/1/C/1-4); the Castleton Household Survey of 1831 (RLSL LA/Z/3/C/1), comprising a local census; Land Tax assessments (LA QDL/S/24); the Castleton township survey of 1844 (RLSL LA/Z/3/C; RLSL LA/Z/3/C/2), which provides the first detailed mapping of the area; the relevant tithe map for the area (LA DRM1/27); nineteenth-century Census Returns (*eg* NA HO 107/550); and references in historical newspapers.

In terms of Cutacre, again, **printed and manuscript maps, and** published and unpublished documentary sources were examined, including: estate records (Bridgewater and Bagot estates; *eg* NRO E(B) 916; MA L 5/4/1/1) and family papers (*eg* NML D/EARLE 9/7); township records for Little Hulton and Middle Hulton (*eg* MA L 5/2/1/2); parish registers and other parish records (*eg* BA PMH 14/1); probate documents (wills and inventories (LA WCW)); Hearth Tax returns and Land Tax assessments (*eg* LA DDKe 2/16/10; LA QDL/S/55); and nineteenth-century Census Returns (*eg* NA HO 107/541). In this instance, the collections consulted comprised: Bolton Archives (BA); Chetham's Library (CL); the Lancashire Archives (LA); Manchester Archives (MA); National Museums Liverpool: Maritime Archives and Library (NML:MAL); Northamptonshire Record Office (NRO); Salford City Archives (SCA); and the National Archives (NA).

Stratigraphic analysis
A detailed analysis of the stratigraphic data was undertaken, which considered each individual excavated context. This analysis included reviewing the primary context records, site plans, and sections, which allowed the relationships between certain deposits, structures, and features, that had broadly been defined during the assessment stage, to be re-examined, refined, and revised. This, in turn, allowed secure site-specific sequences to be determined and enabled the identification of key contexts, containing charred plant remains or charcoal, suitable for scientific dating (*p 14*). Following the programme of dating, and also the artefactual and palaeoenvironmental analyses, the stratigraphic data were then subject to further review and revision, where appropriate, and the digital site databases were updated.

Standing building surveys

In addition to the excavated remains, the survey data on standing buildings were considered as part of the analysis. Most of this was a product of the building surveys at the Kingsway Business Park (*p 7*), and this evidence was reviewed and summarised, allowing it, in some instances, to be integrated with the excavated evidence.

Artefact analysis

The post-excavation assessments identified specific categories of finds that were considered to hold potential for analysis, and these were accordingly considered as part of the post-excavation programme. Principally, analysis was directed towards materials recovered from the Cutacre area, as these were considered to hold the greatest potential. Analysis focused on the sizable assemblage of archaeometallurgical residue from Cinder Hill (*Appendix 3*), although the prehistoric pottery has also been reconsidered from this site in the light of the radiocarbon-dating evidence (*Appendix 4*).

Palaeoenvironmental analysis

During the post-excavation assessments, soil samples were identified which contained sufficient quantities of charred and waterlogged plant remains, and wood charcoal, for analysis, and which were also suitable for scientific dating. The majority of these samples were recovered from prehistoric and medieval features at Cutacre, specifically those at Cinder Hill, and, accordingly, the analysis has concentrated on elucidating the prehistoric and medieval environment and economy there (*Appendix 5*).

In addition to the plant remains from archaeological features, the monoliths extracted from both Cutacre (at Wharton Hall; Fig 7), and Kingsway (Fig 6) were analysed (*Appendix 1*) and dated scientifically (*below*). This provided a means of determining the types of early environments that existed at Cutacre and the Kingsway Business Park.

Scientific dating

A programme of scientific dating was undertaken as part of the post-excavation work, with 20 samples being submitted for radiocarbon assay. Sixteen of these were derived from Cutacre and, of these, seven came from the prehistoric settlement at Cinder Hill (Site 42S; *Ch 2, p 25*), whilst another seven came from the furnaces and associated pits forming part of the Cinder Hill bloomery site (Site 42N; *Ch 3, p 44*). The remaining samples were submitted to date the monolith extracted from the palaeochannel at Cutacare and the peat deposits at the Kingsway Business Park (*above*).

The programme of dating followed those recommendations set out by Patrick Ashmore (1999), in that single-entity short-lived samples were selected. These samples were assayed using the accelerator mass spectrometry (AMS) technique, which was undertaken at the Scottish Universities Environmental Research Centre (SUERC). The resultant data were calibrated using IntCal13 (Reimer *et al* 2013), and OxCal v4.2 (Bronk Ramsey 1995; 1998; 2001; 2009). In some instances, the dates were also subjected to statistical testing, to compare respective dates, and Bayesian chronological modelling (*Appendix 2*). In line with standard procedures, all radiocarbon determinations are cited in this volume as calibrated ranges expressed at the 95% probability level, followed by the radiocarbon age quoted in conventional years BP (before AD 1950), plus the standard error and laboratory code (Stuiver and Polach 1977; Stuiver and Kra 1986).

The Structure of the Volume

This volume deals specifically with the archaeological excavations and standing building surveys completed in advance of development at Cutacre and the Kingsway Business Park. In terms of its structure, a chronological approach has been adopted for the evidence. Hence, *Chapter 2* describes the evidence relating to the early landscapes of the two areas, focusing on the prehistoric remains uncovered at Cutacre, and the evidence derived from pollen analysis and excavation at the Kingsway Business Park.

Chapter 3 discusses the medieval landscapes at Cutacre and Kingsway, specifically considering the evidence for a medieval iron-working site at Cutacre (Site 42N), and the more limited evidence present at the other excavated Cutacre sites. In addition, this chapter describes the evidence for possible medieval routeways at the Kingsway Business Park. The next two chapters detail the evidence for post-medieval activity (*c* 1600-1780) uncovered at the Kingsway Business Park (*Chapter 4*) and Cutacre (*Chapter 5*), and the evidence obtained by excavation and the standing building surveys relevant to this period is presented. Similarly, *Chapters 6-8* present the evidence derived from the excavations and standing building surveys that is relevant to the late eighteenth- and nineteenth-century landscapes that existed at Kingsway and Cutacre.

A final chapter (*Chapter 9*) provides a synthesis of the evidence derived from these two separate landscapes in Greater Manchester, and places the analysed remains within their regional context, through the discussion of several key themes and concepts. This chapter also compares and contrasts these two differing landscape areas in terms of their historical trajectories and associated archaeological remains, which have relevance to the wider archaeology of Greater Manchester.

Each chapter contains interwoven summaries of the specialist post-excavation analyses that were completed, as appropriate, and also summary details of the artefacts that were considered as part of the archaeological assessments. The detailed specialist reports, describing the full range of methodologies and results used during the analysis, are contained in *Appendices 1-5*; *Appendix 4* also provides an overview of the artefacts that were assessed but did not merit analysis.

Project Archives

The project archives from both the Kingsway Business Park and Cutacre contain all of the data and material gathered during the course of the archaeological investigations, which have been collated and indexed in accordance with accepted guidelines (English Heritage 1991; UKIC 1984; Walker 1990; CIfA 2014). This material includes the primary site records, such as context sheets, site and building plans and sections, digital images, and databases, as well as the various documents and reports produced during the project. The Kingsway archive has been deposited with Touchstones Rochdale, whilst that for Cutacre, which relates to Little Hulton (ie the Wharton Hall archive) has been deposited with the Salford Art Gallery and Museum, with the remaining elements being deposited with Bolton Museum.

2

EARLY LANDSCAPES

Richard A Gregory

Prehistoric Activity

Kingsway and the prehistory of the Southern Pennines

The southern Pennines contain a rich body of information relevant to prehistoric archaeology, particularly as the area contains valuable evidence for prehistoric exploitation of the upland landscape. The earliest evidence dates to the Mesolithic period (*c* 8000-4000 cal BC) and primarily consists of small scatters of stone tools, dominated by microliths, which are sometimes associated with hearths, areas of burning, and ephemeral structures (*cf* Hodgson and Brennand 2006, 27-8). These tools and features appear to reflect temporary camps of a highly mobile community of hunter-gatherers, and within the southern Pennines these surface scatters have principally been identified in the uplands to the south-east of Rochdale, between Saddleworth and Marsden (Barnes 1982). However, it is also likely that Mesolithic communities traversed and occupied areas directly adjacent to the River Irwell, and its tributaries, as evidenced by the discovery of Mesolithic tools at the E'es, Radcliffe, which is close to the confluence of the rivers Roch and Irwell, some 12 km south-west of the Kingsway Business Park (Spencer 1950; Fig 8). Closer to the business park, Mesolithic flint tools have also been recovered from the bed of Hollingworth Lake (Greater Manchester Historic Environment Record (GMHER) 290.1.0), Turf Hill, Piethorne Valley (GMHER 297.1.0), New Nook, Blackstone Edge (GMHER 5338.1.0), and Whittaker Moor (GMHER 8867.1.1), and these attest to the movement of Mesolithic groups within the hinterland of the major river systems.

During the Neolithic (*c* 4000-2500 cal BC) and Chalcolithic (*c* 2500-2100 cal BC) periods, and the Bronze Age (*c* 2100-700 cal BC), the region's primeval woodland appears to have been progressively cleared in response to the gradual development of less peripatetic and more rooted communities. At a wider regional level, it is clear that these communities farmed the landscape, and at times created land divisions and territoriality, as well as monumentality, with a range of monuments acting as both arenas of communal interaction and also as receptacles for the dead (*cf* Hodgson and Brennand 2006, 29-45).

Marked and evolving changes in technology also characterised these periods, when ceramics and new forms of stone tools were adopted, with a later shift to the use of bronze in tool and weapon manufacture (*op cit*, 45-50). The evidence for these communities in the southern Pennines is therefore varied, ranging from signals for woodland clearance in the palaeoenvironmental record, to artefacts, such as Neolithic and Bronze Age stone tools, such as those from the E'es (Spencer 1950), Rochdale, and other areas close to the Kingsway Business Park.

In addition, several cast-bronze objects, dating to the Bronze Age, have been recovered from areas close to the Kingsway Business Park, including a flanged bronze axe from the E'es (*ibid*), a bronze palstave from Crompton Moor (GMHER 5926.1.0), and a socketed spearhead from Piethorne, Milnrow (Davey and Forster 1975, entry 107). Other evidence dating to the Bronze Age includes funerary monuments, specifically barrows containing cremation burials, which form another strand of evidence for Bronze Age communities in Greater Manchester (Hodgson and Brennand 2006, 42). Indeed, one such burial probably lay close to the Kingsway Business Park at Low House Farm, Milnrow, where an urned cremation was discovered within a stone cist, that might have originally been sealed by a mound (Platt 1900). This burial was also associated with a perforated stone axe-hammer, which would have been a grave good. Another possible barrow site was found *c* 2.5 km to the south-west of the business park at Thornham Fold (GMHER 9934.1.0), whilst a possible barrow cemetery, comprising six burial mounds, was at Turf Hill in the Piethorne Valley (GMHER 10341.1.0).

The actual settlement sites associated with Neolithic, Chalcolithic, and Bronze Age communities are, however, difficult to detect, though it is possible

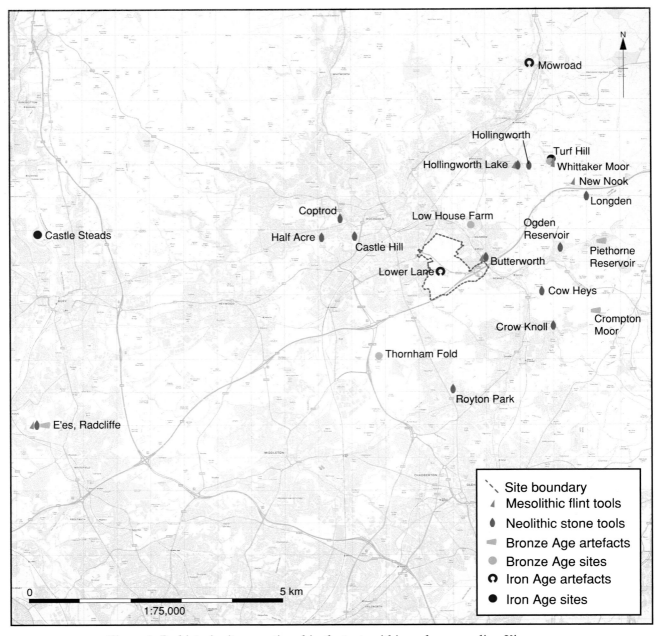

Figure 8: Prehistoric sites mentioned in the text, within and surrounding Kingsway

that several timber structures identified at the E'es, Radcliffe, formed the remains of one such settlement (Spencer 1950; Tyson 1985). This may imply that, more generally, early settlement was concentrated along the major rivers of the area, partly confirmed by the known distributions of Neolithic and Bronze Age artefacts (*cf* Pearson *et al* 1985, fig 4).

During the Iron Age (*c* 600 cal BC-AD 43), the area surrounding Rochdale, including that covered by the Kingsway Business Park, may have been within the tribal territory of the Brigantes, an entity described in several proto-historical sources, such as the accounts of the Roman historian Tacitus (Birley 2009) and the geographer Ptolemy (Knight and Pagani 1990). The Brigantes appear, however, to have occupied a

large territory covering much of northern England and parts of south-west Scotland, and it would seem more likely that this group was a loose confederation of smaller tribal groups (Hartley and Fitts 1988, 1-2).

In the southern Pennines, particularly within Greater Manchester, even though during the later Iron Age the environmental evidence indicates that there was widespread anthropogenic clearance, the evidence for Iron Age activity is sparse (Hall *et al* 1995, 118-19; Haselgrove *et al* 2001, 25; Hodgson and Brennand 2006, 51-2). For instance, Iron Age settlement sites and burial grounds are hard to detect and, in terms of archaeological preservation, the artefacts used by these communities were not particularly durable (Haselgrove *et al* 2001, 25).

There is some evidence for Iron Age activity within and close to the Kingsway Business Park, though. For example, it has been argued that several promontory sites in the Irwell and Roch valleys may represent settlement sites (Hodgson and Brennand 2006, 53), and one of these, Castle Steads, north of Bury, has been subjected to survey and small-scale excavation (North West Archaeological Surveys 1992). This suggested that the promontory was enclosed by a ditched boundary on its gently sloping eastern side and was the site of a late Iron Age/early Roman-period settlement. Closer to the Kingsway Business Park, a possible Iron Age enclosure has been found in the Piethorne Valley, at Turf Hill (GMHER 10337.1.0), whilst a bronze torc of Iron Age date was discovered in the early nineteenth century at Mowroad in Calderbrook (Fishwick 1889, 5).

Tentative evidence for Iron Age activity is also present within the Kingsway Business Park. This consists of a carved stone head, which was discovered beneath a hedge at Castle Farm, to the south of Lower Lane (Arrowsmith and Wilson 1998). This egg-shaped head was carved in a Celtic style, with an open mouth, thick lips, and a triangular flat nose with deep nostrils, and a deep hollow under the right eye (*ibid*). Similar stone heads have been discovered close to the business park, and also close to Cutacre (*cf* Nevell 1992), and although they are difficult to date, it has been suggested that a proportion at least might belong to the Iron Age, that, at a much later date, were incorporated into post-medieval boundaries, where they acted as charms to protect livestock (*ibid*). However, an alternative explanation is that the majority of these stone heads actually date to the post-medieval period, specifically the seventeenth century (Redhead 2003, 76).

It has been further suggested that these potential Iron Age carvings may have originally been placed next to springs or pools, which might have formed significant locales for Celtic rituals (Nevell 1992; Webster 1995, 449). Indeed, there were probably numerous springs in the area, many being known close to Lower Lane and Moor Bank Lane in modern times (Haynes and Tipper 1994, 45). Significantly, these springs probably drained into mossland, and large expanses of peat seem to have existed across the Kingsway Business Park by the Iron Age. These mosses are reflected in the historical place-names applied to the area, including the name Moor Bank, which is found in the southern part of the business park, and Moss Side in its northern portion. Moreover, the name Moss Side may well relate to a fairly extensive swathe of mossland which originally extended from the business park to an area south-west of Rochdale, depicted as 'The Moss' on a map dating to 1754-7, showing the Rochdale glebe land

belonging to the vicarage of the parish (Fishwick 1889, facing 57).

Reconstructing the prehistoric environment at the Kingsway Business Park

Although there is a general absence of direct archaeological evidence for prehistoric activity within the Kingsway Business Park, peat samples extracted from the north of Lower Moss Side Farm (*Ch 1, p 12*) contained pollen evidence relating to the prehistoric environment (*Appendix 1*), dating from the late Mesolithic to the late Neolithic period, from approximately the early sixth to early third millennia cal BC (*Appendix 2*). A mosaic of different woodland types (*eg* hazel-type (*Corylus avellana*-type) scrub, alder (*Alnus glutinosa*), and oak (*Quercus*) woodlands, and birch (*Betula*) woods or scrub; Fig 9) would have presented late Mesolithic and Neolithic communities with sources of food, such as acorns and hazelnuts. The continuous presence of microscopic charcoal also provides evidence of fires and burning, peak occurrences reflecting a greater incidence of fires. Direct evidence for burning came from the occurrence of several specimens of the fungal spore *Gelasinospora* HdV-1, which has been associated with microcharcoal (Innes *et al* 2004). Such burning may have been deliberate and, as a result of these, peat probably expanded on the moor, bordered by alder-carr vegetation. The pollen data suggest that hazel scrub was being burnt, consistent with a decrease in the curve for hazel-type pollen at around 5500 cal BC. At a later date in the late Mesolithic period, the use of periodic fire is again evident in peat deposits dating from *c* 4200 cal BC, both hazel-type and alder being targeted.

Significantly, both of the recorded Mesolithic burning events would have resulted in the development of small cleared areas, possibly given over to grass, within which animals could have grazed. Disturbance events within this period on upland sites in the Central Pennines (Williams 1985) and the North York Moors (Simmons and Innes 1996) have been attributed to the potential seasonal management of vegetation in openings, to improve either the browse or grass-herb ground layers for large mammals, for example red deer. The presence of the fungal spore *Cercophora* HdV-112, which is coprophilous and can also occur on decaying wood, may be used as an indicator for animal dung in the surrounding area (van Geel and Aptroot 2006). Grazing by wild animals could have promoted the development of open areas in or adjacent to the woodland.

Oak woodland appears to have regenerated subsequently, followed by the expansion of birch woods or scrub vegetation during the Early Neolithic period. An increase in birch, replacing alder, has

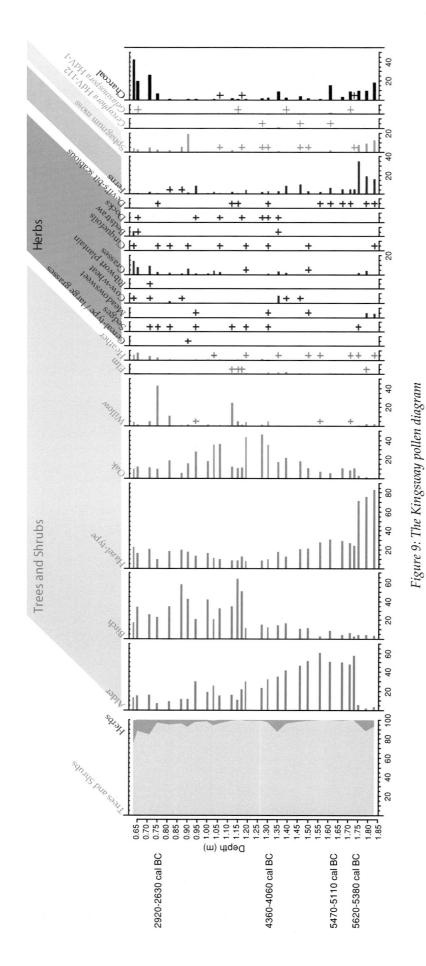

Figure 9: The Kingsway pollen diagram

20

also been identified at Chat Moss (Nook Farm 3) in Greater Manchester (Hall *et al* 1995). During the late Neolithic period (*c* 2800 cal BC), the pollen data show an increase in grassy environments, with a suite of herb taxa consistent with the presence of meadowland, suitable for at least pastoral farming. The diversity of herb pollen, including taxa such as devil's-bit scabious (*Succisa pratensis*), ribwort plantain (*Plantago lanceolata*), cinquefoils, pollen of the bedstraw family (Rubiaceae), and docks/sorrels (*Rumex*), which are representative of wet meadows, heaths, and pastures (Behre 1981; Stace 2010), may suggest the possible use of the land for pasturing animals. Some cereal-type pollen grains are present, suggesting possible cultivation. The pollen curve for heather (*Calluna*) increases towards the top of the profile, possibly around 2500 cal BC, and, together with cow-wheat (*Melampyrum*) pollen, may indicate the growth of these plant types following the fires and the development of acid moorland at the site.

The disturbance events, with intervening forest regeneration, may suggest that the area was revisited, possibly as part of the social territory of late Mesolithic and Neolithic communities (Pollard 2000). Such areas may have been recognised as areas that attracted wild animals, or would provide a source of food.

Cutacre and the prehistory of the eastern Lancashire Coal Measures

Prior to the commencement of the main phase of fieldwork, it was considered that there was little chance of encountering any prehistoric remains within the Cutacre area (UMAU 1996). For example, no prehistoric stray finds, such as flint tools or metalwork, had been recovered from the area, no obvious earthwork sites, marking the position of settlements or burials, were present, and the geophysical surveys and trial trenching had not detected any features that were seemingly related to early activity. It was also assumed during the collation of data for the desk-based assessment that the geology of the area, which comprises heavy, poorly drained superficial deposits of glacial till (*Ch 1, p 6*), was not particularly conducive to prehistoric settlement or agriculture (*ibid*). This latter assumption was based on a more general observation that, in the wider region, those areas that were probably favoured for prehistoric settlement comprised free-draining, easily worked, sands and gravels, adjacent to watercourses or wetlands (*cf* Collens 1999, 39).

Slightly further afield, there is, however, some limited evidence for prehistoric activity (Fig 10). This includes findspots of Neolithic, Bronze Age, and Iron Age material, a possible Bronze Age barrow, and an area that may contain later prehistoric settlement, perhaps dating from the Bronze or Iron Age (*below*). These imply that the area was first cleared and settled by agricultural communities in *c* 4000 cal BC, in a similar manner to those in the southern Pennines (*p 17*), and was then continuously occupied right through to the Iron Age, when the area was probably within Brigantian territory (*p 18*).

The Neolithic objects from the wider region include a stone axe from Deane, *c* 2.8 km north of Cutacre (GMHER 4297.1.0), and a flint polisher, also from the area to the north, in Middle Hulton (GMHER 3621.1.0). The findspot at Deane also produced two perforated stone hammers, which probably date to the Bronze Age, whilst a residual Bronze Age flint flake was recovered from a medieval ditch excavated at Gadbury Fold, Atherton (Connelly 2006). Several other nearby finds may date to the Iron Age, particularly four Celtic-style carved stone heads, comparable to those from the Pennine foothills (*p 19*). Two of these have been incorporated into Deane Church (GMHER 9078.1.0), a third was found in a field boundary at Tyldesley, *c* 2.3 km to the south (GMHER 9082.1.0), whilst the fourth came from Green Lane, *c* 2.6 km to the north-east (GMHER 9071.1.0). Evidence for potential later prehistoric settlement comprises two circular cropmarks in Over Hulton, *c* 1.6 km to the west of Cutacre (GMHER 4558.1.0 and 4560.1.0), whilst a possible Bronze Age barrow is *c* 3 km to the south-east, at Windybank Low (GMHER 515.1.0).

Prehistoric activity and settlement at Cinder Hill

Given the general absence of known prehistoric remains from Cutacre, it was unexpected that clear evidence for prehistoric activity was recognised during the open-area excavations at Cinder Hill, particularly since this site was targeted for excavation as a result of its association with medieval or post-medieval metalworking (*Ch 3, p 44*). The evidence for prehistoric activity took the form of artefacts that were recovered from both the southern (Site 42S) and northern (Site 42N) parts of the site, along with structural remains, which were confined to the southern excavation area (Site 42S; Fig 11). In this latter area, these remains related to a prehistoric settlement, which has been scientifically dated to the Bronze Age (*Appendix 2*).

The two excavated areas (42N and 42S) at Cinder Hill were positioned within a fairly steeply sloping area of ground, which dropped some 15.4 m from *c* 88.7 m aOD, at Site 42N, to *c* 73.4 m aOD, at Site 42S. A deep, narrow valley also lay immediately to the west of the site. The open-area excavations indicated that the superficial geology was dominated by glacial till, which in its northern portion (Site 42N) consisted of a mid-yellowish-pink silty clay, whilst in its southern part (Site 42S) it comprised a mid-orange clayey silt. In the southern part of the site, the glacial till was overlain by two discrete areas of natural gravel (565 and 575; Fig 12)

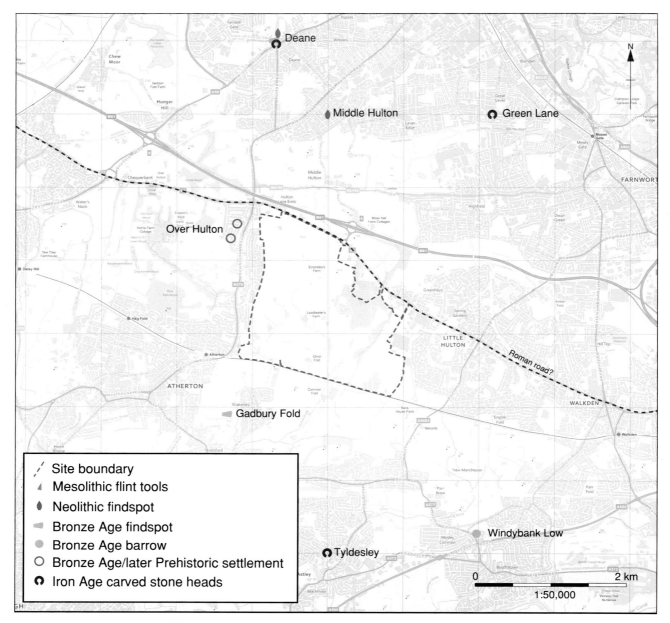

Figure 10: Prehistoric sites mentioned in the text, surrounding Cutacre

and, in other parts, by thin deposits of colluvium, which represent natural material that had been eroded from the upslope area, in the vicinity of Site 42N.

A palaeochannel (**564**) was identified in the southern part of the site (42S). The stream contained had flowed in a southerly direction across the larger of the open-area trenches in this area, which had probably deposited the two areas of gravel on its eastern and western banks (**565** and **575**; *above*), and had cut through deposits of colluvium. The channel had an irregular shape, with a maximum depth of 0.5 m, and was filled by silt, its position suggesting that originally the stream on the western edge of Cinder Hill had braided into two separate channels. Based on the position of the prehistoric settlement (*p 25*), it is possible that it had been active during the Bronze

Age, or had formed a water-filled feature. If this were the case, the settlement would have lain in a triangular pocket of land bounded by two small streams, or a small stream and an area of standing water.

In addition to the palaeochannel, a collection of tree-throws and shrub-root holes was evident within the two trenches in 42S. These were widely scattered, generally irregular in plan, and contained fine greyish-brown silt. Several were within the palaeochannel and appear to have marked the position of small shrubs, which would have colonised the margins of the channel as it gradually dried up. Others, however, were found outside this area, both to its east and west, and a proportion of these may have marked the position of trees that pre-dated the establishment of the Bronze Age settlement (*below*).

22

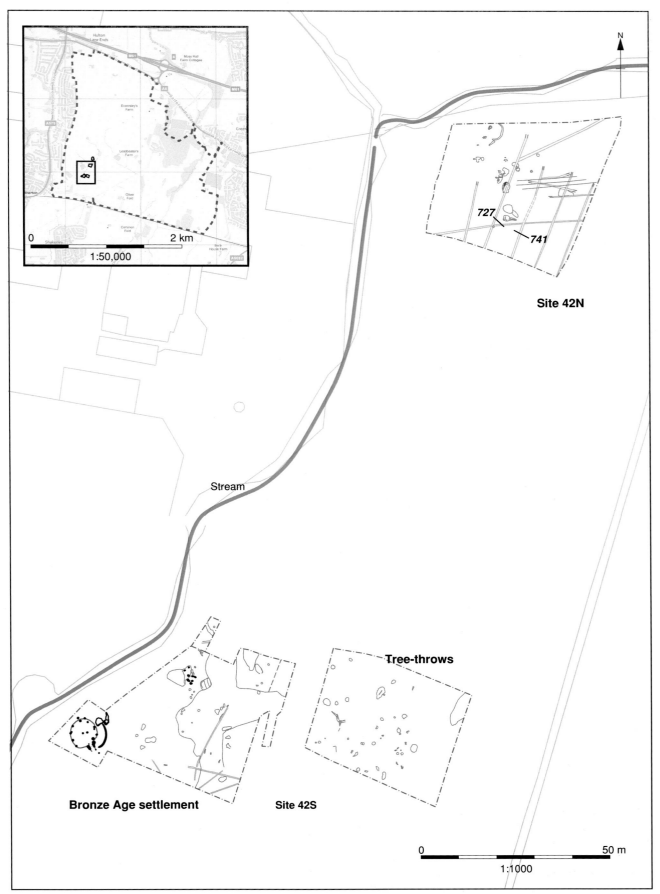

Figure 11: Cinder Hill (Site 42)

23

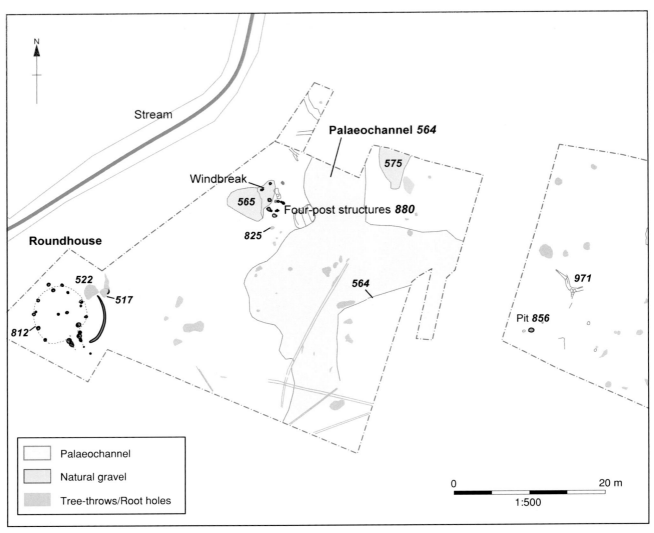

Figure 12: The Bronze Age settlement at Cinder Hill (Site 42S)

Early activity

A small collection of stone tools forms the earliest evidence for prehistoric activity at Cinder Hill, pre-dating the establishment of the Bronze Age settlement, although none was closely dated. This assemblage comprises nine pieces of worked flint and two of worked chert: three flakes; one blade fragment; four scrapers; two microliths; and a bladelet core (*Appendix 4*). Nine of the objects came from the southern part of the site (Site 42S), three being stratified within both natural and anthropogenic features, although three were unstratified, and the other two derived from the topsoil. Two other objects came from the northern part of the site (Site 42N), one unstratified, and the other had been redeposited in a possible modern pit (727; Fig 11; Ch 3, p 50). Most objects were complete, usable tools, rather than debitage, indicating that they had not been worked at the site. In addition to the flint and chert tools, a large pebble was found at Site 42S, though unstratified, which may have been used as a hammer/grinding stone (*Appendix 4*).

The flint varied in colour and quality and probably reflects the opportunistic collection of pebbles from local river-terrace gravels or deposits of glacial till, where this material had been redeposited by fluvial/glacial processes. Given that flint was probably difficult to acquire, it may be significant that a large proportion of cortical pieces is present within the assemblage, suggesting that maximum benefit was made of any available pebbles. Both of the chert pieces were similar in colour and texture, and these were also, perhaps, derived from a nearby source, particularly as chert is present in the local sandstone of the region (Stone 2010). The hammer/grinding stone appears to be made of a type of volcanic basalt, and probably came from a glacial erratic, or a manuport, likely to have originated in Cumbria or Wales (*ibid*; Howells 2007).

Some of these objects can only be placed within a very broad chronological range. For instance, the three flakes could date to anywhere between the late Mesolithic period and the Early Bronze Age, and the scrapers could also have come from the

24

*Plate 3: Pit **856** at Cinder Hill (Site 42S), looking north-west*

same date range, though they are common in early Neolithic assemblages (Rowe 1998; Young 1987, 57-8). Several objects can be dated more precisely, however, including the two microliths, which are probably of late Mesolithic date, and the bladelet core, which dates to either the Mesolithic or early Neolithic period. The hammer/grinding stone is more difficult to date, though it is quite likely that it is prehistoric.

The assemblage has proved difficult to interpret, given this broad chronological range, and because much was effectively unstratified. This might suggest that it relates to the periodic visiting of the site by prehistoric groups over a fairly extended period of time, spanning the Mesolithic and Neolithic periods, into the Early Bronze Age. However, another, more tentative, suggestion, based on the presence of the two late Mesolithic microliths and other broadly dated lithics, which could also feasibly be of Mesolithic age, is that the material is derived from a single phase of Late Mesolithic activity.

Some of the stratified pieces provide cursory details relating to the types of activities that were occurring at the site. A side scraper came from a gully (*971*; Fig 12), which was *c* 5 m in overall length, 0.5 m wide, and no more than 0.25 m deep. Its irregular form suggests that this feature was an animal burrow, rather than man-made. Two flint flakes came from a tree-throw (*517*) and a more closely dated Mesolithic-Neolithic flint blade was also found within a tree-throw (*825*). In addition, it is possible that the end-and-side scraper, from modern pit **727** at Site 42N (*p 24*), was also ultimately derived from an early tree-throw (*741*; Fig 11), which had been disturbed by this later pit.

These objects may suggest that the intentional felling/ uprooting of trees was an activity that was occurring early at the site, although the trees could have been naturally uprooted, and then acted as markers/foci for early activity (*cf* Evans *et al* 1999). Indeed, it has

been argued that many of the tree-throws excavated in England, including an important group from the North West, at Stainton West, in Cumbria, formed receptacles for Mesolithic and early Neolithic acts of intentional deposition (*inter alia*; *ibid*; Bishop 2008; Brown *et al* in prep). Given this, it is possible that this practice also occurred at Cinder Hill.

In addition to the tree-throws, a small pit (*856*; Fig 12; Pl 3) in the southern part of the site (Site 42S) was clearly a product of human activity. This had a diameter of 0.85 m and was 0.18 m deep, corresponding exactly to one of the anomalies detected by the geophysical survey of the site. It was filled entirely with discoloured, fire-cracked stones. Although this remains undated, it could have been a feature associated with earlier prehistoric activity at this locale. One possibility, for instance, is that it was a hearth or cooking pit, perhaps relating to one of the suspected late Mesolithic visitation(s) to the site, particularly as similar features have been discovered at late Mesolithic encampments in the North West, such as that excavated at Stainton West, near Carlisle (Brown *et al* in prep).

The Bronze Age settlement: roundhouse and four-post structures

At Cinder Hill, further, more tangible, evidence for prehistoric activity was present in the form of a small settlement in the southern part of the site (Site 42S). This comprised the remains of a roundhouse, two sequential four-post structures, and a possible fence/windbreak, found within the western trench excavated in this area. These remains were to the west of the palaeochannel (*564*; *p 22*), and immediately east of the stream that defined the western edge of the site.

The principal structure associated with the settlement was a roundhouse (*812*; Pl 4). This was found in the extreme south-western corner of the site, adjacent to the stream, and appears to have been constructed

*Plate 4: Part of Bronze Age roundhouse **812** at Cinder Hill before excavation, looking east*

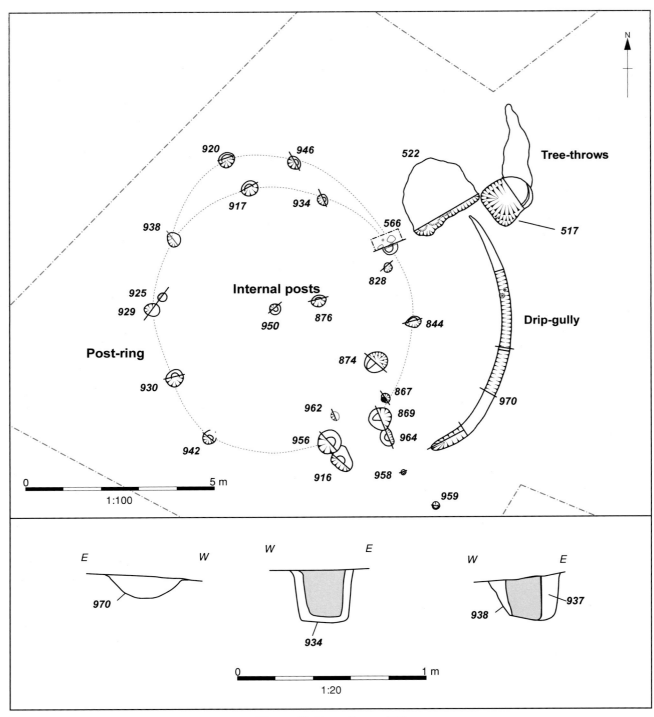

Figure 13: Roundhouse **812**

on a slightly elevated area, in the immediate vicinity of two tree-throws (**517** and **522**; Fig 13), which probably marked the position of trees which had been removed, or died, at a much earlier date, since **517** contained two of the late Mesolithic-Early Bronze Age flint flakes (*p 25*).

The roundhouse was defined by 22 postholes, 17 of which contained post-pipes (Pl 5). The presence of these post-pipes is significant, in that they allow some estimation to be made of the size of the timbers used

in the building. In addition, their presence implies that the main structural elements of the house had rotted *in situ* rather than being removed when the structure was eventually abandoned.

It is evident that 13 of the postholes formed a ring, with a diameter of *c* 7 m, forming the outer wall-line of the structure (Table 1). This would also have provided the main structural support for the roof. The diameters of these postholes ranged between 0.3 m and 0.56 m, and most (11) also contained post-pipes (Pl 6), suggesting

26

*Plate 5: Bronze Age roundhouse **812** at Cinder Hill after excavation, looking north-east. Upright timbers mark the position of the postholes*

Element	Posthole	Posthole dimensions (diameter x depth)	Post-pipe	Post-pipe dimensions (diameter x depth)
Post-ring; external wall-line	*828*	0.45 x 0.29 m	*842*	0.25 x 0.25 m
	830	0.25 x 0.06 m	-	-
	844	0.4 x 0.21 m	*846*	0.3 x 0.21 m
	874	0.56 x 0.25 m	*966*	0.18 x 0.2 m
	917	0.45 x 0.28 m	*919*	0.23 x 0.28 m
	920	0.45 x 0.21 m	*939*	0.15 x 0.17 m
	925	0.23 x 0.12 m	*923*	0.19 x 0.12 m
	929	0.3 x 0.22 m	-	-
	930	0.39 x 0.28 m	*933*	0.18 x 0.15 m
	934	0.33 x 0.28 m	*944*	0.21 x 0.23 m
	938	0.33 x 0.23 m	*936*	0.2 x 0.23 m
	942	0.36 x 0.05 m	*940*	0.16 x 0.04 m
	946	0.34 x 0.12 m	*948*	0.18 x 0.08 m
Porch	*867*	0.27 x 0.1 m	-	-
	869	0.6 x 0. 3 m	*871*	Posthole may have held an upright plank; post-pit measured 0.43 m long, 0.2 m wide, and 0.28 m deep
	916	0.6 x 0.24 m	*915*	0.25 x 0.21 m
	956	0.64 x 0.33 m	*955*	0.26 x 0.27 m
	962	0.28 x 0.1 m	-	-
	964	0.4 x 0.2 m	*968*	0.21 x 0.18 m
Interior posts	*950*	0.33 x 0.2 m	*952*	0.16 x 0.18 m
	876	0.4 x 0.15 m	*878*	0.19 x 0.11 m

*Table 1: The structural elements of roundhouse **812** at Cinder Hill (Site 42S), Cutacre*

*Plate 6: Posthole **917** following half-sectioning, looking east, with post-pipe **919** visible as a dark stain*

*Plate 7: Drip-gully **970**, after partial excavation, looking north*

that the posts used in the wall were 0.15-0.3 m in diameter. It is also possible that this wall-line was repaired on its north-western side, since in this area two sets of postholes were present, implying that, at one time, the wall was defined by posts *934* and *917*, which replaced, or were replaced by, posts *946* and *920* (Fig 13).

Although no artefacts were recovered from the post-ring, several postholes did contain charcoal and charred plant remains (*Appendix 5*). Charcoal from two of the postholes (*828* and *844*) was also subject to radiocarbon assay, returning statistically consistent dates of 1390-1050 cal BC (2989±38 BP; SUERC-56427) and 1410-1200 cal BC (3035±32 BP; SUERC-56655; *Appendix 2*).

A porch projected from the wall-line on its south-eastern side, forming the entrance. This was *c* 1 m wide, aligned north-west/south-east, and defined by six postholes. Its eastern side was defined by postholes *867*, *869*, and *964*, whilst postholes *962*, *956*, and *916* defined its western side. Most appear to have secured posts, although one (*869*) may have held an upright plank. The remains of this were evident as a dark stain within the posthole, which suggests that the plank was *c* 0.4 m wide and 0.2 m thick. The postholes (*867* and *962*) closest to the wall line of the roundhouse were the smallest, whilst the others (*869*, *916*, *956*, and *964*) were larger, and had been positioned directly adjacent to each other, with intercutting postpits. Although the uprights contained within these postholes were probably contemporary, the stratigraphic relationships suggest that postholes *916* and *964* were the first to be erected during the construction of the porch.

Significantly, one of the postholes (*869*) contained two sherds of Bronze Age pottery (*Appendix 4*) and a small assemblage of wood charcoal. This charcoal was analysed (*Appendix 5*), and a sample was also subjected to radiocarbon assay, returning a date of

1370-1050 cal BC (2968±38 BP; SUERC-56428), which was statistically consistent with the two radiocarbon dates obtained from the post-ring (*above; Appendix 2*).

The other two postholes (*950* and *876*; Table 1) associated with the roundhouse were located at its centre. Whilst it is possible that these provided additional support for the roof, because the post-ring probably carried its weight, these may have been only temporary, used when the building was being constructed. They were perhaps removed once a tie-beam had been inserted, possibly to make room for a central hearth, although no evidence for this was identified.

Several features were also immediately adjacent to the roundhouse. These comprised two stakeholes (*958* and *959*), which might have secured a wattle panel close to the porch, and perhaps further emphasised or shielded the entrance. The other feature was an arcing gully (*970*), which enclosed the north-eastern side of the post-ring and also respected the position of the entrance into the house. This was 3.9 m in length, 0.3 m wide, and had a maximum depth of 0.12 m; it clearly formed a drip-gully (Pl 7), which would have collected water falling from the eaves of the roundhouse. This was filled with sandy silt and contained a sherd of Bronze Age pottery (*Appendix 4*), along with a small assemblage of charcoal and charred plant remains (*Appendix 5*).

A cluster of 12 postholes (*880*; Fig 12; Pl 8) was located 31 m to the north-east of the roundhouse, immediately west of the palaeochannel, and just off the crest of a small island of gravel (*565*; *p 22*). Eight were grouped in two parallel rows, and their positions and stratigraphic relationships indicate that they formed two sequential four-post structures (Fig 14). Nationally, such structures have a long chronology of use, being associated with Middle and Late Bronze Age and Iron Age settlement, and they are often interpreted as raised granaries (*cf* Brück 2001; Cunliffe 2005).

*Plate 8: Posthole structure **880**, before excavation, looking north-west*

The earlier of the four-post structures was defined by posts *836, 841, 555,* and *814,* with a ground plan of *c* 1 x 1.65 m, its longer axis being aligned north-east/south-west. Two of the posts (*555* and *836*) had similar diameters, at *c* 0.5 m, defining the western side of the structure; five sherds of Bronze Age pottery were recovered from posthole *555* (*Appendix 4*). The other two postholes (*814* and *841*) were smaller, with respective diameters of 0.25 m and 0.35 m. A post-pipe (*834*) was evident in posthole *836,* indicating that the post had a diameter of 0.25 m.

All of the posts defining the primary four-post structure contained burnt and charred material, including burnt stone, charcoal, and charred plant remains (Pl 9; *Appendix 5*). Charcoal fragments from postholes *555* and *836* were subjected to radiocarbon assay, which returned statistically consistent dates of 1440-1230 cal BC (3091±38 BP; SUERC-56418) and 1430-1230 cal BC (3075±38 BP; SUERC-56419; *Appendix 2*). Significantly, the high proportion of burnt and charred material within these postholes suggests that this structure had burnt down. Indeed, this probably explains the presence of the

second four-post structure, which formed a direct replacement, being constructed on exactly the same site as its predecessor.

The later four-post structure was defined by postholes *839, 853, 811,* and *816.* It was also *c* 1 x 1.65 m and its long axis was, again, aligned north-east/south-west. However, in contrast to its predecessor, the larger postholes (*839* and *853*) were on its northern side, as opposed to the western side (*above*), though the significance of this, if any, is not clear.

The larger postholes associated with the later structure were of similar size, *c* 0.4 m in diameter, and they had been dug directly into two of the earlier postholes (*836* and *841*). One of these (*853*) had a 0.23 m-diameter post-pipe (*851*) and both contained burnt and charred material (*Appendix 5*), and fragments of Bronze Age pottery (*Appendix 4*). It is possible that a proportion of the charred material, and perhaps also the pottery, had ultimately derived from the earlier structure (*above*). A sample of the charcoal from post *853* was analysed (*Appendix 5*), and a charcoal fragment subjected to radiocarbon assay.

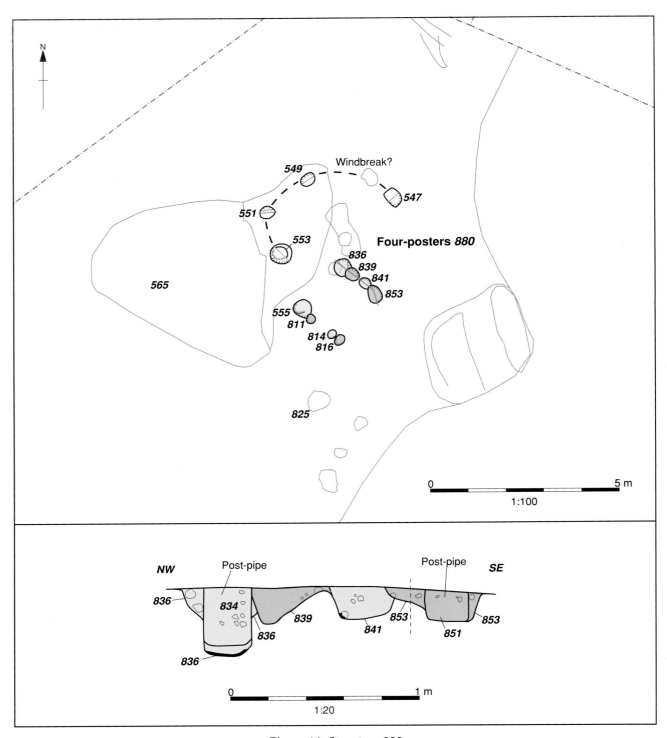

Figure 14: Structure **880**

This returned a date of 1420-1210 cal BC (3052±38 BP; SUERC-56420; *Appendix 2*), which is statistically consistent with the radiocarbon dates obtained from the earlier structure (*p 29*), suggesting that this did not have a long life.

The smaller postholes (*811* and *816*), on the south-western side of the later structure, had diameters of *c* 0.25 m and one (*811*) had been dug through posthole *555*. Both contained fragments of charcoal and *811*

also contained fragments of Bronze Age pottery (*Appendix 5*).

Four postholes (*553, 551, 549,* and *547*), with diameters of between *c* 0.5 m and *c* 0.3 m, were found immediately adjacent to these structures. These probably formed a windbreak, which shielded the area to the north. Significantly, these postholes also contained abundant burnt material (*Appendix 5*), suggesting that this structure had also burnt down, most probably in the

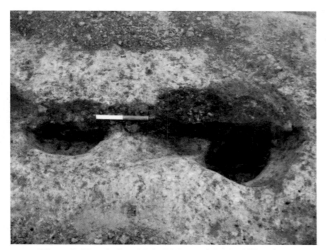

*Plate 9: Postholes **836**, **839**, and **841**, following sectioning, looking south-west*

same conflagration that destroyed the primary four-post structure (*p 29*).

A charcoal fragment from posthole 553 was subjected to radiocarbon assay, returning a date of 1440-1250 cal BC (3092±38 BP; SUERC-56425). Significantly, this date is also statistically consistent (*Appendix 5*) with those derived from the adjacent four-post structures (*pp 29-30*) and also the roundhouse (*p 28*).

Dating the Bronze Age settlement
When all the radiocarbon dates are considered, these indicate that the settlement dates to the latter part of the second millennium BC and that all of its dated features were broadly contemporary (*Appendix 2*). Moreover, modelling of the radiocarbon dates suggests that the settlement was established in *1480-1260 cal BC (95% probability)* or *1420-1300 cal BC (68% probability)*, with occupation ending in *1380-1080 cal BC (95% probability)* or *1290-1170 cal BC (68% probability)*.

Bronze Age pottery from the settlement
The small assemblage of Bronze Age pottery (*Appendix 4*) holds considerable significance, as it represents the only securely dated mid-second millennium BC domestic pottery to date from Greater Manchester (Hodgson and Brennand 2006). It comprises 15 fragments, representing no more than six individual vessels. Of these, five fragments came from one of the postholes (*555; p 29*) of the primary four-post structure; seven fragments were derived from postholes (*839, 811,* and *853*) associated with the replacement four-post structure (*p 29*); and the remaining three were recovered from a posthole in the porch (*869*) and the drip-gully (*970*), both elements of the roundhouse (*p 28*).

The pottery was handmade, having a clay fabric that incorporated coarse-stone inclusions of non-crystalline rock. On those sherds where the surface of the original vessel survived, this had been smoothed, though the coarse inclusions produced an uneven surface. One sherd from the roundhouse (posthole *869*) was, however, finer in character, in that it lacked the large inclusions evident in the other sherds.

Several of the sherds from the primary four-post structure (posthole *555*) and its later replacement (posthole *853*) were coated with thick black deposits, suggestive of burning or heating. Given that the primary four-post structure had seemingly burnt down (*p 29*), it is possible that all derived originally from the structure and were affected by this episode of burning.

Significantly, one rim sherd was present (from posthole *839* of the replacement four-post structure), which provides some indication of the form of the Middle Bronze Age vessels. This rim probably came from a barrel-shaped jar, its form being in keeping with wider Middle Bronze Age ceramic traditions (Gibson and Woods 1990, 104). Indeed, all of the sherds appear to form part of the Middle Bronze Age Deverel-Rimbury tradition. In northern England, this is characterised by plain, or only simply decorated, bucket-shaped vessels, which appear to have been produced using whatever clay and temper materials were available locally, so that there are no particularly distinctive pottery fabrics (Martin and Allen 2001). This tradition is thought to have emerged *c* 1700-1500 BC, though it became increasing popular around 1500-1200 BC (Needham 1996, 133, fig 3), with vessels being used in both settlement and funerary contexts (Gibson and Woods 1990, 104). The date of the vessels from Cinder Hill appears therefore to form part of the main *floruit* of Deverel-Rimbury pottery use, and may well indicate that this ceramic tradition was adopted by at least some, if not all, of the Bronze Age peoples of Greater Manchester.

Plant remains and charcoal from the settlement
In addition to the small assemblage of Middle Bronze Age pottery, a significant assemblage of charred plant remains and charcoal from the Bronze Age settlement was analysed (*Appendix 5*). This, in turn, provides insights into the use of the four-post structures, the agricultural activity associated with the settlement, and those tree species that were selected and utilised.

Analysis of the charred plant remains from the four-post structures proved particularly enlightening, indicating that cereal-rich deposits were present within three postholes (*553, 555,* and *836; pp 29-30*) forming elements of the primary structure, and the adjacent fence/windbreak. The cereals identified comprised barley (*Hordeum* sp), including the naked variety (*Hordeum vulgare* var *nudum*), and the presence of a number of 'twisted' grains indicates that a many-rowed (probably six-row) variety (*Hordeum vulgare* L) was under cultivation. Several wheat (*Triticum* sp) grains were also present (in posthole *553*), though it was not possible to identify these to specific type.

Given that many Middle and Late Bronze Age, as well as Iron Age, four-post structures have been interpreted as raised granaries (*cf* Gent 1983; Brück 2001; Cunliffe 2005), one possibility is that the cereals represent foodstuff that was stored within the primary structure, prior to it being burnt down (*p 29*). However, in damp climates, it was normal to store cereals in a semi-processed state, as a means of protecting the grain (*cf* Hillman 1981), and there was no clear evidence for this within the cereal remains from the three postholes. Indeed, these samples were devoid of cereal chaff and seeds/fruits of crop weeds, which often accompany cereal-processing waste, suggesting that these cereals represent a fully processed crop, rather than grain that was going to be stored (*ibid*).

One distinct feature of the cereal assemblage was that numerous sprouted, or part-sprouted, grains were present, indicating that the cereals had germinated. Whilst this might suggest that they represent a spoilt harvest, another possibility is that they were the remains of intentionally malted grain. There is a significant amount of evidence to suggest that the malting of cereal grains was widely practised in Neolithic Britain and, hence, probably, by extension, also in the Bronze Age (Dineley and Dineley 2000). In this context, malted grain would have acted as an excellent source of B-vitamins and is also the prime ingredient for sweet malt (an ingredient for barley cakes and malt porridge), and for brewing ale (*ibid*).

If the grain was intentionally malted, one possibility is that the four-post structures were integral to this process. Based on the processes used in traditional malting (*cf* Parnell 1835, 11), this would first have involved soaking the grain in a vessel, to increase its bulk by 25%. Water for this process could, therefore, have been obtained from the nearby palaeochannel, which may have contained an active stream, or held standing water, at this time. The next step in the process involved draining the grain and piling it into another vessel, for two to three days, where it began to germinate. After germination had commenced, it was then spread out on a malting floor, within a malting house, and it is possible that the four-post structures functioned as such, supporting raised malting floors. Once on the malting floor, the grain was then turned at intervals, over a two-week period, to achieve an even growth. After this had occurred, the grains would be 'parched' over a hearth, or in an oven or kiln, in order to halt the germination process,

and consequently some may have become charred (Dineley and Dineley 2000).

Although no remains of any hearth or oven, which could have parched the malted grain, were identified, it is possible that such activities, and perhaps also other activities requiring a hearth or oven, may have occurred between the four-post structures and the fence/windbreak. Indeed, this would also explain the requirement for a windbreak in this part of the settlement and, perhaps, also the presence of burnt daub fragments in posthole *555*, associated with the primary structure. In addition, this posthole contained calcined animal bone and metalworking debris, which may also have been derived from activities occurring at the settlement.

Significantly, evidence for the use of the area between the windbreak and primary four-post structure for the parching of cereals was provided by the spatial configuration of the charred-cereal-rich postholes. Of these, two (*555* and *836*; Fig 14) formed the north-western side of the primary structure, whilst the third was from the fence/windbreak, posthole *553* being closest to this side of the structure. Given that none of the other postholes contained cereals, this may suggest that the charred cereals relate to activities that were taking place between the primary four-post structure and the windbreak. In addition, this putative activity may also have eventually resulted in the suspected conflagration that led to the destruction of the primary four-post structure.

Apart from the charred grain, the only other charred plant remains from the primary four-post structure were a single willow (*Salix* sp) catkin from posthole *555*, and two charred hazelnut (*Corylus avellana*) shell fragments from posthole *836*. It is possible that the hazelnut fragments represent a collected food resource that was consumed close to the structure.

Aside from these charred plant remains, small quantities of charred material were also recovered from the roundhouse, specifically from a posthole (*828*) forming an element of its post-ring, and from its drip-gully (*970*; *pp 27-8*). These comprised barley grains, a single cereal culm node, and two seeds, of pale persicaria (*Persicaria lapathifolia*) and corn-spurry (*Spergula arvensis*), which are both considered typical weeds of cultivated ground (Stace 2010). Although these remains were sparse, when allied with the plant remains from the adjacent four-post structure and windbreak, these indicate that both naked barley and wheat, though of unknown type, were the main crops cultivated by the Bronze Age group occupying the settlement. This appears to conform to the wider evidence for Middle Bronze Age cereal cultivation as, for example, seen at other settlement sites in the region, such as the Middle Bronze Age settlement at Irby, on the Wirral (Philpott and Adams 2010). At that site, naked barley and emmer wheat (*Triticum dicoccum*) appear to have been the favoured crops (*ibid*). Significantly, naked barley was perhaps favoured as it is an easily processed food crop, which will grow happily in the climate of northern England (Dickin *et al* 2010). On the down side, it has a low germination rate and produces comparatively low yields, when compared to other types of cereal (*ibid*).

Many of the features in the Bronze Age settlement also contained charcoal, and 13 samples were analysed (*Appendix 5*). This provided insights into both the four-post structures and the roundhouse, indicating that those posts associated with the four-post structures contained abundant quantities of charcoal. Much of this may have been derived from the burning of the primary structure, and also presumably from activities undertaken in its immediate vicinity. This charcoal was predominantly oak, alder/hazel, and/or ash, which may suggest that these species were used in the construction of the structures, and were also burnt in any hearths/ovens that were potentially next to them. Indeed, in this context, oak and ash would have provided both superior structural wood and fuel wood (Edlin 1949). Given this, it is perhaps telling that the analysed postholes contained mixtures of ash and oak heartwood, perhaps representing structural timbers, and oak and ash roundwood, that may have been used as fuel.

It is perhaps also significant that in two of the postholes (*555* and *836*; *p 29*) forming elements of the primary four-post structure, oak was the most abundant species, tentatively suggesting that these postholes originally held oak posts. Furthermore, the charcoal assemblage from posthole *553* (an element of the windbreak) contained larger quantities of alder roundwood, suggesting that these posts may have secured a wattle panel of alder.

There was no evidence that the roundhouse had been burnt, rather that its posts had rotted *in situ* (*p 26*), and thus it is likely that the charcoal present represents fuel wood. Therefore, this charcoal perhaps derived from the roundhouse's hearth, although this was not identified, and/or from burning taking place in its immediate vicinity. The assemblage was dominated by mature oak, but also contained small oak twigs, and frequent to common alder/hazel roundwood.

Interpreting the Bronze Age settlement
The remains uncovered by the excavation at Cinder Hill are highly significant, in that they represent the first definitive example of a Bronze Age settlement that has been examined in Greater Manchester. The settlement appears to have consisted of a single

roundhouse, which probably housed an extended family, constructed between the fifteenth and thirteenth centuries BC, a period which is traditionally characterised as the Middle Bronze Age (*cf* Needham 1996). The house was of a typical Bronze Age form (*Ch 9, p 224*) and its main structural elements were built of oak and ash timbers. Although its wall line was seemingly repaired at some stage, this house was eventually abandoned and left to rot. The inhabitants who occupied the house were certainly engaged in cereal cultivation, and grew both naked barley and wheat. It also seems quite possible that the sequential four-post structures to the north-east of the roundhouse acted as malting floors, where sprouted barley was turned, to promote sprouting and growth. This barley could then have been used to make beer and/or sweet malt.

Roman Activity

Although across Greater Manchester the general pattern of Iron Age settlement and land-use may have changed comparatively little during the Roman period (AD 43-*c* 450), this period is typified by the construction of forts by the Roman military, and a concomitant network of roads (*cf* Philpott 2006, 59). In addition, items of Roman material culture, such as coins, pottery, metalwork, and glass, were introduced into the region, and the indigenous communities of the area gradually adopted some of these objects (*ibid*).

Perhaps the most significant of the Roman military installations was the auxiliary fort established at Manchester in *c* AD 79, which may well have been garrisoned until the end of the Roman period (Bryant *et al* 1986; Gregory 2007). Its significance lay in the fact that it formed the central hub for a network of major Roman roads, which radiated out from it, linking this fort with several other Roman military installations across the region (Fig 15).

Although no known Roman roads directly traverse the Cutacre site, the probable line of the Manchester to Wigan road (road 702; Margary 1967, 369) lies *c* 600 m to the south (Fig 16). A second putative road may also have lain immediately to the north of Cutacre, on the line of the modern A6. This road may have branched from the Manchester to Wigan road, possibly at Chorlton Fold near Worsley, and led to Blackrod, from where it may have joined the Wigan to Walton-le-Dale road (road 70c; *op cit*, 368), at a point north of Wigan (Watkin 1883, 46-7). To the north-east of Cutacre, the line of this road is suggested by the place-names Stanney Street, in Walkden, and Street Gate, in Little Hulton. In addition, between these points, Watkin (*op cit*, 46) reported that in Little Hulton

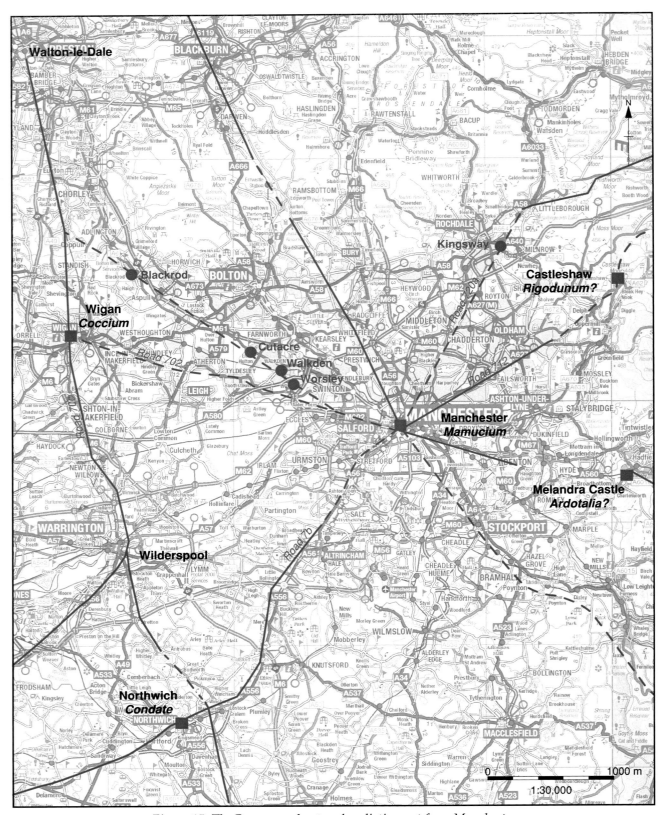

Figure 15: The Roman road network radiating out from Manchester

the road was uncovered during the construction of the railway and was found to be 'only ten feet wide and paved'. Between this point and Lane Ends (to the north-west of Cutacre), it had been traced 'by slight remains' (*op cit*, 47).

In contrast, a possible Roman road (road 720a; Margary 1967, 403) is suspected to have traversed the Kingsway Business Park (Fig 15). This seemingly ran from Manchester, perhaps branching off the main York-Chester Roman road (road 712 in its section

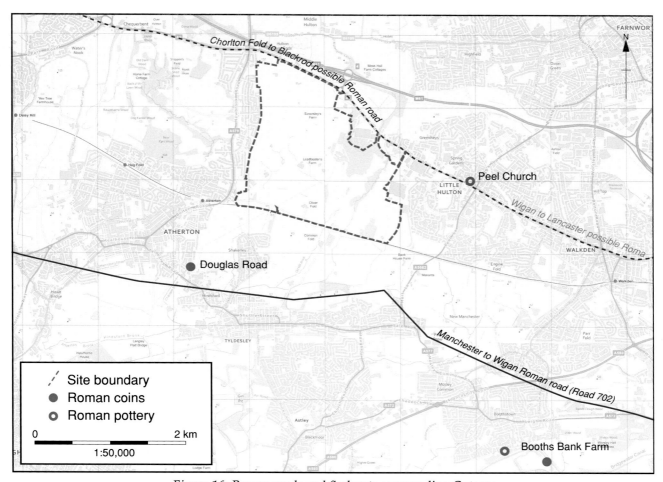

Figure 16: Roman roads and findspots surrounding Cutacre

between Manchester and Castleshaw; *ibid*), across the Pennines towards Ilkley, and then on to Aldborough (*ibid*). However, the origins of this road are contentious, particularly along one of its better-preserved sections. This extends between Littleborough and Huddersfield, across Blackstone Edge, where it forms a 4.9 m-wide paved road, composed of stone setts 'supported by kerbs and having a remarkable middle rib of large flat stones of millstone grit carved with a central groove or trough which shows considerable wear' (*ibid*). This paved road was argued to be Roman in date by several eighteenth-/nineteenth-century antiquarians (*inter alia*: Whitaker 1773; Colley-March 1883) and also by the eminent Roman archaeologist Sir Ian Richmond (Richmond 1925). However, documentary research suggests that this section, at least, might date to the eighteenth century, forming part of a turnpike, and that this may have followed the route of a medieval packhorse road (Pearson *et al* 1985, 125-8). Needless to say, it is still possible these routes followed the course of an earlier road that was perhaps established in the Roman period.

Unsurprisingly, a few Roman artefacts are also known from both the Cutacre and Kingsway Business Park areas, though these are not seemingly associated with identifiable settlement sites. At Kingsway, these include several coin hoards and coins, querns, a bronze bracelet, and the arm from a small silver statute, possibly dedicated to the VI Legion Victrix, that was discovered at Tunshill to the east of the business park (Fig 17; Fishwick 1889, 12; Pearson *et al* 1985, 111-12). In addition, a stone with a late Roman inscription, possibly derived from a temple or shrine, was discovered at Low House Farm (GMHER 2730.1.1).

The evidence from the Cutacre area is also minimal (Fig 16). It includes a piece of grey-ware pottery from Peel Church, Little Hulton, which may date to the first century AD (Mullineux 1964, 10-11), two late third-century coins from Douglas Road, Atherton (GMHER 4297.1.0), and a hoard of 1070 Roman coins from Booths Bank Farm, Worsley, that was deposited in the AD 290s (GMHER 476.1.0).

Investigating the putative Roman road at the Kingsway Business Park

One aim of the archaeological investigation at the Kingsway Business Park was to uncover any evidence of the Roman branch road that was postulated to cross this area. With this in mind,

35

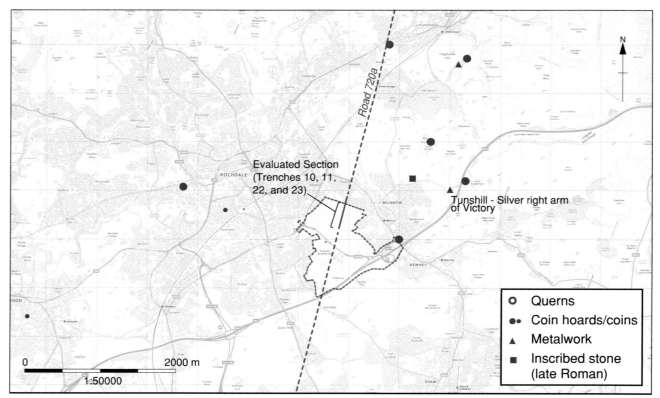

Figure 17: Roman roads and findspots within and surrounding the Kingsway Business Park

four evaluation trenches were excavated across its suggested line (10, 11, 22, and 23; Fig 17). However, no remains relating to this road were discovered, the only features present relating to a former field boundary and nineteenth-century drainage ditches. This may, therefore, suggest that no such road crossed this area. Indeed, it is quite possible, given the doubtful Roman nature of the Blackstone Edge road (p 35), that no such route existed in the Roman period.

3

MEDIEVAL LANDSCAPES

Richard A Gregory, Peter Arrowsmith, and Ian Miller

The programme of archaeological excavation at Cutacre revealed important evidence of medieval activity, which has significance both to the local area and the wider region. The evidence related to both the early medieval period, an era that is generally under-represented in the archaeological record of the North West (R M Newman 2006), and the later medieval period.

The evidence for the earlier period came from palaeoenvironmental remains, derived from Cinder Hill and Wharton Hall, which provide insights into the environment and, importantly, its exploitation by the early medieval communities of the area. Indeed, this evidence holds particular significance as, more generally, 'little is known about land-use, landscape, and climate change from the fifth to eleventh centuries, on both a regional and national level' (Newman and Brennand 2007, 79).

Evidence for the later medieval period was also present at Cinder Hill and Wharton Hall. Although at the latter site this was scant, Cinder Hill contained important remains relating to late medieval iron production. This evidence has great regional significance as, although late medieval bloomeries probably formed a fairly frequent component of the medieval landscape, only a few have been excavated in Greater Manchester and the wider North West (C Newman 2006, 132-3). Moreover, nationally, the evidence from Cinder Hill represents an important addition to the corpus of excavated late medieval bloomery sites (*cf* Dungworth 2015, 22), which did not employ waterpower in the ironworking process (*ie* to power the bellows of smelting furnaces and, in some cases, hammers, which were used in smithing; *cf* Paynter 2011).

Although no direct evidence for medieval activity was uncovered by the archaeological excavations at the Kingsway Business Park, several landscape features were identified, which may have their origins in the late medieval period. These features formed the subject of a topographical survey (*p 56*).

Medieval Cutacre

The early medieval landscape (early fifth to late eleventh centuries)

Prior to the archaeological investigations, the evidence for early medieval activity in the Cutacre area was scant, being confined to the place-names of the three townships in which the development was situated. Of these, the township of Tyldesley cum Shakerley, now in the Metropolitan Borough of Wigan, covered the southern part; the township of Middle Hulton, now in Bolton, covered its north-western part; whilst its eastern part fell in Little Hulton, now in the City of Salford (Fig 18). Tyldesley and Shakerley both contain the element *-ley*, derived from the Old English *leah*, meaning a 'woodland' or 'clearing in a wood' (Gelling and Cole 2003, 220), whilst Little Hulton, Middle Hulton, and the township of Over Hulton, to the west, share the same name, originally Hilton. The first element is the Old English *hyll*, a hill, which clearly refers to the local topography (*op cit*, 192). The second element is the Old English *tun*, a term for a settlement, with meanings including a 'farmstead' and 'estate' (Kenyon 1991, 106).

Significantly, the *tun* and *leah* elements appear to have first come into common use in about the mid-eighth century (Gelling and Cole 2003, 237) and, as such, they suggest that settlement dating to this period existed in the Cutacre area, or its environs. *Leah* place-names, though plentiful in Cheshire, are relatively rare in Lancashire, although Tyldesley and Shakerley form part of a band of such names, which also includes Worsley and Kearsley to the east, Astley to the south, and Leigh and Hindley to the west (Kenyon 1991, 104). They imply a relatively late survival of woodland, which on the west may have adjoined a more open landscape, suggested by the element *feld* in the place-name Makerfield (*ibid*). Where *leah* place-names are clustered, as in this instance, the relevant meaning is understood to be a 'clearing', with the name denoting a settlement within a wooded environment (Gelling and Cole 2003, 237).

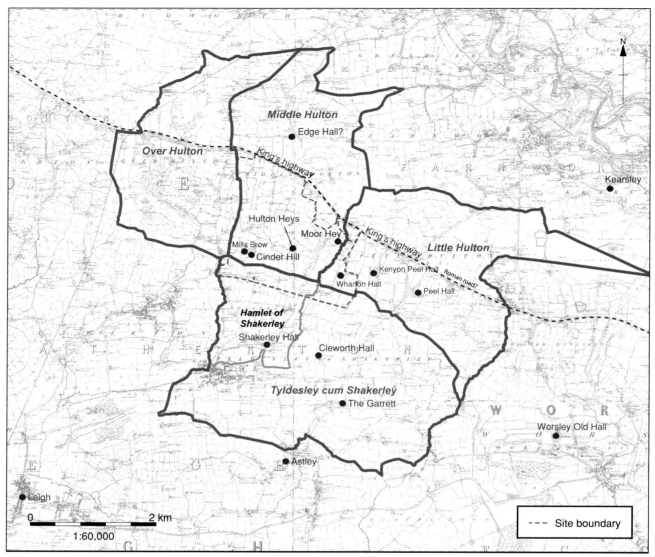

Figure 18: Medieval townships and sites within the Cutacre area, superimposed on the OS first edition six-inch maps (1849; 1850a)

Reconstructing Cutacre's early medieval landscape: the palaeoenvironmental evidence

Significantly, the archaeological investigations provided corroboration for the presence of early medieval settlement in the Cutacre area, confirming the place-name evidence (*p 37*). Although no direct remains for settlement were recovered, palaeoenvironmental evidence indicates that the Cutacre area was probably settled and farmed during this period.

The evidence for this was derived from Cinder Hill and Wharton Hall (Fig 18). At Cinder Hill, a small fragment of residual alder charcoal was recovered from a late medieval gully (**700**; *p 49*), which perhaps related to the clearance of woodland; it returned a radiocarbon date of cal AD 540-660 (1451±38 BP; SUERC-56416). This putative phase of clearance may therefore equate to the period when the area was first subsumed into the Anglo-Saxon kingdom of Northumbria during the seventh century (R M Newman 2006, 91).

At Wharton Hall, evidence for both the medieval environment and human activity could be discerned in a pollen monolith extracted from a palaeochannel (*Appendix 1*). This palaeochannel (**1305**; Fig 19) was aligned north-east/south-west and extended along the eastern limit of the field once occupied by the hall. It was 1.5 m deep, and may have contained an active stream in the later prehistoric or Roman period. It also had waterlogged wood (**1304**) towards its base and was sealed by a relict soil (**1001**), which began to form in the latter part of the sixteenth or early seventeenth century (*Ch 5, p 126*).

Radiocarbon dating (*Appendix 2*), and the pollen signatures, indicate that the channel filled during the medieval period, pollen and non-pollen palynomorphs (NPP) being incorporated into the sediments, allowing some palaeoenvironmental reconstruction. Four distinct pollen zones have been identified that relate to the former environment,

38

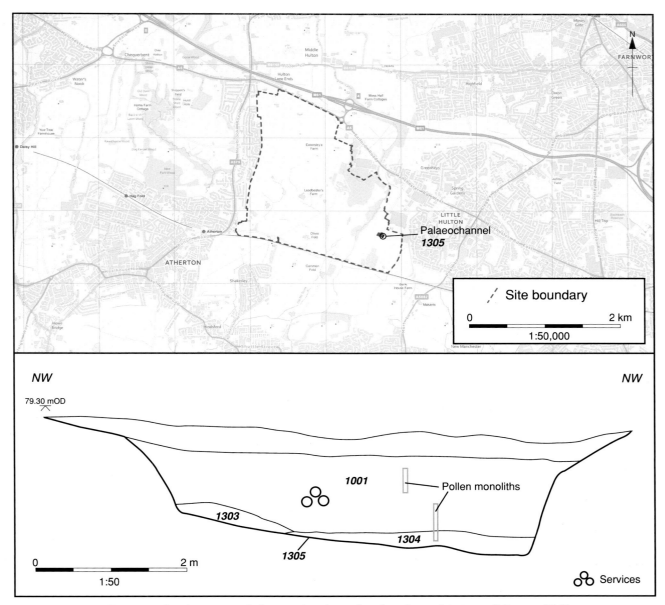

Figure 19: South-western-facing section through palaeochannel **1305**, *at Wharton Hall*

revealing some interesting events, which may be interpreted in terms of human interaction with the landscape (Fig 20).

Two of the zones (Cu-a and Cu-b; *Appendix 1*) appear to date to the early medieval period, and may contain evidence relevant to the landscape between the eighth and tenth centuries. The earlier (Cu-a) was dated by a radiocarbon assay on humic acid within the organic sediment, returning a date of cal AD 770-990 (1139±30 BP; SUERC-58092; *Appendix 2*).

There was also evidence for arable cultivation nearby, implying that the Cutacre area had witnessed early medieval settlement of some description. Cereal-type pollen suggested the cultivation of barley and wheat/oats, assuming that these were not derived from wild grasses (Andersen

1979), and the consistency of its occurrence might relate to crop processing in the vicinity of the palaeochannel.

Early medieval pastoral farming was also apparent within the earliest pollen zone, in that abundant grass pollen (Poaceae) was present, as well as that of ribwort plantain, which is a potential indicator for this type of agricultural activity (*cf* Behre 1981; Tipping 2002). Other open-ground flora consisted of a range of herbs, some (*eg* sedges (Cyperaceae) and bedstraw) known to inhabit wet areas, whilst others (docks/sorrels, cinquefoils (*Potentilla*-type), mints (*Mentha*-type), common knapweed (*Centaurea nigra*), daisy-types (*Aster*-type), and dandelion-types (*Taraxacum*-type)) may grow in a wide variety of habitats, including hedgerows, field edges, footpaths, and ruderal communities (Stace 2010).

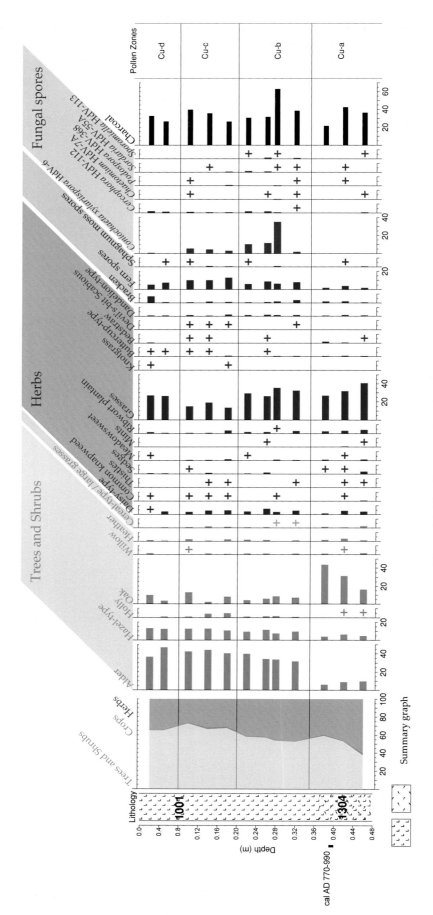

Figure 20: The Cutacre pollen diagram

40

Although there were clearly significant open areas available for agriculture, a major part of the landscape was wooded, primarily with oak, but lesser quantities of alder, hazel, and a range of other trees and shrubs was recognised, including willow (*Salix*). The earliest pollen zone also contained evidence for burning, with moderate quantities of microcharcoal being identified. This presumably also derived from an early settlement, or may reflect intentional woodland clearance.

Significantly, the pollen evidence from the second zone (Cu-b) suggests that there was more extensive clearance of the area's oak woodland than in the preceding period. Evidence from the palynological assemblages also suggests that dead oak may have been infected by fungi and possibly burnt as fuel. It appears that, following the clearance of oak, alder carr became established and was persistent throughout the remainder of the pollen zone. In addition to alder, these clearances also appear to have contained hazel-type scrub and ferns (evidenced by monolete fern spores (Pteropsida), bracken (*Pteridium*), and polypody ferns (*Polypodium vulgare*)), and grassland areas that would have been suitable for grazing. Indeed, more specific evidence for pastoral farming was present, as ribwort plantain was consistently recorded, suggesting grazing activity (Tipping 2002).

Further confirmation for this was also provided by the presence of a range of fungal spores known to exist on animal dung (*eg Sporomiella* (HdV-113), *Cercophora* (HdV-112), *Chaetomium* (HdV-7A), *Podospora* (HdV-368), and *Sordaria* (HdV-55); van Geel and Aptroot 2006). Apart from the grazing of livestock, there was also evidence for arable agricultural in the form of cereal-type pollen. However, the pollen counts for this were generally low, becoming slightly more frequent within the upper part of the pollen zone. This therefore suggests the existence of small-scale cereal cultivation, or crop processing, close to the Wharton Hall palaeochannel in the medieval period.

Late medieval Cutacre (late eleventh to early sixteenth centuries)

Some indication of the form of the late medieval landscape of the Cutacre area, and its medieval landholdings, can be derived from the documentary evidence for its component townships of Tyldesley cum Shakerley, Middle Hulton, and Little Hulton (Fig 18).

Tyldesley

Tyldesley, in the parish of Leigh, is first documented in the early thirteenth century as a manor held by the de Tyldesleys, who took their name from the place. Subsequently, in 1301, Henry de Tyldesley divided the estate between his two sons and thus effectively created two manors within the same township (Farrer and Brownbill 1907, 439-44). These manors contained separate halls, though these were beyond the study area. One manor contained the hall known as the Garrett, and a hall is still present at this site, though it is clearly a building of the sixteenth century and later, although it probably stands on the site of its medieval predecessor (*ibid*). The other 'reputed' manor lay in the northern part of the township and included the freehold estate of Cleworth Hall (*ibid*). The hamlet of Shakerley was also in this north-western part of the township, and was given in the early thirteenth century by the de Tyldesleys to Cockersand Abbey, under which it was held by the de Shakerley family, living at Shakerley Hall (*ibid*). The history of the Shakerley family also provides early evidence for the working of the local Coal-measures. For example, in 1429, Hugh Tyldesley, who then held the 'reputed' manor, accused Robert Shakerley and others of digging his land in Tyldesley and taking away sea coal (*op cit*, 444 n9).

Hulton

Middle Hulton and Little Hulton lay within the medieval parish of Eccles and later in the parish of Deane, created in 1541 (Farrer and Brownbill 1911a, 3). Along with the township of Over Hulton to the west, they appear to have originally formed a single post-Conquest manor of Hulton (*op cit*, 25). The prefixes Nether (later Little), Middle, and Over are all documented by the sixteenth century (Ekwall 1922, 43), by which time the original manor had long been divided. Hugh Putrell gave land in Hulton and in the neighbouring township of Worsley to Richard, son of Elias de Worsley, between 1195 and 1212. This grant appears to have been of the whole of the manor of Worsley and those parts of the manor of Hulton which became the later townships of Middle and Little Hulton. The remainder, which became Over Hulton, was in the lordship of the de Hulton family (Farrer and Brownbill 1911b, 376-7; 1911a, 26).

The de Worsley family held their share of the manor of Hulton until the early fifteenth century, when their estates passed by marriage to the de Masseys. These families had a manor house in Worsley, probably on the site of the present Worsley Old Hall (Walker and Tindall 1985, 148).

Halls and farms in Middle Hulton

There is documentary evidence in the late thirteenth to mid-fourteenth centuries of a hall of the de Worsleys in Middle Hulton. This includes a reference in 1354 to Wood Hall, and parts of its demesne named Wood Hey and Moor Hey (Farrer and Brownbill 1911a, 29 n58). The names suggest that the hall was a late medieval creation, which was established on assarted (cleared and enclosed) land. Fields named

Moor Hey are shown on a *c* 1764 Bridgewater estate plan of Middle Hulton, in the north-east part of the study area, with two others on the township's northern boundary (SCA BW/E/1).

In the early fifteenth century, a survey of the de Masseys' estate in Middle Hulton referred to 'le Egge hall' (*ie* Edge Hall), tenanted by John 'del Egge' and Richard his son (Partington 1909a, 2, 7). It is believed that this was situated at the site of the later Edge Fold, in the northern part of the township, and it has also been supposed that Edge Hall was originally the hall of the de Worsleys (*ibid*). In addition to a manor house, there is documentary evidence for a mill in Middle Hulton at which the tenants of the de Worsleys would have been obliged to take their corn and pay for it to be ground. The mill was in existence by 1296 (Farrer and Brownbill 1911a, 29 n58), and in 1341 it was described as a water mill situated on the north side of the king's highway, the present A6 (Partington 1909a, 3). Although the origin of the name, Mills Brow Farm, is not known, it might relate to an early mill in the Cutacre area.

The de Massey survey also indicates that in the early fifteenth century there were at least six tenements in Middle Hulton in addition to Edge Hall, but their locations are not specified (*op cit*, 7). Other documentary evidence suggests that one late medieval settlement may have been located at the later Hulton Heys farm, within the Cutacre development. 'Le Hulton hey' (*ie* the 'enclosure of Hulton') is mentioned in the early fifteenth-century survey, and is described there as being divided into separate parcels (*op cit*, 2, 7). In 1467 and 1484, leases of land in 'Hulton Hey' were made by William de Massey and Geoffrey de Massey respectively. The 1484 grant gave the lessees the right to build on and marl the ground, while de Massey undertook to maintain hedges and ditches (Farrer and Brownbill 1911a, 30 n58). The extent of the medieval 'Hulton Hey' is unclear, but the name of Hulton Heys implies the general location and suggests that the farm itself may have been of late medieval origin.

Wharton Hall: Little Hulton
The eastern part of the Cutacre area, in the township of Little Hulton, contained the site of Wharton Hall, which was excavated archaeologically (*p 43*). This was one of three halls in this township, the others being Peel Hall, also known as Wicheves, which is documented from the thirteenth century, and Kenyon Peel Hall, recorded from *c* 1600 (Farrer and Brownbill 1911a, 30-3). Both Peel Hall and Kenyon Peel Hall were moated sites.

Sources in the post-medieval period show that Wharton Hall was the centre of a freehold estate.

This principally comprised a belt of land along the western boundary of the Little Hulton township, on the south extending into the township of Tyldesley cum Shakerley. On the east, it also met the estate of Kenyon Peel Hall (SCA BW/T 7/1; BW/T 7/14; Fig 21). In addition to Wharton Hall itself, this estate contained several farm tenements and other dwellings.

The earliest known explicit mention of Wharton Hall dates from 1582, when the hall and its estate were in the ownership of William Warton (SCA BW/T 7/1). However, there is a succession of references in the medieval period to the de Warton, or de Waverton, family as local landowners, making it likely that the site dates back to that time. The 'clausura' (*ie* enclosure) of William de Waverton in Little Hulton is documented in 1295 and is believed to refer to the Wharton Hall estate (Partington 1909a, 4, 78), whilst a messuage and land in Wharton of John de Warton are mentioned in 1356 (Farrer and Brownbill 1911a, 30 n60). In the early fifteenth century, Denis Warton is also recorded as a free tenant of the lordship of Worsley, to which he was liable to give a pair of gloves as the annual rent, and in 1446 the same Denis granted all his lands in Hulton and Tyldesley to trustees on behalf of his son and heir, Ralph (Farrer and Brownbill 1911b, 379 n33; 1911a, 30 n60).

The late medieval environment: Wharton Hall

The pollen monolith extracted from the palaeochannel at Wharton Hall (*p 38*) also provided evidence for the late medieval environment surrounding Cutacre's medieval settlements, and details relating to changing medieval farming regimes. It appears that two of the pollen zones identified (Cu-c and Cu-d; Fig 20) contained evidence relevant to this period (*Appendix 1*). Although these two sequential zones were not directly dated, they certainly post-dated the early medieval period, whilst the uppermost zone (Cu-d) was also sealed by a relict horticultural soil (**1001**), which dates to the latter part of the sixteenth or early seventeenth century (*Ch 5, p 126*). The evidence therefore suggests that pollen zones Cu-c and Cu-d contained palynological evidence relevant to the later medieval period.

The earlier zone (Cu-c) contained a marked pollen signature, which can be equated with known historical climatic events. This was defined by relatively abundant quantities of holly pollen (a thermophilous shrub; Godwin 1994), which suggests that a comparatively warm climate was in existence when this pollen zone formed. It is therefore likely that this relates to the 'medieval climatic optimum', within England estimated to have occurred in *c* 1150-1350 (Mann 2002). If these warmer temperatures existed, it is perhaps no coincidence that the counts

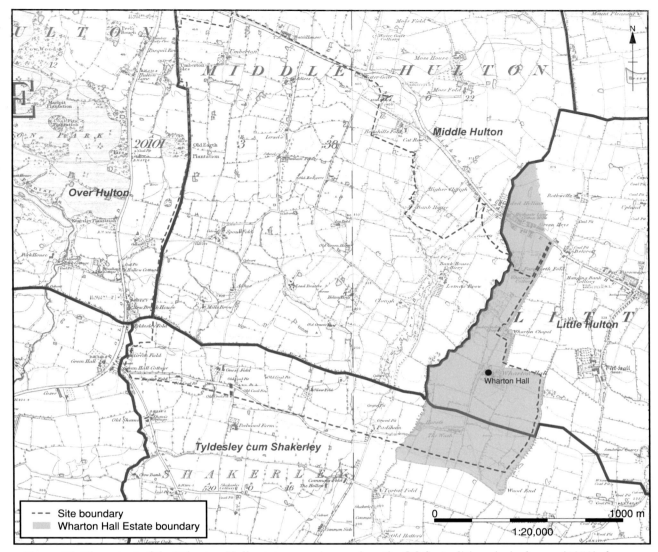

Figure 21: The extent of the Wharton Hall estate, superimposed on the OS first edition six-inch map (1850), from an 1881 deed of sale

for cereal pollen slightly increased within this zone, when compared with the preceding zone (Cu-b; *p 39*). The pollen of knotgrass was also present, which is a weed that is often association with cereal growth and cultivated land (Behre 1981; Gaillard 2007). This evidence suggests that arable farming may have become a more prominent feature of the Cutacre landscape between the mid-twelfth and mid-fourteenth centuries. This apparent increase in arable agriculture also appears to correspond to a possible decrease in pastoral farming, as evinced by decreasing pollen values for ribwort plantain, grass pollen, and also the fungal spores associated with animal dung. Apart from pollen associated with agricultural activity, there were indications that there was an increase in alder during this period.

In contrast, the succeeding pollen zone (Cu-d), which may relate to the period extending between the mid-fourteenth and sixteenth centuries, indicates that cereal farming dramatically decreased. Moreover,

evidence suggests that the landscape was dominated by grassland areas, perhaps with some hedgerows, and was primarily used for pastoral farming.

Medieval activity at Wharton Hall

The documentary evidence suggests that a late medieval estate was centred on Wharton Hall, which may have been the site of the medieval hall occupied by the de Warton family (*p 42*). The known site of the post-medieval hall (*Ch 5, p 121*) formed the focus of open-area excavation, one aim of this work being to determine the presence of any remains that might relate to the suspected medieval dwelling.

Although a fairly extensive area was excavated, which exposed the main body of the post-medieval hall, no medieval structural remains were encountered, which could be equated either with a medieval hall, or other early buildings or structures. However, a small assemblage of medieval artefacts was recovered, which suggests that there had been activity at the

43

site in that period, and it is possible that its remains had been comprehensively destroyed in the early post-medieval period, during the rebuilding of the Hall. Significantly, this artefactual material included 14 fragments of medieval window glass, from the foundation trench of a seventeenth-century wall (*1133*; *Ch 5, p 134*), which came from a leaded window, the design preserved on one fragment suggesting a simple grisaille pattern. This technique was popular in the thirteenth to fifteenth centuries, and was increasingly associated with secular houses of some status in this period (Crewe 1987, 19). It is therefore highly likely that this material was derived from a window in the medieval hall, or from a family chapel (*Appendix 4*).

As well as the glass, a small assemblage of medieval pottery was recovered from the site, although all from residual contexts. Five sherds came from the topsoil (*1108*), and also a seventeenth-century relict soil (*1109*) and drain (*1284*). All of the sherds were in a gritty fabric and some had the remains of a pale green glaze coating them. These are part of the Northern Gritty tradition (Fabrics 1, 2, and 4; *Appendix 4*), which was widely distributed across northern England and was produced between the twelfth and fourteenth centuries (McCarthy and Brooks 1988). In addition, two post-medieval pits also contained fragments of probable daub, which could conceivably have derived from medieval buildings (*Appendix 4*).

Cinder Hill: a late medieval bloomery site

During the preliminary stages of the archaeological investigation, it was suggested that Cinder Hill might contain evidence for early industry, based on its field-name, which appears on a 1722 survey of the area (*Ch 1, p 8*). It was suspected that the name 'cinder' could denote the site of medieval or early post-medieval kilns or furnaces, which were, in turn, responsible for creating large quantities of industrial residues. This suggestion was initially confirmed by a magnetometer survey of the site (*Ch 1, p 8*), which detected an area of magnetic debris at the northern end of the field, thought to reflect industrial activity. Subsequently, the presence of early industry was confirmed by trial trenching, which exposed numerous fragments of slag (*Ch 1, p 10*).

Based on the results of the trial trenching, the site was extensively excavated, resulting in the discovery of a late medieval bloomery. The remains were largely concentrated at the northern end of Cinder Hill (Site 42N), upslope from the Bronze Age settlement (Site 42S; *Ch 2, p 25*), within a *c* 50 x 43 m open-area trench (Fig 22); only one late medieval feature was present in the southern part of the field (Site 42S). All of these features were, however, cut into natural deposits of glacial till, and those at the northern end of the field were concentrated in a north-west/south-east line

along the brow of the gentle slope that declined to both the south and west. Several tree-throws (*559, 574, 717, 728, 738*, and *741*; Fig 23) were also evident in the vicinity of the late medieval remains. Although it is possible that these marked the position of trees that were present when the iron-smelting was in operation, given the suspected presence of prehistoric tree-throws in the southern part of Cinder Hill (*Ch 2, p 22*), some may actually date to this earlier period.

Sherds of medieval pottery in the Northern Gritty-ware tradition were recovered from several features, suggesting that they dated to sometime between the twelfth and fourteenth centuries (*Appendix 4*). In addition, fragments of charcoal were subjected to radiocarbon assay from five features (*Appendix 2*). Aside from one fragment, which appears to represent an early medieval residual ecofact (*p 38*), the other charcoal samples confirmed the late medieval date of the bloomery site. Moreover, when these radiocarbon dates are statistically ordered, they suggest that at least three broad phases of activity occurred at the Cinder Hill site (*Appendix 2*).

The bloomery

The remains relating to the late medieval bloomery were fairly extensive. In the northern part of the site (Site 42N), they included two furnace bases, which were associated with tapping pits, three possible furnace bases, a heat-affected feature that might represent the remains of a reheating hearth, and other possible structures. More limited remains relating to the bloomery were also evident downslope, to the south (Site 42S), in the form of charcoal clamp *864* (Fig 22).

The furnaces

Two definitive, and three possible, furnaces were identified, in which iron ore would have been smelted, to produce wrought-iron blooms. The two definitive furnace bases were fairly well defined (*588/581* and *722/720*; Fig 23) and contained some of the major components relating to the processes of medieval iron smelting. Both were of similar form, and were possibly contemporary (*Appendix 2*), each comprising two circular, conjoining pits, one forming the base of the furnace's firing chamber, the other a tapping pit, where the molten slag was collected during the tapping of the furnace. Both of the furnaces and associated tapping pits had been cut directly into the natural clay, which had been discoloured by oxidisation during firing (Pl 10).

In the case of furnace *588/581*, the southern pit (*588*; Fig 24) formed the chamber, with a diameter of *c* 0.9 m. It was *c* 0.4 m deep and, although it was not lined, it contained three sequential deposits of gritty clay, intermixed with slag, which may represent the remains of the collapsed, or demolished, clay

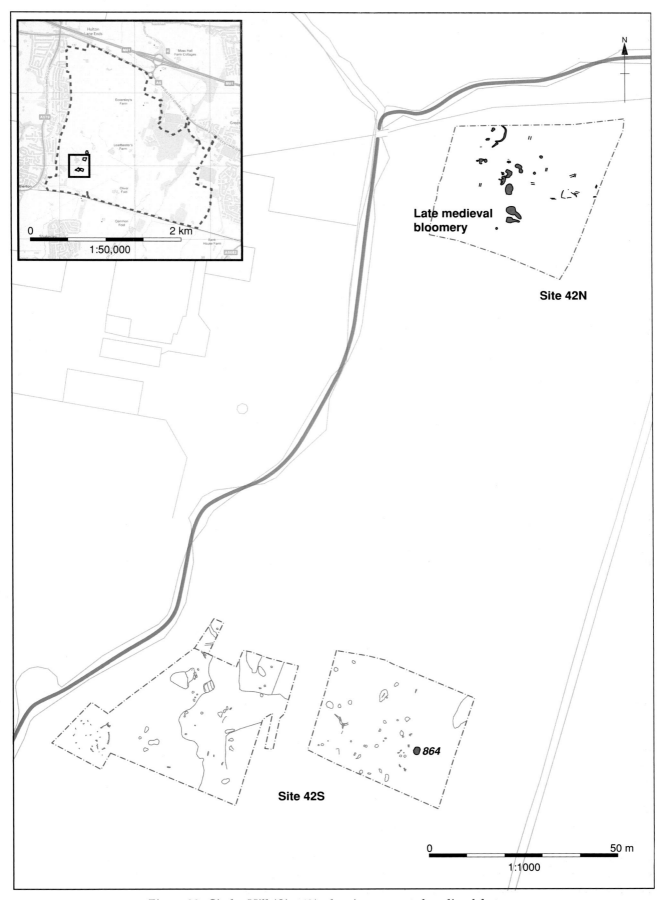

Late medieval
bloomery

Site 42N

Site 42S

● 864

0   2 km

1:50,000

0   50 m

1:1000

Figure 22: Cinder Hill (Site 42), showing excavated medieval features

45

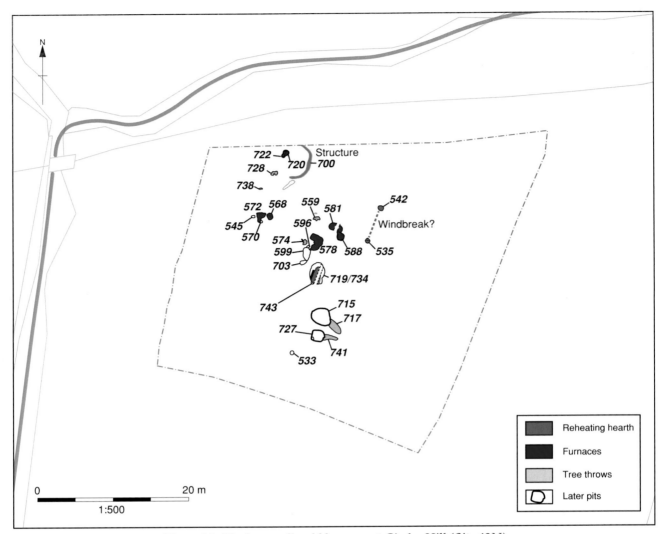

Figure 23: The late medieval bloomery at Cinder Hill (Site 42N)

superstructure. A fragment of alder charcoal from the uppermost fill (*591*) returned a radiocarbon date of cal AD 1050-1280 (828±38 BP; SUERC-56410; *Appendix 2*).

An opening, or mouth, was also apparent, which was fairly wide at *c* 0.5 m across. It may be significant that this opening was on the north-western side of the furnace, and hence did not face the prevailing wind. This probably indicates that the furnace did not use any natural draughts, but instead was solely reliant on forced-draughts. It is therefore likely that one or more bellows were employed to pump air into the chamber, and that the furnace mouth was only opened during the tapping of slag.

Significantly, evidence for this slag-tapping process was present in the form of a 0.3 m-wide channel, which extended from the mouth of the furnace chamber into the conjoined tapping pit (*581*). This lay to the north and had been partially removed by a post-medieval field drain. It had an oval plan, measuring *c* 1.7 x 1 m, and contained several charcoal-

and slag-rich deposits. A fragment of alder charcoal from one of these (*587*) produced a radiocarbon date of cal AD 1150-1280 (817±38 BP; SUERC-56415), which was statistically consistent with the date derived from the adjacent firing chamber (*above*; *Appendix 2*).

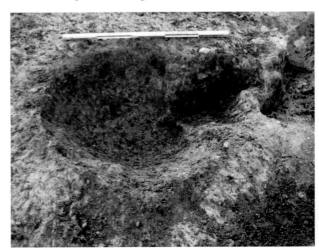

*Plate 10: Furnace chamber **588** at Cinder Hill (Site 42N), looking south-west*

46

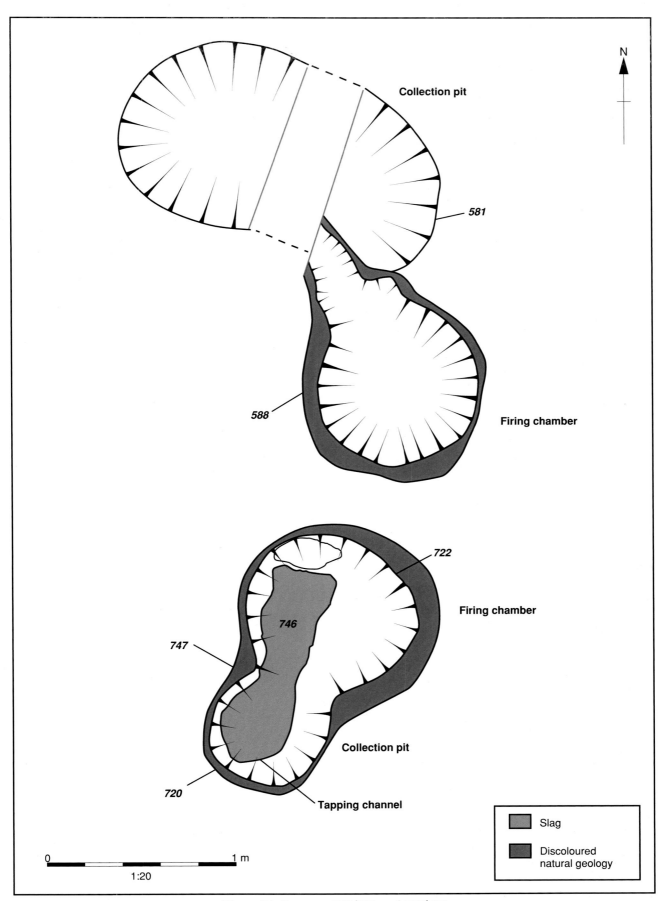

N

Collection pit

581

588

Firing chamber

722

Firing chamber

746

747

Collection pit

720

Tapping channel

Slag

Discoloured
natural geology

0   1 m

1:20

*Figure 24: Furnaces **588/581** and **722/720***

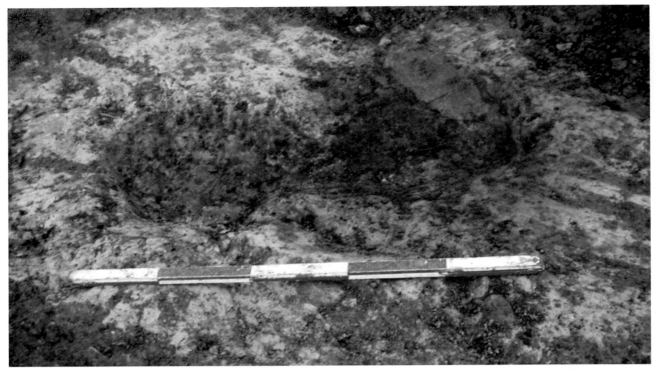

*Plate 11: Furnace **722** and tapping/rake-out pit **720** at Cinder Hill (Site 42N), looking north*

Furnace **722/720** (Pl 11) lay some 12 m to the north-west of furnace **588/581** (Fig 23). It comprised a furnace-chamber (**722**), which had a diameter of 0.7 m and was *c* 0.15 m deep. The mouth of the furnace was 0.5 m wide, and faced the prevailing south-westerly wind (Fig 24). Therefore, this might suggest that the furnace partly utilised natural draughts, in addition to forced-draughts, as has been proposed for several late medieval furnaces at Stanley Grange, Derbyshire (Challis 2002, 40-1). The general form of the Cinder Hill furnace seemed more akin to one that utilised forced-draughts, however, as it did not appear to have been provided with a long flue emanating from the furnace mouth.

The furnace chamber contained a charcoal- and slag-rich fill and also an *in situ* lump of slag (**746**), which was contained within a *c* 0.15 m-wide tapping channel, extending from the chamber into the adjacent tapping pit (**720**). This pit was at the mouth of the furnace and was *c* 0.4 m in diameter. Apart from the *in situ* lump of slag, it also contained two sequential charcoal- and slag-rich deposits, a fragment of hazel charcoal from the uppermost fill (**721**) returning a radiocarbon date of cal AD 1050-1280 (832±38 BP; SUERC-56417; *Appendix 2*).

The three possible furnaces (**568, 572,** and **578**; Fig 23) were less complete and appear to have been partly disturbed by later activity. This later, destructive, activity seems to have included post-medieval ploughing, which was evidenced by plough furrows, and intrusive fragments of post-medieval pottery,

present within one of the late medieval features (*Appendix 4*).

Two of the potential furnace bases (**568** and **572**) were adjacent to each other and were defined by two oval-shaped, shallow pits. Each measured *c* 0.9 x 0.7 m, and base **572** was partially surrounded by a halo of heat-affected clay. The other putative furnace base lay to east, defined by a *c* 0.8 m-wide L-shaped pit (**578**), which might have formed the base and tapping pit. This was 1.7 m long, east/west, by 2 m, north/south, and also contained a large concentration of archaeometallurgical residues (*Appendix 3*), including concentrations of lining, providing further confirmation that it was the site of a furnace (*p 51*).

Reheating hearth(?)
A shallow, *c* 0.2 x 0.3 m, scoop (**743**), which was surrounded by a halo of heat-affected natural clay and contained a slag-rich fill, was identified at the centre of Site 42N (Fig 23). This feature had, however, been largely destroyed by later pit digging and thus proved difficult to interpret (*p 50*). Given its heat-affected character, it might have been the remains of a furnace base, although it is equally possible that it formed a hearth, where the blooms derived from one or more of the furnaces were reheated and then compacted.

Evidence for the use of **743** as a reheating hearth, although admittedly slim, comprises a lump of smithing slag, which came from a later pit (**719**; *p 51*) that had disturbed the feature. Analysis indicates

*Plate 12: Charcoal clamp **864** at Cinder Hill (Site 42S), looking south-west*

that the slag relates to the early stages of bloom compaction (*Appendix 3*), which may have involved reheating blooms.

Apart from this slag, further evidence for reheating and compaction was also found in the central part of the site. A small, indistinct scoop (*596*), which was *c* 5 m north-west of putative reheating hearth *743*, contained a concentration of archaeometallurgical residues and also, significantly, a probable iron bar or billet (*p 51*). The presence of this object indicates that at least some of the blooms produced at the site had been reheated and hammered.

Charcoal clamp

One other feature relating to the bloomery was found downslope, to the south of the furnaces, in one of the open-area trenches excavated at the southern end of Cinder Hill (Site 42S; Fig 22). This was a charcoal-burning pit or 'clamp' (*864*; Pl 12), which comprised an oval pit, 2.15 x 1.6 m, with a maximum depth of 0.18 m. It contained very fine charcoal ash and a few fragments of charcoal, one of which returned a radiocarbon date of cal AD 1220-1390 (720±38 BP; SUERC-56421; *Appendix 2*).

Potential structures

Aside from the furnaces and charcoal clamp, the remains of several potential structures were identified at the northern end of Cinder Hill (Site 42N), which were perhaps contemporary with the furnaces. These included a curving gully (*700*; Fig 23), set some 2.5 m east of furnace *722/720* (*p 48*); it was 7 m long by 0.6 m wide, had a maximum depth of 0.25 m (Pl 13), and might have formed a small drainage ditch, or could conceivably have secured the timbers of a light structure. It produced late medieval pottery and slag, suggesting it was contemporary with the furnace, although it also contained apparently intrusive fragments of post-medieval glass, and a residual fragment of early medieval charcoal (*p 38*). The

*Plate 13: Gully **700** at Cinder Hill (Site 42N), looking north-east*

medieval pottery, which was probably contemporary with the gully, included sherds in the Northern Gritty-ware tradition, which can be broadly dated to the twelfth to fourteenth century (McCarthy and Brooks 1988; *Appendix 4*).

Another potential structure was recognised to the south-west of putative furnaces *568* and *572* (*p 48*). This was defined by two small pits (*545* and *570*), spaced *c* 1.6 m apart, both with diameters of *c* 0.4 m; they also both contained slag-rich fills, suggesting that they were contemporary with the adjacent furnaces. It is possible that these were postholes that, given their positions, may have secured a north-west/south-east-aligned windbreak. Another small pit (*535*), some 2 m east of furnace *588/581*, was itself 4 m south of a second pit (*542*). Both had diameters of *c* 0.6 m, and contained slag fragments, again suggesting they were contemporary with the nearby furnace. Although their precise function is not clear, they did not appear to be directly associated with heating processes, and thus they may have been postholes, perhaps forming elements of a fence, windbreak, or structure. A similar-sized pit (*533*), also perhaps a posthole, was excavated *c* 16 m south-west of pit *535*.

Other pits
Five shallow, oval-shaped pits (*599*, *703*, *715*, *727*, and *719/734*) were also present at the bloomery site in the immediate vicinity of the furnaces. Two of these (*599* and *703*) formed adjacent features, one of which (*599*) had been dug into the extreme south-western end of putative furnace *578* (*p 48*), and also partially cut through scoop *596* (*p 49*). Both pits contained slag and charcoal, and a charcoal fragment from pit *703* returned a radiocarbon date of cal AD 1250-1400 (698±38 BP; SUERC-56411; *Appendix 2*). Two other pits (*715* and *727*) were found to the south, which had disturbed earlier tree-throws (*717* and *741* respectively). Again, both were filled with slag and charcoal, and a fragment of charcoal from the uppermost fill of pit *715* returned a radiocarbon date of cal AD 1300-1440 (544±38 BP; SUERC-56426; *Appendix 2*). Medieval pottery was also recovered from these pits, and from the covering topsoil, comprising sherds in the Northern Gritty-ware tradition, dating to the twelfth to fourteenth centuries (*Appendix 4*). In addition, pit *727* produced a residual flint tool (*Ch 2, p 24*) and post-medieval pottery and glass. Pit *719/734* had been dug into, and largely destroyed, putative reheating hearth *743* (*p 48*), and it contained a lump of smithing slag that may originally have been derived from this earlier hearth.

The function of these shallow pits is uncertain, as they do not appear to have been directly related to iron production. Although they contained slag

and charcoal, it is highly likely that, since the site was littered with archaeometallurgical residues, this material was ultimately derived from iron production. One possibility is that the pits were dug at a much later date, which would certainly explain the presence of eighteenth- and nineteenth-century pottery in pit *727*. Indeed, it is conceivable that the earlier archaeometallurgical residues were being actively targeted and removed, perhaps for resmelting in blast furnaces, or for other reasons.

Fuelling the furnaces
Analysis of the wood charcoal from several features provided valuable insights into the fuel that was used at the bloomery site. In total, five samples were considered (*Appendix 5*); two of these came from the slag-tapping pits associated with furnaces *588/581* (*p 46*) and *722/720* (*p 48*), two from pits *715* (*above*) and *535* (*above*), and one from charcoal clamp *864* (*p 49*).

All of the charcoal samples were dominated by mature, slow-growing oak wood, at least 50 years in age (*Appendix 5*). This indicates that oak was the preferred wood type for the production of charcoal, which is perhaps not surprising given that oak charcoal provides an intense, almost smokeless, and easily controlled fire that would have been ideal for the smelting of iron (Edlin 1949). The majority of the oak wood also had closely spaced growth rings, suggesting the use of trees that were under stress. Small amounts of alder and/or hazel, and holly charcoal were also recovered, though these may represent fuel used for kindling.

Iron-production processes
Most of the features associated with the late medieval bloomery contained archaeometallurgical residues that were clearly associated with iron production (*Appendix 3*). In addition, an assemblage of archaeometallurgical residues was retrieved from the topsoil, although the concentration fell away from the area of the furnaces at the top of the slope, towards the stream to the west. This may, to some extent, represent the original deposition of this material, but might also be as a result of the effects of later ploughing dislodging it from features or spreads.

Given the preponderance of archaeometallurgical residues (a total of 200 kg of material), and its importance for understanding the iron production at Cinder Hill, this was subjected to a full programme of analysis (*Appendix 3*). Significantly, this indicated that the assemblage compares closely with other known residue assemblages of the twelfth to fourteenth centuries (*cf* Young 2014a; 2015; Young and Poyner 2014). The majority of the material (>72% by weight) represented tapped bloomery iron-smelting slags, which were approximately evenly divided into denser and more vesicular varieties, and they also included a variety of dense slags in sheets and plano-convex to biconvex cakes. Although these latter types superficially resembled smithing slags, analysis suggested that most were probably part of the smelting assemblage, and represented slag 'bowls', formed at the base of the furnace.

Apart from tapped bloomery iron-smelting slags, some secondary-processing smithing slags were also present. One of these was unstratified, derived from the topsoil, whilst the other came from a pit (*719*; *p 50*), which had disturbed an earlier heat-affected feature (*743*; *p 48*). The discovery of the smithing slag in the later pit might suggest that *743* was indeed a hearth where blooms were reheated prior to compaction. Both of these smithing slags were very iron-rich, suggesting they derived from the early stages of bloom compaction. Moreover, that derived from the topsoil was a particularly large biconvex example, rich in metallic iron, set in wustite-rich slag, suggesting an accumulation of bloom fragments. Although no typical smithing-hearth cakes were recorded (*ie* with a more fayalitic composition) that would relate to the hammering of blooms into iron bars/billets, one possible iron bar/billet was present in the assemblage. This was an irregular fragment of iron, with a strong internal fibrous structure within the corrosion layer, which was recovered from scoop *596* (*p 49*).

The other residues from the site included furnace linings, which were particularly concentrated in furnace chambers *588* (*p 44*) and *722* (*p 48*), putative furnace base *578* (*p 48*), and scoop *596* (*p 49*). Small quantities of ore were also recorded, including claystone ironstone nodules and magnetic claystone ironstone.

As part of the investigation into the residues, chemical analysis of 11 examples of smelting slags, one example of a smithing slag, one example of furnace lining, and two samples of claystone ironstones was completed. The microstructure of four of the smelting-slag samples was also investigated with a scanning electron microscope (SEM). This suggested that the ore samples were rather weathered examples of Coal-measures claystone ironstones.

The chemical composition (both of major and trace elements) of one of these provided a very good match for the composition of the slag. The textural and compositional range of the smelting slags was also similar to that from other medieval sites that smelted Coal-measures claystone ores. The plano-convex slag blocks lay at the iron-rich end of the compositional range, with the externally tapped slags having a more evolved, iron-poor composition.

Interpreting the late medieval bloomery

The excavations at Cinder Hill exposed a significant late medieval bloomery, within the township of Middle Hulton. A broad date range for the activity was provided by the medieval pottery, and the fragments of charcoal which returned radiocarbon dates. Although many of the pits were seemingly unrelated to the bloomery site, it is highly likely that they contained residual materials derived from medieval iron production, and ultimately some of the undated furnace bases and associated features.

Modelling of the radiocarbon dates suggests that the dated materials relate to at least three separate episodes of iron production (*Appendix 2*). More specifically, the earliest dated episode may have been the use of furnaces *588* and *722*, which appear to be contemporary features. Charcoal clamp *864* seems later than the furnaces, perhaps representing a second episode of activity; it is possible that the dated material from pit *703* was also contemporary with this charcoal clamp. Finally, a third episode of iron production may be reflected in the dated medieval material from pit *715*. Given the spread of these dates, it seems likely that the site was visited repeatedly.

Importantly, the Cinder Hill site appears to have contained many features and archaeometallurgical residues associated with the initial production of iron. The primary raw materials for this process were iron ore and charcoal, and analysis of the archaeometallurgical residues suggests that the site was probably smelting the local Carboniferous claystone ironstones from the Coal measures (*Appendix 3*). Prior to smelting, the ore would need to be roasted, which would remove its water content, reduce its sulphur content, and also fracture it into managably sized fragments, ready to be smelted in the nearby furnaces (*cf* Crossley 1981, 31). This process would have employed a roasting pit, though there was no clear evidence for such a feature within the excavated areas.

The direct production of charcoal was, however, evident at the site, in the form of charcoal clamp *864*. It is likely that this clamp comprised wood fuel, initially stacked vertically around a central split log. This wood was probably arranged to form a flattened dome, which could be sealed by an airtight covering of bracken, dead leaves, and turf, followed by a layer of soil. The central stake was then removed to form a flue, and burning coals could be poured down the hole, which lit the wood fuel. The flue was then plugged and the stack would be left to smoulder for two days, to remove the moisture and volatile material from the wood fuel, and convert it to charcoal (**Bowden 2000, 23**; Gregory 2014, 18).

51

The age of the oak charcoal indicates that it was not derived from coppiced woodland, and this in itself may hold some significance. For instance, in iron-producing areas, such as the Lake District, this type of managed woodland was often found in tandem with bloomeries and it provided the main source of fuel required for iron smelting and reheating (Bowden 2000, 6). Therefore, the lack of coppiced wood at Cinder Hill may suggest that there were no managed woodlands in the vicinity of the bloomery site and that iron production would, in turn, only be possible once adequate supplies of fuel were available. If this was the case, this might explain the repeated use of the site, apparently on at least three separate occasions (*Appendix 2*). These perhaps equate with periods when specific stands of oak woodland had adequately regenerated and could be exploited for charcoal production.

At Cinder Hill, once the raw materials had been assembled, iron smelting could commence, and the evidence from the site clearly indicates that this process occurred within charcoal-fuelled furnaces. Several of these also appeared to have been associated with light structures, which may have acted as windbreaks or perhaps even shelters. Based on the known form of medieval iron furnaces (*cf* Bowden 2000, 39; Paynter 2011), along with the remains of two of the better-preserved furnaces at the site (*588/581* and *722/720*), it is likely that the Cinder Hill furnaces

Plate 14: A reconstructed medieval furnace, perhaps comparable in form to those found at Cinder Hill (Courtesy of Tim Young)

comprised small cylindrical structures (Pl 14), and both probably had upper walls constructed of wood and thick clay. The walls formed the body of the furnace and also acted as a chimney, perhaps standing to a height of 1-2 m (Bowden 2000, 40).

It is highly probable that, following the lighting of the charcoal within the Cinder Hill furnaces, to attain the required smelting temperatures (*c* 1200°C), a continual supply of charcoal was added and air was probably also blown into these structures, using bellows, through a blow hole, which would have been provided with a pipe, or *tuyère* (Paynter 2011, 2). Although in some medieval furnaces firing might also have been partly reliant on natural draughts, in addition to the forced-draughts provided by bellows (*cf* Challis 2002), no firm evidence for this specific type of practice was evident at Cinder Hill.

Once the furnaces were at the correct temperature, ore could be placed within them, through their open tops, and the smelting process would begin. This specifically involved the reduction of iron oxide within the ore to produce a bloom of metallic wrought iron (Bowden 2000, 39). During this process, the use of charcoal as a fuel was essential, as this produced carbon monoxide, which acted as the reducing agent (Bayley *et al* 2008, 43).

An integral part of the smelting process was the production of slag, which represents the gangue (worthless) elements derived from the ore, and some of the iron oxide. Above 1200°C, the slag melts and separates from the bloom, allowing it to be tapped off from the bottom of the firing chamber, through an opening and into a shallow pit. Once this process had been completed, the bloom could be removed from the furnace (Bowden 2000, 39). Evidence for slag tapping was abundant at Cinder Hill, both in the archaeometullurgical residues, which were dominated by tapped bloomery iron-smelting slags, and the presence of slag-tapping pits associated with furnaces *588/581* and *722/720*. Within both of these furnaces, their evident mouths would have been opened, once smelting had been achieved, to allow slag to be tapped along channels, which were also associated with each of these furnaces. In addition, some of the slag in the Cinder Hill furnaces appears to have accumulated directly at the base of furnaces and formed slag 'bowls'.

The presence of slag 'bowls' might be significant in that these hint at a previously unrecognised aspect of twelfth-fourteenth-century iron smelting. This may have entailed the formation of a 'puddle' of slag within a hollow in the floor of the furnace, as opposed to the slag bowl being positioned at a higher level in the furnace base, supported by ash and charcoal (*cf* Sauder and Williams 2002). However, it is perhaps significant that the formation of a slag bowl in direct contact with the base of the furnace would probably cause problems with the preparation of the furnace for any subsequent smelt. It is thus possible that the Cinder Hill slag bowls were created by accident, and were not intended to be left on the furnace base. Moreover, their presence may have been a reason why certain of the furnaces were abandoned.

Although it is sometimes possible to estimate the efficiency and scale of iron production from the slag residues recovered, this was not achievable for the Cinder Hill assemblage. Attempts to construct a mass balance for the smelting reaction failed due to the absence of a suitable roasted-ore sample (*cf* Thomas and Young 1999a; 1999b). Likewise, it was clear, based on comparison with other analysed late medieval bloomery sites (*eg* Young 2014a), that the 200 kg slag assemblage recovered from the site only represents residues from just 13 smelts. However, in reality, each of the furnaces would have been capable of being used for many tens of, and probably several hundred, smelts.

Following the removal of the bloom from the furnace, it was normal for it to be compacted, through hammering, to remove any remaining slag impurities and also consolidate the bloom. Some initial refining might have occurred immediately after the bloom had been removed from the furnace, when it was still hot (Bowden 2000, 40). However, some medieval-bloomery sites, although by no means all, also contained hearths where the wrought-iron blooms could be reheated and hammered into an iron billet (*op cit*, 3).

Significantly, the archaeometallurgical residues from Cinder Hill (*Appendix 3*) contained some evidence for these secondary refining processes, in the form of two wustite- and/or metallic iron-rich cakes. These slags appear to have been formed early in the process of bloom compaction, one being derived from a pit (**719**) that had disturbed an earlier heat-affected feature (**743**; *p 48*). Given the presence of the smithing-slag cake, this heat-affected feature might therefore represent a potential hearth, which was used to reheat the blooms prior to compaction.

In addition to the slag cakes, a fragment of bar iron was also recovered, which could only have been produced using a reheating hearth. Indeed, experiments into ancient iron-working techniques indicate that a cold 2 kg bloom might require 20 to 25 heats before it could be brought up to the correct temperature for final consolidation into a billet (Crew 2013, 36). Therefore, the fragment of bar iron

provides further confirmation that a reheating hearth was present at the site, which presumably could be represented by feature **743** (*above*), particularly as the bar iron was found in a scoop in its immediate vicinity.

Following the cessation of iron production, the site would have contained piles of metallurgical waste. Indeed, other comparable medieval iron-production sites, such as that at Culmstock Road, Hemyock, Devon (T Young *pers comm*), produced an estimated 22 tonnes of slag, and it is probable that Cinder Hill originally contained equivalent or greater amounts. It appears, however, that the majority of this waste was targeted and removed by later activity, and as such the site's iron-producing legacy was only preserved through its place-name. This slag 'waste' would, however, have been rich in iron and may, therefore, have been removed from the site and converted into cast iron within a blast furnace, a more sophisticated form of iron-smelting furnace, that was introduced into the North West in the late seventeenth century (Bowden 2000, 7).

The Medieval Landscape at the Kingsway Business Park

The evidence for activity across the Kingsway Business Park, and indeed the wider area, during the early medieval period is scant and is based largely on place-name evidence and the Domesday Survey of 1086. However, in terms of land divisions and territories, it is clear that during this time the area covered by the business park lay within the parish of Rochdale (Fishwick 1889, 1). This formed the most extensive of those within the Hundred of Salford, which was a large Anglo-Saxon territorial unit immediately north of the River Mersey, encompassing the Irwell Valley (*ibid*). Although the origins of this parish are unclear, it was possibly created in the seventh to ninth centuries, when the wider area was incorporated into the Anglo-Saxon kingdom of Northumbria (Pounds 2000, 3; R M Newman 2006, 91).

The major early medieval settlement within Rochdale parish was probably in the area now covered by the modern town. Rochdale is mentioned by name as '*Recedham*' in the Domesday Survey, the '*ham*' element of the place-name being Old English in origin, referring to a settlement, which perhaps originated in the seventh or eighth century (Ekwall 1922; Kenyon 1991). Similarly, although the element '*Reced*' might have been the Celtic name for the River Roch, it is also possible that it has an Old English origin, meaning 'hall' (Ekwall 1922, 55). The presence of an Anglo-Saxon settlement at Rochdale also tallies well with the dedication of its parish church to St Chad, the late seventh-century bishop of Lichfield (Fishwick 1889, 127). If this is correct, it is possible that a settlement existed surrounding this church, close to the centre of the modern-day settlement, on the southern bank of the River Roch.

During the early medieval period, the parish of Rochdale was divided into several smaller townships, and those with suspected Anglo-Saxon origins can again be discerned by the place-name evidence. One of these was Butterworth, immediately east of, and partly bounded by, the Stanney Brook, which was also within an area partly covered by the Kingsway Business Park (Fig 25). This place-name is probably pre-Norman in origin and may refer to 'enclosed pastureland [*worth*] that provides good butter' (Mills 1976, 69). Significantly, several other place-names incorporating the element '*worth*' are known from the south-west Pennine fringe and it has been argued that these may reflect the presence of late Anglo-Saxon enclosures, which were used seasonally for livestock farming (Kenyon 1991, 137). However, no physical evidence for such an enclosure can now be discerned within the Kingsway Business Park.

Immediately prior to the Norman Conquest, the manor of Rochdale, which was probably co-extensive with the parish, was in the possession of Gamel, the theyn, who held his land directly from King Edward the Confessor, and appears to have belonged to a family that had fairly extensive landholdings in northern England (Fishwick 1889, 14; Morgan 1978, R6). For instance, Gamel may also have held land in Bebington, Cheshire, and Elland, West Yorkshire, whilst his father held Cheadle and either Mottram St Andrew or Mottram in Longdendale (Morgan 1978, R6). The Domesday Survey indicates that by 1086 he retained reduced landholdings in Salford Hundred, under the Norman lord Roger de Poitou, which may have included those in the parish of Rochdale (Fishwick 1889, 14; Farrer and Brownbill 1911a, 189). Rochdale also became the focus of post-Conquest settlement, with construction of a motte-and-bailey castle at Castle Hill, to the south of the River Roch, perhaps to the west of the original settlement (*above*). It is also possible that an original church was rebuilt during this time, as fragments of Norman masonry were reputedly discovered during early nineteenth-century renovation work (Farrer and Brownbill 1911a, 194).

It is likely that during the late eleventh/twelfth century, following the construction of the Norman castle, the administrative units within the parish were formalised into four main townships, the process perhaps being undertaken by the de Lacy family, who held the manor of Rochdale between 1080 and 1311 (Fishwick 1889, 16,

18; Farrer and Brownbill 1911a, 187). These townships were Butterworth, Hundersfield, Spotland, and Castleton. This latter township is first documented in the twelfth century (*cf* Fishwick 1889, 9) and was probably named after the motte-and-bailey castle at Castle Hill (Mills 1976, 70-1). It lay immediately west of, and was partly bounded by, Stanney Brook and therefore encompassed the portion of the Kingsway Business Park beyond Butterworth township. It is also possible that during this period the townships were subdivided into smaller units, forming hamlets (sub-manors) or freehold estates. Within the area covered by the Kingsway Business Park, these included Butterworth (later referred to as Butterworth Hall), in Butterworth township, and Buersill in Castleton township. In addition, a very small portion of the hamlet of Newbold was situated at the far northern end of the Kingsway Business Park, which also lay in Castleton township.

Following the death of Henry de Lacy, Earl of Lincoln, in 1311, Rochdale passed, by marriage, to the earls of Lancaster, who held the manor until the end of the fifteenth century, except for between 1322 and 1327, when it was forfeited to the Crown (Fishwick 1889, 21). During the fifteenth century, the manor was also leased to various stewards, and from 1462 until 1616 these were members of the Byron family, who were influential locally, with significant landholdings in Butterworth and Castleton townships, and whose later lineage included the late eighteenth-century Romantic poet Lord Byron (*op cit*, 21, 26; Fishwick 1913, xiii; *p 56*).

Late medieval hamlets and landholdings

Documentary evidence dating from the thirteenth to fifteenth centuries allows some insights into the character of the various hamlets within the Kingsway Business Park, suggesting that they contained land held by freeholders, tenants, and the monastic orders, and that there were also areas of common land. Butterworth Hall, for example, formed the central hamlet within the medieval township of Butterworth, which also contained the settlements of Milnrow, Lady House, Wildhouse, Clegg, Belfield, and Lowhouse, though these were all immediately to the east and north of the Kingway Business Park (Farrer and Brownbill 1911a, 213; Fig 25).

During the medieval period, Butterworth township contained a mix of freeholders and tenants who owed service to the lord of the manor (*ibid*). Indeed, the township was divided historically into two sub-districts, Butterworth Freeholdside and Butterworth Lordshipside, which reflected the ancient terms of tenure (*ibid*). Fairly large areas of the medieval township were also held by the Hospitaller Order of monastic knights, whilst smaller portions were

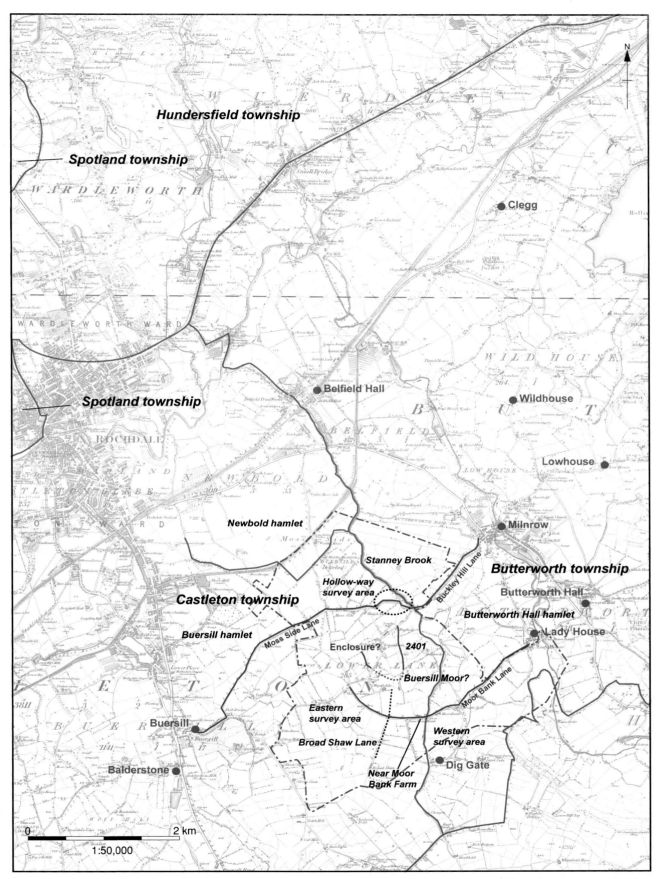

Figure 25: Medieval townships, hamlets, sites, and landscape features within the Kingsway area, superimposed on the OS first edition six-inch map (1850)

held by the Cluniac monks of Bretton in Yorkshire and the Cistercian monks of Stanlaw Abbey, on the Wirral, Cheshire, who moved to Whalley Abbey in Lancashire in the 1290s (Fishwick 1889, 113, 119). Similarly, the Hospitaller Order was a significant landowner in Buersill hamlet, to the west of Stanney Brook, whilst the monks of Stanlaw Abbey held some land in Newbold hamlet (op cit, 72, 74; Farrer and Brownbill 1911a, 203). Newbold also contained Newbold Hall, which may date from the sixteenth century, to the north of the Kingsway Business Park (Farrer and Brownbill 1911a, 203).

Several landowners in this area took their name from Butterworth township, the first lord on record being Reginald de Butterworth, who has been credited with building the original Butterworth Hall in 1148 (Robertson 1881). He was succeeded in 1166 by Robert de Butterworth, whilst Gilbert de Butterworth occurs in records dated 1203 (ibid). According to Baines (1825, 205), Butterworth Hall was occupied by the family of that name until 1274, when Geofrey de Butterworth sold it to the Byrons and moved to nearby Belfield Hall, situated just over 2 km to the north-west. The family retained the Belfield estate until 1728, when Alexander Butterworth died without issue (Fishwick 1889, 341-2).

The medieval townships of Butterworth and Castleton also contained a fairly large area of common land, and this probably encompassed much of what is now covered by the Kingsway Business Park. This was known as Buersill Moor, and it is documented as covering portions of the hamlets of Buersill, Butterworth, and Newbold, which all extended into the area of the Kingsway Business Park, as well as part of the hamlet of Balderstone, lying to the west (Fishwick 1889, 73).

Many of the early historical references to Buersill Moor have been collated (Fishwick 1889. 71-3; 1913, ix, 30-4) and these indicate that, initially, medieval rights to the moor were in the hands of various owners/occupiers. It is also clear that some encroachment onto this common land had occurred by the mid-fourteenth century, since there are documentary references to buildings. From the early fourteenth century onwards, the rights to Buersill Moor began to be accrued by the Byron family, who would eventually become the stewards for the manor of Rochdale (below). In 1327-8, 'Henry de Baldeston conveyed to Richard de Buron all the lands which he had in the hamlet called Berdesile in Castelton [sic]' (Fishwick 1889, 71), and these probably included all his part of the waste of 'Buerdsall Moore', with all the buildings and appurtenances that are mentioned in an undated deed describing a conveyance between the two men (Fishwick 1913, 30-1). Further early

references to the Byrons' acquisition of land in this area date to 1342-3, when 'William de Sclake granted to Richard Burun, knight, his lands in Buerdsall moor in Castleton for the accustomed service' (Fishwick 1889, 71).

Sir John Byron was granted the stewardship of the manor of Rochdale in 1519 by Henry VIII (op cit, 21) and one of his first acts was the construction of a dyke, to enclose part of Buersill Moor, probably the earliest act of enclosure in this area. However, it was contentious, and certainly viewed as an infringement of the rights of others to this area of common land. For example, it is noted in the 'ancient deeds' relating to the moor, contained in a 1626 survey of Rochdale (Ch 4, p 65), that following this act of enclosure 'certain women and children in peaceable manner did cast doun the sayd Dyke lately made by the commandment of the sayd Sir John Byron' (Fishwick 1913, 32). This led to them being 'wrongfully indited' as it was noted in the deeds that the moor 'hath ben tyme out of mynd of any man pastured & occupied with all manner of bests & catalls...& never was incloses' (ibid).

Despite this incident, the acquisition and enclosure of Buersill Moor by the Byrons continued throughout the sixteenth century, again evidenced through reference to the 'ancient deeds' for the moor. This phase of acquisition began in 1539 when Sir John Byron acquired James Garside's Buersill Moor holdings whilst, in 1555, 300 acres of land and 12 houses held by John Stafford and others were conveyed to Sir John Byron (op cit, 31-2; Haynes and Tipper 1994, 35). This was then followed by the enclosure of 1260 acres of the moor by Sir John Byron in 1560 (Haynes and Tipper 1994, 35).

The 'ancient deeds' for Buersill Moor contained in the 1626 survey also make reference to areas of potential medieval settlement (Fishwick 1913, 30-4). These include Dig Gate (originally Dyke Gate), just outside the southern boundary of the business park, and Lady House, which lies to the east. In addition, the 'ancient deeds' also refer to areas of early enclosure that may fall within the business park, including le Blackley Hey and le Layst, in the vicinity of Lady House, and le Inhurst, Calfe Hey, and le Carr.

Medieval landscape features

Prior to the construction of the Kingway Business Park, several landscape features were identified which may have had their origins in the medieval period. One of these was a possible early enclosure, potentially relating to Sir John Bryon's enclosure of Buersill Moor in 1519 (above). The assessment suggested that several earthworks and relict field boundaries defined the eastern, southern, and

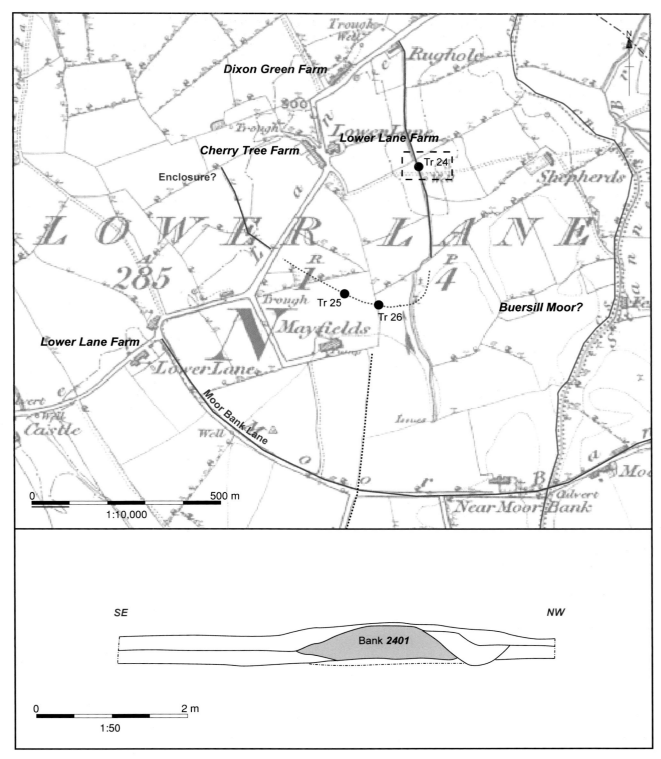

Figure 26: The evaluation trenches across the possible early enclosure at Kingsway, superimposed on the OS first edition six-inch map (1850)

western sides of a large oval enclosure, which surrounded three seventeenth-century farms known as Cherry Tree Farm (*Ch 4, p 70*), Lower Lane Farm (*Ch 4, p 70*), and Dixon Green Farm (Haynes and Tipper 1994, 47). Three evaluation trenches were excavated across its postulated boundary, to investigate its form and date (Fig 26). One of these

trenches (Tr 24) was excavated through an extant bank (**2401**), which may have formed the eastern side of the enclosure. The bank was 2.1 m wide by 0.5 m high, and was constructed entirely of earth, with no associated ditch; no dating evidence was recovered. The other two trenches (Tr 25 and Tr 26) were excavated in the area of the southern extent of

57

Plate 15: Moss Side Lane trackway, looking west (by Profile 1)

the enclosure. However, no archaeological features were encountered in either trench.

Other potential landscape features with medieval origins were two routeways, crossing the business park. One was Moss Side Lane (Fig 25), which the first edition Ordnance Survey (OS) map (1850b) indicates ran in an easterly direction from Buersill (where it was known as Stiups Lane) and eventually joined, close to the Stanney Brook, with Buckley Hill Lane, leading to Milnrow. Although this route is not depicted on Yates' map of 1786, a section of it, to the east of Haigh Field (*Ch 6, p 146*), formed a green lane, or hollow-way, suggesting that it might have an early origin, perhaps being established in the medieval period as a route across Buersill Moor. Moreover, to the west of Stanney Brook, it was lined by several early farms, such as Moss Side Farm (*Ch 4, p 70*) and Higher Moss Side Farm (*Ch 4, p 68*), which were perhaps established in the seventeenth century, and might therefore further attest to its antiquity. The section to the east of Haigh Field was subjected to a topographic and photographic survey. Generally, it had a sinuous form, and extended in a roughly west/east direction between a corner of the paved lane in the west, and a field boundary to the south of Stanney Brook in the east (Pl 15). It was *c* 190 m long and was up to a maximum of 9 m wide.

The earthwork consisted of two raised earthen banks on either side of a sunken hollowed-out trackway (Fig 27; Pl 16). The banks were up to 2.5 m wide by up to 0.4 m high, and the hollowed trackway was up to 0.6 m deep. The banks had also probably been hedged in the past, as the last remnants of an overgrown hedge-line were visible during the survey. In general terms, the southern bank survived better, though both banks had been actively eroded by pedestrian traffic, manifested by grooved depressions on top of each bank. Although this 'green lane' had undoubtedly been a routeway for some considerable time, the depth of the hollowed-out track was not considerable in size, though this may be partly a result of the fact that the routeway crossed comparatively flat ground.

The other potentially early routeway was Moor Bank Lane. This is depicted on Yates' map of 1786 and the first edition six-inch OS map (1850b) as a curving route from Lower Lane to the settlement at Lady House (Fig 25), and it may have defined the edge of Buersill Moor. As with Moss Side Lane, this route was also lined by several early farms, such as Near Moor Bank Farm (*Ch 4, p 88*), the known ancestry of which dates back to the early part of the seventeenth century, and these provide a *terminus ante quem* for its construction. It was therefore surveyed as part of the archaeological investigation and proved to be over 980 m long, and for much of its length it could

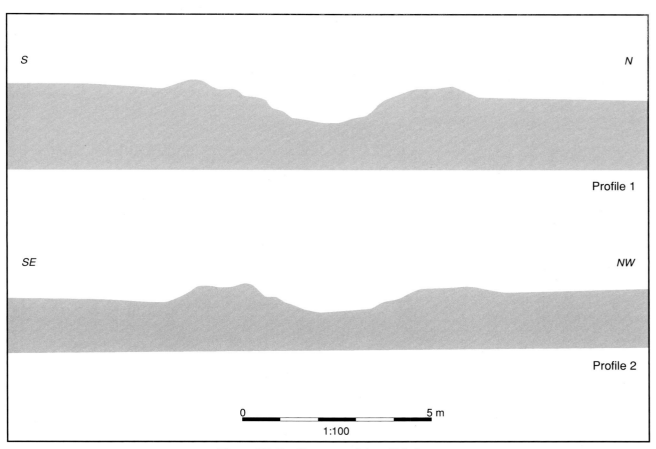

Figure 27: Profiles across Moss Side Lane

Plate 16: The sunken trackway (Site 25) of Moss Side Lane, looking north-east (by Profile 2)

Plate 17: Moor Bank Lane, looking north-east (by Profile 3)

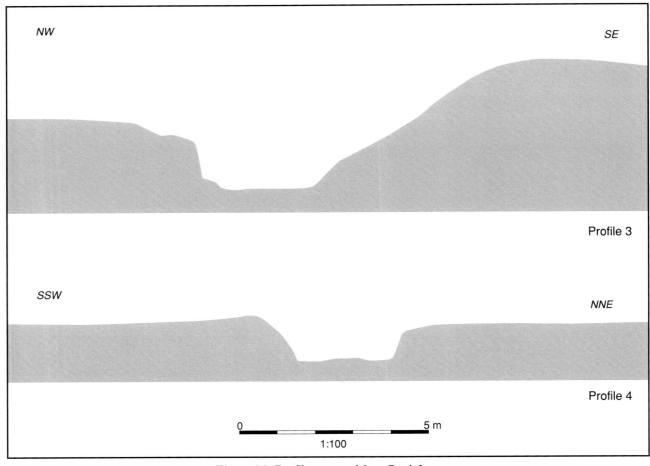

Figure 28: Profiles across Moor Bank Lane

Plate 18: Moor Bank Lane, looking south-east (by Profile 4)

be characterised as a sunken lane with a base width of approximately 2.5 m. This incorporated a surface of surviving stone setts (mostly on the western side; Pl 17), which had probably been inserted in the post-medieval period, the grooves from wheeled traffic being visible within the surface profile (Fig 28).

The western half of this sunken lane had a steep-sided profile, often with a small vertical stone retaining-wall at its base. The upper edge of the lane was hedged on both sides, and the remnants of an upcast bank survived on the north side. One surveyed profile (Profile 4) indicated that the lane was approximately 0.8 m deep, with the upcast northern bank measuring 1.5 m wide by up to 0.25 m in height.

In the eastern half of the sunken lane (to the east of the junction with Broad Shaw Lane), the profile varied, but essentially it remained 2.5 m wide at its base. Between Broad Shaw Lane and Moor Bank, the lane was sunken by between 1 m and 1.5 m, with almost vertical sides. To the east of Moor Bank, it flattened out as it continued over the course of Stanney Brook, and to the east of this, it ran uphill within a deep cutting towards Lady House (Pl 18). The cutting was through a large bank, with the sides angled at *c* 45°, extending down from the field to the south, while the northern edge was retained by an almost vertical stone wall, up to 1.4 m in height. The lane was approximately 3.3 m deep from the field to the south, and 1.8 m deep from the field to the north, but it returned to a depth of approximately 1.5 m at the top of the hill by Lady House.

4

POST-MEDIEVAL LANDSCAPES 1: KINGSWAY
BUSINESS PARK – *c* 1600-1780

Richard A Gregory, Michael Nevell, and Ian Miller

The Changing Rural Landscape

The seventeenth and eighteenth centuries witnessed a series of significant changes to the form and use of the landscape within the Kingsway Business Park. This period represents an era of progressive agricultural expansion, which is defined by the eventual enclosure of the moorland and the construction of a scattering of rural dwellings, farm buildings, and associated routeways. The upland character suggests that it was utilised primarily for the rearing of stock, which formed the principal farming activity in other parts of the Pennine foothills (*inter alia*; Pearson 1985, 33; Redhead 2003, 70). This involved a mixture of dairy and sheep farming, with sheep being dominant in the moorland areas (*ibid*). The process of seventeenth-century enclosure was intimately linked to the acquisition of medieval landholdings by yeoman farmers, an emerging class of Lancashire landowners. The yeomen, who were the small farmers of the region, held the land either as a freehold, copyhold, or leasehold (Allen 1992; *Ch 9, pp 231-2*). Yeoman farmers often employed labourers, who, in turn, normally leased portions of the yeoman's holdings and/or may have rented property.

In addition, it appears that most areas of common land, such as that at Buersill Moor (*p 65*), had been enclosed completely during either the seventeenth or early eighteenth century (*ibid*), or else enclosure was anticipated. A notice printed in a newspaper in 1815, for instance, advertised the sale of land in the manor of Rochdale, and specifically in the townships of Butterworth, Castleton, and Spotland, belonging to the Newstead Abbey Estate. This land comprised,

> over about 45,000 acres, of which about 33,000 acres are enclosed lands, and 12,000 acres are moors, commons and wastes which, in the case of enclosure, will add considerably to the value of the estate... (*Morning Chronicle*, 5 May 1815).

In east Lancashire and what is now Greater Manchester, this process of enclosure and agricultural expansion appears to have been largely completed by the mid-eighteenth century. Yates' map of Lancashire (1786) depicts a rural landscape containing a plethora of farmsteads and hamlets, along the Pennine foothills, connected by an extensive network of roads (Fig 29).

Another significant feature pertinent to the seventeenth- and eighteenth-century rural economy in east and south-east Lancashire was the development of the domestic-based textile industry, which took place alongside farming and often formed a much-needed supplementary source of income (*cf* Redhead 2003, 70-1). In the Lancashire Pennines, this industry appears to have emerged in the mid-late sixteenth century and involved the production of woollen textiles, whilst in other parts of the Pennines both woollen and linen cloth were produced (Pearson 1985, 35).

In the sixteenth century, Walloons fleeing the Low Countries and Huguenots escaping persecution in France sought refuge in England, brought their looms and their weaving trade, specialising in making complicated threads and tapes (Wadsworth and Mann 1931, 102). They settled initially in the south, in Canterbury and London, but soon transferred their trade to south-east Lancashire, centred on Manchester, a move presumably stimulated by the lack of regulation and guilds. This skilled immigrant workforce, using complicated Dutch looms, effectively added a new dimension to the area's traditional textile industry (*ibid*).

The introduction of new technology from mainland Europe coincided broadly with the start of a decline in the weaving of pure woollens in south Lancashire in favour of mixed fabrics classed as smallwares and fustians. Linen yarn formed the warp for both of these fabrics, and whilst worsted was usually selected for the weft in smallwares, cotton became frequently used in fustians; the earliest known reference to cotton in the wider region dates from 1601, when it was mentioned in the will of George Arnould, a Bolton fustian weaver (*op cit*, 15).

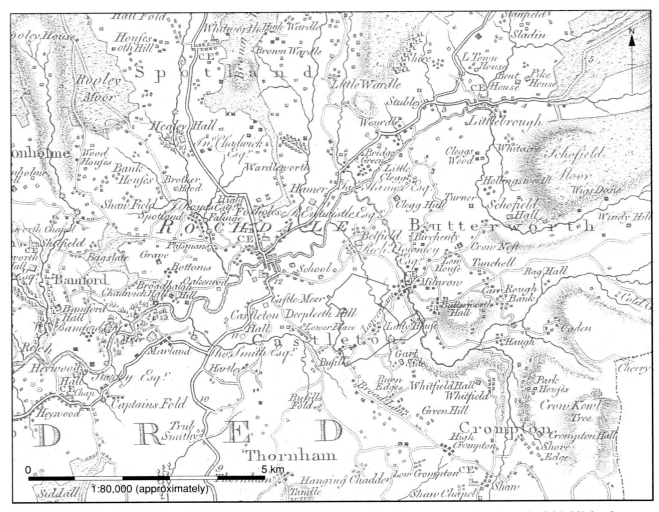

Figure 29: Yates' map of Lancashire (1786), with the position of the Kingsway Business Park highlighted

Production of textile goods on the Pennine fringe appears to have occurred in the substantial houses occupied by yeomen farmers, and also lesser-status dwellings (Pearson 1985, 35), and, given this, it would certainly have occurred within a large proportion of the farms that were established to the south-west of Rochdale in the seventeenth century. Indeed, it has been suggested that, across the Pennines, the textile industry may have been an important stimulus for house building during the late sixteenth century (*op cit*, 36), and presumably this also applied to house building in the seventeenth century.

The technology and organisation of labour employed in this industry was relatively simple and normally involved the preparatory processing of the flax or wool, such as the disentangling, or scribbling, of the woollen fibres, and then the hand carding of the fibre by women and children. This was followed by the hand spinning of yarn using simple machines such as a great wheel or a treadle wheel, usually operated by women, and then the weaving of cloth, typically by a male weaver, who used a frame loom (Giles and Goodall 1992, 6-15).

During the eighteenth century, significant technological advances occurred in the textile industry, and these had a marked effect on the domestic-based textile industry in the Lancashire Pennine fringe (Benson 1983, 9-12). Foremost amongst these was the invention of the flying shuttle, patented by John Kay in 1733, which doubled the productive capacities of the loom (Smith 1973, 19).

Mechanisation was introduced to the woollen-textile industry in the mid-eighteenth century, in the form of hand-powered scribbling and carding machines (Giles and Goodall 1992, 6-15), which during the late eighteenth century were often water powered, undertaken in purpose-built mills (*Ch 6, p 137*). Another significant technological advance during the mid-eighteenth century was the development of the spinning jenny, invented in 1764 by James Hargreaves (Smith 1973, 20), which provided significant advances in the spinning of cotton yarn, as it allowed a group of eight spindles to be operated together. The jennies were hand-powered, and were therefore suitable for use in a domestic setting, although groups of jennies housed in a single building effectively represented the emergence of the 'proto-factory' production of yarn.

Together, these mid-eighteenth-century advances resulted in an abundance of raw yarn, which was available for weaving using improved machinery. In consequence, in many parts of central and south-east Lancashire, handloom weaving emerged as an important feature of the rural economy (*Ch 6, p 137*).

The manor of Rochdale and its townships were leased by Sir John Byron at the very beginning of the seventeenth century. However, Sir John Byron let this lease expire in 1616 as a result of his poor financial situation, and control of the manor reverted to the Crown (Fishwick 1913, xii). In 1625, Charles I sold the manor to the trustees of the Earl of Holderness, who then immediately sold it to Sir Robert Heath, the Attorney General, who, in turn, mortgaged it to Sir John Byron's eldest son, another John Byron (*ibid*). The manor was then sold to Sir John Byron, the mortgagee, in 1638 for £2500, and the Byron family then owned the manor until 1823 (*op cit*, xiii).

Sir Robert Heath commissioned a survey of Rochdale in 1626, during his time as owner of the manor, and from this some details of the character of the early seventeenth-century landscape covered by the Kingsway Business Park can be gleaned. This survey indicates that the part of Buersill Moor which lay to the west of Stanney Brook, in Castleton township, had been sold off by Sir John Byron in the early 1600s to tenants, they being yeomen farmers (*op cit*, 24-34). In total, 30 freeholders are listed, along with their dwellings and fields (*ibid*). Similarly, the survey lists 82 freeholders in Butterworth township and several of these probably held land immediately east of the Stanney Brook, in the area covered by the business park (*op cit*, 35-71).

It has, though, proved impossible to relate the majority of these seventeenth-century fields and dwellings to later map evidence. For instance, one useful source of information might have been the nineteenth-century tithe awards, which normally include a township map and schedule, listing the owners, their properties, and field-names, the latter of which could potentially be related to the field-names present in the 1626 survey. However, no such award exists for Castleton township, and the Butterworth tithe-award schedule (LA DRM 1/27) does not include field-names. Furthermore, an 1844 township plan of Castleton (RLSL LA/Z/3/C) only lists owners and occupants and also does not include field-names. This said, the location of one the properties (Near Moor Bank Farm) that formed the focus of the archaeological investigation is documented in the 1626 survey (*above*). There are also seventeenth-century deeds for some of the properties that formerly stood within the Kingsway Business Park, and although it has not been possible to locate these deeds recently, they were examined by Haynes and Tipper (1994).

Late eighteenth-century Land Tax assessments also mention several of the properties in the study area, although only a few entries specify individual farms. The Land Tax was first introduced in 1692, together with several other personal taxes, to raise revenue from personal estates, public offices, and land (Mathias 1967). The tax was calculated initially on the actual rental values of land and individual tax assessments were made, but in 1697-8, fixed quotas for each county were established, with Land Tax Commissioners being appointed, and the quotas were apportioned to the hundreds and then to the individual parishes or townships. Assessors were appointed for every constablewick or township. It has been calculated that the funds raised from land tax formed approximately 35% of the national revenue, although this figure had fallen to around 17% by the 1790s (*ibid*). The earliest Land Tax assessments for the Kingsway area dated from the early 1780s (*Ch 6*).

The Post-medieval Properties

The archaeological investigation of the Kingway Business Park afforded an opportunity to examine ten post-medieval properties within the townships of Castleton and Butterworth (Fig 30). These were associated with three major routeways, Lower Lane, Moss Side Lane, and Moor Bank Lane, of which the latter two might have had their genesis in the medieval period (*Ch 3, p 58*). These properties appear to typify dispersed settlement and its evolution across a wider area of the Pennine foothills of south-east Lancashire. Several of the farmhouses originated in the seventeenth century and were expanded and adapted in the eighteenth century, whilst others were solely a product of the eighteenth century, and some were also associated with the domestic-based textile industry. The investigative techniques employed comprised an initial survey of any upstanding buildings, which was then supplemented by archaeological excavation, following the demolition of the respective properties. However, in some instances, particular circumstances dictated that only one of these investigative techniques could be employed.

Moss Side Lane properties
Lower Moss Side Farm
Lower Moss Side Farm (originally Middle Moss Side Farm) stood on the north-western side of

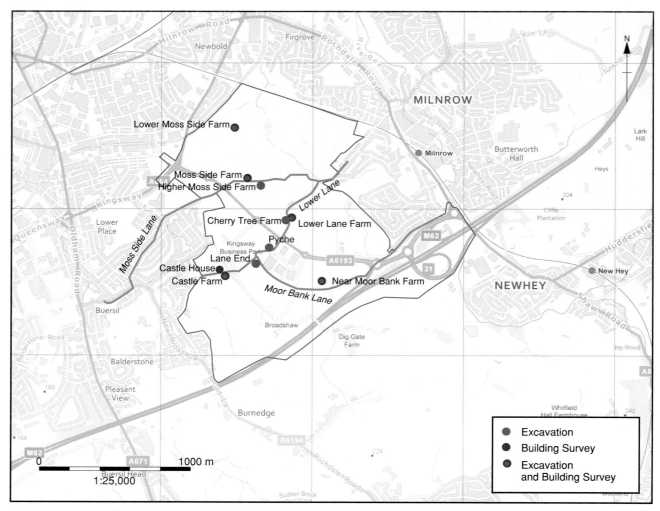

Figure 30: The post-medieval buildings investigated at the Kingsway Business Park

the Kingsway Business Park (SD 9147 1256), in the township of Castleton, approximately 150 m to the south-east of the Rochdale Canal. It was situated at a height of 147 m aOD, on a flat platform surrounded on the east, south, and west by a wide hollow, which to the west carries a small stream that flows into the Stanney Brook. A raised track led from the ancient hollow-way of Moss Side Lane (*Ch 3, p 58*) through to the farmstead, with another grassed-over track joining that to Waith Field to the north. The surrounding fields were mainly of pasture with gardens and a cobbled yard close to the building. The adjoining fields to the east showed traces of ridge and furrow, denoting late medieval or post-medieval agricultural practice.

The archaeological investigations indicate that a seventeenth-century farm existed at this site, which was later rebuilt as a farmhouse and adjoining cottage (*Ch 6, p 140*). It appears, however, that no documentary evidence relating to this early post-medieval settlement exists. Presumably, though, it formed one of the seventeenth-century dwellings that was constructed on land that was formerly part of Buersill Moor (*p 65*).

Archaeological investigation: building survey and excavation

In 2005, this site contained an extant two-storeyed farmhouse and adjoining cottage, with a barn to the north-east, all of which were subject to a building survey, undertaken immediately prior to their demolition. Although the exterior of the farmhouse and cottage was rendered, largely obscuring the details of the materials used to construct them, the building survey did identify elements that were probably associated with a seventeenth-century farmhouse, which had been comprehensively rebuilt in the mid-nineteenth century, to create two adjoining cottages (*Ch 6, p 140*).

An open-area excavation was then undertaken across the footprint of the buildings, following their demolition. This was designed to expose any remains that would assist in interpreting the development of this complex. Although the remains were fragmentary, they did produce valuable evidence relating to the seventeenth-century farmhouse, which, when combined with the building survey data and cartographic evidence, allow the ground plan to be reconstructed.

The evidence for a possible seventeenth-century farmhouse was in the form of two isolated stretches of stone walling, visible within the fabric of the upstanding brick-built nineteenth-century structures (Fig 31). One of these formed the southern wall of a cellar beneath the eastern bay of the nineteenth-century building. The cellar possessed a flagstone floor and contained several internal features, though these probably dated to the nineteenth century (Ch 6, p 142). The second, disturbed, stretch of stone walling was at the base of the northern elevation of the nineteenth-century structure. This wall was at the junction between the two later buildings and originally would have extended in a north/south direction, indicating a possible north/south range.

The archaeological excavation exposed further elements of the seventeenth-century farmhouse, in the form of drystone walls (**101**) defining the complete extent of the cellar, which measured *c* 8.5 x 5 m, and had a depth of 2.2 m below the modern ground surface. It was entered from the east via a set of four steps, keyed into the inside of the north wall of the building (Pl 19). These steps were *c* 1 m wide and were largely of stone, but incorporated some handmade bricks, apparently part of the original construction. The third step up the stairway incorporated a rebate on the southern side, and it would seem likely that this provided space for a wooden upright forming part of a doorframe near the top of the stairs (Pl 20). The interior of the cellar contained the partial remains of

Plate 19: Lower Moss Side Farm: steps into the seventeenth-century cellar, looking east

a flagstone floor, a continuation of that recorded in its western section during the building survey (*above*), and also a short length of stone walling. This wall created a small partitioned area, measuring *c* 2 x 1 m, at the south-eastern corner. A final interior feature was a drain, beneath the western wall of the cellar.

The excavation also uncovered further sections of drystone walling to the east of the cellar (Fig 31). These comprised a *c* 2 m long east/west wall, the

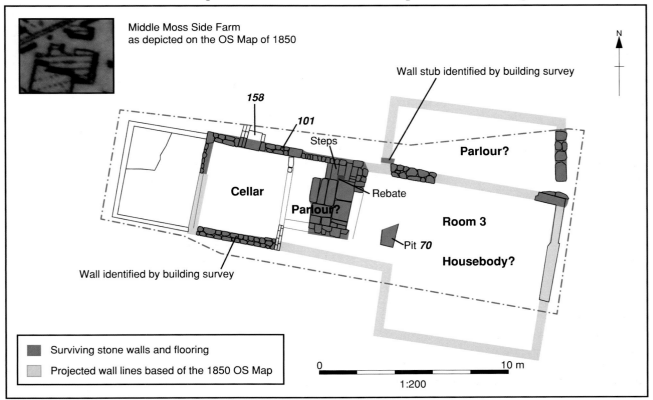

Figure 31: Seventeenth-century farmhouse at Lower Moss Side Farm

Plate 20: Lower Moss Side Farm: rebate in the side of the cellar steps, looking north

alignment of which corresponded to the northern wall line of the adjacent cellar, another east/west-aligned wall stub, *c* 4.5 m to the east, probably representing a continuation of this wall, and another length of walling immediately north of this, extending northwards for *c* 4 m. Significantly, this latter wall appears to have formed the eastern side of a range, the western wall of which was defined by the wall stub identified by the building survey, in the northern elevation of the later building (*p 67*).

Taken together, these remains suggested that the seventeenth-century farmhouse was L-shaped in plan, and contained at least three ground-floor rooms, one of which had a cellar beneath. Further details relating to its original form are provided by the first edition six-inch OS map (1850b), which depicts Middle Moss Side Farm, as it was then called, as a T-shaped building, with two small outshuts appended to that part of the building containing the cellar. Significantly, the seventeenth-century remains identified by the archaeological investigations correspond to the building depicted on this map, implying that it was still extant in the mid-nineteenth century. Based on the combined evidence, the seventeenth-century farmhouse appears to have comprised a main north/south range, divided into two rooms, with the larger room to the south probably forming the main housebody (living room and kitchen), with a smaller room to the north, perhaps functioning as a parlour. An additional cellared room was to the west, which may have been an additional parlour. However, it is clear from later mapping that the seventeenth-century farmhouse had been demolished by 1889-91 (OS 1893a). Indeed, following its demolition, it appears that some of the stone from its fabric was reused to construct a barn, to the east (*Ch 6, p 144*).

In addition to the seventeenth-century walls, the excavation also exposed a rectangular pit (*70*; Pl 21) in the larger of the rooms within the north/south range. This contained successive lenses of humic material, with inclusions of degraded felt, and yielded fragments of clay-tobacco pipes and pottery, which were in use during the seventeenth century (Table 2). Although the original dimensions and the intended function of the pit are unknown, as its northern end had been destroyed by later activity, it is tempting to suggest that it was associated with textile manufacturing, which may have occurred in the seventeenth-century farmhouse. Indeed, one possibility is that this formed the vestiges of a bleaching pit, or a feature that was used in another form of textile finishing.

Higher Moss Side Farm

Higher Moss Side stood in the north-west of the Kingsway Business Park, in the township of Castleton, on the southern side of Moss Side Lane (SD 9165 1215; Fig 30). The farm was *c* 250 m to the south-west of the Stanney Brook, at a height of *c* 150 m aOD. At the time of the archaeological investigation, there were no extant buildings, and an open-area excavation was undertaken to record any buried remains relating to the farm. This excavation comprised two trenches, one across the site of the farm and the other over the site of an associated weaver's cottage, which probably dated to the late eighteenth century (*Ch 6, p 161*). The documentary evidence (*p 69*) suggests that a seventeenth-century farm existed at Moss Side, and the archaeological excavations indicated that this was probably at Higher Moss Side Farm. This building was, however, demolished and rebuilt in the late eighteenth century (*Ch 6, p 155*).

*Plate 21: Lower Moss Side Farm: pit **70**, looking north*

Pottery	Date of pottery	Clay tobacco pipe
Cream-coloured earthenware hollow-ware vessel. Yellow-glazed on interior, black-glazed on exterior with red slip-trailed decoration under black glaze – experimental?	Seventeenth-eighteenth century	Clay tobacco-pipe stem, wide bore (sixteenth-eighteenth century)
Fine black-glazed red earthenware hollow-ware vessel	Seventeenth-early twentieth century	
High-fired purplish blackware(?) hollow-ware vessel; Staffordshire-type sherd	Seventeenth-eighteenth century	

*Table 2: Stratified post-medieval artefacts from pit **70**, Lower Moss Side Farm*

Documentary evidence

The early history of Moss Side can be partially discerned through documentary sources, which record the Butterworth family as cloth-makers at Moss Side in 1656 (Haynes and Tipper 1994, 48). Similarly, in 1673, a Samuel Dewhurst of Moss Side, who was a woollen merchant, is recorded as being in dispute with a Mary Taylor, a cloth-maker of Wardlehurst, who claimed that he had provided bad wool, which led to her getting into debt and being imprisoned at Lancaster Castle (*ibid*).

Archaeological excavation

Several early remains were present in the excavation (Pl 22), which probably date to the seventeenth century. The earliest remains comprised a *c* 0.8 m-wide gully (*53*; Fig 32), aligned north-west/south-east, which appeared to curve at its north-western end, at which point a small posthole (*76*) was recognised.

Following the natural silting of the gully, it was subsequently cut by a north/south-orientated stone wall (*41*; Pl 23). Significantly, this wall had been partly

*Plate 22: Higher Moss Side Farm: gully **53** and posthole **76**, looking west*

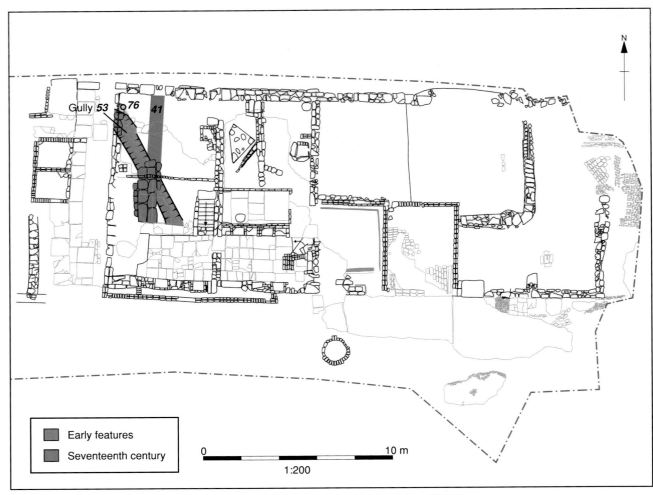

Gully *53* *76* *41*

Early features

Seventeenth century

0   10 m

1:200

Figure 32: The early remains at Higher Moss Side Farm

robbed at its northern end and was cut by the walls of a late eighteenth-century farmhouse (*Ch 6, p 155*). The wall was 1 m wide and was constructed of drystone blocks, which had a rough horizontal coursing. Small stone wedges were present on either side, though their function is not particularly clear. Although its date could not be directly ascertained, it is quite possible that it formed part of a seventeenth-century farmhouse, rebuilt in the late eighteenth century. Confirmation of this was provided by a reused stone-mullioned window, discovered within the fabric of the late eighteenth-century farmhouse, which probably derived from this earlier building (*Ch 6, p 159*).

Moss Side Farm
Moss Side Farm stood immediately west of Higher Moss Side Farm, on the northern side of Moss Side Lane (SD 9158 1220; Fig 30), and was also investigated archaeologically. This comprised a building survey of the extant farmhouse and an adjacent barn, and, following their demolition, an archaeological excavation across their footprints. Whilst this work indicated that the farmhouse probably dated to the late eighteenth century, it also located remains that pre-dated its construction.

Archaeological excavation
Several features were identified that pre-dated the construction of a late eighteenth-century farmhouse (*Ch 6, p 151*). These comprised a shallow ditch (*85*; Fig 33), aligned north-west/south-east, the remains only surviving within the interior of a later extension to the farmhouse (*Ch 6, p 152*). This ditch was *c* 2 m wide, had silted naturally, and contained a fragment of pottery that may date to the eighteenth century. A posthole (*89*) on its eastern edge, and a square pit (*79*) to the south, which may also have originally been placed on the ditch's eastern edge (Pl 24), were the only features associated.

Lower Lane properties
Lower Lane hamlet: Lower Lane Farm and Cherry Tree Farm
A hamlet existed on Lower Lane (centred on SD 9184 1192; Fig 30), at the centre of the Kingsway Business Park, at a height of 154 m aOD, in the township of Castleton. Historically, this comprised two adjacent farms, on either side of Lower Lane, approximately 75 m south of the junction with Moss Side Lane. The farm on the eastern side was Lower Lane Farm (SD 9185 1194), whilst Cherry Tree Farm (originally known

Plate 23: Higher Moss Side Farm: wall **41**, looking north

Plate 24: Moss Side Farm: section excavated across pit **79**, looking west

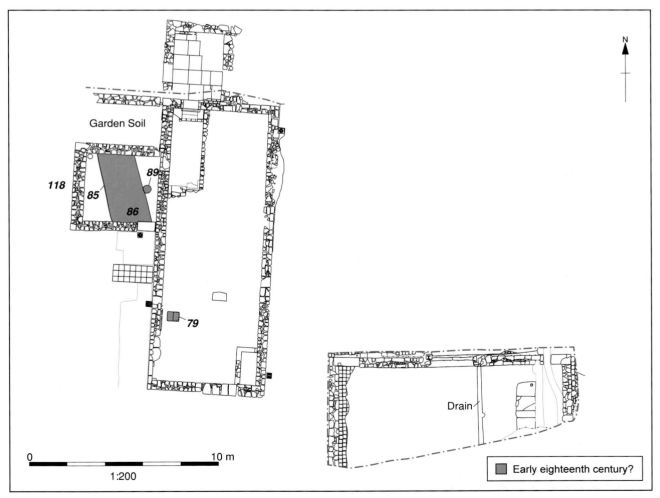

Figure 33: The early eighteenth-century remains at Moss Side Farm

First floor

Remains identified by the building survey

Projected walls

Pit *189*

Beams

Housebody

Parlour

Doorway

Entrance

Roof beam

Fireplace

0   10 m

1:200

Ground Floor

Figure 34: Seventeenth-century remains at Lower Lane Farm

as Yew Tree Farm) stood to the west of this route (SD 9182 1192); both were investigated archaeologically.

The archaeological investigation at Lower Lane Farm comprised a building survey and subsequent open-area excavation, following demolition. However, it was only possible to undertake an open-area excavation at Cherry Tree Farm, as the buildings there had been demolished prior to the major scheme of archaeological investigation within the Kingsway Business Park.

Significantly, these investigations, together with the documentary evidence, indicated that there was a late seventeenth-century farmhouse at Lower Lane

Farm, which was modified and substantially rebuilt during the mid-eighteenth century. Similarly, an early building was present at Cherry Tree Farm, in the form of a laithe-type house, dating to either the seventeenth or eighteenth century, which was then extended later in the eighteenth century. Some evidence for activity pre-dating this building was also apparent.

Documentary evidence
The earliest known deeds for Lower Lane Farm date to 1694, indicating that the locale was then known as Great Wickenshaw (Haynes and Tipper 1994, 46). Great Wickenshaw is also mentioned in the 1626 Rochdale survey (*p 65*) as being a close held by John Roade, granted to him by Robert Milne of Lady House,

Plate 25: Lower Lane Farm: the seventeenth-century mullioned window, at ground-floor level, in the southern elevation

though there is no mention of a messuage (dwelling) (Fishwick 1913, 29). Other documentary material that can be associated firmly with Lower Lane Farm is scant, although a reference in the probate records of the Archdeaconry of Chester dated to 1719 refers to John Holt, a yeoman, at Lower Lane, Castleton (LA WCW/Infra/C1392/31). A slightly later reference mentions Robert Holt of Castleton, described as a merchant, who agreed in 1759 to lease a plot of land 'in the little Calfhey' to James Taylor, a weaver in Buersill (LA DDX 409/30); Holt is named in late eighteenth-century documents as the proprietor of two properties at Lower Lane (*Ch 7, p 167*), whilst James Taylor is listed in the Land Tax assessment for 1780, where he is accredited with erecting a 'new house (LA QDL/S/24).

Although the early history of Cherry Tree Farm is not particularly forthcoming, it has been suggested that an early farm, known as Yew Tree Farm, was established there, which was also used as an inn (Haynes and Tipper 1994, 47). The mid-nineteenth-century first edition six-inch OS map (OS 1850b) suggests that this farm may have formed part of a linear range fronting a small lane at its junction with Lower Lane.

Archaeological investigations at Lower Lane Farm: building survey and excavation
The documentary evidence indicates that, in the late seventeenth century, a farmhouse existed at this site and, although this building appears to have been comprehensively rebuilt in the early eighteenth century (*p 74*), the building survey identified structural elements within the fabric of the upstanding eighteenth-century building that might date to this period. Although these elements were fairly piecemeal, these may suggest that this farmhouse was a stone-built rectangular building, which might, based on the dimensions of the later rebuild, have measured 8.8 x 4.8 m (Fig 34).

The potential elements relating to this early building survived in the southern elevation, in an area that would later form the western bay of the mid-eighteenth-century farmhouse (*below*). At ground-floor level, these included a long, narrow window, with roughly chamfered stone mullions, with three irregular narrow lights, and two chamfered stone mullions (Pl 25). Above this, set close to the eaves, was a similar long, narrow window, with roughly chamfered mullions, which originally had four narrow lights (Pl 26). These were to the east of a doorway, which could also conceivably have formed an element of the seventeenth-century house. This was covered by a modern porch, and was square-headed with stone jambs and lintel; the jambs and lintel were of large blocks of ashlar bevelled along the edges. Immediately to the east of the door were traces of a stone plinth at ground level, which probably formed an element of the seventeenth-century farmhouse, indicating that its walls were set on a wide stone foundation.

Another feature probably belonging to the seventeenth-century house was a massive, crudely cut timber, which was visible on the interior side of the southern elevation at first-floor level. This ran the full length of the southern wall and appeared to have derived from a tree that was not specifically grown for timber (Pl 27). The wood had been cut with an axe or adze and the under-surface was roughly bevelled. Given its position, this timber may have formed an element of the roof of the seventeenth-century building.

Two similar crude timber beams were also identified at ground-floor level, which were probably used to support the upper floor. It is also noteworthy that the position of these beams equated with a wide chimney stack, and it is therefore quite likely that this was also seventeenth-century in date. The chimney was probably at the centre of the early building, and it is quite possible that the eastern bay of the mid-

Plate 26: Lower Lane Farm: the seventeenth-century mullioned window, at first-floor level, in the southern elevation

Plate 27: Lower Lane Farm: the irregular beam running the length of the first-floor ceiling

Two stone-mullioned windows, roughly chamfered, were also recorded in the northern elevation, in addition to the windows in the southern elevation. One of these, at ground-floor level (Pl 28), appears to have had three narrow lights, whilst the other, at first-floor level, had two narrow lights (Pl 29). Although these windows were in that part of the building which dates to the eighteenth century (*below*), such small stone-framed windows, with their roughly chamfered mullions, are typical of the seventeenth century (*cf* Miller 2002, 158), and one possibility is that they were removed from the demolished section of the earlier farmhouse, and reused during the eighteenth-century rebuilding.

The excavation also revealed a feature to the west of the seventeenth-century farmhouse, that might also date to this period. This was an elongated sub-circular pit (*189*), which had been partially destroyed by the footings of a small cottage, appended to the mid-eighteenth-century farmhouse in the late eighteenth century (*Ch 7, p 169*). This pit contained a dark fill, with humic lenses, and it may have been used in textile finishing.

eighteenth-century farmhouse was a direct rebuild of an earlier bay (*below*). If this was the case, the seventeenth-century building was a two-cell house, within which the western bay was a heated room (the housebody), whilst the eastern bay may have been an unheated parlour. Access between these bays was probably through a doorway to the south of the chimney, which was retained in the mid-eighteenth-century farmhouse. To the north of the chimney was a dividing wall, which again might be a seventeenth-century feature. Access to the upper floors, as in other comparable two-cell houses, was probably not by stairs *per se*, but via ladders at the back of the housebody (*cf* Pearson 1985, 81).

The building survey and excavation suggested that, during the mid-eighteenth century, the late seventeenth-century farmhouse was comprehensively rebuilt. This new structure also had two bays (western and eastern), with a small cellar at the rear of the house, partially beneath the western bay (Fig 35).

It appears that the eastern bay of the earlier house was completely rebuilt, demonstrated by the surviving architectural features in its southern elevation, which were typical of the eighteenth century. At ground-floor level, these included a wide window of two lights, with a narrow square-profiled stone mullion and stone surrounds, whilst above

Plate 28: Lower Lane Farm: the lower stone-mullioned window in the northern elevation

Plate 29: Lower Lane Farm: the upper stone-mullioned window in the northern elevation, the lower part blocked with handmade bricks

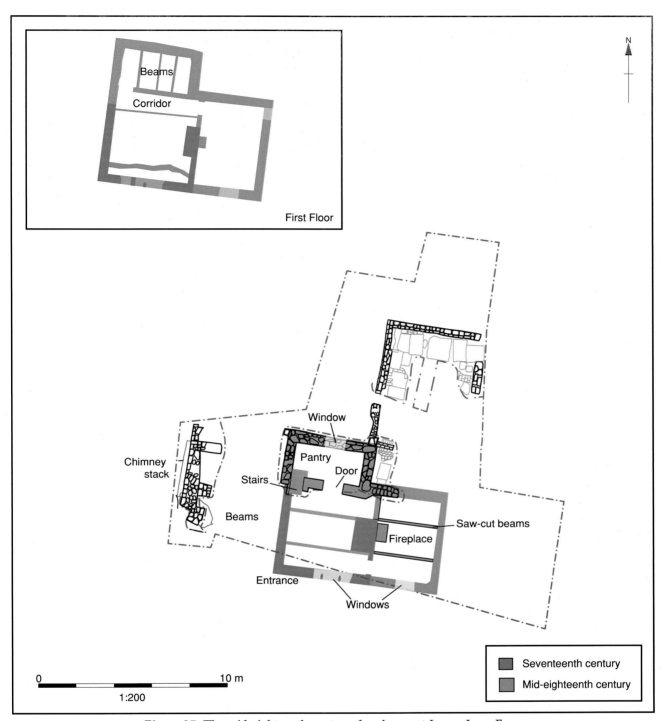

Figure 35: The mid-eighteenth-century farmhouse at Lower Lane Farm

this, on the first floor, was a tall wide window of three lights, with two thin stone mullions.

Part of the northern elevation, in the area occupied by the western bay, projected outwards, and formed a gable end, constructed of roughly dressed blocks of random rubble set in courses. This projecting elevation contained the two stone-mullioned windows, on the ground- and first-floor levels, that may have originally derived from the seventeenth-century farmhouse (p 74). Significantly,

the eighteenth-century date of this elevation was confirmed during the open-area excavation, which revealed that its foundation trench contained pottery of that date (p 76).

The northern elevation of the eastern bay was obscured by a nineteenth-century barn (Ch 7, p 171), although at ground-floor level it was clearly stone-built. The nature of the stonework was obscured by white paint and washes, but there appeared to be a change in build in the centre of the elevation,

Plate 30: Lower Lane Farm: the eighteenth-century door in the western bay

wide planks with a narrow architrave, hung on handmade L-shaped hinges. There were also traces of what may have been an original wooden handle on one side of the door. The smaller room did not contain a fireplace and may thus have originally functioned as a pantry. The room did, however, contain a short, steep narrow staircase, which allowed access from its north-west corner up to the floor above.

The cellar beneath the possible pantry was examined by both the building survey and open-area excavation, it measuring *c* 3.6 x 1.8 m internally, being accessed down a flight of stairs from the larger room in the western bay. These steps, which led into the south-west corner of the cellar, were of handmade brick with well-worn stone treads. The main walls were composed of roughly dressed blocks laid in irregular courses, without bonding material, whilst its floor, which was 1.8 m below the ground surface, was composed of irregularly sized local flagstones. Its roof was a single barrel vault of handmade brick, at least two bricks deep.

During the excavation, the walls of the cellar were found to have been built within a foundation cut, and a small collection of eighteenth-century pottery was recovered from the backfill (**184**) of this (Table 3). Significantly, this material provides a *terminus post quem* for the rebuilding of the farmhouse, indicating that this most likely occurred in the mid-eighteenth century.

Various niches were also present within the cellar walls. The northern elevation had two, which may originally have been windows or small light wells, later blocked with loose brick (Pl 31). The eastern and western elevations also both had a single small niche; the eastern one was blocked, while the western one appeared to have a base and surround in stone (Pl 32). The niche in the southern elevation was again blocked with brick. A line of brick against the south-east wall may also have marked the position of a stone-slab table.

which might either represent a break between the seventeenth- and eighteenth-century elements of the farmhouse, or could denote the position of a former doorway. Both the eastern and western elevations were obscured, but were constructed of large, roughly dressed blocks of stone.

The western bay was divided at ground-floor level into two rooms, with the smaller room to the rear, above the cellar (*below*). This room had also been raised above the level of the larger room, and access between them was via two stone steps, leading up from the larger room, and then through a doorway. The door there (Pl 30) appeared to date from the eighteenth century, being constructed from three

Pottery	Date	Clay tobacco pipe
Beaded creamware	Mid-late eighteenth century	Clay tobacco pipe, medium bore (sixteenth-nineteenth century)
White salt-glazed stoneware	Eighteenth century	
Slip-decorated red earthenware dish with wavy incised decoration	Eighteenth century	
Fine brown stoneware	Eighteenth century	

*Table 3: Stratified post-medieval artefacts from backfill **184**, Lower Lane Farm*

Plate 31: Lower Lane Farm: the northern elevation of the cellar, showing the two brick-blocked niches

The main housebody, to the south, was essentially retained from the seventeenth-century farmhouse (*p 74*), and it continued to contain the main chimney stack, along with a doorway to the south and dividing wall to the north (*p 74*). However, several features were apparent which might date to the eighteenth century. These included a very narrow skirting board around the base of the room, and a crude oval-section picture rail.

The ground-floor of the eastern bay may, like its seventeenth-century predecessor, have continued to function as a parlour. However, in the eighteenth century, this room was heated by a fireplace that had been built against the back of the earlier central stack. The position of this fireplace was marked by a small chimney breast, which contained a twentieth-century fireplace (Pl 33).

The ground-floor of the eastern bay was accessed through a doorway to the south of the chimney, containing an eighteenth-century door. Its three planks were hand-sawn, braced by four solid bars

Plate 32: Lower Lane Farm: the western elevation of the cellar, with a niche with a stone surround set into the wall

of wood, with handmade nails and L-shaped hinges. Other potential mid-eighteenth-century features in the eastern bay included two saw-cut timber beams extending in an east/west direction across the ceiling.

The first-floor contained three rooms, the arrangement of which largely followed that of the ground-floor, albeit with the addition of an east/west corridor allowing access into all the rooms. They all may originally have functioned as bedrooms, as they were probably too poorly lit to have been workshops. Original features included an eighteenth-century fireplace in the eastern bay (*p 74*) and a doorway, set between the chimney and the northern wall. The door was probably eighteenth century in date, built of three wide planks, with a handmade iron latch. A central narrow ridge purlin of saw-cut wood, with other purlins on either side, was also visible in the small first-floor room at the rear of the house.

Archaeological excavation at Cherry Tree Farm
All of the historic buildings at Cherry Tree Farm had been demolished prior to the major scheme of archaeological investigation in 2005. The site was, however, visited in 1998 (*Ch 1, p 6*), and at this time a one-and-half-storeyed linear building range was extant, constructed in stone (Arrowsmith and Wilson 1998). This appeared to be a post-medieval building, probably that once known as Yew Tree Farm (*p 73*). In addition, at that time, two small nineteenth-

Plate 33: Lower Lane Farm: the eighteenth-century ground-floor chimney-breast

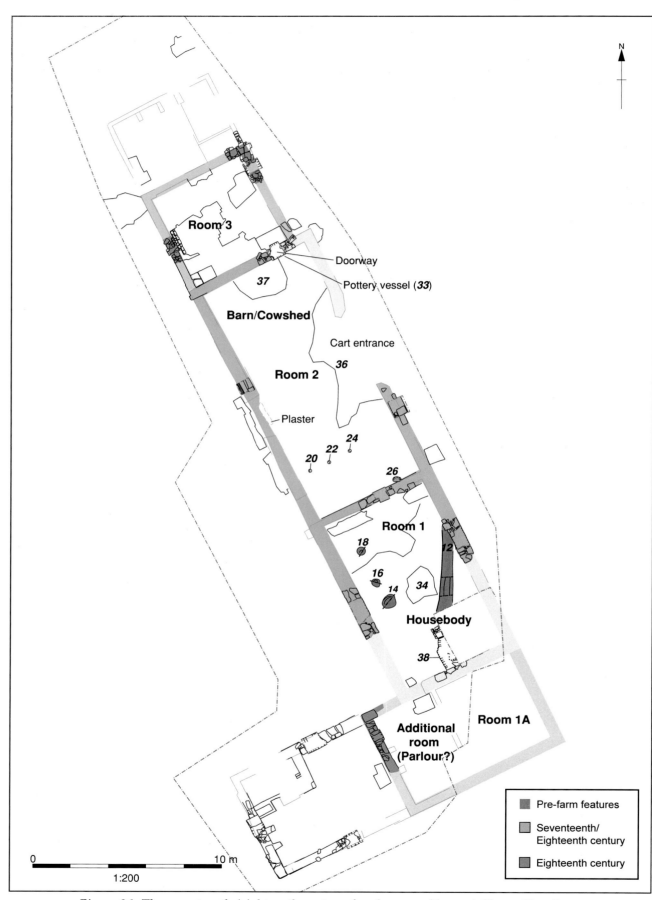

Room 3

Doorway

Pottery vessel (*33*)

37

Barn/Cowshed

Cart entrance

36

Room 2

Plaster

24

22

20

26

Room 1

18

12

16

34

14

Housebody

38

Room 1A

Additional
room
(Parlour?)

Pre-farm features

Seventeenth/
Eighteenth century

Eighteenth century

0   10 m

1:200

Figure 36: The seventeenth-/eighteenth-century farmhouse and barn at Cherry Tree Farm

Plate 34: Cherry Tree Farm: gully 12, looking south

century cottages and a larger cottage were standing at the southern end of the range (*Ch 7, p 174*). The site of these buildings therefore formed the focus of an open-area excavation, which uncovered the fragmentary remains of the range and also the later buildings (*Ch 7, p 172*).

The site was unusual, in that it had witnessed an early phase of activity prior to the construction of Yew Tree Farm (Fig 36). This was demonstrated by the discovery of several 'negative' features beneath the flooring of the later farm, cut into the natural geology. In particular, there was a narrow gully (*12*; Pl 34), aligned north/south, *c* 0.7 m wide, which was not associated with any artefacts but did contain organic material, and had been cut by the walls of the later stone-built farm, suggesting that it was comparatively early in date. Immediately to the west were three circular pits (*14, 16,* and *18*), with diameters ranging between 0.4 m and 0.8 m, which had been filled with slag and clinker, whilst a comparable pit (*26*) was found 4 m to the north-east. These features also contained no artefactual material, though *26* was cut by a later wall, indicating that it pre-dated the construction of the stone-built farm.

The external wall of the farm was of drystone construction, an average of 0.7 m wide, which had been built above a series of levelling layers composed of gravel, sand, and clinker. The building was subdivided by a *c* 0.5 m-thick drystone wall into two 'rooms' (1 and 2; Pl 35).

It is likely that the smaller of these 'rooms' (1), which measured internally 9.5 x 5.8 m, was the dwelling, whilst the larger (2), 13.3 x 5.8 m, acted as an attached barn/cowshed. A sondage excavated across the wall separating the dwelling and barn produced

Plate 35: Cherry Tree Farm: Rooms 1 and 2, looking north-west

Pottery	Date	Clay tobacco pipe
Fine mottled ware(?) vessel, exterior almost black	Seventeenth-eighteenth century	Clay tobacco pipe, medium bore (sixteenth-nineteenth century)
Fine black-glazed red earthenware with zigzag(?) white slip-trailed decoration, hollow-ware	Seventeenth-eighteenth century	
White-glazed thin wall(?) tile, relief-moulded and green painted	Twentieth century	

Table 4: Artefacts from the sondage excavated at Cherry Tree Farm

artefactual material indicating that it was constructed either in the later seventeenth or eighteenth century (Table 4). This sondage also produced a piece of twentieth-century wall tile, although this must have been intrusive.

Several features were identified within the probable barn/cowshed ('Room' 2), which appear to have been contemporary with its use during the seventeenth/eighteenth century. These included a line of three postholes (*20, 22,* and *24*), parallel with the southern wall, possibly defining a stall or pen, *c* 2.5 x 2.2 m. One clear doorway was also identified, *c* 1 m wide, in the gable end of the barn, close to its north-eastern corner, defined by a flagstone and handmade-brick threshold. A complete pottery vessel (*33*) had also been placed beneath the floor, directly adjacent to this threshold. This was a black-glazed red

earthenware crock, with a broad date range spanning the seventeenth to twentieth centuries. In addition, a larger, centrally positioned, cart entrance may have existed on the eastern side of the barn, as a *c* 4 m-wide break in this wall line was present.

At some stage, perhaps during the eighteenth century, the barn was extended, as an additional room (3) was added to its north-western end (Pl 36); this was *c* 6 m square. Its external walls butted onto the earlier gable end of the house and were composed of irregularly coursed drystone blocks. The north-eastern wall was 0.6 m thick, the south-western wall being narrower, at 0.45 m, and the room contained a flagstone floor. Access into it was through the doorway close to the north-eastern corner of the barn (*above*), and it is possible that it was a store.

Plate 36: Cherry Tree Farm: Room 3, looking west

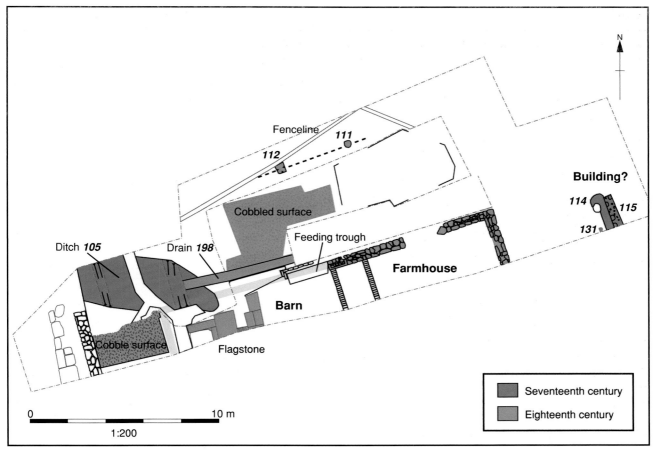

Figure 37: The seventeenth- and eighteenth-century farmhouse and barn at Pyche

It also seems likely that, during this period, the south-eastern end of the house was extended, involving the construction of an additional room (1A), which had been converted in the early nineteenth century into two cottages (*Ch 7, p 174*). Evidence for this extension was postulated during the 1998 archaeological assessment, when it was noted that the then extant cottages were constructed of sandstone at ground-floor level, 'possibly incorporated from an earlier building (perhaps part of the rear range)' (Arrowsmith and Wilson 1998, 12). This was confirmed during the excavation, when a 0.5 m-thick drystone wall, defining the north-western corner of the building, was uncovered. This suggests that the additional room at the southern end of the house was probably *c* 9 m long and *c* 5.5 m wide.

Pyche farm
The site of Pyche farm was immediately north of Lower Lane (SD 9171 1173), approximately 150 m to the east of the junction of Lower Lane and Moor Bank Lane (Fig 30). This is depicted on mid-nineteenth-century mapping (OS 1850b) as a linear range, and a photograph, taken prior to its demolition, indicates that it possessed two storeys, with chimneys on each gable wall, and a centrally positioned doorway (Haynes and Tipper 1994, 46, fig 5.18). The form of the house suggests that it was constructed in the

eighteenth century. The photograph also indicates that a single-storey building was attached to its western side, which probably functioned as a barn.

The house and barn were demolished prior to 1998, the remains being visible as a grassed-over platform, this being targeted for excavation. However, given ecological constraints, it was only possible to excavate an open-area trench, 30 x 9 m, over the rearward section of the former farm. This exposed potential seventeenth-century remains, relating to a possible building and field boundary, and the footings of the eighteenth-century farmhouse.

Archaeological excavation of the seventeenth-/eighteenth-century farm
The excavation uncovered several early features at the western and eastern ends of the site that potentially relate to seventeenth-century occupation. A small group of seemingly contemporary features were present at the eastern end of the trench, which may have been the fragmentary remains of a building. These included a posthole (*131*; Fig 37), which contained a large number of clay tobacco-pipe stem fragments and stamped clay-pipe bowls dating to the mid- to late seventeenth century. The stamps on the bowls were exclusively of a design incorporating the letters 'I.B.' (*Appendix 4*). To the east, a linear

81

*Plate 37: Pyche farm: ditch **105**, looking west*

Plate 38: Pyche farm: the wall defining the north-eastern corner of the eighteenth-century farm, looking north

spread (**115**) was noted, in a north/south alignment, composed of some dressed-stone blocks, apparently denoting the position of *c* 0.45 m-wide drystone wall. Immediately to the west of, and parallel with, this spread, was a gully (**114**), which may either represent a robber trench or the remains of a drain contemporary with the wall.

At the western end of the trench, the early remains comprised the terminus of an east/west ditch (**105**; Pl 37), perhaps also dating to the seventeenth century. This had a maximum width of 2.7 m, and contained two sequential deposits of silt, the lower of which also contained fragments of ceramic building material. It may well have formed an early field boundary, contemporary with the putative seventeenth-century building to the east.

The footings of the eighteenth-century farmhouse lay between the possible seventeenth-century remains (*above*), though these were also fragmentary. They included a right-angled section of drystone wall (Pl 38), with a *c* 1.8 m-wide break in its northern stretch. It was *c* 0.6 m wide and appears to have formed the north-eastern corner and northern side of the linear range depicted on mid-nineteenth-century mapping. At its far western end, this wall

also incorporated a stone feeding trough in its fabric. The probable eighteenth-century date of the farm was confirmed, through the discovery of artefacts dating to this period, which were recovered from infill (**103**) adjacent to the eastern wall of the building (Table 5).

A small area of flagstones was uncovered to the west of the farmhouse, which may have been the original floor within the barn attached to the dwelling. The walls of this barn did not survive, however, though a cobbled surface was located to the west of the flagstones, presumably forming part of a yard on the western side of the barn.

Several other contemporary features were also revealed to the north of the farmhouse and attached barn. These included a cobbled yard surface, set above a 0.30 m-thick clinker levelling layer (**100**), associated with an eighteenth-century horseshoe drain (**198**). This drain cut the earlier boundary ditch (**105**; *above*) and was seemingly parallel with the northern side of the barn. Two postholes (**111** and **112**) were to the north of the cobbled surface, one of which (**112**) contained a deposit of clinker comparable to the material used as a levelling deposit beneath the cobbled yard, whilst the other (**111**) contained the vestiges of a wooden post. These posts were spaced *c* 5 m apart and might have formed elements of a fence bounding the northern side of the yard.

Lane End
The site of Lane End Farm was close to the centre of the Kingsway Business Park (SD 9162 1163),

Pottery	Date of pottery	Clay tobacco pipe
Press-moulded red earthenware dish, pie-crust edge, red, orange, and white-slip decoration	Seventeenth-eighteenth century	Clay tobacco pipe, wide bore (sixteenth-eighteenth century)

*Table 5: Stratified post-medieval artefacts from infill **103**, Pyche farm*

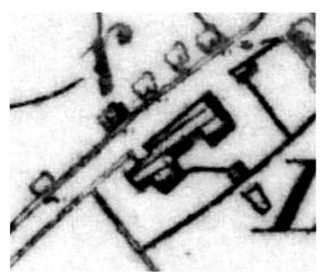

Plate 39: Extract from the OS first edition six-inch map (1850), showing Lane End Farm

on Lower Lane, immediately south-west of the junction with Moor Bank Lane (Fig 30). The documentary evidence (*below*) indicates this farm had a fairly extended history, dating back to the early seventeenth century, and it seemed possible that an L-shaped range depicted on the first edition six-inch OS map (OS 1850b) was the seventeenth-century

farm (Pl 39). Although farm buildings were present at this site throughout the nineteenth and twentieth centuries (Arrowsmith and Wilson 1998, 10), these had been demolished in 1980. The footprint of the farm buildings fronting Lower Lane was targeted by an open-area excavation, in an area measuring some 15 x 14 m, which appeared to confirm the postulated sequence of development, in that the features uncovered were of an early building, possibly dating to the seventeenth century.

Documentary evidence
Deeds dating to 1634 give reference to a timber-framed property in the locality, and it is possible that this was the 'Half Acre Gate' referred to at Lane End in 1626, being then owned by the Clegg family (Haynes and Tipper 1994, 45-6). They were in tenure until the nineteenth century.

Archaeological excavation of the seventeenth-century farm
The early farm had an L-shaped plan (Fig 38) and appears to have been composed of a dwelling with an attached barn/cowshed on its north-eastern side (Pl 40). The external walls (**202** and **214**) were constructed of regularly coursed, roughly hewn stone, bonded with white, fine mortar, which had an average thickness of 0.6 m. They were fragmentary,

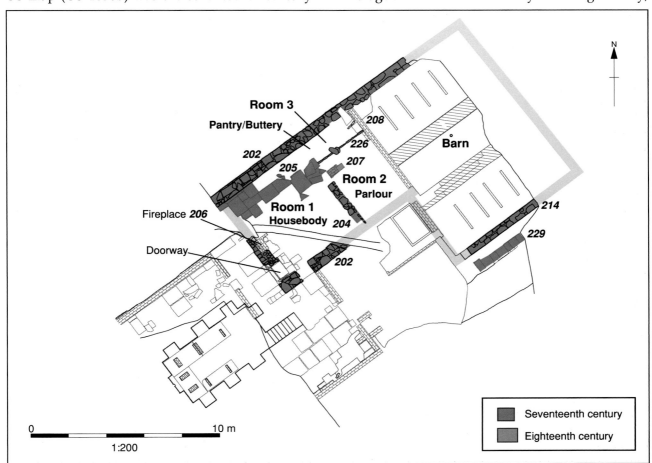

Figure 38: The seventeenth-century farmhouse and barn at Lane End Farm

Plate 40: Lane End Farm: the possible seventeenth-century farm, looking south-east

though those that did survive defined the front (north-western) elevation of the dwelling and barn (**202**), parts of the gable end (south-western elevation) and rear (south-eastern) walls of the dwelling (**202**), and the south-eastern wall (**214**) of the barn. All of these walls had seemingly been placed directly onto the natural geology and were not contained in foundation trenches. In contrast, the wall (**208**) that separated the dwelling from the barn was constructed of handmade brick. This therefore appears to represent a later replacement of an earlier stone wall, and it is possible that it was inserted in the late eighteenth century, when major modifications were being undertaken at the farm (*Ch 7, p 186*).

The seventeenth-century dwelling had a rectangular plan, internally *c* 7.6 x 5 m, forming a two-celled house (*cf* Pearson 1985, 81-2). Internally, the house was divided by a *c* 0.4 m-thick stone wall (**204**), parallel with the gable-end of the building, creating eastern and western cells. The western cell (Room 1) was the larger, measuring 5 x 4.5 m, and this formed the housebody. The original doorway into this room was positioned on the gable wall, allowing access into the southern corner of the dwelling. This doorway was *c* 0.8 m wide, marked by two stones which contained slots for securing the uprights of the doorframe. The interior floor of the housebody

was of large stone flags (**205**) measuring up to 0.9 x 0.70 m. It is also possible that a fireplace (**206**) originally existed on the gable wall, which had been removed at a later date and replaced by a setting of machine-made bricks.

The smaller eastern cell was divided into two rooms (2 and 3) by a stone wall (**226**) parallel with the north-western elevation of the dwelling; it is probable that these functioned as a parlour and pantry/buttery. The parlour (Room 2) was the larger, measuring 3.6 x 2.8 m, accessed from the housebody (Room 1) through a doorway positioned at its north-western corner. Immediately inside this doorway was a stone and brick plinth (**207**), which was possibly added during the eighteenth century. The probable pantry/buttery was to the north-west and measured 2.8 x 1.2 m, again accessed directly from the housebody. At its eastern end was a single surviving flagstone with two adjacent upright stones.

Aside from the external walls (*above*), the remains relating to the barn attached to the dwelling were sparse, as its internal area had been substantially modified during the twentieth century. That said, it is likely that its entrance was on its north-eastern side and that it was served by a stone-lined drain (**229**) immediately adjacent to its south-western wall.

Castle hamlet: Castle House and Castle Farm

Castle hamlet lay in the south-western portion of the Kingsway Business Park (centred on SD 9141 1156) and comprised two separate building complexes, one on either side of Lower Lane (Fig 30). Castle House (SD 9140 1166) was on the northern side of the lane, where a series of buildings was extant until 2007, which were subjected to a building survey. This indicated that the building complex had a fairly long history, the earliest element being a house dating to the mid-late seventeenth century, which was then modified in the late eighteenth century (*Ch 7, p 188*).

The other building complex was Castle Farm (SD 9143 1156), immediately opposite Castle House, on the southern side of Lower Lane. Again, at this site, a standing building was present in 2007, which was subjected to a building survey, though it was clear that this dated to the late eighteenth century and functioned as a weaver's cottage (*Ch 7, p 190*). However, the building survey also identified some

limited evidence for an earlier building at the site, adjoining the northern side of the standing building. Significantly, the position of this building is plotted on nineteenth-century mapping (OS 1850b) and it was probably a farmhouse, present at the site prior to the late eighteenth century. Following the demolition of the standing building, the site was therefore stripped to examine additional details regarding its construction and date. The site of a probable outbuilding was also stripped, which historical mapping indicates was present in the nineteenth century, being demolished in the earlier part of the twentieth century. This building stood directly adjacent to Lower Lane, and the excavation suggested that some of its elements were contemporary with the early farmhouse.

Building survey at Castle House

During the building survey, *in situ* elements of a mid-late seventeenth-century house were identified, which appears to have been of two bays (Fig 39) and was single-storeyed. However, these elements were only apparent in the north-eastern and south-western elevations of the extant building, as the other two

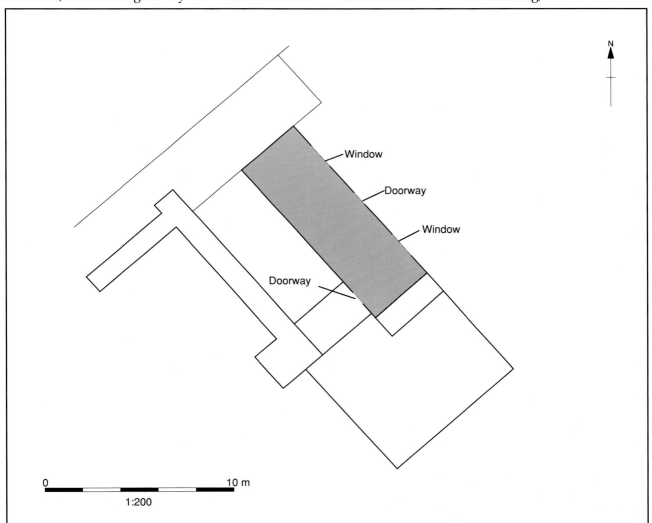

Figure 39: The Castle House building ranges, showing the seventeenth-century building

Plate 41: Castle House: the seventeenth-century ground-floor window surround, with eighteenth-century saw-cut mullions

Plate 42: Castle House: the north-eastern elevation of the seventeenth-century cottage

elevations were obscured by a modern building used as an abattoir. In addition, no evidence for the internal arrangement of the early cottage was present, as the interior of the building had been completely altered during the twentieth century.

The seventeenth-century elements included the ground-floor walls, which were composed of coursed drystone blocks. Within the north-eastern elevation, which formed the façade of the cottage, other seventeenth-century features (Pl 41) were two single stone-built windows, on either side of a later doorway that had been inserted in the late twentieth century (Pl 42). However, given the position of the windows, it is possible that the later doorway replaced an original seventeenth-century feature, providing access into the property. In both instances, the window surrounds were formed of mason-dressed stone and also contained saw-cut stone mullions, clearly eighteenth-century replacements (*below*). That to the south-west of the door was a single stone-mullioned window, whilst its counterpart to the north-east had a double stone mullion.

The south-western elevation also contained a doorway that was probably seventeenth-century in date. This was at the southern end of the elevation and had a mason-dressed stone surround. A broad wrought-iron draw-bar bracket was present on the western stone architrave (Pl 43), whilst two original heavy gudgeons were in the opposing architrave.

Aside from the *in situ* elements, it also appears that elements of the original roof had been reused in the raised late eighteenth-century roof of the house (*Ch 7,*

p 188). A seventeenth-century truss was identified, forming a king post, with brackets (Pl 44), which was double pegged to the tie beam, as were the principal rafters. However, there were vacant purlin saddles at both ends of the principal rafters, strongly suggesting that it had been removed from the earlier building and reused (Pl 45). In addition to the roof truss, there was also a single floor-bridging beam that had been reused as a roof purlin in the southern section of the south-western roof pitch.

Archaeological investigation at Castle Farm: building survey and excavation

Evidence for an early farmhouse was identified during the building survey at Castle Farm. This took the form of a 'ghost' gable outline (Pl 46), visible on the north-western elevation of a late eighteenth-century weaver's cottage (*Ch 7, p 190*),

Plate 43: Castle House: the wrought-iron draw-bar bracket

Plate 44: Castle House: the king-post roof truss

which indicates that the earlier farmhouse was two storeys in height.

The footprint of the farmhouse was also stripped as part of the open-area excavation, which indicated that it was a rectangular range, *c* 9 x 12 m (Fig 40). The footings for the north-eastern and north-western external walls of the building survived, composed of unbonded stone, which incorporated some handmade brick; this latter material would suggest that the building dated to the eighteenth century and, on balance, a mid-eighteenth-century date is favoured for its construction. A *c* 1.2 m-wide doorway was also visible on the north-eastern wall, close to that corner of the building. The remains of

a partition wall were also present, which divided the house into two bays. The larger bay occupied the northern end of the building, and was *c* 7 m wide, whilst the smaller bay to the south was *c* 5 m wide. A stone-capped drain was also present in the larger bay.

To the north of the farmhouse, the open-area excavation exposed the footings of a small outbuilding, measuring 7 m square. Its walls were constructed of unbonded stone in a similar manner to the farmhouse, and, as such, it was probably contemporary in date.

Plate 46: Castle Farm: the north-western elevation and south-western gable end of the weaver's cottage, with a ghost roof line visible on the north-western elevation

Plate 45: Castle House: the reused bridging beam

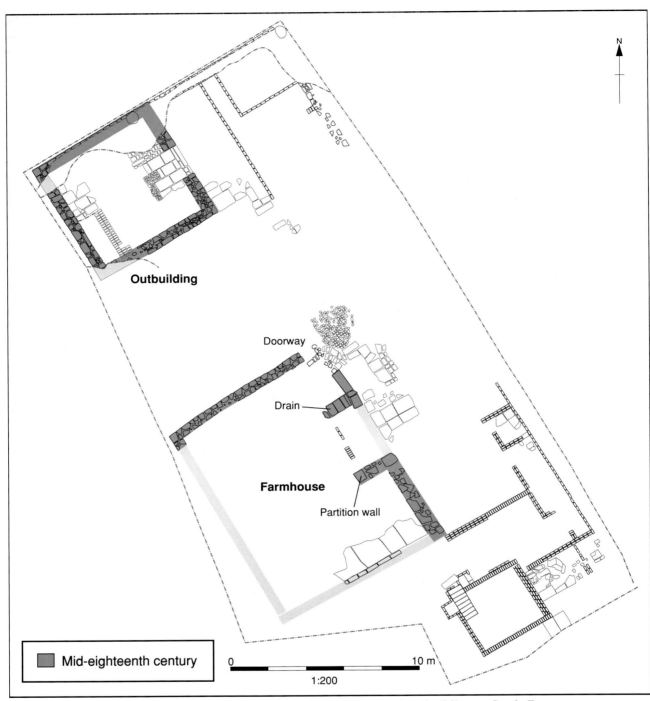

Figure 40: The mid-eighteenth-century farmhouse and outbuilding at Castle Farm

Moor Bank Lane
Near Moor Bank Farm

Near Moor Bank Farm was situated in the south-eastern part of the Kingsway Business Park (SD 9207 1147), on the northern side of Moor Bank Lane, at a height of 160 m aOD (Fig 30). Another farm, named Moor Bank Farm, stood approximately 140 m to its east, on the southern side of the lane. This was probably established at a slightly earlier date (*p 89*). In addition, another early farmhouse was opposite Moor Bank Farm, on the northern side of Moor Bank Lane, known as Further Moor Bank, and later Moor

Bank, following the demolition of Moor Bank Farm in the mid-nineteenth century (Haynes and Tipper 1994, 44). Whilst Near Moor Bank Farm stood on the eastern edge of the historic township of Castleton, the other farms were part of the adjacent township of Butterworth.

The archaeological investigation at Near Moor Bank Farm initially comprised a detailed building survey in 2005 of the farmhouse at the site. A barn and stable were attached to this, though these had been gutted by a fire in 2002, and therefore were not recorded as they were structurally unsafe. Following demolition of all of the buildings, the sites of the farmhouse and barn were subjected to open-area excavation.

Significantly, the building survey and excavation, together with the documentary evidence, indicated that a seventeenth-century farmhouse, built in 1632, had once stood at this locale. This farmhouse was partly rebuilt and extended in the late eighteenth century (*Ch 7, p 198*).

Documentary evidence
The origins of Near Moor Bank Farm can be confidently traced back to the seventeenth century as, prior to its demolition, a datestone was recorded over the main entrance of the farmhouse bearing the inscription 'I M M 1632'. It seems likely that the initials refer to the Milne family, possibly James Milne, who is recorded as owning a house at Moor Bank in 1626, together with 24 acres of land on the moor (Fishwick 1913, 28-9). However, it is likely that this property was actually Moor Bank Farm, to the east, which was also owned by the Milne family (Haynes and Tipper 1994, 44). Another possibility

is that Near Moor Bank Farm was constructed by John Milne, who died in 1664 (*ibid*). After this date, the property was possibly occupied by John Milne's son, another John, who died in 1679 and was an important woollen clothier (*op cit*, 23). The Milne family continued to own all of the Moor Bank farms during the latter part of the seventeenth century, though documentary evidence indicates that one of these properties was leased by James Buckley, recorded as a weaver in 1656, and later the Taylor, Gartside, and Grindrod families (*Ch 7, p 197*). The Milne family appears to have continued to own all of the Moor Bank farms throughout the eighteenth century (*ibid*).

Archaeological investigation: building survey and excavation
At the time of the building survey, it was evident that some elements of the 1632 farmhouse were still extant (Fig 41). These comprised the façade (southern elevation), the eastern and western exterior walls, and some interior features of the farmhouse. Its northern elevation had, however, been rebuilt in the late eighteenth century, as part of a scheme designed to widen the building (*Ch 7, p 198*).

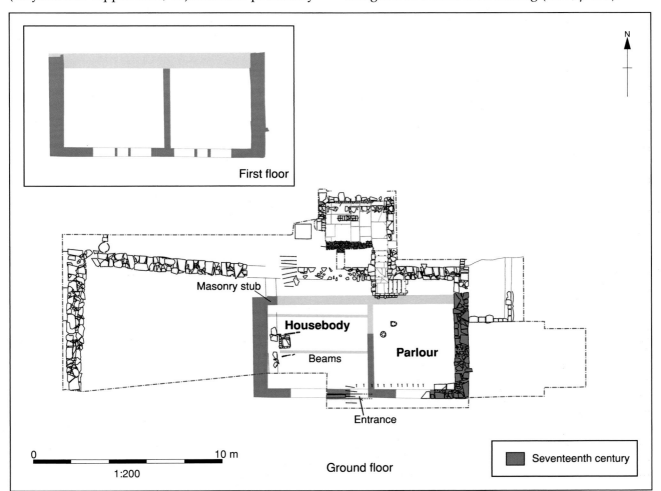

First floor

Masonry stub

Housebody

Beams

Parlour

Entrance

0   10 m

1:200

Ground floor

■ Seventeenth century

Figure 41: The seventeenth-century farmhouse at Near Moor Bank Farm

Plate 47: Near Moor Bank Farm: the centrally positioned doorway on the southern elevation, with the 1632 datestone above

Plate 48: Near Moor Bank Farm: the multi-light mullioned first-floor window in the southern elevation of the western bay

As this façade had been rendered in cement and painted white, the main feature visible was the centrally positioned front door (Pl 47). The door surround had quoins with a moulded band (strap) to the inner door surround, with a depressed (flat) double-pointed arch, whilst the lintel had a simple broken pediment containing the initialled datestone, with a horizontal capstone. The door within the surround was a late twentieth-century reproduction. Although the windows on either side of the door were late twentieth-century replacements, at first-floor level there were two long horizontal windows with two stone-slab mullions, which formed three-light windows dating from the seventeenth century (Pl 48).

Some details relating to the seventeenth-century eastern and western elevations were exposed during the open-area excavation. This indicated

Plate 49: Near Moor Bank Farm: the external walls of the seventeenth-century farm, exposed during the excavation, looking south

that the walls forming these elevations, along with that defining the southern façade, had an average thickness of 0.7 m and were composed of neatly coursed and roughly dressed local sandstone, which had not been bonded with mortar (Pl 49). A short stub of masonry extending from the western gable formed the only surviving remains of the northern elevation of the seventeenth-century farmhouse.

Some elements relating to the interior were also recorded during the building survey. It was evident, for example, that the farmhouse had been divided at both ground- and first-floor level, by a cross-wall on the eastern side of the centrally positioned doorway. This created two bays within the house, the larger of which formed the western bay. Within this, at ground-floor level, there were two original seventeenth-century beams between the eastern and western walls of the bay. Both were bevelled on one side and had a simple mould strip at the arris on the opposite side (Pl 50).

Based on the combined evidence, it therefore appears that the 1632 farmhouse was a two-celled structure, which was accessed through a centrally positioned entrance. At ground-floor level, the larger western bay probably formed the housebody, and presumably originally had a fireplace, which would have been positioned opposite the entrance. The smaller eastern bay was probably a parlour, which may well have been

Plate 50: Near Moor Bank Farm: the seventeenth-century ceiling beam

unheated. The two chambers above were presumably originally accessed via a ladder.

5

POST-MEDIEVAL LANDSCAPES 2: CUTACRE *c* 1600-1780

Richard A Gregory and Peter Arrowsmith, with Andy Phelps and Chris Wild

The Settled Landscape

The documentary evidence for the North West substantially increases in the sixteenth to eighteenth centuries, allowing greater insight into the settlements in the Cutacre area, the patterns of land ownership and tenancy, and associated industry. During this period, the main settlement in the eastern part of the area, in the township of Little Hulton, continued to be Wharton Hall (*p 121*), although a nearby farmstead, known as Hursts after its early occupants, was also present (Fig 42). This farmstead was part of the Wharton Hall estate and the Hurst family are recorded as tenants in 1582 (SCA BW/T 7/1). Several farmsteads are also known in the township of Tyldesley cum Shakerley, which can be traced back to the late sixteenth or seventeenth century. These included Oliver Fold, which is believed to have been the tenement of John Marsh, who died in 1597 (Lunn 1953, 48), and Guest Fold. This was named after the Guest family, a John Guest being a resident of Shakerley in *c* 1670 (*op cit*, 72).

The majority of the Cutacre area was in the township of Middle Hulton, and during the post-medieval period, the manor of Middle Hulton remained in the hands of the lords of Worsley (*Ch 3, p 41*). Therefore, much of the information about this area derives from the documents of the Egerton family, who held that lordship in the seventeenth and eighteenth centuries. In 1639, John Egerton, the first Earl of Bridgewater, inherited the Worsley estates from his aunt, Dorothy Legh. The second earl (another John Egerton) then gave these estates to his younger son, William, in 1674 (Farrer and Brownbill 1911a, 380-1), who, in that year, married Honora Leigh, and under the marriage settlement she was granted a number of farms in Worsley, Middle Hulton, and Kearsley (LA DDX 75/17, DDX 643/1; NRO E(B) 916). In 1711 she, in turn, gave these to her daughter Honora Egerton, on her marriage to Thomas Arden Bagot (MA L 5/1/1/8). William

Egerton's only male heir, John, died in childhood in 1700 and the rest of William's estate reverted to the main Egerton line (Fletcher and Arrowsmith 1995, 6-9). In 1720, Scroop Egerton was made Duke of Bridgewater, Francis Egerton, the third and last Duke, who succeeded to the title in 1748, being the most famous of his line. He was the 'Canal Duke', whose pioneering navigation was originally built to link his Worsley coal mines with Manchester (Malet 1977). Following his death in 1803, his estates were managed for a century by trustees.

As a result of the early eighteenth-century partitioning of the Egertons' estate, the tenements within Middle Hulton, including those within the Cutacre area, had divided ownership, with some being still part of the Bridgewater lands, but others now in the possession of the Bagots. Indeed, the latter remained in Bagot ownership until 1895-6, when they were sold to the Bridgewater Trustees (SCA BW/T 7/19).

Fortunately, the Bagot properties are shown in pictorial form in a book of early estate plans (MA L 5/4/1/1). Although this is undated, it was compiled for Egerton Bagot, who held the estate in 1734 and died in 1775, and includes a summary list of his tenements dated May 1772. A set of early plans also exists for the Bridgewater estate (SCA BW/E/1), probably of *c* 1764, and these can be cross-referenced to a Bridgewater estate survey of 1722, which itself refers back to the marriage settlement of William Egerton and Honora Leigh (NRO E(B) 916). As a consequence, it is known that the pattern of farms in Middle Hulton shown on the mid- to late eighteenth-century Bridgewater and Bagot estates plans was already established by 1674. The properties in both estates are also described in a survey of Middle Hulton of the early nineteenth century (Partington 1909b, 39-63). Together, these various sources also clearly indicate that the prominent form of local farms by the latter half of the eighteenth century was of a house with a detached barn.

Although the inhabitants were probably principally engaged in agricultural activity, there is evidence

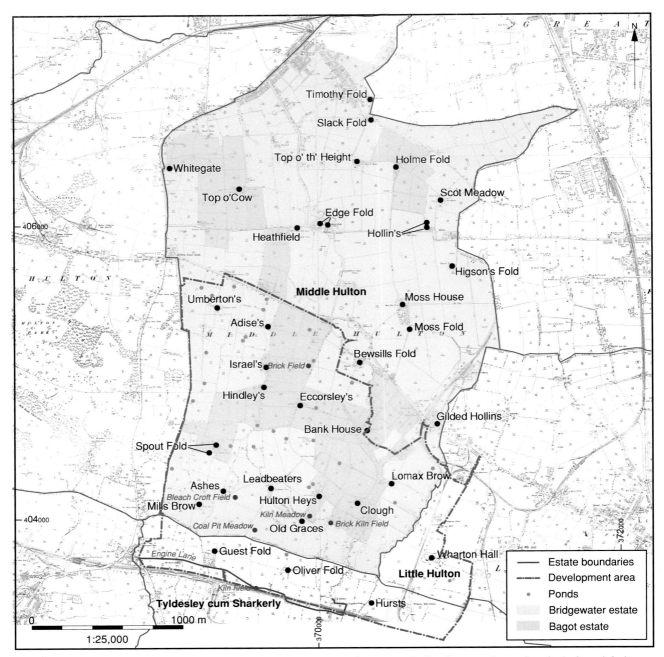

Figure 42: Middle Hulton, with the sixteenth- and seventeenth-century halls, farmsteads, and early industrial sites, and the division between the Bridgewater and Bagot estates

for other industries that may have regularly supplemented some tenants' farming income. For instance, textile manufacture appears to have formed one of the principal cottage industries, evidenced by the 1606 probate inventory of Thomas Hurst of Shakerley, which lists 'linen towe and yarn to the value of 40s 4d, and a small pair of looms with heald and other implements at 24s' (Lunn 1953, 50). In addition, in 1597 the will of John Marsh, possibly of Oliver Fold, listed flax, which also indicates that linen weaving occurred (*op cit*, 48). Moreover, textile manufacturing appears to have been a persistent feature of the rural economy, as later evidence shows that handloom weaving continued within the Cutacre

area into the nineteenth century. Textile finishing was another feature, particularly as a Bleach Croft field is documented at Ashes in *c* 1764 (SCA BW/E/1), indicating a site where the locally produced cloth was bleached. The Mort family, who were tenants there in the seventeenth and eighteenth centuries (*p 95*), also made a living as tanners (*pp 96-7*).

Field-names, such as Brick Field, Brick Kiln Field, Kiln Meadow, and Kiln Field, suggest locations at which bricks were manufactured, probably on an *ad-hoc* basis to meet immediate local needs (GMAU 1991, 7). The historical mapping also depicts numerous ponds in the area. Some of these may have been dug to extract clay for brick making, whilst others might have been marl pits, from which calcareous clay was extracted to be spread as a fertiliser in neighbouring fields.

Although there is mention of the mining of coal in the locality in the late medieval period, the industry is better documented from the second half of the sixteenth century. In 1556, a coal pit was the centre of a dispute between Elizabeth Hulton, the widow of the former lord of Over Hulton, and Adam, her son and heir (Farrer and Brownbill 1911a, 28 n41). In leasing land to tenants, local landowners reserved the mining rights, an early example being provided by leases granted in 1571-84 by the owner of the Peel Hall estate in Little Hulton (Crofton 1889, 42-3). The reservation of mining rights and the right of access to any coal workings were also specified in later leases given by the Bridgewater and Bagot estates. The involvement of local landowners in the industry is illustrated by the will of Dorothy Legh in 1639, which included a gift of 10s to each of the workmen 'in or at the coalepitts and cannel pitts' in her manor of Middle Hulton. Her probate inventory included 'coales cannell and basse upon the banke at Hulton', worth £106 3s 2d, and lists a collection of mining gear: 'two stithes, two payre of bellowes, windles, ropes, chaines, arks, timber, and other things there', valued at £5 8s 8d (Piccope 1861, 209-10).

In the Cutacre area, the location of one early mining site is indicated by the name Coal Pit Meadow, which is listed as part of Leadbeaters farm in the Bridgewater estate survey of 1722 (NRO E(B) 916) and is shown on the c 1764 estate plans (SCA BW/E/1). A lease of 1795 for the Bankhouse tenement of the Bagot estate mentions an old sough, ie a tunnel for draining mine workings (MA L 5/2/1/2).

The Farmsteads Investigated

As part of the archaeological work at Cutacre, four post-medieval farmsteads were investigated (Fig 43) by a combination of archaeological techniques. Two of these farms, Ashes and Hulton Heys, had been demolished prior to the archaeological work, although the standing buildings at Hulton Heys had been described as part of the original archaeological assessment that was completed in 1991 (Ch 1, p 6). Archaeological excavation was undertaken at both sites, with the site of Ashes forming the subject of an open-area excavation, whilst, in contrast, an archaeological evaluation was completed at Hulton Heys. Although this latter evaluation exposed early post-medieval remains, subsequent excavation

was not undertaken, as no further development was scheduled (as of 2019), which might have an impact on these buried remains. Mills Brow and Spout Fold were the other two Cutacre farmsteads investigated, which still contained extant buildings in early 2016. Accordingly, these were the subject of building surveys, recording the buildings prior to their anticipated demolition.

Ashes

The site of Ashes was adjacent to a small brook in the south-western portion of the area investigated (SD 6938 0420), at a height of c 85 m aOD. Significantly, Cinder Hill was immediately to the south, on the opposite side of the brook, confirming that this area had witnessed a fairly protracted period of activity in both the prehistoric (Ch 2) and medieval (Ch 3) periods.

Documentary evidence

Ashes was tenanted by members of the Mort family of Middle Hulton from the seventeenth until the early nineteenth century (below). As a result of its long connection with that family, the farm was sometimes referred to as Mort Fold, a name which is found in the Census Returns as late as 1881 (NA RG 11/3819). It seems likely that this Mort family had a common ancestry with the Morts of Wharton Hall (p 122), but the precise relationship is not known. The name Ashes is documented from at least the eighteenth century (MA L 5/4/1/1; BA PMH 14/1), and the proximity of the farm to the late medieval bloomery site at Cinder Hill (Ch 3) suggests a possible origin for its name.

Ashes was among the tenements which remained under Bridgewater control when the Middle Hulton estate was partitioned in the early eighteenth century (Fig 42). Its earliest known occupant was Henry Mort, who is recorded in the 1674 marriage settlement of William Egerton (NRO E(B) 916, no 18). He paid an annual rent of £8, a figure which remained unchanged until the beginning of the nineteenth century. He was possibly living at Ashes as early as 1639, when John, the son of Henry Mort of Middle Hulton, was baptised at Deane parish church (Sparke 1916, 25). Henry's name is also found in the Hearth Tax records for Middle Hulton. In the returns for 1663 and Lady Day 1664 he was assessed at only one hearth, in common with the majority of householders in the township (LA Mf 27-29). This is probably an under-estimate, since in September 1664 the surviving slips for individual households show him with two hearths. The same figure is found in the returns of 1673, but in the intervening years, in 1666, as many as three hearths are set against his name (LA DDKe 2/16/11). Henry Mort died in 1685, and no

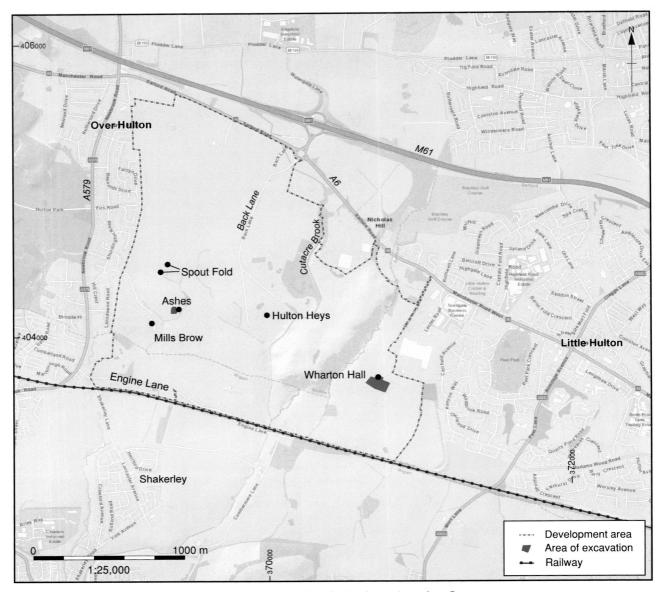

Figure 43: The post-medieval sites investigated at Cutacre

surviving probate documents are known (Sparke 1917, 465). However, it is evident that he had an occupation in addition to farming, for in 1654 he is described as Henry Mort of Middle Hulton, tanner (LA DDHu 19/30).

John Mort of Middle Hulton, presumed to be Henry Mort's son, died in 1691 (Sparke 1917, 474). His probate inventory mentions a 'parlor (sic)', 'chamber over parlor', 'litle parlor', 'the great parlor', 'the fire house' (which contained 'one great table' and was presumably the housebody, or hall), and 'the buttery' (LA WCW/Infra/C1363/71). It also refers to the 'back house' or 'bark house'. The latter reading would be further evidence for the family's involvement in tanning.

The Bridgewater estate survey of 1722 names the tenant as Robert Mort, paying the same rent of £8 as

Henry Mort in 1674 (NRO E(B) 916, no 18). Robert was probably the son of John Mort of Middle Hulton, who was baptised at Deane in January 1680 (Sparke 1916, 96). He died in August 1728 and was buried at Deane, where a gravestone recorded his age at death as 49 (Sparke 1917, 538; Bolton and District Family History Society 1983, no 874). In his will, he described himself as a tanner (LA WCW/Supra/C345A/30). The 1722 survey lists Robert Mort's farm as containing '9 bays of building' (NRO E(B) 916, no 18). Additionally, in the will compiled shortly before his death, he named his son John as his heir and instructed that his wife Margaret 'shall have the little house in the fould where I now dwell in Middle Hulton for a dwelling place dureing her chast [sic] widowhood' (LA WCW/Supra/C345A/30). The implication is that there was a second dwelling, the 'little house', at Ashes at this date in addition to the main farmhouse.

John Mort, Robert Mort's son and successor, remained the tenant until his death in 1784. Information about the farm during his lifetime is chiefly provided by the *c* 1764 Bridgewater estate plan, which depicts two main structures at the farmstead (Fig 44, no 32). These were the farmhouse and a range to the north, which functioned as a barn. In a Window Tax assessment of 1760, John Mort was charged for nine windows, the number that seems to have been charged to the majority of householders in the township (BA PMH 7/4). In his will, drawn up in March 1784, John Mort described himself as a yeoman, and this term is also used of him in a lease of 1758 (LA WCW/Supra/C517B/59; NRO E(B) 1218). Other evidence implies that, like his predecessors, he was not totally dependent on

Plate 51: Ashes, following excavation, looking south-west

farming. Among the field-names at Ashes which appear on the *c* 1764 estate plan were Bleach Croft and Tan Pit Croft, referring to two adjoining plots situated on the east side of the farm buildings. Tan Pit Croft provides a further indication of the Morts' involvement in tanning, while the Bleach Croft indicates that the family were also involved in the domestic-based textile industry. Neither field-name is found in the 1722 survey, but one of these two plots is listed there as the Bake House Croft, possibly a corruption of 'back house' or 'bark house' (*p 93*).

Archaeological excavation

As part of the programme of archaeological investigation, Ashes was targeted for open-area excavation, examining an area covering some 40 x 32 m (Pl 51). This exposed the seventeenth- and eighteenth-century remains of the farmstead that had been occupied by the Mort family (*above*). The excavations revealed three main phases of development in the farmhouse, Phase 1 being a single-depth range; Phase 2 a two-bay addition against the southern elevation; and Phase 3 a western extension.

The mid-seventeenth-century farmhouse (Phase 1)

In its earliest form, the farmhouse comprised a two-celled stone-footed rectangular building (Fig 45), measuring 10.25 x 3.75 m, with a substantial cellar. Only the footings (Pl 52) and basement of this building survived, but these show that it was either entirely constructed in stone, or that the stone footings supported a timber-framed structure. Based on the documentary evidence (*above*), this farmhouse was probably constructed in the mid-seventeenth century, the Hearth Tax records of 1664 and 1673 (LA Mf 27-29) indicating that it contained two hearths. One of these hearths would have been in the housebody, which was almost certainly the larger cell, containing the cellar, whilst the other would have heated a parlour. The smaller excavated cell was presumably this latter room, and it contained

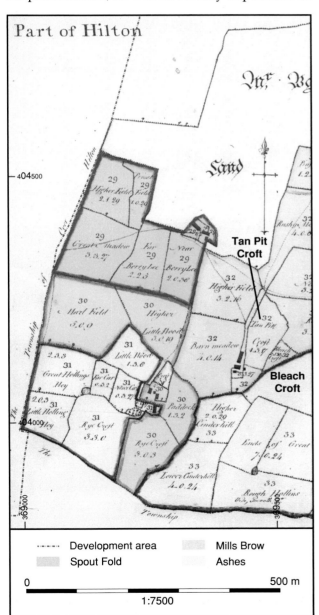

Part of Hilton

Development area · · · · · · ·
Spout Fold
Mills Brow
Ashes

0   500 m
1:7500

*Figure 44: Ashes, Mills Brow, and Spout Fold, on the
c 1764 Bridgewater estate plan*

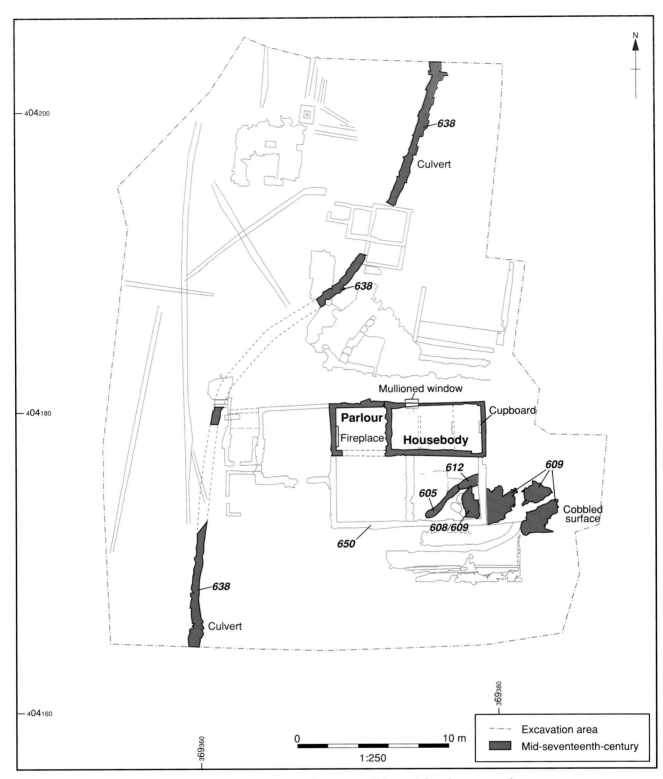

Figure 45: The mid-seventeenth-century (Phase 1) farmhouse at Ashes

the remains of a fireplace on its western wall. Although the three hearths recorded in the Hearth Tax records for 1666 (*ibid*) might be indicative of a larger dwelling, it is possible that this additional hearth was actually situated in a separate smaller dwelling, suggested by the reference in 1728 to 'the little house in the fould' (NRO E(B) 916, no 18).

The cellar was the best-preserved feature relating to the Phase 1 building, and was originally a single room, with a stone-flagged floor. It was 6 x 2.8 m in plan, aligned east/west, and had 0.4 m-thick stone walls surviving to a height of 1.5 m. A mullioned window situated in its northern wall was 1.05 m wide and 0.8 m high, being built of stone slabs for

Plate 52: Ashes: stone-built foundations of the western walls of Room 10 of the seventeenth-century farmhouse, looking south

the sills and lintel, with a single upright creating two lights; these were later blocked when alterations were made (*Ch 8, p 205*).

A recessed storage cupboard was also evident in its eastern wall (Pl 53), clearly part of the original structure. This was 1.4 m long by 0.6 m high, with a maximum depth of 0.3 m, and was similar in style to the mullioned window (*above*), in that it was constructed of stone slab-built sills and lintels. The cupboard had been divided into three compartments, which were defined by two upright slabs, and it may have been used for storing materials for the suspected cottage industries that occurred at the site, textile manufacturing and/or leather working (*pp 96-7*).

Several potentially contemporary features were also present beyond the farmhouse, seemingly of late seventeenth-century date. A curvilinear, stone-built culvert (*638*; Fig 45), aligned approximately north/south, was found to the north and west of the farmhouse. It extended for over 43 m, was on average 0.7 m wide, and was built of stone slabs laid horizontally over smaller stacked stones. It was clearly designed to divert water to a stream, which flowed to the south, though whether it functioned solely as a drain, or provided a managed water source for activities at the farmstead, is uncertain.

Plate 53: Ashes: the cellar with the stone cupboard, and the later dividing wall and stone-shelved cupboard, looking east

*Plate 54: Ashes: cobbled surface **609**, looking west*

Plate 55: Ashes: the easternmost Phase 2 room, which may have been a parlour, looking east

The remains of a cobbled surface (**609**; Pl 54) were excavated to the south-east of the building, laid on a bedding deposit (**608**), which contained fragments of early post-medieval pottery (Table 6). This surface was a maximum of 6.08 m east/west by 3.74 m north/south and had been partly destroyed by a wall (**650**) forming part of a late seventeenth-century extension (*below*). A small pit (**612**), immediately to the north-west, had been cut by a gully (**605**), seemingly also an early feature. A fragment of slag from the gully suggests that metalworking activities occurred at the site during this period, whilst pit **612** contained a fragment of daub, perhaps suggesting that timber buildings may have accompanied the original farmhouse.

Late seventeenth-century expansion (Phase 2)
In Phase 2, the original farmhouse was extended to the south, and based on the rooms listed in the inventory of John Mort in 1691 (*p 96*), which included two, or possibly three, parlours, as well as the housebody and buttery, it can be concluded that

this expansion had occurred by that date. It entailed the construction of a stone wall (**650**), of similar form to those defining the original farmhouse (Pl 55), creating two additional rooms. The farmhouse then measured approximately 10 x 8 m (Fig 46).

The remains of this extension had been badly disturbed and the positions of doorways, thresholds, and windows could not be determined. What is clear, however, is that part, and probably all, of the extension contained a flagged floor (**614**), which survived in the eastern room. This was set on two sequential bedding layers (**602** and **603**), which sealed the earlier external cobbled surface (**609**), gully **605**, and pit **612** (*above*). Layers **602** and **603** contained artefacts that have a date range spanning the sixteenth to nineteenth centuries (Table 6).

Outside, and to the south of, extension **650** was an east/west, 6 x 3 m, band of cobbles (**610**; Pl 56), which post-dated cobbled surface **609** (*above*), and

Phase	Context	Pottery	Date of pottery	Other material
1	Bedding layer **608** for cobbles **609**	Staffordshire slipware (red paste) sherd	*c* 1660	
		Cistercian-ware/Blackware sherd	Fifteenth/seventeenth century	
		Marbled slipware	Seventeenth/eighteenth century	
		Staffordshire/Staffordshire-type sherd		
	Pit **612**			Fragment of fired-clay daub
	Gully **605**			Slag fragment
2	Bedding layer **602**; Room 1	Blackware sherds	Sixteenth/nineteenth century	
	Bedding layer **603**; Room 1	Blackware sherds	Sixteenth/nineteenth century	

Table 6: Stratified artefacts from the seventeenth-eighteenth-century farmhouse at Ashes, Cutacre

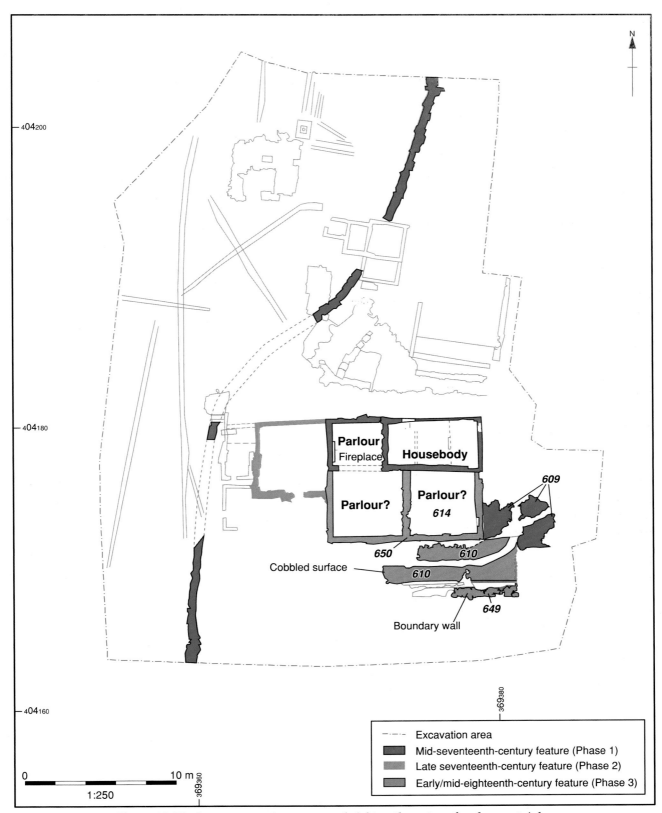

Figure 46: The late seventeenth-century and eighteenth-century farmhouse at Ashes

appeared to respect a stone-built boundary wall (**649**), being on an identical alignment. Although surface **610** had been disturbed by a number of services, it was clearly associated with the second phase of the farm building.

Early/mid-eighteenth-century expansion? (Phase 3)
It is probable that during the early/mid-eighteenth century, the farmhouse was once again extended. Although no documentary evidence has been found for this work, it is evident that this involved

*Plate 56: Ashes: cobbled surface **610**, looking west*

the construction of an additional room, which abutted the western side of the mid-seventeenth-century farmhouse and its late seventeenth-century extension (Fig 46). This 'new' room was square, measuring 4.85 x 4.85 m, and was defined by a stone-built wall patched with bricks. These were clearly later, as large parts of the farmhouse appear to have been substantially rebuilt in brick in the late eighteenth/early nineteenth century (*Ch 8, p 205*).

Hulton Heys

The site of Hulton Heys was set within a rectangular enclosure, which was accessed from a nearby routeway (Back Lane) via a short trackway (Fig 43). A small reservoir was immediately to the north of the site, whilst two ponds were present a short distance to the north-west, and a well immediately to the south.

Documentary evidence

Hulton Heys was originally part of the Bridgewater estate but passed to the Bagots when the estate was partitioned in the early eighteenth century (*p 93; Fig 42*). It is quite possible that a late medieval farm had been established at this site (*Ch 3, p 42*), though clearer evidence for its occupation dates to the seventeenth and eighteenth centuries, when it was occupied by successive members of the Mather family. In the Hearth Tax returns for Middle Hulton in 1666, John Mather, assessed at two hearths, was described as 'of Hulton Heys', thereby distinguishing him from another individual of the same name at Umbertons Farm (LA Mf 27). Mather was also named as the tenant of Hulton Heys in William Egerton's marriage settlement in 1674 (NRO E(B) 916). The probate inventory of John Mather of Middle Hulton survives from 1675, and mentions the 'parlor', 'house', 'buttery', and 'chamber over the parlor', but it is uncertain if these formed elements of the Hulton Heys farmstead (LA WCW/Supra/C203/53). A John Mather of Hulton Heys was also the constable and overseer of the

poor for Middle Hulton in 1703. The farm was subsequently occupied by the widow, Margaret Mather, who is listed as the constable in 1713 (BA PMH 14/1), remaining at Hulton Heys until her death in 1767 (MA L 5/2/4/1; LA WCW/Supra/C460B/41). Two buildings are depicted on the Bagot estate plan of *c* 1772 (MA L 5/4/1/1), comprising a house and barn, the house being shown with a smaller wing to its rear (Pl 57).

By 1778, the tenancy was held by Thomas Eckersley (BA PMH 14/1). He was given a new lease on the property, for ten years, in 1792, but died later that year and the farm passed instead to William Lomax (LA QDL/S/56; MA L 5/2/4/2; Sparke 1940, 1066). William Lomax's tenure was particularly long-lived, for he was still the farmer there at the time of the 1841 census (NA HO 107/541).

Standing-building assessment

The post-medieval farmhouse and barn (along with a later cartshed) were extant in 1991, being described during an archaeological assessment undertaken at that time (GMAU 1991). It was noted that the farmhouse, on the east side of the yard, was two-storeyed, with ridge and gable chimneys, and with an outshut of one and two storeys to the rear. The front elevation was rendered, but other parts displayed early brickwork. This was almost certainly the house depicted on the *c* 1772 Bagot estate plan (*above*), complete with rear outshut. The barn, which is recognisable in plan on late eighteenth- and nineteenth-century mapping (*eg* OS 1849), was aligned north/south, on the west side of the yard. It was brick-built and had four bays, with a cart door and opposed winnowing door in bay 2; bay 3 was a rebuild; and bay 4, which included honeycomb brickwork, appeared to be an addition to the original structure. At right-angles to bay 1, on the south side of the yard, was a brick-built cartshed and stables, which probably dated to the nineteenth century.

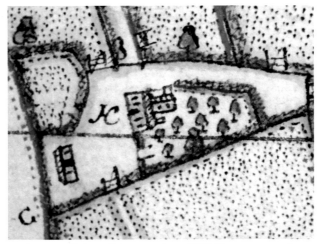

Plate 57: Hulton Heys, on the c 1772 Bagot estate plan

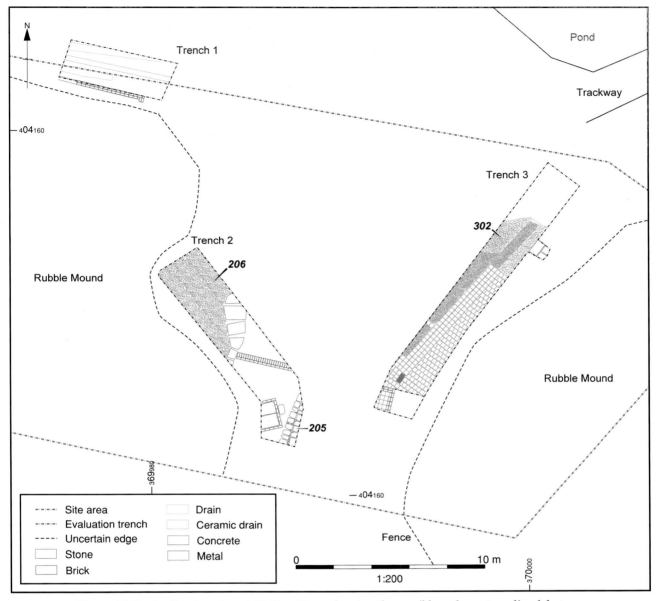

Figure 47: Evaluation trenches at Hulton Heys, showing the possible early post-medieval features

Archaeological excavation

In 2014, the site was subjected to archaeological evaluation, which involved excavating three trial trenches. One of these (Trench 1) was positioned across the barn, another (Trench 2) across a later cartshed, whilst the third trench (Trench 3) was placed immediately west of the farmhouse (Fig 47). Possible early post-medieval remains were exposed in Trenches 2 and 3, comprising a metalled surface (*206/302*), consisting of very compact small pebbles of varying sizes, set into a layer of clay. This may well represent an early floor or yard surface, particularly as it was partially sealed by a later cobbled yard. In addition, a seemingly early wall (*205*) was present in Trench 2 (Pl 58). This was 0.87 m wide, orientated north/south, and comprised a foundation with a stone core but no apparent mortar. Given the small area exposed, the exact function of this wall is not clear,

though it was certainly earlier than a nineteenth-century cartshed which had stood in this part of the site. However, given its form, it may well date to the early post-medieval period, and presumably formed

Plate 58: Hulton Heys: the early stone wall exposed during the archaeological evaluation

103

an element of a stone-footed building. If this is the case, it probably relates to a building that pre-dated the farmhouse and barn depicted on the Bagot estate plan of *c* 1772.

Mills Brow

Mills Brow stood at the western edge of the Cutacre reclamation area (Fig 43). It was at 85 m aOD, approximately 400 m north of Engine Lane, within an area of irregular, predominantly pastoral, fields.

Documentary evidence

This farm appears in the marriage settlement of William Egerton in 1674 as a tenement occupied by William Halliwell (NRO E(B) 916, no 17), who was assessed for one hearth in the Hearth Taxes of 1663 and 1664, and two in 1666 and 1673 (LA Mf 27-29; DDKe 2/16/11). When the Middle Hulton estate was partitioned the farm remained under Bridgewater ownership (Fig 42). The farm

'commonly called or known by the name of Halliwells Tenement' was taken over by Edward Aldred, husbandman, at some date prior to 1722, when the lease was renewed (NRO E(B) 980, 981). The Bridgewater estate survey of 1722 described the farm as containing '7 bays of building' (NRO E(B) 916).

Edward Aldred remained the lessee until his death in 1759 (*below*), but in the later years of his life he lived in Atherton, leaving Mills Brow to be worked by his sons, John and James. Each held half of the tenement, with separate houses and outbuildings. The precise date at which this division occurred is uncertain, since the rent and taxes for the farm continued to be collected under Edward's name until the time of his death (BA PMH 14/1; SCA BW/M 2/5/1/5). The division of the farm was confirmed by Edward in his will of 1755, in which he bequeathed to his son James 'that part of Mills

Plate 59: Ashes, Mills Brow, and Spout Fold, on the c *1764 Bridgewater estate plan, showing the division of Mills Brow*

104

Brow where he now dwells', with 'the outhousing called the Old Shop', and to John 'that dwelling house where he now dwelleth…with the barn and shippon att (*sic*) the north end of his house for his outhousing'. Edward also instructed that the two sets of buildings were to be physically separated by the construction of a fence from the north end of John's barn (LA WCW/Supra/C433A/7). It is clear from the *c* 1764 estate plan (SCA BW/E/1) that John held the fields in the south-west of the farm (Pl 59, no 31). James died in 1762 (Sparke 1940, 977) and, therefore, at the time of the survey, his portion was in the hands of Elizabeth Aldred, holding the fields in the north and east (Pl 59, no 30).

Three main ranges are shown on the *c* 1764 plan. One, aligned north/south, belonged to John Aldred's share, and the buildings standing and surveyed in 2016 stood within this portion (*below*), whilst the two, to the north, belonged to Elizabeth Aldred's share. In the 1760 Window Tax assessment for Middle Hulton, John Aldred and James Aldred were each charged for nine windows (BA PMH 7/4). By 1765, following James Aldred's death (*above*), the two halves appear to have been reunited under John Aldred (BA PMH 14/1).

Building survey of the early to mid-eighteenth-century farm
Andy Phelps and Chris Wild

At the time of the survey, the core of the surviving farmstead comprised a two-storey farmhouse with an attached barn to the north (Fig 48; Pl 60), which appears to have been built at the same time as the farmhouse. It is likely, given the documentary evidence, that these were constructed no later than 1755 (*p 104*). The original post-medieval farmstead would have lain to the north, which, based on historical OS mapping (OS 1849; 1893b), was demolished in the late nineteenth century.

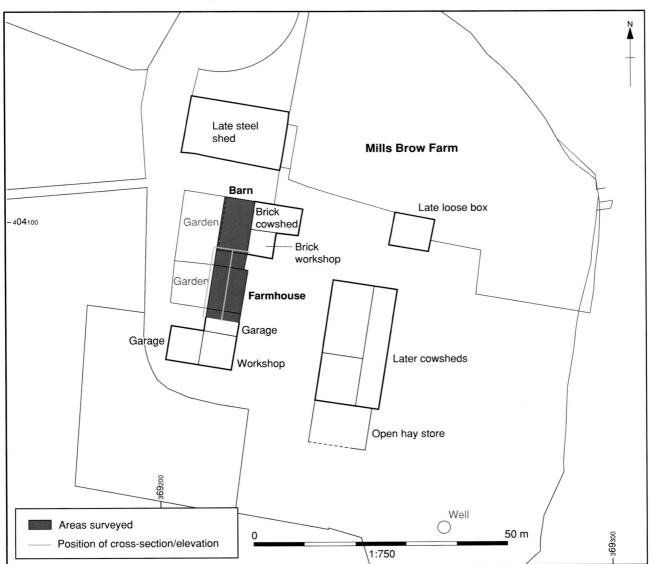

Figure 48: Mills Brow, and the surveyed eighteenth-century buildings

Plate 60: Mills Brow: facing south-east

The eighteenth-century double-pile farmhouse

The farmhouse was erected on a double-pile plan to a height of two storeys, with a cellar. It was built of handmade brick, bonded in a four-stretcher English Garden Wall style with lime mortar, and its gable roof was covered in slate tiles to the west and sandstone flags to the east.

Its western elevation had a central doorway (Fig 49; Pl 61), which was originally enclosed within a single-storey porch, with a ground-floor window on either side, with sandstone sills. The first floor had an identical window at each end and a narrower window in the centre, above the ground-floor doorway. The eastern elevation was arranged in an identical manner, with a central door flanked by a pair of ground-floor windows, and by first-floor windows at each end, with another at the centre (Pl 62).

In contrast, the southern (gable) elevation had no visible openings, though it did possess an integrated rectangular chimney stack rising from its apex. This elevation was also abutted by a single-storey twentieth-century flat-roofed garage (Fig 48). The majority of the northern elevation had been enclosed within the adjoining threshing barn (p 110), but it again had an integrated chimney stack

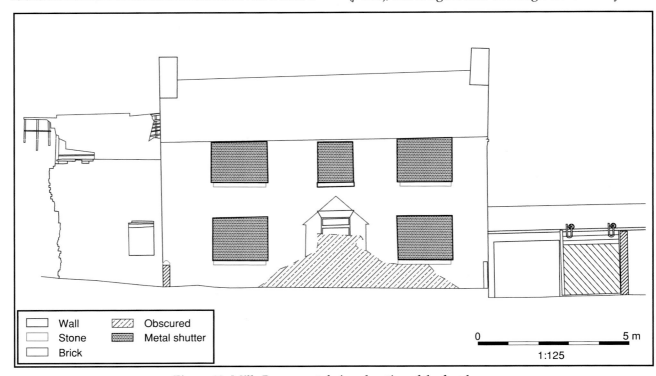

	Wall		Obscured
	Stone		Metal shutter
	Brick		

0   5 m

1:125

Figure 49: Mills Brow, west-facing elevation of the farmhouse

Plate 61: Mills Brow: farmhouse, western elevation

Plate 62: Mills Brow: farmhouse, eastern elevation

Plate 63: Mills Brow: northern elevation of the farmhouse from within the adjoining threshing barn

at the apex, slightly larger than the opposing southern example. At the base of the elevation, to the west of centre, there was a small aperture framed with cast-iron, approximately 1 m above the ground (Pl 63). This opening had been blocked, but may have related to the maintenance of the fireplace behind.

Inside the building, a hallway at ground-floor level extended between the two central doorways (Pl 64; Fig 50). Two pairs of rooms, on either side of the hallway, could all be accessed from the entrance lobby. The largest of these was in the north-western corner of the house and was probably the principal living area. On the northern wall of this room, a heavily remodelled fireplace had removed much of the original chimney breast. Opposite this room, in the south-west corner of the house, was a smaller room, perhaps originally the parlour. This was also heated, as a chimney breast projected from the centre of its southern wall, containing a blocked fireplace. The remaining two ground-floor rooms, in the north-east and south-east corners of the house, were narrower, the north-eastern room being in a poor condition. It was, however, evident that this was probably the kitchen, as the remnants of a small fireplace were visible on its northern wall, projecting from a chimney breast, adjacent to a cupboard inserted into the recess to the east. The south-eastern room was the smallest of the ground-floor rooms, and may originally have acted as the dairy or pantry.

Plate 64: Mills Brow: entrance hall, facing east

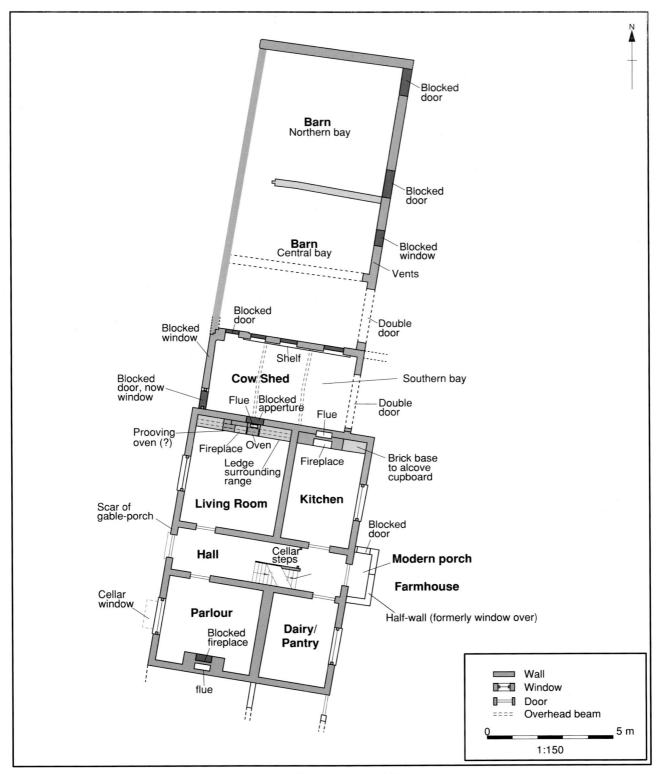

Figure 50: Mills Brow, ground-floor plan

Labels in figure:
- Blocked door
- Barn **Northern bay**
- Blocked door
- Blocked window
- **Barn** Central bay
- Vents
- Blocked door
- Double door
- Blocked window
- Shelf
- **Cow Shed**
- Southern bay
- Blocked door, now window
- Flue
- Blocked apperture
- Flue
- Double door
- Proving oven (?)
- Fireplace
- Oven
- Fireplace
- Brick base to alcove cupboard
- Ledge surrounding range
- **Living Room**
- **Kitchen**
- Scar of gable-porch
- Blocked door
- **Hall**
- Cellar steps
- **Modern porch**
- **Farmhouse**
- Cellar window
- **Parlour**
- **Dairy/ Pantry**
- Half-wall (formerly window over)
- Blocked fireplace
- flue

Legend:
- Wall
- Window
- Door
- Overhead beam
- 0 5 m
- 1:150

The hallway also contained a single-flight staircase providing access to the first-floor (Fig 51). This contained four rooms, mirroring those on the floor below, which functioned as bedrooms. Three contained blocked fireplaces, whilst there was no evidence for heating in the south-eastern bedroom, above the suspected pantry. This floor also contained a small bathroom at the western end of the landing, though this was clearly a modern insertion.

The south-western corner of the farmhouse also contained a cellar (Fig 52), beneath the parlour, which could be accessed via a flight of sandstone-

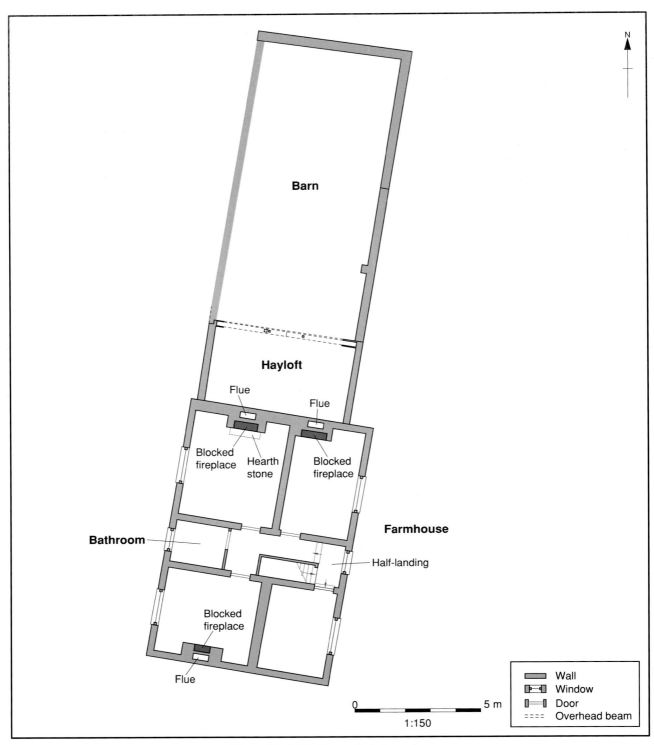

Figure 51: Mills Brow, first-floor plan

flag-capped brick steps beneath the staircase in the hallway. This was a brick-lined structure with a slightly pointed barrel-vaulted roof (Fig 53), and a cellar light on its western wall. Features within it included two brick piers, supporting the fireplace in the parlour above, and a drain. There was also a partially bricked-up opening at the centre of the western wall, coinciding with the apex of the vault, which served as a coal chute.

The eighteenth-century Lancashire barn

The building to the north was a combination, or Lancashire, barn, for both threshing and stalling cows (*cf* Brunskill 1987, 111). The threshing area was in the northern part of the structure, whilst the cow house formed its southern end.

It extended from the northern gable of the farmhouse and was constructed in a similar handmade brick,

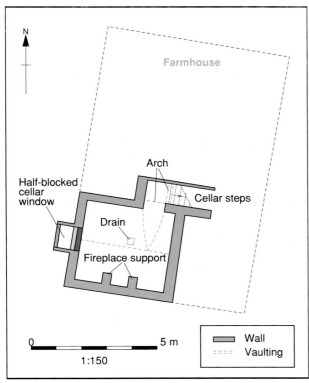

Figure 52: Mills Brow, cellar plan

Plate 65: Mills Brow: Lancashire barn from the north-west

laid in a four-stretcher English Garden Wall style and bonded with a lime-based mortar (Pl 65). Originally, the building was two storied over three bays, but the northern gable wall and two-thirds of the western wall had been demolished, leaving the eastern wall intact, along with the entire southern bay. The surviving portion of roof was covered in grey slates, overhanging at the eaves.

The central and northern bay formed the threshing barn. The principal access into this was through a low cart doorway, in the central bay on the eastern wall, which had been modified at a later date (Pl 66). Two smaller doorways once allowed access into the northern bay, but had later been blocked.

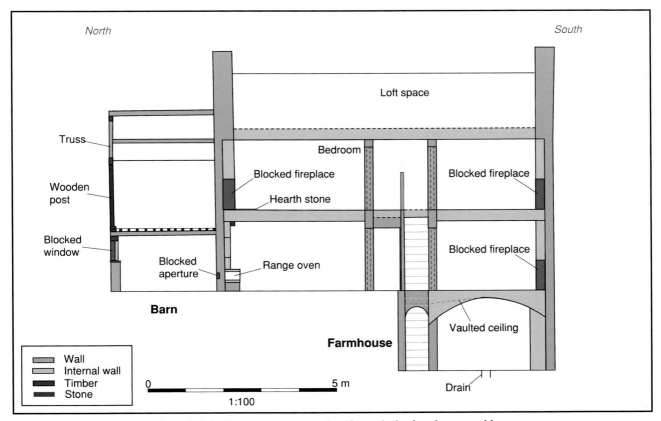

Figure 53: Mills Brow, cross-section through the farmhouse and barn

Plate 66: Mills Brow: Lancashire barn, eastern wall, facing east

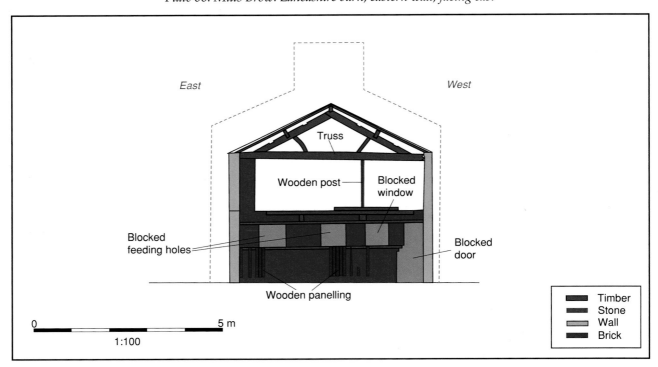

Figure 54: Mills Brow, cross-section through the barn

The eastern elevation also contained several other features, including diamond-shaped vents at ground and first-floor height, used to ventilate the northern bay, along with an adjacent ground-floor window or hatch.

The southern bay formed the cow house, and could be accessed via a large double-width entrance on the eastern wall; it was, however, evident that this doorway had been inserted at a later date. Above this were the remnants of a diamond vent. A ground-floor window on the surviving western elevation appeared to have been converted from an original doorway.

Internally, the cow house comprised a cattle stall, with a mezzanine floor above, supported on two chamfered beams, which probably functioned as a hay loft (Fig 54). Empty mortice sockets on the underside of the beams indicated the former position of posts forming elements of two north/south-aligned timber partitions within the cattle stall. Four rectangular feeding holes were present within the brick wall on the northern side of the stall, which formed the partition with the adjacent barn; one of these had been modified from an earlier doorway (Pl 65).

The cow house also contained the only surviving roof truss within the barn. This comprised a simple pegged A-frame timber truss with curved braces from the tie beam to the principal rafters, suggesting that it was an original feature (Fig 54).

Spout Fold

The farmstead at Spout Fold stood at the western edge of the Cutacre site (SD 6930 0447; Fig 43) at a height of 100 m aOD. It originally consisted of two adjoining farmsteads, forming a small settlement. The buildings surveyed comprised the southern farmstead, as the northern farm been demolished prior to the archaeological assessment of 1991 (Ch 1, p 6). When the Middle Hulton estate was partitioned in the early eighteenth century, Spout Fold had a divided ownership, with the southern farm remaining in Bridgewater hands, but the northern farm passed to the Bagots (p 93; Fig 42).

Documentary evidence

In the eighteenth century, the northern farmstead was known as Morris's, or the Spout (MA L 5/4/1/1; L 5/2/6/1-2), the first name suggesting that this was the tenement in Middle Hulton occupied by Richard Morris in 1674 (NRO E(B) 916). The Bagot estate plan of c 1772 depicts two buildings there, comprising a house and barn (MA L 5/4/1/1).

The earliest known occupant of the southern farmstead was Giles Halliwell, husbandman, who was buried at Deane in November 1656 (Sparke 1917, 413). By 1674, this farm was in the hands of Richard Edge, who had married Halliwell's daughter Katharine (NRO E(B) 916, no 12; Sparke 1916, 38, 291). Richard held the lease until his death in 1705, but at that date he was living at the Moss, in the northern half of Middle Hulton. He left that tenement to his son James, and the 'tenement called Halliwells' to

his son Giles, together with 'one stone trough at Halliwells house and a large Bible' (LA WCW/Supra/C281B/17).

In the Bridgewater estate survey of 1722, Giles Edge's farm was listed as having '8 bays of building' (NRO E(B) 916, no 12). Giles remained the occupant of Spout Fold until his death in 1753 at the age of 80 (Bolton and District Family History Society 1983, no 277), and perhaps because of the length of his occupancy, the farm continued to be known as Giles Edge's Tenement for many years after. In his will, compiled in 1736, he bequeathed the farm to his wife Sarah, who was some 17 years his junior. She continued to hold the farm until c 1764, when it passed to her son-in-law Ralph Seddon (LA WCW/Supra/C416A/11; NRO E(B) 1199; BA PMH 14/1).

Seddon was the tenant when the c 1764 estate plan was compiled, which shows his farm as containing two buildings (Pl 59, no 29). He was already the tenant and occupant of Edge Fold in Middle Hulton when he took over the lease, and he continued to live at that property until his death in 1775, sub-letting Spout Fold. He left Spout Fold to his son Richard Seddon in his will, and instructed that Edge Fold was to be used to fund his bequests to other family members (BA PMH 14/1; LA WCW/Supra/C489A/41). In 1776, a year after receiving his inheritance, Richard Seddon married Elizabeth Eckersley and the couple set up home at Spout Fold (Sparke 1940, 874; BA PMH 14/1).

Building survey
Andy Phelps and Chris Wild
The surviving portions of this farmstead had an irregular form, with the buildings scattered around a central yard (Fig 55; Pl 67). The eighteenth-century elements were the farmhouse, at the south side of the yard, and a three-bay threshing barn with integrated cow house on its western edge. Later twentieth-century structures, which were not considered as part of the building survey, included an L-shaped range to the north, comprising a single-storey cowshed and large two-storey brick barn, and a small square brick-built loose box at the centre of the yard.

The farmhouse and barn can be confidently identified on mapping of the 1840s onwards, beginning with the Middle Hulton tithe map of 1844 (LA DRM 1/59). Two buildings are shown on this site on the c 1764 Bridgewater estate plan (SCA BW/E/1), and presumably these relate to the farmhouse and threshing barn, since the position of the latter in particular equates well with one of the buildings on this map. However, the latest

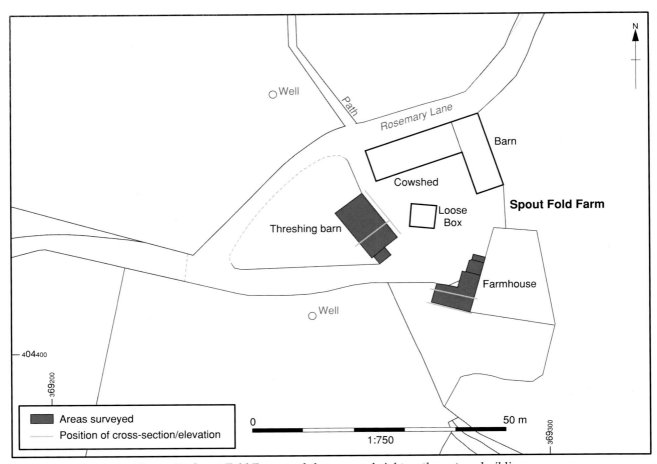

Figure 55: Spout Fold Farm, and the surveyed eighteenth-century buildings

Plate 67: Spout Fold Farm: farmhouse, looking north-west

farmhouse was on a slightly different alignment to that depicted on the estate plan and, on balance, it seems likely that it post-dated the *c* 1764 plan. If that was the case, it may have been built by

Richard Seddon, perhaps as a home for himself and his new wife Elizabeth in *c* 1776 (*p 113*).

The eighteenth-century farmhouse (c 1776?)
The farmhouse, on the south side of the yard, was L-shaped, with single-storey domestic extensions projecting from the north elevation (Pl 68). These date from the nineteenth century (*Ch 8, p 209*), the farmhouse originally forming a two-celled dwelling.

Although its exterior was covered with a modern concrete render, examination of its interior indicated that it was constructed of handmade bricks, laid with no discernible bond, cemented with lime mortar. The principal (south) elevation (Fig 56; Pl 69) had a slightly off-centre doorway, with short vertical windows within the bays of each floor, and a smaller dropped window above the doorway, all of which had sandstone sills. The eastern and western gable elevations both had a central projecting chimney, and the western elevation also contained single ground-floor and first-floor windows, identical to those in the principal elevation (Pl 68).

The internal layout of the farmhouse reflects its modest status, with two rooms on each floor, on either side of a centrally placed lateral staircase

114

Plate 68: Spout Fold Farm: farmhouse, from the rear, with multiple extensions to the left

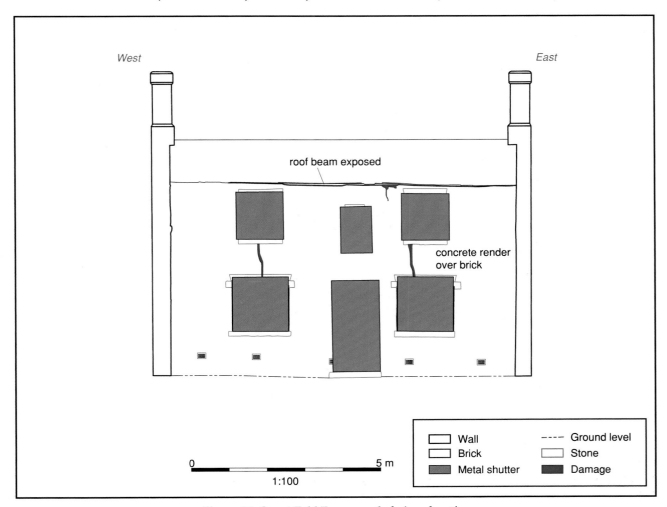

Figure 56: Spout Fold Farm, south-facing elevation

Plate 69: Spout Fold Farm: farmhouse, principal elevation

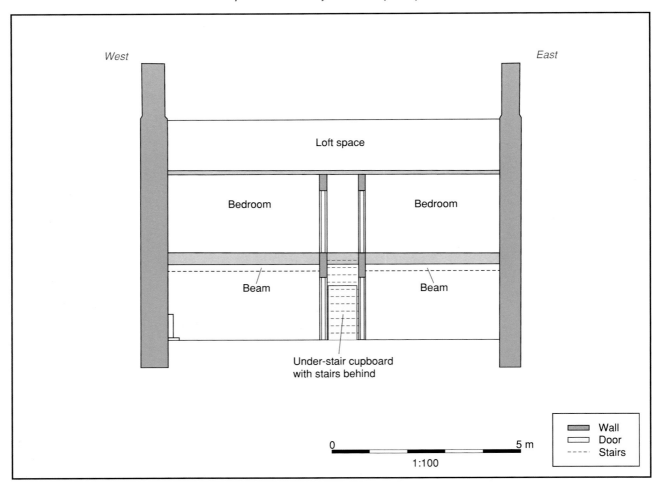

Figure 57: Spout Fold Farm, cross-section through the farmhouse

116

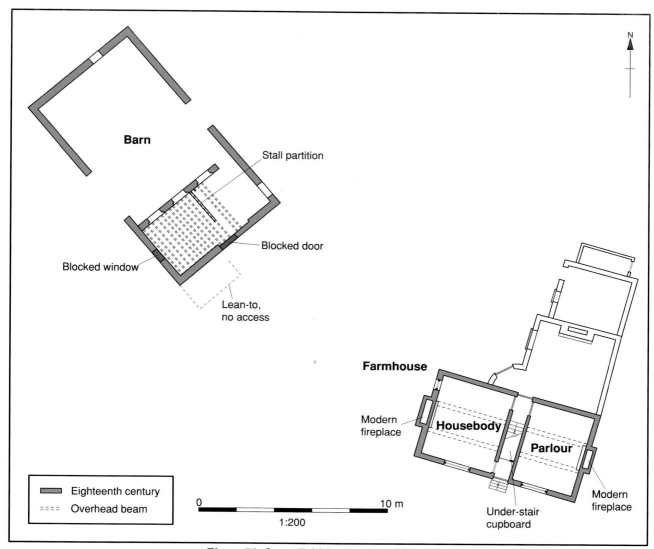

Barn

Stall partition

Blocked door

Blocked window

Lean-to,
no access

Farmhouse

Modern
fireplace

Housebody

Parlour

Modern
fireplace

Under-stair
cupboard

Eighteenth century
Overhead beam

0　　　　　　　　　　　　10 m

1:200

Figure 58: Spout Fold Farm, ground-floor plan

(Fig 57). The main entrance led into a small vestibule, which created a baffle entry, designed to reduce draughts into the rest of the house, and the larger of the ground floor rooms, which could be accessed from this entrance, lay to the west (Fig 58). This room would have formed the housebody. Although slightly narrower, the eastern ground-floor room was of a similar form to that to the west. This room, however, was accessed from under the staircase landing at the centre rear of the house. It was apparent that both these rooms were heated, though the original fireplaces had been blocked and converted to house modern gas fires, with the loss of all original detail. The first-floor rooms were bedrooms, accessed from a small landing at the top of the staircase, and lit by the window at the centre of the southern elevation (Fig 59). Both rooms were similar to those below, with modern finishes throughout, although the eastern room was slightly bigger and incorporated the space over the stairs at the northern side of the building. The western room was served by an additional first-floor window on the western gable.

The eighteenth-century Lancashire barn

The barn (Fig 58) comprised a two-storey, three-bay threshing barn and cow house, and thus was another example of a combination or Lancashire barn (Brunskill 1987, 111). Its roof had been all but destroyed by fire and its fragile state prevented detailed internal investigation. It was, however, evident that it was constructed of handmade brick, laid in four-stretcher English Garden Wall style, bonded with lime mortar; in the upper storey this brickwork was blackened, as a result of the fire that had destroyed the roof. Of the long elevations, the eastern was the better preserved (Fig 60; Pl 70). This possessed a large central cart entrance, a window serving the south-eastern bay, and six diamond-patterned ventilators distributed across the head of the wall, with a further two at ground-floor level at the north-western end. The opposing long western elevation seems to have mimicked its eastern counterpart, though part of the elevation had collapsed above the cart entrance.

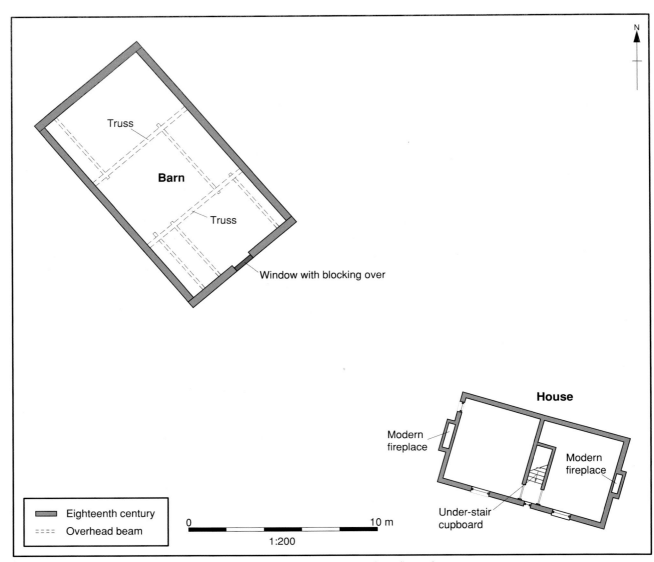

Figure 59: Spout Fold Farm, first-floor plan

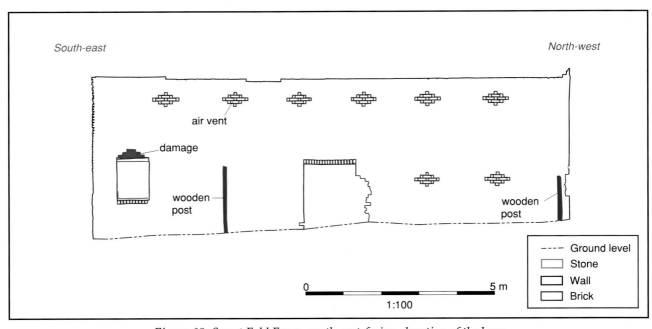

Figure 60: Spout Fold Farm, north-east-facing elevation of the barn

118

Plate 70: Spout Fold Farm: Lancashire barn, looking north-west

Both the southern and northern gable elevations contained single doorways. The southern gable also contained a rectangular pitching hole immediately above the doorway, and there was a small single-storey brick lean-to to the north (Pl 71), whilst the northern elevation had a pair of vents below the eaves and two more at ground-floor level. A smaller opening towards the apex probably served as an owl hole.

A sufficient portion of the charred roof timbers survived to indicate that there had been a king-post truss on either side of the central bay (Fig 61). The trusses were held together with threaded iron bolts with square-plate washers.

Internally, the southern bay of the barn was partitioned off from the remainder with a brick wall, defining what presumably had served as cattle stalls, with a hay loft above (Pl 72). A doorway at the eastern end of the partition provided access into the stalls, with three small, rectangular feeding holes along the remainder of its length. The stalls were also divided by a substantial timber plank partition wall (Pl 73).

It is likely, based on these remains, that this part of the barn provided accommodation for six cows, tethered in pairs within three stalls. The cattle probably entered the building through the central doorway in the southern gable and would have faced north, towards

the feeding holes in the brick partition. Typically, there would have been a drought at the rear of the stalls, which could have been cleared through the side door in the eastern elevation. When required, the feed would have been dropped over the northern side of the loft, from where it could have been served to the cattle through the feeding windows. There may

Plate 71: Spout Fold Farm: Lancashire barn, central doorway in the southern gable, with lean-to structure

119

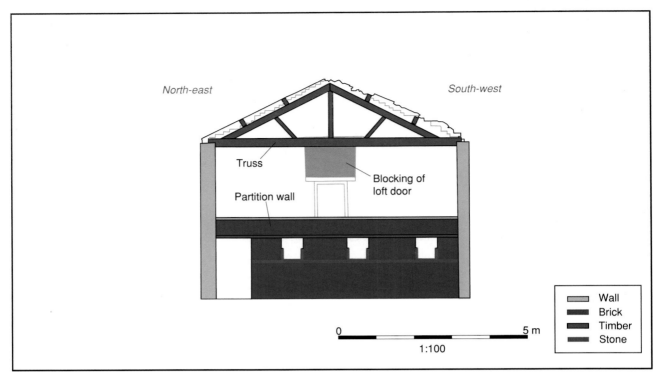

North-east   South-west

Truss

Blocking of loft door

Partition wall

	Wall
	Brick
	Timber
	Stone

0   5 m

1:100

Figure 61: Spout Fold Farm, cross-section through the barn

Plate 72: Spout Fold Farm: Lancashire barn, internal partition

Plate 73: Spout Fold Farm: Lancashire barn, internal stalling

also have been a hatch above the stalls to facilitate the laying of fresh straw bedding.

The remainder of the barn would have been used for numerous tasks, with threshing carried out in the central bay, using the two opposing doors to create the through draught necessary for the winnowing process. Threshing was generally undertaken in the winter months, and the full-height cart entrance to the west would have provided sufficient light to work by. It would also have allowed a fully laden cart to enter the building and was specifically positioned to the west, on the access track from the surrounding fields.

Wharton Hall

An integral element of the Cutacre project was open-area excavation at the site of Wharton Hall (Fig 43), to examine its possible medieval origins and post-medieval development. Although the evidence for medieval activity was scarce, the artefactual evidence suggests that there had probably been a medieval hall at the site (*Ch 3, p 43*). However, all the structural remains that survived were of the post-medieval hall. It therefore appears that the putative late medieval hall was comprehensively destroyed in the early post-medieval period, to be replaced by a 'new' hall. This early post-medieval hall probably occupied the same footprint as its predecessor, being constructed on the brow of a small hill that could be accessed via Wharton Lane to the west.

Owners and residents
The Wartons and Ashtons
Wharton Hall remained in the possession of the Warton family, the medieval owners of the estate (*Ch 3, p 42*), until the late sixteenth century. In June 1587, William Warton leased his lands to Ralph Ashton, or Assheton, of Great Lever, and Thomas Mort of Little Bolton (SCA BW/T 7/1). Ralph Ashton was the fourth in a line of family members of that name who held the manor of Great Lever, near Bolton, from the mid-fifteenth century onwards. His estates included the former abbey of Whalley in east Lancashire, inherited from his uncle, Richard Ashton (Farrer and Brownbill 1911a, 183-4). In the 1590s, accusations of high treason were brought against William Warton for support of the Catholic church, and his lands were seized by the Crown and leased to John Cotton, of the queen's wardrobe (*ibid*). In February 1596, the lease was transferred to William Grenevile of Wiswell Eaves in Lancashire, and in September of that year to the fifth Ralph Ashton of Great Lever (SCA BW/T 7/1).

The Wharton Hall estate was subsequently returned to the ownership of the Warton family, and in 1613 was sold by John Warton of Portsmouth to Ralph Ashton (SCA BW/T 7/1). In 1616, it was listed in Ashton's *Inquisition Post-mortem*, as being held of the lordship of Worsley for the annual rent of a pair of gloves, the same rent as paid by Denis Warton in the early fifteenth century (Rylands 1887, 287-9). It seems likely that at this period Wharton Hall was occupied by a namesake of William Warton, the declared traitor, as in 1614, when Ralph Ashton agreed to confirm the current leases on the estate, heading the list of tenants was a William Warton and his daughter Alice (SCA BW/T 7/1). Probate documents of this William Warton have survived, and in his will, drawn up in April 1630, he described himself as a husbandman, a term used of a tenant farmer, of Little Hulton (LA WCW/Supra/C104C/37). The main beneficiaries were his wife Margaret and daughter Alice. To his grandson Ralph Rothwell he left goods, deriving from Wharton Hall, which included 'one irone chimney and the furniture thereunto belonging' and 'one corne arke standing in the barne'. His probate inventory had a total value of £68 5s 4d. The 'house' (*ie* the housebody, or hall) and 'chamber' are mentioned by name.

The Morts

The sixth Ralph Ashton was made a baronet in 1620, and preferred to live at Whalley, where the former monastic buildings had been converted into a new dwelling, rather than at Great Lever Hall, and in 1628 he sold his estates in south-east Lancashire (Farrer and Brownbill 1911b, 184). The manor of Great Lever was bought by John Bridgeman, rector of Wigan and bishop of Chester (*ibid*). The Wharton Hall estate was sold to Adam Mort, of Dam House in Tyldesley, and his son Thomas Mort (SCA BW/T 7/1; LA WCW/Supra/C122C/37).

The Ashtons belonged to the old feudal gentry, but Adam Mort's wealth and social status appear to have been largely gained during his lifetime. Details of his family background are provided by a pedigree compiled by William Dugdale in the 1660s (Raines 1872, 211). According to this, Adam was a younger son of the Mort family of Highfield in Farnworth, a township bordering Little Hulton, and was heir to Dr Mort, the chamberlain of the bishop of Chester. The pedigree also identifies Adam's wife Janet as the daughter and heir of Thomas Mort of Dam House, in Tyldesley. In 1595, Adam bought the Dam House estate and in 1606 purchased the neighbouring manor of Astley (Farrer and Brownbill 1907, 446). By the time of his death in 1631, he owned land in 11 townships in south Lancashire, and also in Lymm in Cheshire (Lunn 1968, 22). Mort was also a local benefactor and founded a chapel of ease in Astley, which was

consecrated in 1631, after his death. In addition, in his will he provided for a school, which was built in the chapel yard (*op cit*, 24). His probate inventory shows that the bulk of his goods were at Dam House, with 'goods at Warton Hall' being valued at only £1 (LA DDKE/29/6).

On Adam Mort's death, the family estates passed to his son Thomas. He was married to Margaret, the daughter and heir of Robert Smith, a wealthy nailer, of Smithfold in Little Hulton (LA WCW/Supra/C98C/29). For a while after his marriage Thomas lived at his wife's family home, to judge from his description as 'of Smithfold' in documents of 1631 and 1635 (CL Booth 2/1/1/1; LA QDD 43/F3). However, he also added to the Mort estates by purchasing Peel Hall, or Wicheves, in Little Hulton, and the inventory compiled after his death in 1638 makes it is clear that this had become his principal residence (LA WCW/Supra/C122C/37). While it lists some goods at Dam House, Wharton Hall, and Smithfold, the majority were at Peel Hall. The items at Wharton Hall had a total value of only £1 9s 0d, and included a cheese press, various boards, two arks, and a 'hart's head', presumably a hunting trophy, but no furniture such as beds and chairs.

The hall was not, however, unoccupied during this period. The parish register of Deane records the burial of James Boardman of 'Worton Hall' in Little Hulton in September 1637 (Sparke 1917, 381). Probate documents of this James Boardman have survived, and describe him as a husbandman. His inventory had a total value of £41 16s 8d, mostly comprising ready money and debts owing. In addition to his personal apparel, his modest goods consisted of pewter and brass valued at 16s, treen ware at 2s, a bed and bedding at £1 5s, and an ark at 1s. His will, drawn up in 1634, shows that he shared his place of residence, for he appointed as his executor James Grundy, 'with whom I now do dwell', and made bequests to Grundy's sons (LA WCW/Supra/C118A/22).

That the Grundy family were tenants at Wharton Hall is also shown by a lease granted in November 1637 by Thomas Mort's widow Margaret (SCA BW/T 7/1). Under its terms, Francis, the widow of James Grundy, and Richard Grundy her son were to hold certain named parts of Wharton Hall and its farmland for a term of three years. Rooms included in this lease were 'the hall, the great parlour, the butterie and the storehouse, and all the romes [*sic*] over them, the entrie betwixt the dores, the litle parlour beneith the old wyves house, and the lofte over the said entrie'. Also included were 'three bayes at the south end of the barne and the half of the bay of that barne in which the dores are, all the housinge upon the south syde of the fould, the orchard, garden and backsyde' (ibid).

In his will, Thomas Mort instructed that his estates were to be divided between his four sons. The eldest, Adam Mort, aged 15 at the time of his father's death, inherited the Dam House estate. Peel Hall passed to Thomas Mort, the second son, and Wharton Hall to the third son, Robert Mort. The youngest son, John Mort, was given property in Astley (LA WCW/Supra/C122C/37; Lunn 1968, 25-6). Peel Hall also remained the home of Thomas's widow Margaret until her death in 1675 (SCA BW/T 7/1; LA WCW/Supra/C203/66).

Robert Mort is a significant figure in the story of Wharton Hall, in that he is the first of the Mort family who is known to have lived there. He is believed to have been baptised at Bolton in November 1627 and therefore would have come of age by 1648 (Lunn 1968, 44). However, in the 1650s he lived for a time at Ringley, near Prestwich, as a result of what appears to have been a combination of family and religious ties. Ringley was where a chapel was built in 1625 by Nathan Walworth, and in November 1654, Robert Mort married Mary Walworth, a great-niece of the founder, in Prestwich parish church (Fletcher 1880, ix; Brierley 1909, 179). The couple were living in Ringley in November 1655, when the Prestwich register records the baptism of their daughter Anna (Brierley 1909, 50). In 1658, Robert was made an elder of the Ringley congregation (Lunn 1968, 44).

From the 1660s until his death in 1692, the evidence shows that Robert Mort lived at Wharton Hall. The baptism of his younger daughter, in November 1663, took place at Deane parish church, with the register describing Robert as of Little Hulton (Sparke 1916, 54). Surviving Hearth Tax records for Little Hulton from 1663-73 list him as the occupant of a dwelling within the township (below). Elsewhere, he is explicitly described as of Wharton Hall, for example, in his own will in September 1688 (LA WCW/Supra/C259B/37).

Under Robert Mort, Wharton Hall became a place of Nonconformist worship. He allowed the minister James Wood to preach there, after he was ejected from the chapel at Chowbent in Atherton, following the Act of Uniformity in 1662 (Nightingale 1892, 110). The ministers Matthew Henry and Henry Newcombe of Manchester were also visitors during this period. In May 1672, Edward Richardson, who had been ejected from Manchester collegiate church, was licensed to be a Presbyterian teacher at Robert Mort's house in Little Hulton, ie Wharton Hall (Crofton 1889, 68).

Robert Mort was predeceased by Thomas, the older of two sons, who died in 1688 (Sparke 1917, 470, 475;

LA WCW/Supra/C262A/36). On Robert's death in February 1692, the succession passed to the younger son Nathan. He lived at Wharton Hall until the 1700s but then moved to Atherton. Deeds for the mortgage of other properties, to which Nathan was a party, date the move to between 1701 and 1709, describing him as of Wharton Hall in the earlier year, and of Atherton in the later (BA ZFL 5/2-6; LA DDX 349/29). Entries in the Deane parish registers narrow the date range, with Nathan being 'of Little Hulton' in April 1704 and 'of Atherton' in November 1707 (Sparke 1916, 142; 1917, 501). At Atherton he lived at Alder Fold, now known as Alder House (Lunn 1968, 51). This was constructed for Ralph Astley, an Atherton ironmonger, in 1697, and is a stone-built three-storey house distinguished by its multiple gables and early double-pile plan (Pollard and Pevsner 2006, 138-9).

Owners and residents in the eighteenth century
Nathan Mort shared his father's nonconformity. In January 1709, he obtained a licence for Wharton Hall to be a dissenters' meeting place, used for Presbyterian services (LA QSP 985/7; QDV 4/22). In that same year it was said that 'One half of Farnworth and Kersley and Middle Hulton and more goe to Wharton Hall and to Mr Burns ery [sic] Sundey' (LA DDHu 10/6). In 1723, a purpose-built chapel was constructed to the north of the hall, adjacent to Wharton Lane, rebuilt in 1901 (Nightingale 1892, 109-11; Farrer and Brownbill 1911a, 34), but demolished in the late twentieth century, although the graveyard remains. Nathan Mort also supported the Presbyterian congregation at Chowbent, in his new home of Atherton (Lunn 1971, 93-5), where he built a chapel which now has the best-preserved eighteenth-century ecclesiastical interior in south Lancashire (Pollard and Pevsner 2006, 137). Its vestibule also contains a pulpit, which was brought from a Unitarian chapel in Manchester, but was originally at Wharton Hall (ibid).

In December 1722, Nathan Mort conveyed the Wharton Hall estate to his son Adam (NML D/EARLE 9/7). Like his father, Adam lived in Atherton. His son Nathan did not survive infancy, and when Adam died in 1734 he left his property in Atherton to his brother John Mort, and the Wharton Hall estate to his daughter Mary (Sparke 1917, 523; LA WCW/Supra/C365A/54). In 1754 she married Thomas Earle, a younger son of a prominent family of Liverpool merchants, and under the terms of their marriage settlement, the Wharton Hall estate was held by trustees on Mary's behalf. Following their marriage, Mary and Thomas Earle lived for some years at the Italian port of Leghorn (Livorno), before returning to Liverpool in 1766 (Earle 1890, 39-44). Thomas died in 1781, Mary in 1785, and the family's estates, including Wharton Hall, were divided between their two daughters as co-heirs. Maria, the older, married her cousin Thomas Earle of Speaklands, while her sister Jane Elizabeth was the wife of Richard Gwillym of Bewsey Hall, near Warrington (*ibid*; SCA BW/T 6/22; NML D/EARLE 10/5). The Wharton Hall estate continued in the joint ownership of these two families and their representatives until its sale in *c* 1870 (Nightingale 1892, 109).

The marriage settlement of 1754 described Wharton Hall as in the occupation of James Horridge, who may have been the James Horridge who married Mary Hindley at Deane parish church in April 1745. The church register also records the baptism of James Horridge in April 1717, his father Thomas being described there as 'of Little Hulton' (Sparke 1916, 35, 165), suggesting that he may have been the previous tenant. James Horridge is named again as the occupant of Wharton Hall in 1776, but in 1780 John Green is recorded there, either as sole or joint tenant (BA ZZ 640/1-2; LA QDL/S/55). The hall was subsequently occupied by successive generations of the Green family until the close of the nineteenth century (*Ch 8, p 211*).

Investigating Wharton Hall
Historical development
The historical evidence for the appearance of Wharton Hall partly comprises sources from the nineteenth and twentieth centuries, the earliest ground plans of the site appearing on mapping of the mid-nineteenth century. In addition to the Little Hulton tithe map of 1844 (LA DRM 1/58) and the first edition six-inch OS map (1850a), these include a larger-scale plan of the Wharton Hall estate of 1844 (BA ZJA 752; Pl 74). A few photographs of the hall are also known, the earliest from 1876 (Pl 75), the latest from 1959, shortly before the building was

demolished (Pl 76). There appear to be few written descriptions, though, the fullest being that in the *Victoria County History* for Lancashire published in 1911 (Farrer and Brownbill 1911b, 30).

These various sources show the hall to have been a two-storey house, consisting of a central range, aligned north/south, with two east/west-aligned gabled cross-wings, positioned at either end of the central range. The west elevation of the south wing, facing Wharton Lane, was jettied and coved at the first-floor level. The *Victoria County History* reports that timber framing was still present in the lower part of this wing and that the original timber-framed construction was also evident at both ends of the north wing, but otherwise the house had been refaced in brick, covered with a wash, and painted in parts to resemble timber framing (*ibid*). These external alterations to the building are also evident on the 1876 photograph (Pl 75). It is possible that the refacing in brick had occurred prior to the 1830s, when Edward Baines described the hall as 'a simple but venerable building' (Baines 1836, 41). As to the original date of the building, in the early 1890s, Rev Nightingale reported that 'some years ago the date 1629 was found upon an old beam, but it is thought that the Hall was erected much earlier by a member of the Wharton family' (Nightingale 1892, 109).

The north wing was extended on the north prior to 1844, and a single-storey lean-to was added against the west elevation of the extended wing. The line of the old gable was still visible at both ends of the north wing in the early twentieth century (Pl 77). The south wing had also been extended on the east by that date. The *Victoria County History* noted that 'with its yellow-washed walls, grey stone slate roofs and red brick chimneys, the house has rather a picturesque if tumble-down appearance, emphasised to some extent on the back by the addition of low modern outbuildings' (Farrer and Brownbill 1911b, 30).

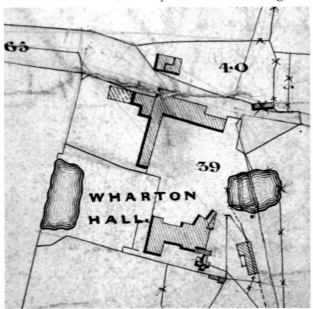

Plate 74: Wharton Hall on the 1844 colliery plan

Plate 75: Photograph of Wharton Hall taken in June 1876

Plate 76: Photograph of Wharton Hall taken in May 1959

Plate 77: Photograph of Wharton Hall taken in 1930

In addition to the nineteenth- and early twentieth-century sources, there is a body of information from the seventeenth century. The earliest known reference to rooms within the hall is provided by the probate inventory of the tenant, William Warton, in 1631, which mentions the 'house' and a 'chamber' (WCW/Supra/C104C/37). More informative is the lease of 1637 (*p 122*), by which Francis Grundy and her son Richard were given certain rooms (SCA BW/T 7/1). In addition to the hall, these included two parlours (the great and little parlour), two service rooms (the buttery and storehouse), and an entrance (*p 122*).

Externally, a barn is also mentioned in the will of William Warton (WCW/Supra/C104C/37). The lease of 1637 to Francis and Richard Grundy included the 'three bayes at the south end of the barne and the half of the bay of that barne in which the dores are' (SCA BW/T 7/1). This suggests a building seven bays long and aligned north/south. It possibly stood opposite the hall and immediately alongside Wharton Lane, where a probable north-east/south-west-aligned barn is shown on later mapping (*eg* OS 1850a). Also included in the 1637 lease was 'all the housinge upon the south syde of the fould'. The later mapping shows that the likely barn was adjoined at its southern end by a south-east/north-west-aligned range, so that these buildings formed two sides of a yard in front of the hall. The lease suggests that in the seventeenth century one or more buildings had stood in approximately the same location as that east/west range.

No document which names rooms and outbuildings later than the 1637 lease is known, although such evidence might have been provided by the probate inventory of Robert Mort, who died in 1692. He was the only member of the Mort family who both owned Wharton Hall and resided there at the time of his death, but while his will has survived, an inventory has not (WCW/Supra/C259B/37). However, it is from Robert's time that one other important source of information derives: the Hearth Tax records.

In the surviving returns for Little Hulton, Robert Mort is listed with three hearths in 1663, four on Lady Day 1664, six on Lady Day 1666, and six again in 1673 (LA Mf 27-29; Tait 1924, 91). Such variations are not untypical in the returns for Lancashire, with assessments for individual householders often being higher in later years. The frequency of such instances suggests that they are at least in part due to a change in the method of assessment, or in the efficiency of the recorders (Tait 1924). However, in the case of Wharton Hall, there is evidence that in the 1660s the number of hearths did actually increase. The

original slips giving the total for each household in Little Hulton survive from September 1664, and the slip for Wharton Hall records that 'I Robert Mort give Account to the Constable that there is in my house five fire hearths whereof on[e] was lately Erected'. To this has been added, in a separate hand, '3 more hearths erecting where newer hearth was' (LA DDKe 2/16/11).

The Hearth Tax records reveal that by 1664 Robert was undertaking new building works at the house. In doing so he may have been following the example of his elder brother, Adam, who had rebuilt Dam House, and perhaps also his father Thomas, who may have been responsible for the rebuilding of Peel Hall (*p 122*). The Rev Nightingale's reference (*p 124*) to the discovery of the date 1629 on a beam at Wharton Hall (perhaps an inglenook bressumer?) suggests that an earlier phase of building work had been carried out shortly after the Morts first acquired the property, and that Robert's work in the 1660s retained at least part of that earlier house.

In comparison with the Morts' other houses, at Dam House and Peel Hall, Wharton Hall was neither particularly large nor architecturally distinctive. Such considerations may have influenced Nathan Mort's decision in the early eighteenth century to move to Atherton, where he lived at the more striking Alder House (*p 123*). Wharton Hall itself was subsequently leased to farmers and other tenants, and the extensions to the building reflect that later use.

Archaeological excavation
The excavated structural remains of Wharton Hall largely conformed to the description contained in the *Victoria County History* and the photographic evidence (*pp 124-5*). However, they did provide additional chronological details, and also revealed the sequence of construction during the course of the early post-medieval period.

Phase 1: The early seventeenth-century hall (constructed in 1629?)
The earliest structural remains (Phase 1; Fig 62; Pl 78) identified at the site were cut into a naturally deposited yellow clay (*1255*), or a red-brown clay (*1001/1109/1160/1162/1230*) that overlay it, which formed a relict horticultural soil. Significantly, this soil, which also extended across areas to the east, south, and west of the hall, and sealed the adjacent palaeochannel (*1305*; *Ch 3, p 38*), provided a *terminus post quem* for the Phase 1 remains. Although it contained a collection of chronologically diverse artefacts, its initial formation probably dated to the late sixteenth or earlier seventeenth century, on the basis of characteristic early post-medieval pottery types, particularly Midlands Purple-type pottery,

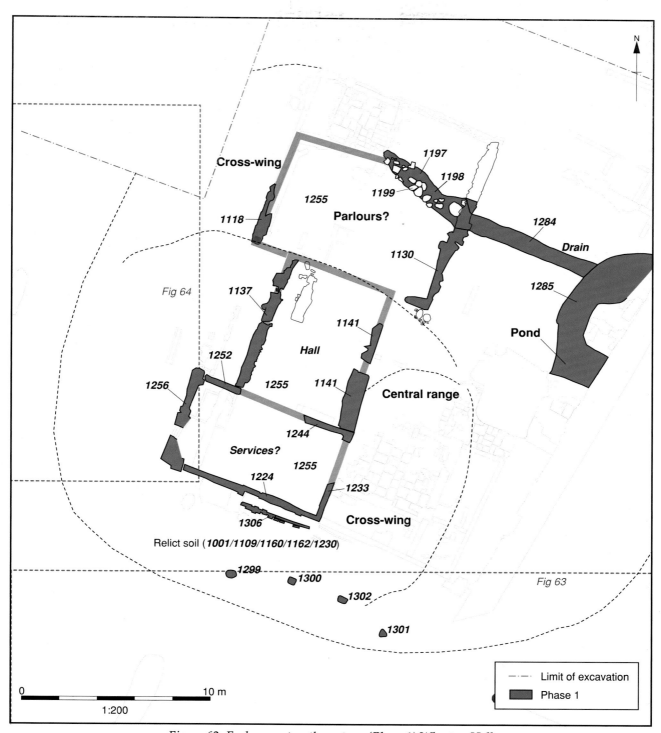

Figure 62: Early seventeenth-century (Phase 1) Wharton Hall

Yellow-bodied wares, and early Staffordshire trail-slipware (Table 7; *Appendix 4*). Sherds of medieval pottery were also recovered from the eastern extent of the layer, and these may be a residual trace of earlier activity (*Ch 3, p 43*). However, following the construction of the Phase 1 hall, this relict soil continued to be worked around the early post-medieval building for a fairly extended period of time and therefore received additional inputs of artefactual material. This included a fairly large

assemblage of eighteenth- and nineteenth-century pottery and clay-tobacco pipe fragments, which probably derive from the later occupation of the hall (*Ch 8, p 211*).

Based on this dating evidence, the Phase 1 remains appear to date to sometime in the late sixteenth or early seventeenth century (*p 126*). Although it is theoretically possible that this hall may have been constructed by either the Wartons, the Ashtons,

Plate 78: The excavated remains of Wharton Hall, with its stone foundations, looking south-east

Context	Post-medieval pottery types	Clay tobacco pipe	Other material
Relict soil *1001/1109/1160/1162/1230*	Creamware Dark-glazed red earthenware Glazed white earthenware Self-glazed brown earthenwares Speckled red-glazed wares Mottled ware White salt-glazed ware Staffordshire-type slipware Industrial slipware Tin-glaze ware Stoneware (includes green stoneware; manganese-speckled salt-glazed stoneware; Brampton-type stoneware; Nottingham-type stoneware; and imported stoneware) Porcelain Yellow ware Hand-trailed slipware Blackware Midlands Purple-type ware Coarse brown-glazed red ware Light green speckled ware Feather-trailed press-moulded slipware Redware Unglazed red-slipped white ware	Narrow- and medium-bore stems, two small spurs, glazed mouthpiece, possibly derived from a mid-seventeenth-century Dutch pipe, mid-nineteenth-century bowl (1650–1900)	Copper-alloy items and ironwork

*Table 7: Stratified post-medieval artefacts from relict soil **1001/1109/1160/1162/1230** and Phase 1 structural remains at Wharton Hall*

Context	Post-medieval pottery types	Clay tobacco pipe	Other material
Fill *1132* in foundation trench *1131*; contained wall *1130*	Thin-walled purple-red Blackware Light red coarse earthenware Midlands Purple-type ware Dark-glazed red earthenware		Ironwork
Fill *1138* in foundation trench *1139*; contained wall *1137*	Staffordshire-type hand-trailed slipware Blackware Possibly imported green stoneware		
Fill *1198* in foundation trench *1197*	Midlands Purple-type ware		
Wall *1233*	Dark-glazed coarse red earthenware		
Fill *1235* in foundation trench *1236*; contained boundary wall *1237*	German stoneware Trailed slipware Yellow-slip-trailed Blackware Blackware Dark-glazed red earthenware	Large-bore stem (1850-1900)	
Fills *1150* and *1232* in boundary *1149/1239*	Midlands Purple-type ware Blackware Dark brown-glazed red ware		
Fill *1259* in culvert *1238*	Industrial slipware Glazed white earthenware Stoneware Mottled ware		
Fill *1283* in drain *1284*	Cistercian-type Blackware		
Fill *1301* in posthole *1302*	Lead-glazed fine dark red earthenware		
Fill *1307* in drain *1306*	Midlands Purple-type glazed ware Trailed slip in red fabric		

*Table 7: Stratified post-medieval artefacts from relict soil **1001/1109/1160/1162/1230** and Phase 1 structural remains at Wharton Hall (cont'd)*

or the Morts (*pp 122-3*), it is highly likely that these remains actually date to the early seventeenth century, based on the discovery of the beam inscribed with the date of 1629 (*p 124*). If this is the case, this indicates that the early seventeenth-century hall was constructed by Adam and Thomas Mort, after they acquired the property in 1628 (*p 122*).

The surviving remains of this early seventeenth-century hall comprised **truncated stone walling and tumble**, which defined its eastern (*1130*, *1141*, and *1233*), western (*1118*, *1137*, *1252*, and *1256*), and southern (*1224*) external walls (Fig 62). These varied in thickness, between 0.38 m and 0.6 m wide,

and were composed of rectangular, rounded, and square-hewn sandstone blocks. The best-preserved sections of walling defined the eastern and south-western sides of the hall, three courses high (0.5 m). In addition, an east/west-aligned foundation trench (*1197*; Pl 79), filled with sediment (*1198*) and large rounded boulders (*1199*), marked the position of the northern wall, which was eventually removed during the eighteenth century (*p 135*).

Foundation trench *1197* contained a sherd of Midlands Purple-type pottery, which can be dated no later than the seventeenth century (Hurst and Wright 2011), whilst the foundation trench for wall *1137* contained

*Plate 79: Wharton Hall: foundation trench **1197**, looking north*

several sherds which could also date to that period. Midlands Purple-type pottery was also recovered from the foundation trench for wall **1130**, whilst seventeenth-century pottery was associated with wall **1233** (Table 7).

When taken together, the walls and foundation trench indicate that the seventeenth-century hall was *c* 19 m in overall length. Its form also corresponded closely to the early twentieth-century descriptions of the site (*p 124*), in that it comprised a central range with projecting northern and southern cross-wings, creating an H-shaped plan. The central range was 6 m in width, whilst the southern cross-wing was

9 m long and 5 m wide, projecting to the north-west, but ending flush with the central range in the south-east. The northern cross-wing was 10 m in length, 6 m wide, and projected out from the central range to both the north-west and south-east. Based on the form of these remains, and the seventeenth-century documentary evidence (*p 122*), it is quite likely that the central range contained the hall, whilst two parlours were in one cross-wing, probably that to the north, and the other contained two service rooms, based on the position of the later (Phase 2) kitchen (*p 134*).

Few contemporary features survived within the interior of the Phase 1 hall. Although there were no floors, traces of compacted natural clay (**1255**) were present across the footprint of the building, and stone wall **1244**, butting the southern end of east wall **1141**, created the subdivision between the central range and the southern cross-wing.

Several contemporary features were also present outside the hall. To its east, these comprised a shallow east/west-aligned channel (**1284**), filled with sandy clay (**1283**), containing medieval pottery, and two almost complete Cistercian-ware-type bowls dating to the seventeenth century (Table 7). This channel ran below the eastern wall of the northern cross-wing (**1130**), and was probably a drain. It

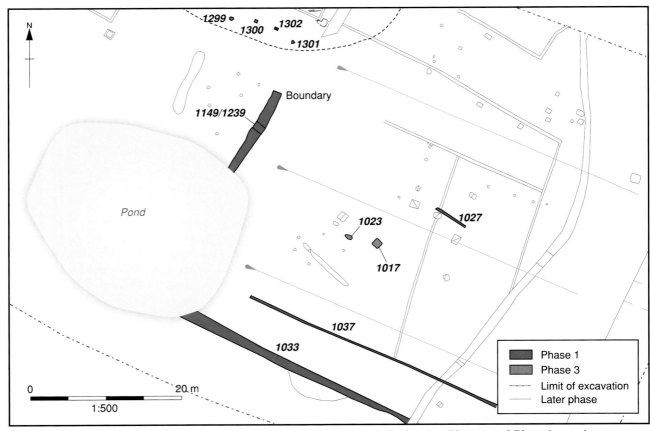

Figure 63: The excavated area to the south-east of Wharton Hall, showing Phase 1 and Phase 3 remains

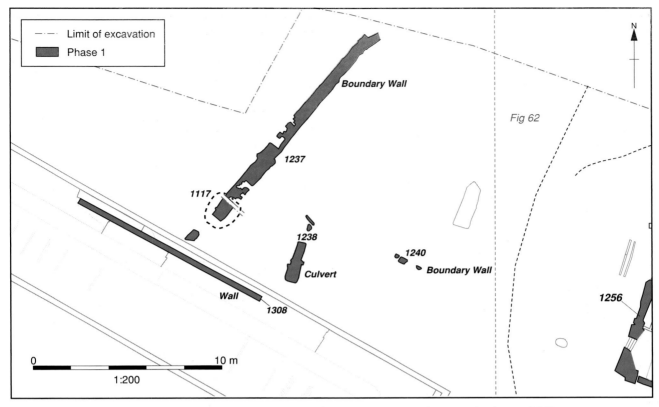

Figure 64: Early seventeenth-century (Phase 1) remains to the west of Wharton Hall

appears that it fed water into a small pond (*1285*), to the east of the hall.

Several other Phase 1 drains were also identified. These included a brick-built drain (*1306*) immediately south of the building, parallel with the southern wall of the southern cross-wing. This drain was exposed over a distance of 3 m, and contained fragments of Midlands Purple-type ware and Metropolitan-type hand-trailed slipware (in drain fill *1307*), suggesting that it had silted no later than the late seventeenth century (Table 7).

A second pond also existed 30 m south of the hall (Fig 63) and, although it is first depicted on nineteenth-century mapping (*eg* OS 1850a), it is possible that it was contemporary with the seventeenth-century hall, or even pre-dated it. It was under water at the time of excavation, which prohibited investigation, although an external diameter of 13 m was established. Two east/west-aligned drains (*1033* and *1037*) extended from this pond (*below*), draining water from this feature, one of which (*1033*) contained pottery dating to the seventeenth to nineteenth centuries. Other land drains were also found in this area, some of which were potentially contemporary with the earliest phase of the hall. However, few of these drains yielded dating evidence, other than field drain *1027*, which contained fragments from a seventeenth-century Yellow-ware bowl and a Blackware cup (*Appendix 4*).

Four postholes (*1299-1302*) were also found to the south of the hall (Fig 62) and possibly formed elements of a fence, which surrounded a small garden. One of these (*1302*) contained three sherds of late seventeenth- or early eighteenth-century pottery (Table 7). The other Phase 1 features external to the hall consisted of the remains of two boundaries and a stone building. A boundary was found between the hall and pond (Fig 63), defined by a north/south-aligned gully (*1149/1239*), which was exposed for a distance of 10 m. It contained pottery spanning a broad date range between the fifteenth and nineteenth centuries (Table 7). However, this boundary also contained fragments from a late seventeenth-century wine bottle, suggesting that it began to fill during this period.

A stone building had stood to the north-west of the hall (Fig 64), and was probably the building range mentioned in the seventeenth century, which adjoined a north-east/south-west-aligned barn (*p 122*). Although the building had been comprehensively demolished and replaced in the early part of the twentieth century by a shippon, some elements of an external wall survived, which, based on mapping, defined the northern side of the building range. This wall was a single course of stone foundation (*1308*), extending for 10 m. It is also possible that a culvert (*1238*), uncovered to the north, was associated with the drainage of this

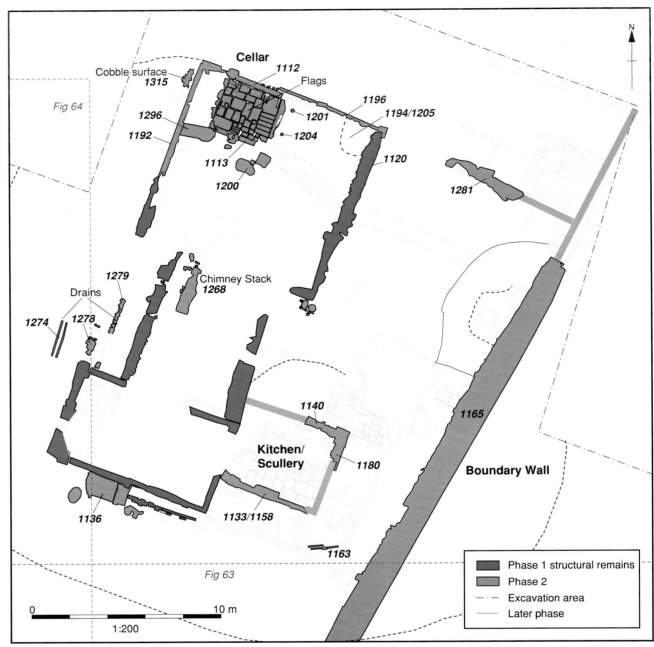

Figure 65: Late seventeenth-century (Phase 2) Wharton Hall

early building. It comprised a channel with brick sides and a slate base, capped with sandstone flags, and fragments of pottery from its backfill (**1259**) included mottled ware and industrial slipware, which suggests that it also functioned as a drain during the eighteenth and nineteenth centuries (Table 7).

A contemporary boundary was defined by a length of stone walling (**1237**), identified *c* 25 m to the west of the hall, which extended from the northern side of the stone building range (*p 131*). This wall was followed for 15 m and, significantly, its foundation trench contained sherds of pottery (in fill **1235**) that suggest that it was built in the late seventeenth century (Table 7), although it

also contained a fragment of nineteenth-century clay tobacco-pipe, which was probably intrusive. Intriguingly, the vestiges of a buried gravel surface (**1117**) were exposed beneath the south-western end of this wall, which may represent an earlier track. A line of three flat sandstone blocks (**1240**) were also excavated some 9 m to the east, which were possibly associated with the wall.

Phase 2: late seventeenth-century rebuilding (1662-4?)
During the possession of the Mort family in the late seventeenth century, it seems that the original early seventeenth-century building was modified and extended. This work principally involved rebuilding and extending its northern cross-wing, and

Plate 80: Wharton Hall: the late seventeenth-century cellar, looking north-east

constructing an additional extension on the south-eastern side of its southern counterpart (Fig 65). Significantly, the documentary evidence provides further insights into this phase of modification, as this suggests that this programme of rebuilding was probably undertaken by Robert Mort at some point between 1662 and 1664 (*p 126*).

The modifications at the northern end of the hall comprised the demolition of its original northern wall (represented by foundation trench *1197*; *p 129*), followed by a fairly substantial programme of rebuilding, which resulted in an extended and enlarged northern cross-wing. Indeed, it is possible that this rebuilding was necessitated by a fire, which damaged the northern end of the Phase 1 hall, since traces of charcoal (*1205*) were found within the north-eastern corner of the late seventeenth-century extension, overlying a clay levelling layer (*1194*).

The northern extension extended the hall by 3 m, as shown on an early twentieth-century photograph (Pl 77). This also demonstrates that the extension had substantial chimney stacks on each of the gables and also at its centre, and a ground-level doorway in its northern wall. However, the only remains which

might be associated with these features were two large flagstones (*1200*), possibly the foundations for the extension's central chimney stack.

The most substantial feature present within the northern extension was a cellar in its western half. This measured approximately 3 x 3 m and was 1.6 m deep, being floored with flagstones (Pl 80). Three of its walls were constructed from stone, while the northern wall utilised stone and brick. It was accessed from the south-eastern corner by a flight of five sandstone steps, descending to a flagstone platform, 0.8 m long, 0.15 m above the floor. The remains of a probable window were visible in the northern wall, although much of it had been removed. The space had been partitioned, with internal brick walls being attached to the northern and southern walls (*1112* and *1113*), creating small chambers for storage. The chambers on the southern side were bordered by a narrow, 0.5 m-wide shelf, lined with slate, which was probably damp coursing. The cellar may have been used for storage of victuals and perhaps for the products of any cottage industry undertaken at the hall. Directly adjacent was a gully (*1296*), perhaps a foundation trench, which contained eighteenth/nineteenth-century pottery.

Plate 81: Wharton Hall: the late seventeenth-century
extension, early eighteenth-century reflooring, and
nineteenth-century additions, looking north-west

The other late seventeenth-century extension involved the construction of an additional ground-floor room abutting the south-eastern wall of the southern cross-wing (Pl 81), which was probably a kitchen. This measured 4.7 x 3.9 m and was defined by three stone walls (*1140*, *1133/1158*, and *1180*), surviving only as single courses.

Another feature which probably also dates to the late seventeenth century was a chimney stack (*1268*). Its foundations were identified on the north-western side of the central range, comprising two north/south-aligned rows of sandstone, 2.2 m long and 0.6 m wide.

Beyond the hall, the excavation detected several other features that may date to the late seventeenth century.

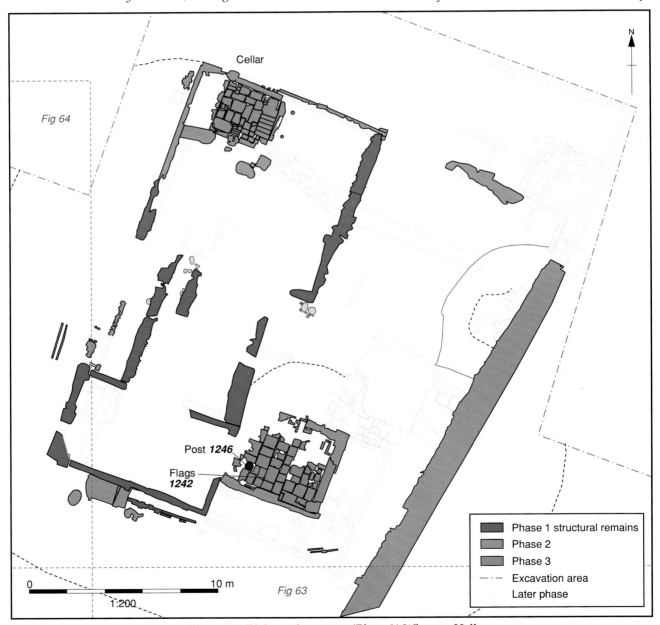

Figure 66: Eighteenth-century (Phase 3) Wharton Hall

One of these comprised an east/west-aligned wall to the east of the northern cross-wing, composed of three roughly hewn sandstone courses (*1281*), 4 m long and 0.45 m wide. This had been built over levelling material similar to that found beneath the northern wall of the extended cross-wing, suggesting that it dated to a similar period. Although its function is not entirely clear, it probably formed either a boundary or the remnant of a dismantled ancillary building. It is possible that this wall also joined a more substantial boundary wall (*1165*) to the east, which was aligned north-east/south-west. This was of drystone construction, with some later handmade brick repairs, and survived to a maximum height of 0.8 m, above relict soil *1109* (*p 126*). It extended for a distance of 22 m, its position being depicted on the first edition six-inch OS map (1850a), indicating that it continued to function as a boundary during this later period. This map also suggests that it may have formed the western boundary of a walled garden.

Immediately outside the hall, another potential late seventeenth-century feature was a small section of cobbled surface (*1315*), along the western side of the building, above relict soil *1109* (*p 126*). Although this had been disturbed by later development, it perhaps formed the remnants of a path that extended around this side of the hall.

Phase 3: eighteenth-century modifications
It appears that several minor modifications were made to the hall in the eighteenth century. Principal amongst these was the insertion of a flagstone floor (*1242*; Fig 66), within the late seventeenth-century extension at the south-eastern corner of the hall (*p 134*). This floor presumably replaced an earlier surface and survived over an area of 4 x 3.3 m, set on a bedding layer (*1241*), which contained fragments of coal and eighteenth-century pottery. The upper surface of the flags along the eastern side of the room had been coated in pitch, perhaps denoting the position of kitchen apparatus. Another feature within this floor was an *in situ* wooden post (*1246*), with a diameter of 0.2 m, in its south-western corner. Its function is not particularly clear, however.

Two pits (*1017* and *1023*; Fig 63) were also present to the south of the hall, which contained seventeenth- and eighteenth-century pottery, and, as such, probably relate to Phase 3 activity. One of these (*1017*) also contained a fragment of burnt daub, which was probably residual (*Ch 3, p 44*).

6

LATE EIGHTEENTH- AND NINETEENTH-CENTURY LANDSCAPES 1: KINGSWAY BUSINESS PARK - MOSS SIDE LANE

Richard A Gregory, Ian Miller, and Michael Nevell

It is clear from the cartographic evidence that, in the townships of Butterworth and Castleton, the major post-medieval routeways (*Ch 4*) continued to form prominent features within the late eighteenth- and nineteenth-century landscape. These comprised Moss Side Lane, Lower Lane, and Moor Bank Lane (Fig 67). Along these routes, it is also evident from the cartographic sources that the majority of post-medieval settlements (*Ch 4*) continued to be occupied during this later period, whilst some additional dwellings were constructed during the late eighteenth and nineteenth centuries. Those late eighteenth- and nineteenth-century properties which existed along Moss Side Lane are considered below.

Background: Kingsway Business Park

Throughout the late eighteenth and nineteenth centuries, farming formed the economic mainstay of the rural area around Rochdale, which was supplemented by various other activities, principally small-scale textile production. However, although in essence this mimicked the situation in earlier centuries, from the late eighteenth century onwards it is clear that textile production, particularly the weaving of cloth, became an increasingly important element of the rural economy; this led, in the Kingsway area, to the appearance of several specialised, semi-domestic buildings, which were designed specifically to facilitate such activities. These are known locally as weavers' cottages, and they form a common element of this period within the rural landscapes of historic Lancashire (*cf* Timmins 1977; 2004). These structures reflect wider economic changes that were occurring across Lancashire in the late eighteenth century, with the rise of industrialisation in the textile sector leading to a radical transformation of the character of Lancashire. The move to the mechanisation of spinning, starting in the mid-eighteenth century (*Ch 4, p 64*), resulted in a sharp rise in the demand for handloom weavers, which boosted the rural cottage

industry (Walton 1987, 104) and was the impetus which led to the appearance of large numbers of weavers' cottages.

Aside from these semi-domestic loomshops, another defining feature of the late eighteenth century is the appearance of purpose-built textile mills within the Rochdale area, during the 1780s, which were another clear expression of industrialisation (Williams with Farnie 1992, 42). Indeed, the site of one such mill is within the Kingsway Business Park though, as this was not affected by the development, it was not subjected to archaeological investigation. This was at Broad Shaw and may have been Rochdale's first purpose-built cotton mill (Haynes and Tipper 1994, 44-5). It stood next to an early seventeenth-century farmhouse and barn, and was constructed in 1782 by Francis Ashworth (*ibid*). Reputedly, it was no bigger than an outhouse and was used initially for the carding of cotton, though Ashworth used it subsequently for the scribbling of wool (*ibid*). Both carding and scribbling were preparatory processes, whereby a stiff wire brush, on a carding machine, was used to disentangle fibrous material to create a sliver, which in the spinning process were drawn out and twisted into yarn (Phelps *et al* 2017, 113).

The site of another comparable mill may also have existed in the business park, known as Lower Lane Mill. This also dates to the 1780s and was possibly a woollen mill, owned by John Wild (Haynes and Tipper 1994, 46). However, archaeological evaluation at the site indicated that its remains had been completely obliterated by later development (OA North 2012). It seems that John Wild also had property interests, as he is listed in the Land Tax assessments for Castleton for 1780 as the owner of three newly erected cottages in the area (LA QDL/S/24).

During the nineteenth century, industrialisation progressed rapidly across the wider Rochdale area and there was a shift to the manufacture of cotton goods, which was greatly advanced following the introduction of steam power in the early nineteenth

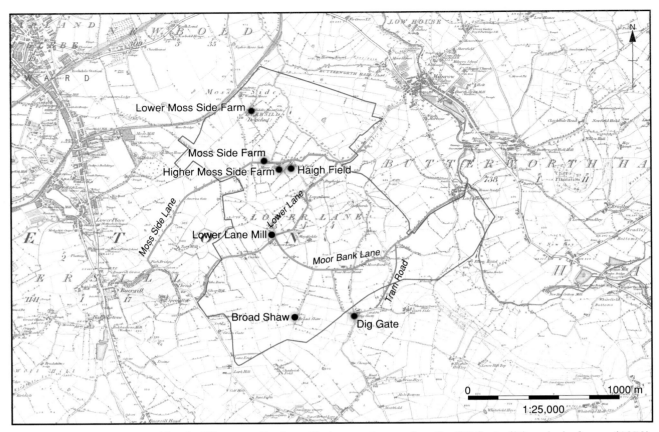

Figure 67: The area covered by the Kingsway Business Park, superimposed on the OS first edition six-inch map (1850)

century, coupled with a downturn in the woollen trade in the mid-nineteenth century (Haynes and Tipper 1994, 71). Indeed, Rochdale became one of the major cotton-spinning centres within Lancashire during the late nineteenth century, along with Oldham, Bolton, and Bury (Williams with Farnie 1992, 46, table 1). One significant advance in the weaving of both cotton and wool during this period was the introduction of a successful power-loom in the 1820s, which mechanised the process, and eventually allowed it to be undertaken within large single-storey weaving sheds (*op cit*, 11). Such sheds were either constructed adjacent to a spinning block, to form an integrated spinning and weaving mill, or were stand-alone structures within a weaving mill. Across Lancashire, integrated mills began to appear in the late 1820s and early 1830s, and were fairly abundant by the mid-nineteenth century (Phelps *et al* 2017). Similarly, purpose-built weaving mills appeared at the same time as integrated mills, although their uptake was slower. However, by the middle of the century they began to be built in large numbers (*ibid*).

The focus for the production of cotton goods was the Rochdale Canal, adjacent to the Kingsway Business Park. This canal was authorised by an Act of Parliament in 1794 and was designed to link Manchester with the canal system of West Yorkshire,

with the section close to Kingsway, between Sowerby Bridge and Rochdale, being completed in 1798 (Paget-Tomlinson 1993, 182). It proved to be a great stimulus to the area's nineteenth-century cotton industry and a series of large cotton mills was established in its vicinity from the 1820s onwards (Haynes and Tipper 1994, 74-9; Fig 68). To the west of Kingsway, the earliest of these included mills such as Wellfield Mill (built in the late 1820s; *op cit*, 74) and Moss Mill (built in 1827; *op cit*, 77), though mill building continued in this area throughout the second half of the nineteenth century, as witnessed by those mills depicted on the 1893 OS map (1893a). However, although the factory-based system of textile production was imposed on the area, within Kingsway, semi-domestic textile working continued to form a feature of the rural economy. Indeed, cottages such as those at Mayfields (*Ch 7, p 175*) and Moss Side (*p 147*) continued to be occupied by handloom weavers during the first half of the nineteenth century, with references to such weavers at Mayfields in the 1861 Census (NA RG 9/3035; *Ch 7, p 177*).

Coal mining was another industry within the Kingsway area during nineteenth century. The first edition six-inch OS map (1850b) depicts coal pits close to Dig Gate, and an associated tram road running north from there, terminating at Moor Bank

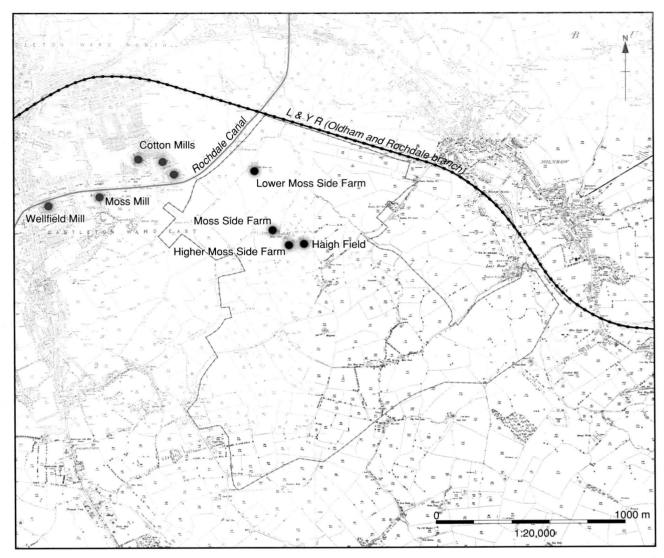

Figure 68: The area covered by the Kingsway Business Park, superimposed on the OS first edition 1:2500 map (1893)

Lane (Fig 67). Further evidence for coal mining is provided by the nineteenth-century Census Returns, which record several miners living in Castleton township, including three at Lower Lane and one at Castle House in 1851 (NA HO 107/2244), and others at Lower Lane and Moss Side in 1861 (NA RG 9/3035). It is not known when coal mining commenced in the area, although a James Smith of Butterworth, Rochdale, described himself as a collier in his will dated June 1719 (LA WCW/Infra/C1392/47). However, at Kingsway, the coal pits and tram road are absent from the first edition 1:2500 OS maps (1893a; 1893c; Fig 68), suggesting that the small-scale nature of the local mining activity had been superseded by the deep coal pits sunk across the Manchester and Oldham coalfields (Phillips and Smith 1994, 274-5).

Other nineteenth-century developments relevant to the area related to infrastructure, specifically the construction of the rail link between Manchester and Leeds, which was authorised in 1836 (Haynes and Tipper 1994, 54). This railway was owned initially by the Manchester and Leeds Railway Company, though later in the nineteenth century it formed part of the Lancashire and Yorkshire Railway (L&YR), established in 1847 through an amalgamation of several different railway companies (Marshall 1969). In 1863, the Oldham and Rochdale Branch was opened, with a station at Milnrow (*ibid*), and the route now bounds the north-eastern edge of the Kingsway Business Park.

In the light of the industrial expansion of Lancashire, it is unsurprising that the population in some of the rural areas on the Pennine fringe expanded quite dramatically during the late eighteenth and early nineteenth centuries. According to F R Raines (1805-78), vicar of Milnrow, for instance, the chapel of Butterworth was only calculated to accommodate 100 persons in 1715, 'which would be the major part of the inhabitants' (CL GB418/2). However,

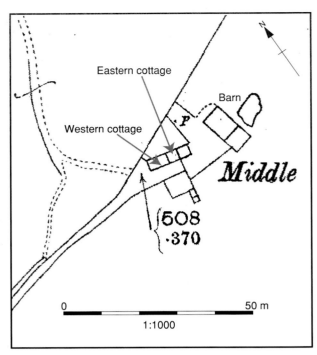

Figure 69: An extract from the OS first edition 1:2500 map (1893), showing Lower Moss Side Farm

a Census of 1801 recorded that the inhabitants of Butterworth township totalled 3923, a figure that had increased to 4872 by 1811 (*ibid*). Of this latter total, Raines calculated that 133 families were engaged in agriculture and 725 were employed primarily in 'trade, manufactures, or handicraft' (*ibid*). By 1821, the population of the township had increased to 5554 persons, comprising 987 families that occupied a total of 943 houses (*ibid*). The population of Butterworth increased steadily to a total of 5786 recorded in the Census of 1851, with 1115 houses being occupied, 129 uninhabited, and 11 in the process of construction (NA HO 107/2244).

The Moss Side Lane Properties

Lower Moss Side Farm

Lower Moss Side Farm was known as Middle Moss Side Farm during the nineteenth century, and is named as such on the first edition six-inch (1850b) and first edition 1:2500 (1893a) OS maps. The earlier of these maps plots the position of a seventeenth-century farmhouse (*Ch 4, p 65*), though by the time of the publication of the 1:2500 edition this had been demolished and replaced by a 'new' farmhouse and cottages (Fig 69). These buildings were extant in 2005 and were recorded by a building survey. In addition, the later map (1893a) also indicates that by 1893 a barn had been constructed to the east. This building was also extant in 2005 and was thus recorded as part of the building survey. Additional

details relating to these buildings were revealed subsequently by archaeological excavation.

Documentary evidence

A building in the approximate position of Lower Moss Side Farm is shown on early nineteenth-century mapping of the area, including the surveys by Greenwood and Hennet, published in 1818 and 1830 respectively. Both of these, however, were produced at a scale that does not enable details of the component buildings to be elucidated. The first edition six-inch OS map does, however, show the farmstead, as a T-shaped range, with a small detached building to the north (1850b), which was probably a barn. These buildings were remodelled or demolished subsequently, and by 1881 the replacement farmhouse and cottage were occupied by two families: the Shepards; and the Hardikes. Fred Shepard is listed in the 1881 Census Returns (NA RG 11/4103) as a 29-year-old coal carter from Rochdale, whilst his 25-year-old wife, Selina, was a power-loom weaver, presumably employed in a nearby textile mill. Their neighbour, Thomas Hardikes, was from Staffordshire, and was employed as an iron turner, perhaps at the nearby St George's Foundry. Hardikes shared Lower Moss Side with his 28-year-old wife and their three young children. It is of note that neither of these families earned a living from agriculture.

The Census Returns for 1891 (NA RG 12/3329) indicate that Middle Moss Side was then occupied by a single family, comprising John Glover, his wife, and four young children. John was from Chorley in Lancashire originally, whilst his wife was born in Bolton, and their children were born in Hindley, Astley Green, and Rochdale, implying that the family had moved around south Lancashire. John Glover is described as an agricultural labourer.

The Census Returns for 1901 (NA RG 13/3833) provide slightly more detail than earlier records. These demonstrate that Lower Moss Side Farm was occupied by Edmund Farrow, a 31-year-old farmer from Whitworth in Lancashire. The adjacent property, Lower Moss Side Cottage, is marked 'uninhabited'.

Archaeological investigation: building survey and excavation

The building survey and cartographic evidence suggested that a seventeenth-century farmhouse was demolished in the mid-nineteenth century and replaced by two adjoining two-bay cottages (Fig 69; Western Cottage and Eastern Cottage). Both of these elements were two-storeyed, though the western bay of Western Cottage was slightly higher than that to the east, and also of the bays of Eastern Cottage (Fig 70). A barn was also erected in the nineteenth century (*p 145*).

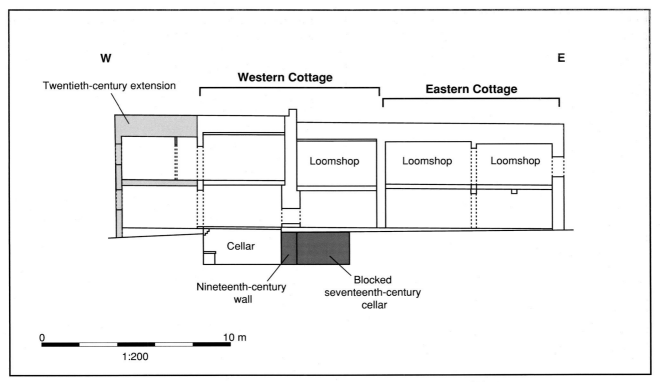

W

Twentieth-century extension

Western Cottage

Eastern Cottage

E

Loomshop

Loomshop

Loomshop

Cellar

Nineteenth-century
wall

Blocked
seventeenth-century
cellar

0   10 m

1:200

Figure 70: Cross-section through the cottages at Lower Moss Side Farm

The Western Cottage
The northern and southern exterior elevations of the two-bayed Western Cottage were recorded, although its western elevation was obscured by a twentieth-century extension. The western bay of Western Cottage on the north (Pl 82) had a single wide window on the ground floor, with modern window frames and glazing. Below this was a set of steps, which led down to a doorway partially below ground level, giving access into a cellar. On the upper floor were a small, but tall, window and another rectangular window. At ground-floor level, the eastern bay had a single rectangular window, whilst the upper floor had a small window and a tall narrow window, from the level of the ground-foor ceiling to near eaves level. As far as could be ascertained, all the windows had modern frames and glazing.

The western bay also had a square-headed narrow central door on the south, accessed by a short set of steps (Pl 83). A small window was immediately to the east of the door, whilst another small but tall window was to the west. Marks in the render around the door suggest there may once have been a surrounding porch. Above the central door was a wide rectangular window. At ground-floor level, the eastern bay possessed a long single window, whilst its upper floor had a long narrow window, directly below the eaves (Pl 84). Both of these are characteristic of multi-light windows, which were constructed to provide light for workshops in the local textile industry (*cf* Timmins 1977).

Inside, it was evident that an original chimney breast (covered with modern cladding) lay between,

Plate 82: Lower Moss Side Farm: northern elevation of the farmhouse and cottage

Plate 83: Lower Moss Side Farm: the southern elevation of the western bay of the western cottage, with abutting twentieth-century extension (left)

Plate 84: Lower Moss Side Farm: the southern and eastern elevations of the farmhouse and cottage

and separated, the eastern and western bays, with a fireplace at ground-floor level, open on both sides, allowing both bays to be heated (Fig 71). Two beams extended across the ground-floor room in the eastern bay, which had been clad with modern planking. At ground-floor level, access between the two bays was through a doorway, positioned to the north of the chimney breast. Access to the first-floor was via a staircase in the north-eastern corner of the eastern bay. Access between the upper two rooms was through a doorway in an identical location to the internal doorway on the ground floor.

The cellar was beneath the western bay of the Western Cottage, although this dates to the seventeenth century (*Ch 4, p 67*), but had been clearly modified during the

nineteenth-century programme of rebuilding. It is apparent that the construction of the western cottage required the insertion of a north/south-aligned wall, which acted as the foundation for the wall dividing its eastern and western bays, and effectively divided the cellar into two (Fig 70). The excavation demonstrated that it was composed of handmade brick, bonded with sand and lime mortar, and cut the southern wall of the seventeenth-century cellar, and following its construction, only the western portion of the original cellar was used. Significantly, the construction of this wall also blocked the original cellar entrance, and hence access to the remodelled cellar, during the nineteenth century, was via an external entrance on the northern wall of the Western Cottage, which was itself remodelled in the twentieth century (Fig 71).

During the building survey, several features were also recorded within the interior of the remodelled cellar that might have been eighteenth-century in date. These included stone-slab benches, supported on stone and brick pillars, along its western and southern walls. Two other brick pillars were designed to carry the joists supporting the floor of the ground-floor room above. However, the original joists had been replaced by modern timber beams.

The Eastern Cottage
The building survey recorded the northern, eastern, and southern elevations of the two-bayed Eastern Cottage. The western elevation formed the linking wall to the Western Cottage (Fig 70).

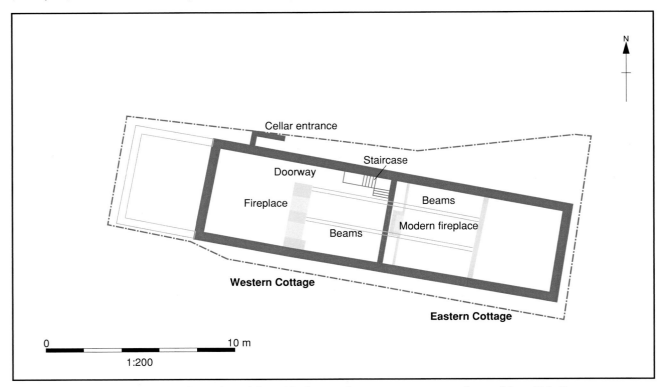

Figure 71: Ground-floor plan of the mid-nineteenth-century cottages at Lower Moss Side Farm

Plate 85: Lower Moss Side Farm: eighteenth-century handmade brick wall with seventeenth-century stone wall below, looking south

The western bay had a single small window in the lower northern elevation, with another of similar dimensions directly above, set close to the eaves. There was also one other small rectangular window on the upper floor of this bay. The eastern bay had two rectangular windows on the ground floor, but none on the upper floor (Pl 82). The eastern elevation contained a square-headed doorway on the ground floor with no windows at that level, but a single rectangular window on the upper floor was in the centre of the elevation (Pl 84). The open-area excavation indicated that the wall forming this elevation was constructed of handmade brick, and had been partly built upon the drystone walling dating to the seventeenth century (Pl 85).

The building survey indicated that the main doorway to the south was in the western side of the eastern bay, with a rectangular window to the east (Pl 84). Above the door was a long rectangular window set high under the eaves. The western bay had two similar long rectangular windows, one on the ground floor, the other on the upper floor close to the eaves. These windows were multi-light, indicating that workshops were present in these parts of the cottage (*p 141*).

No original features remained in the interior of the cottage at the time of the building survey. All remaining features were twentieth-century in date.

The nineteenth-century barn

The barn stood to the east of the cottages (Fig 69), separated by a yard paved with setts, and was recorded as part of the building survey in 2005 (Fig 72). Following its demolition, an open-area trench was excavated across its footprint, although this did not uncover any additional remains to aid the interpretation of its development.

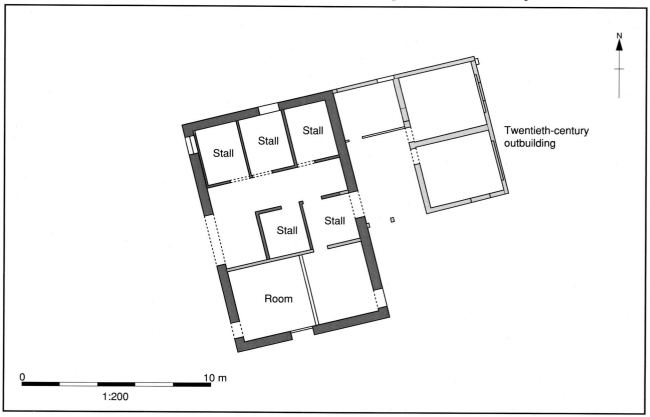

Figure 72: Ground-floor plan of the nineteenth-century barn at Lower Moss Side Farm

Plate 86: Lower Moss Side Farm: reused stone in the eastern interior wall of the barn, probably from a mullioned window

It was a large rectangular, two-storey stone building with an inscribed datestone above its door (*p 145*). An early twentieth-century brick-built outbuilding had also been added to its eastern side, which had been modified in the late twentieth century. Although it is possible that parts of the barn may have been used for threshing, it seems more likely that, during the nineteenth century, it was associated with the keeping of animals. It is also possible that the upper floor functioned as a processing area or workshop.

The stonework of the barn was mainly narrow rectangular hammer-dressed blocks laid to course using a soft lime-rich mortar. Significantly, it was also apparent that it contained reused stone from another building, including long narrow blocks, possibly from the demolished seventeenth-century farmhouse (*Ch 4, p 68*). These reused materials were observed in the northern and eastern elevations of the building (Pl 86).

The northern elevation showed a distinct difference in build at the ground-floor level, where the blocks

Plate 87: Lower Moss Side Farm: the northern and eastern elevations of the barn and brick outbuilding

were slightly wider, with two courses of much larger stones forming a distinctive band just above door height (Pl 87). A single square-headed doorway had a lintel of flat-faced stone and was blocked with machine-made brick. The upper north-eastern corner had quoins of larger blocks; this was the only part of the building with quoins. At the centre of the north gable end, below the apex, was a small opening for birds, perhaps providing a pigeon loft.

Although the eastern elevation was obscured at ground-floor level by the later outbuilding (*above*), a centrally positioned, square-headed ground-floor doorway was visible, with a wooden lintel. The timber was reused from elsewhere and had notches for fittings, and the number '44' engraved on it (Pl 88). This elevation also contained another square-headed doorway, at the south-eastern corner of the building. This had a wooden frame and wooden-planked door that was possibly an original feature (Pl 89). On the upper floor, towards the centre of the eastern elevation, was a tall narrow opening, possibly a window, or taking-in door (Pl 87). This had a wooden slot with a slate base, set in the top of the opening.

The southern gable elevation had a series of beam slots above door height, which had been partially blocked with machine-made brick (Pl 90), indicating that an outbuilding had also originally stood against this elevation. This building is depicted on the first edition 1:2500 OS map (1893a; Fig 69). A square-headed doorway with a wooden lintel was also present on the ground floor of this elevation, although the door surrounds were much damaged and the wall above was collapsing. To the immediate east, a block of stone may indicate where stone door surrounds like those on the western elevation had been removed. In each corner of the gable end were two square-

Plate 88: Lower Moss Side Farm: the underside of a timber used as a lintel for the doorway in the eastern elevation of the barn

Plate 89: Lower Moss Side Farm: the eastern elevation of the barn

first edition 1:2500 (1893a) map. Just below the apex in the centre of the gable was a small bird hole.

The main front, the western elevation, had a central cart entrance with a segmental arch, with a projecting key stone above (Pl 91). This had a date of '186?' or '188?', indicating that the barn was built in either the 1860s or 1880s. The archway had large ashlar surrounds and the remains of a set of double plank doors that may have been original. Two doorways with square heads and ashlar surrounds were towards the ends of the elevation, some of the stone surrounding the southern doorway having been removed.

A ridged roof of graded stone covered the barn, with a small glazed panel in the south-western slope. Internally, it had trusses and collar beams, held in place by iron ties; the whole was typical of the nineteenth century.

Internally, the barn consisted of three (northern, central, and southern) bays and two floors, with no obvious staircase (Fig 72). The cart entrance opened into a space, open to the roof, in the central bay, and was thus for taking in, whilst in the south-west corner, in the southern bay, was a separate room, only accessible by an exterior door in the southern end of the western elevation. The floor of this room was badly damaged, but appeared to have been flagged originally, with brick repairs and modern concrete. Several animal stalls were also present, with three in the northern bay, and two in the central bay, though these were clearly modern additions. The northern and southern bays possessed a first-floor area, both of which would have been accessed from the central bay, via a movable ladder. At the time of the survey, access to the upper floor was not possible, though from the ground-floor area, several damaged partitions were visible that were attached to the trusses.

headed doorways, at first-floor level, with wooden timber surrounds and lintels. Some of these timbers had the same pattern of notches as the lintel of the ground-floor opening on the eastern elevation (*p 144*), and it is possible that these derived from wooden loom frames used in the domestic textile industry, probably from machinery originally housed in the adjacent cottages (*p 140*). To the side of each of these upper doors was a small rectangular slot, possibly intended to take drive belts from a small stationary or traction steam engine that may have been housed in a demolished southern outbuilding shown on the

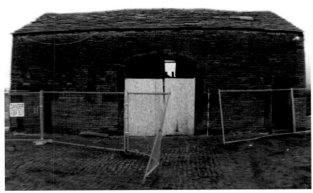

Plate 90: Lower Moss Side Farm: the southern elevation of the barn

Plate 91: Lower Moss Side Farm: the western elevation of the barn

Moss Side hamlet: Moss Side Farm, Higher Moss Side Farm, and Haigh Field

Cartographic evidence indicates that a hamlet existed at Moss Side (centred on SD 9162 1219) by the late eighteenth century. William Yates' map of 1786, for instance, shows a group of four buildings along Moss Side Lane, although the OS first edition map (1850b) shows just three building complexes (Fig 67): Moss Side Farm was on the northern side of Moss Side Lane; Higher Moss Side Farm on the southern side; and Haigh Field to the east of this latter farm. All of these sites were subjected to archaeological investigation, which included excavation at Higher Moss Side Farm and Haigh Field, and also a building survey at Moss Side Farm.

The archaeological excavation at Higher Moss Side Farm indicated that this was probably the earliest element of the hamlet, as it originally was a seventeenth-century farmhouse (Ch 4, p 68). It was also evident from the excavation that this early farmhouse was demolished during the late eighteenth century and replaced by two adjoining cottages, and an adjoining barn. In addition, during this time, a separate weavers' cottage was constructed immediately to the east, which was also excavated. The archaeological investigation and the cartographic evidence suggest that the cottages and barn remained in use during the nineteenth century, and that they were subjected to a series of modifications. By the time of the publication of the second edition OS map (1893a), an outbuilding had also been constructed to the rear of the farm (Fig 73). This was extant at the time of the 1998 archaeological assessment and was noted as being two-storeyed and stone-built (Arrowsmith and Wilson 1998). It had, however, been demolished prior to 2005.

Similarly, the archaeological excavations indicated that Moss Side Farm dated to the late eighteenth century and that it was also subjected to some late eighteenth-century modification. Following this, it continued to be occupied in the nineteenth century, and several additions and extensions were made during this period. Furthermore, during the nineteenth century, a stone barn was constructed, next to the farmhouse (Fig 74), which was recorded during the building survey. The buildings reputedly incorporated a datestone inscribed '1831' (Haynes and Tipper 1994, 48) but since the major elements of the farmhouse were constructed in the eighteenth century, one possibility is that this was associated with the barn (below). The building survey also identified a series of reused timbers that had been incorporated into a twentieth-century agricultural building, which appear to have been derived from an earlier building, possibly this barn. Following demolition, the site of the barn was subjected to open-area excavation.

Haigh Field (SD 9173 1218) originally stood on the south-western side of a small lane, which joined the southern side of Moss Side Lane. At the time of the 1998 archaeological assessment, the farm contained a single extant building, though it was covered by a modern render and also had modern windows (Arrowsmith and Wilson 1998). The building was demolished prior to 2005. Nineteenth-century cartographic evidence indicates that it comprised two adjoining cottages, which the archaeological excavation indicated probably dated to the late eighteenth century.

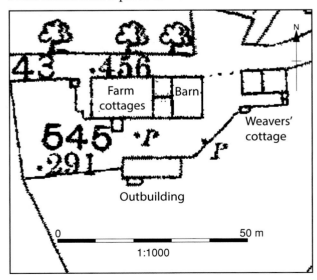

Figure 73: An extract from the OS first edition 1:2500 map (1893), showing Higher Moss Side Farm

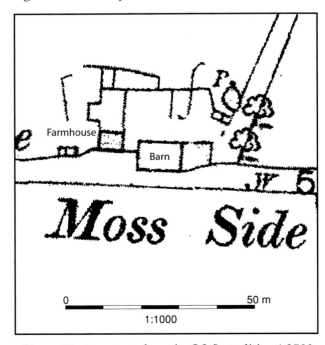

Figure 74: An extract from the OS first edition 1:2500 map (1893), showing Moss Side Farm

Documentary evidence

Moss Side

Documentary sources such as the Census Returns very rarely differentiate between Moss Side Farm, Lower Moss Side, and Higher Moss Side Farm, and even when 'Moss Side Farm' is referenced it is not entirely clear which of the farms this refers to. Similarly, three different properties are listed simply as Moss Side in the Land Tax assessments compiled in July 1790 (LA QDL/S/24). The first of these was occupied by Robert Ashworth and owned by 'Mr Walmsley', and the other two properties were occupied by John Stott and Robert Turner, and owned by Hollows Hamer Esq and Ralph Harrison respectively. The tax on Hollows Hamer's property was 6s 6d, whilst that of Ralph Harrison was only 3s 10d, indicating it to have been a smaller landholding. It seems likely, however, that the latter property was actually Haigh Field (situated a very short distance to the east of Moss Side Farm), as Ralph Harrison is given as the proprietor there in the Land Tax assessment for 1797, with Robert Turner as the occupier (*ibid*). Land Tax assessments compiled in June 1791 similarly list John Stott at Moss Side, although the occupants of other properties in the hamlet are given as James Wild and James Stott, with Richard Townley Esq and Thomas Chadwick as the respective proprietors (*ibid*). James Stott is listed at Moss Side, occupying a property owned by Thomas Chadwick in the Land Tax assessment for 1782, whilst in the same year Samuel Wild is given as the occupant of Richard Townley's property at Moss Side (*ibid*).

An early nineteenth-century reference to Moss Side Farm occurs in a newspaper advertisement of 1823, when 'several valuable freehold and tithe-free farms in the townships of Castleton, Butterworth and Crompton' were advertised for sale in 35 lots. Lot 28 concerned 'a farm called Moss Side in the township of Castleton in the occupation of Benjamin Taylor' (*Manchester Mercury*, 13 May 1823). The Taylor family had been long-established in Castleton, and are mentioned in documents throughout the post-medieval period. In the mid-eighteenth century, for instance, the freehold estates in the parish of Rochdale belonging to the late Samuel Hamer were advertised for sale in a series of lots, including 'two cottages or dwelling houses in the several tenures of Robert Taylor' in Buersill. Another lot comprised 'a messuage and outhouses, with six closes of ground, containing about eleven acres', in the 'possession of widow Butterworth, or her undertenants' (*The Leeds Intelligencer*, 17 April 1764).

The nineteenth-century Census Returns provide a flavour of Moss Side's social composition. The Census Returns for 1841 (NA HO 107/550), for instance, record William Griffiths as a farmer at Moss Side, together with his wife and two adolescent children. William Slater, a 20-year-old agricultural labourer, is also recorded as part of the Griffiths' household. Other farmers at Moss Side listed in the 1841 Census include Mary Taylor and her two daughters, Edward Taylor (occupying a separate dwelling with his family), Ann Stott, and Richard Whitaker. The occupation of the heads of five other families recorded at Moss Side is given as weaver, including a John Butterworth.

The detail provided by the Castleton township plan of 1844 (Pl 92) and its accompanying schedule (RLSL LA/Z/3/C; LA/Z/3/C/2) provides some clarification, and shows that the heart of the Moss Side hamlet comprised two groups of buildings. That on the south side of Moss Side Lane (Plot 2010; referred to as Higher Moss Side Farm) comprised a farmhouse and attached agricultural building, with two detached cottages to the east, and a small detached farm building to the south, with a pump in the central farmyard. Thomas Wilson Hardwin is identified as the owner, and Richard Whittaker and others as the occupiers. The property is described as 'houses, buildings, garden and yard'. On the opposite side of the lane is another farmhouse and detached agricultural building (Plot 2004; known as Moss Side Farm), described as 'houses, building, garden and yard', owned by John Chadwick and occupied by Ann Stott.

Situated across several fields to the north was another farm complex, identified as 'Middle Moss Side' (Plot 1299; now referred to as Lower Moss Side Farm), which had a farmhouse, and attached agricultural building, together with a detached cottage to the north. The schedule identifies the site as 'Middle Moss Side House, buildings, garden and field', which was in the ownership of Richard Holford Holt and occupied by Edmund Taylor. Higher Moss Side Farm is shown on the 1844 township plan to the north of the Rochdale Canal and beyond the area of the later Kingsway Business Park; Richard Holford Holt is also given as the landowner, whilst William Griffiths is named in the schedule as the occupant.

The Census Returns for 1861 (NA RG 9/3035) similarly give Moss Side Farm as the residence of several families. These include William Griffiths from Clitheroe, described as a 56-year-old farmer of 14 acres, who occupied the farm with his wife, grandson, and two lodgers; based on the information from the 1844 township schedule, it seems likely that Griffiths and his family lived at Higher Moss Side, to the north of the Rochdale Canal. Another building was occupied by Thomas Shephard, a farmer of 18

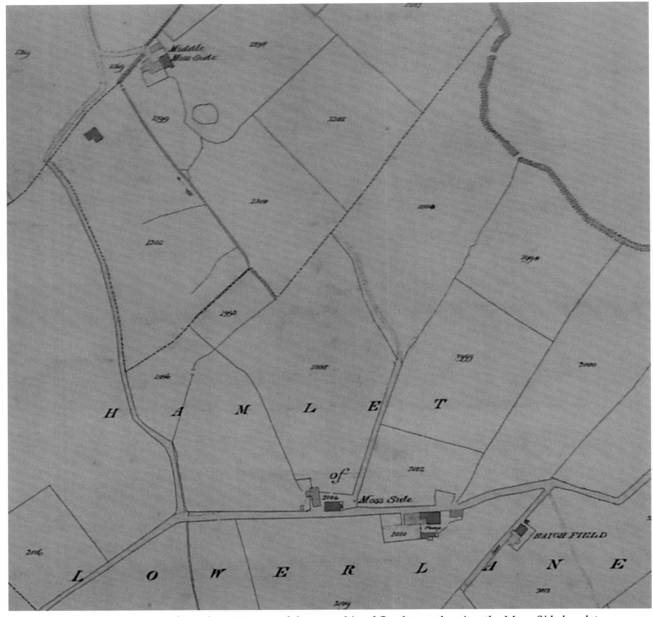

Plate 92: An extract from the 1844 map of the township of Castleton, showing the Moss Side hamlet

acres, together with his wife and 20-year-old son, who was employed as a book-keeper.

Edmund Taylor from Heywood is also recorded in the 1861 Census Returns as a farmer at Moss Side Farm, responsible for 18 acres (*ibid*); it is probable that this was Middle Moss Side. He occupied the farm with his wife, Martha, who was originally from the Spotland area of Rochdale. There were several members of the wider Taylor family residing in Moss Side during this period, including James Taylor, who is described as a 'manufacturer' in a notice published in 1859, advertising the marriage of his daughter, Ann, to Mr Abraham Turner of Dearnley (*The Leeds Times*, 13 August 1859). Similarly, John Taylor, a farmer of Moss Side in Castleton, is mentioned in a newspaper article that describes a burglary in

1840. The 'bad character' was apprehended in the farmhouse, and also confessed to having committed a burglary at Haigh Field (*Manchester Courier*, 27 June 1840).

Richard Whittaker is another farmer listed at Moss Side Farm, with a land holding of 36 acres. Whittaker probably lived in the farmhouse referred to subsequently as Higher Moss Side Farm, situated on the south side of Moss Side Lane. Richard was originally from Grindleton, near Clitheroe in the Ribble Valley, but appears to have lived in Bolton, where his wife and 27-year-old daughter were born, before moving to the Castleton area. He also shared the house with his two grand-daughters and an 18-year-old male servant. The Whittaker family is also recorded in the 1851 Census Returns

(NA HO 107/2244), which lists Richard Whittaker's 20-year-old son as an agricultural labourer, although he had evidently moved by 1861. A separate house was occupied by John Whittaker, probably a relative, who was also employed as an agricultural labourer.

In addition, Edmund Brierley is listed at Moss Side Farm, with 'farm labourer' given as his occupation. Thomas Bellfield, sharing a house at Moss Side Farm with his widowed mother, is also described as an agricultural labourer.

Other occupants of Moss Side in 1861 that were not engaged directly in agriculture were Thomas Howarth, a calico block-printer from Oakenshaw, Anthony Hailwood, a retired block-printer who originated from Liverpool, and John Lambert, a coal miner from Wakefield, who shared a house with a 52-year-old female servant (NA RG 9/3035). Another resident of Moss Side in 1861 was John Metcalfe, a 63-year-old handloom woollen weaver, a survivor of a rapidly disappearing traditional skilled occupation that had been supplanted by mechanisation. This trend is exemplified by the Farrow family, which also lived in Moss Side. John Farrow, his wife Hannah, and five of their eight children all worked in textile factories, variously as woollen spinners, woollen piecers, and woollen and cotton weavers.

The 1871 Census Returns (NA RG 10/4116) record the households of eight separate houses at Moss Side, and show that few of the occupants recorded at Moss Side in 1861 remained. The Whittaker family were still farmers, with the largest landholding of 30 acres, although the farm was then being run by Mary, Richard Whittaker's widow, together with her grandson and grand-daughter. The family evidently enjoyed a level of relative affluence, as they employed a 'farm servant' and a 'domestic servant', who also lived in the farmhouse. John Whittaker, the agricultural labourer listed in the earlier Census Returns, appears in the 1871 Returns as an 'outdoor labourer'. Several other residents of Moss Side were occupied as farm labourers, although a John Butterworth and his wife were both listed as cotton weavers, presumably in a local mill.

The 1881 Census Returns show some changes to the socio-economic status of the residents of Moss Side, and indicate that there had been a slight reduction in the number of households to eight families (NA RG 11/4103). James Whittaker, originally from the Ribble Valley, had taken over the responsibility of farming the family's 30 acres, together with his wife, son, and daughter. The other farmer at Moss Side at this date was Benjamin Hurst, who was responsible for 14 acres, together with his wife. Two of his children, however, appear to have

been employed in a woollen mill, whilst a third was described as an apprentice boiler-maker. The members of the other five households in the Moss Side hamlet were all engaged in the local factory-based woollen and cotton industries. The Census Returns for 1891 similarly record seven households at Moss Side (NA RG 12/3329), two of which resided as Moss Side Farm. The farmers were the Green and the Kershaw families, whilst all the other residents worked in local textile factories.

By 1901, Moss Side Farm was occupied by Abraham Houldsworth and his wife Hannah, who had both been born in Aden Hildwick, Yorkshire (NA RG 13/3833). The Census gives farming as Abraham's occupation, and the Returns also provide explicit reference to Higher Moss Side Farm. These indicate that, by 1901, this was occupied by William Dawson, a 48-year-old farmer from Yorkshire, and his 42-year-old wife from Shropshire. They had clearly lived in the local area for some time as all of their six children, with ages ranging from four to 18 years old, had been born in Rochdale. William is listed as an employer, implying that he paid labourers to assist with the running of the farm, one of whom lived at Higher Moss Side (ibid). With the exception of one of his daughters, who worked as a cotton weaver, none of the children had an occupation listed in the Census, suggesting that they also worked on the farm.

Entries in early twentieth-century trade directories suggest that only a few of the farms in the area were still occupied by farmers. Amongst those listed in a directory for 1907, however, is Moss Side Farm, which was still occupied by Abraham Houldsworth (Clegg 1907, 126). Haynes and Tipper (1994, 48) provide some details relating to the twentieth-century history of the farm, suggesting that there was a fire in 1914, although precisely which building this affected is uncertain. They further indicate that this farm was occupied during the latter half of the twentieth century by the Halliwell family, who farmed cattle and ran a wholesale meat business from the premises (ibid). Intriguingly, they also allude to a block of three, three-storey weavers' cottages that was demolished in the 1970s after being damaged by fire, and note that there were two other cottages, one-up and one-down, that were knocked through, but still retained their original stairs (ibid). It has not been possible to locate these cottages within the Moss Side hamlet, though.

Haigh Field
The documentary sources do not provide any firm evidence for the origins of Haigh Field, although a building in its approximate position is shown on William Yates' map of 1786. The cottage appears

to be listed in the Land Tax assessment for 1780, which identifies Robert Turner as the occupier and Mr Harrison as the proprietor (LA QDL/S/24); the same entries occur in the Land Tax assessment for 1797 (*ibid*). Turner also appears in the Land Tax assessment for 1790, and whilst he is named as the occupier of a property owned by Ralph Harrison at Moss Side, it seems likely that this entry actually refers to Haigh Field. The property's tax assessment rate was 3s 10d, indicating that it was relatively small (*ibid*).

Haigh Field seems to be depicted on Greenwood's survey of 1818 and Hennet's map of 1830, although the detail provided by these is far from clear. The earliest detailed plans of the building are provided by the Castleton township plan of 1844 (RLSL LA/Z/3/C) and the OS first edition map (1850b). These show a short linear range comprising two adjoining cottages, accessed via a short track leading off Moss Side Lane. The schedule accompanying the township plan describes the property as 'Hagg Field, house, building, yard and occupation road', owned by Thomas Wilson Hardwin, and occupied by Richard Whittaker and others (RLSL LA/Z/3/C/2).

By the mid-nineteenth century, Haigh Field was occupied by Alexander McEwan, who is listed in the Census Returns for 1851 (NA HO 107/2244) as a civil engineer, with no indication that he was involved in any textile- or agricultural-related occupations. He was 33 years old at the time of the Census, and had been born in Wigan. His 35-year-old wife, Sarah, was also from outside the local area, having been born in Manchester. In the same year, however, Alexander was declared insolvent, the printed notice describing him as a 'civil engineer and coal proprietor' (*Lancaster Gazette*, 4 October 1851). This seems to hint that McEwan had interests in the small-scale local coal-mining industry, though this may have been a subsidiary occupation as he also, in partnership with William Lancaster, worked as an engineer and millwright at the Horrock's Works in Blackburn (*Blackburn Standard*, 8 October 1851). McEwan appears to have left Haigh Field shortly afterwards, and is listed in the Census Returns for 1861 as a 'director of mines', residing in the Piccadilly area of Manchester. The 1851 Census Returns do not record any occupants of a second cottage at Haigh Field (NA HO 107/2244).

By 1861, Haigh Field was occupied by Joseph Butterworth, a 62-year-old agricultural labourer from Heywood in Lancashire, together with his two daughters and three sons (NA RG 9/3035). The eldest daughter, aged 37, is also listed as an agricultural labourer, whilst his three sons (with ages ranging from 14 to 18) were all employed as power-loom cotton weavers, presumably in local mills.

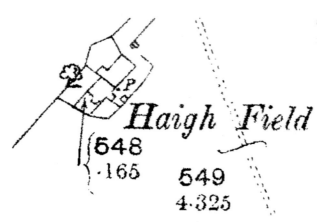

Plate 93: An extract from the OS first edition 1:2500 map (1893), showing Haigh Field

The Census Returns for 1861 also show that the adjacent cottage at Haigh Field was occupied by Thomas Clegg, a 29-year-old labourer in an iron foundry, together with his 26-year-old wife, Sarah, who was employed as a power-loom cotton weaver (*ibid*). Both were of local origin; Thomas had been born in Butterworth, and Sarah in Castleton. It is possible, although unconfirmed, that Clegg worked at the large St George's Foundry, on the north bank of the Rochdale Canal, *c* 1 km to the north-west of Haigh Field. It is notable that none of the residents of Haigh Field in the early 1860s were employed in the domestic textile industry.

Joseph Butterworth was still residing at Haigh Field in 1871 (NA RG 10/4116), together with his two daughters and youngest son, who was employed as a cotton weaver. There are no records pertaining to the adjacent cottage, suggesting that it may have been uninhabited. The Census Returns for 1891 similarly record just a single family at Haigh Field, comprising William Parkinson (a 46-year-old railway goods porter), his wife, and two children (NA RG 12/3329). His 20-year-old son was a general labourer and his 19-year-old daughter was employed in a cotton mill.

Haigh Field is annotated on the first edition 1:2500 OS map (1893a), although it is difficult to establish whether the footprint of the buildings is different from that shown on the first edition six-inch map (OS 1850b). The 1893 map clearly shows Haigh Field as comprising two adjoining buildings (Pl 93), although only a single family was living there in 1901. This was William Parkinson, a railway worker from Milnrow, and his wife Martha, also from Milnrow (NA RG 13/3833).

Archaeological investigations at Moss Side Farm: building survey and excavation
A late eighteenth-century weavers' cottage? (Phase 2a)
Following the silting of an early eighteenth-century ditch (*Ch 4, p 70*), a levelling layer (**86**),

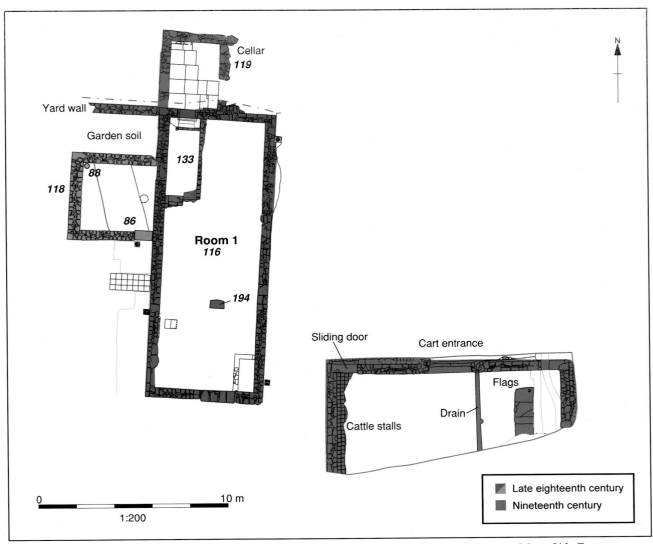

Figure 75: The late eighteenth- and nineteenth-century cottage and warehouse/barn at Moss Side Farm

was deposited before the construction of Moss Side Farm (Fig 75). This contained numerous fragments of pottery with an extended currency, dating anywhere in the seventeenth and eighteenth centuries, and also a fragment of clay tobacco-pipe, which dates to the mid-late eighteenth century (Table 8). This later item therefore provides a *terminus post quem* for the construction of the building, implying that it dated to the latter half of the eighteenth century; on balance, a late eighteenth-century date seems most likely.

This building was surveyed and there was also an open-area excavation following its demolition. It is clear from both that the main body of the building was one bay wide and three bays long, measuring 17 x 7 m. It was two storeyed, and the excavation indicated that the external walls of the main range had an average width of 0.6 m and consisted of dressed drystone blocks, encasing a rubble core, which had been arranged in a fairly regular fashion.

The building survey indicated that the eastern elevation was the front, with a doorway at the southern end of the northern bay, and two small rectangular windows on the ground floor to the north of the door. Above these was a single, wide rectangular window set close under the eaves, whilst the central bay had a single ground-floor window with two wide rectangular windows in the floor above. These upper windows had proportions reminiscent of the multi-light mullioned windows of weavers' cottages, indicating that the building may have been used for this purpose, with a workshop on the first floor. The southern bay was partially obscured by a roofed-over area linking to a later stone barn (*p 153*), and only one rectangular window on the ground floor was visible.

The rear western elevation was partly obscured by a later extension, which probably also dated to the eighteenth century (*p 152*). To the north, on the ground floor, was a single rectangular window, and above this was a long rectangular window set close under the eaves, presumably once a multi-light

Pottery	Date	Clay tobacco-pipe
Everted-rim globular jar, high-fired purplish-brown-glazed purple earthenware	Seventeenth-eighteenth century	Clay tobacco-pipe with wide bore, flat spur, and bulbous bowl (mid-late eighteenth century)
Yellow-glazed cream-coloured earthenware tankard (?) with red slip-trailed decoration	Seventeenth-eighteenth century	
Red slip-coated cream-coloured earthenware dish with white slip-trailed alternating motifs	Seventeenth-eighteenth century	
Fine cup (?) rims, yellow-glazed cream-coloured earthenware with trailed and combed red and white slip on exterior	Seventeenth-eighteenth century	
Yellow-glazed red slip-decorated lid (?) rim	Seventeenth-eighteenth century	
Trailed and combed slip-decorated hollow-ware vessel	Seventeenth-eighteenth century	
Yellow-ware press-moulded dish (?) with moulded circular motifs	Seventeenth-eighteenth century	
Fine black-glazed red earthenware cup (?)	Seventeenth-early twentieth century	

*Table 8: Stratified post-medieval artefacts from levelling layer **86**, Moss Side Farm*

mullioned window, whilst the central bay had a similar arrangement. The southern bay had two wide rectangular windows, one on each floor, although the upper window was set at a lower level than the upper windows of the central and northern bays.

The northern gable elevation was blind, except for a single large rectangular window on the ground floor at the western end, probably a modern insertion. Similarly, two modern bay windows had been inserted into the southern elevation. However, there was a small rectangular window on the upper floor, which may have been an original feature.

All the internal features recorded by the building survey were modern, apart from some potentially original roof beams, visible in the upper rooms. These included two very roughly hewn irregularly shaped timbers, which appeared to be little more than roughly dressed tree trunks chamfered along their lower edges. They were visible in the central and northern bays, parallel with and adjacent to the front of the house. Significantly, the form of these beams suggest that they pre-dated the eighteenth century, and it is quite possible that they were reused from an earlier building. Other, smoother, timber beams were visible parallel and adjacent to the rear of the building in all of the bays.

Some further evidence for the arrangement of the late eighteenth-century building was revealed during the excavation. This included the base for a fireplace (*194*), which heated either the southern or central bay.

Late eighteenth-century extension (Phase 2b)
Later in the eighteenth century, an extension (*118*), 5 x 4.5 m, was added to the west side of Moss Side Farm. Its external walls were 0.6 m wide and were constructed of drystone blocks (Pl 94), and each of its elevations contained a single window, all with modern window frames. A complete kitchenware storage jar (*88*; Fig 75), of probable eighteenth-century date, was discovered close to the north-west corner.

Late nineteenth-century additions and modifications to the cottage
Several fairly major modifications were made to the northern end of the cottage in the latter part of the nineteenth century. These may have been undertaken to convert it into a farmhouse, which also included the conversion of a nearby outbuilding (possibly a small warehouse) into a barn (*p 153*). One of these modifications involved the construction of a small extension on the northern elevation. This is first depicted on the first edition 1:2500 OS map (1893a); it was demolished in the early twentieth century, and hence its remains were only identified during the open-area excavation.

These comprised a cellar (*119*), with drystone walls (Fig 75), those to the east and west containing alcoves, whilst the north wall had a large flat flagstone near the existing ground surface, which may have been a sill for an original cellar light. The floor was composed of flagstones, at a depth of 1.9 m below the existing ground surface. There were also traces of two parallel brick piers, against the west wall, which may well have supported a stone table top. Access to the cellar

152

Plate 94: Moss Side Farm: the excavated external walls of the late eighteenth-century extension, looking east

was via a steep stairway constructed of flagstones and handmade bricks, which were contained within a substantial construction cut (Pl 95). The cellar beneath the northern bay was abandoned in the twentieth century and backfilled with material that contained pottery from the 1930s (*Appendix 4*). The steps down into the cellar were also blocked by the insertion of a new brick wall, which was butted by flagstones.

Another modification, which was probably added at the same time as this extension, involved the construction of a partially sunken room (*133*) within the north-western corner of the eighteenth-century cottage, directly opposite the stairs into the cellar. This measured *c* 4.8 x 2 m, was defined on its eastern side by a narrow stone wall, and appears to have contained a flagstone floor (Pl 96).

Another probably contemporary structure was an east/west-aligned wall footing that extended westwards from the northern elevation. This probably enclosed a yard.

An early nineteenth-century warehouse/workshop?
A stone barn to the east was first depicted on the first edition six-inch OS map (1850b), and it may have been erected in 1831, based on the presence of the datestone (*p 146*). Another possibility, however, is that this building was originally constructed as a small warehouse/workshop area, given the adjacent weaver's cottage, that was later converted into an agricultural building.

The building survey indicated that originally it was two-storeyed, though it had been reduced in height

and considerably altered in the late nineteenth or early twentieth century. The partial footprint of this building was also subject to excavation.

Its external walls were constructed of drystone blocks, with an average width of 0.5 m (Pl 97). Although it was only possible to record the building's northern and southern elevations, as the other two were obscured by brick outbuildings dating to the twentieth century, it was evident that it may have originally contained a cart entrance on the north side. This was visible as a large opening to the full height of the building, which had been much altered in the late nineteenth or early twentieth century, perhaps when it was converted to an agricultural building. As part of these later alterations, a wooden sliding door had been added to the north-western corner of the building, which gave access to a low room containing two cattle stalls. A circular window may also have been inserted when the roof was lowered, perhaps originally an owl hole or for hay. The southern elevation was constructed of rectangular ashlar blocks, and also contained evidence for a cart entrance with a depressed arch, which had been blocked with machine-made bricks. Internally, there was also a small rectangular opening or recess blocked with machine-made brick.

Two cattle stalls were present at its western end, which had been added in the late nineteenth or early twentieth century (*above*). Traces of an earlier doorway and at least one small blocked rectangular opening were observed on the western wall of the building, features associated with the early nineteenth-century structure. The excavation uncovered an internal flagged surface at its eastern end, and an absence of

Plate 95: Moss Side Farm: the cellar steps, looking south-east

*Plate 96: Moss Side Farm: sunken room **133**, looking south-east*

Plate 97: Moss Side Farm: foundations of the barn, looking north-east

internal partitioning, which may suggest that the early nineteenth-century building possessed an open plan.

Although at the time of the survey there was no roof, it was apparent that the surviving roof timbers were a later addition, presumably when the building was reduced in height (*p 153*). These consisted of massive timber trusses set in the walls and sloping towards the south. Some of the main timbers also had shallow round recesses partially drilled into two sides of the beam, possibly to reduce the weight of the timbers.

It is quite possible, however, that when the building was reduced in height, building materials were removed and then reused within another agricultural structure. For instance, a twentieth-century cattle shed to the north of the farm contained an unusual roof of latticed timber struts that may well have originally derived from the barn. The large timber pillars supporting the roof also came from elsewhere, as these appeared to have been cut-down floor trusses, with the sockets for the floor joists clearly visible. It is possible that these may originally have been part of an upper floor that had been removed from the early nineteenth-century stone building, as part of a scheme of modification in the early part of the twentieth century.

Archaeological excavation at Higher Moss Side Farm
The late eighteenth-century buildings
During the late eighteenth century, the early farmhouse at Higher Moss Side Farm was demolished and replaced by a 'new' building complex (Fig 76), which was largely constructed in stone. The excavation uncovered the ground plan of this complex and

its construction date was partly confirmed by the discovery of a shallow square pit (*43*), which was cut by one of the internal walls (*64*; Pl 98). This pit contained fragments of clay tobacco-pipe, dating to 1784, which provides a *terminus post quem* for the construction of this wall and, in turn, the late eighteenth-century building.

The complex had a rectangular plan, measuring 31.5 x 11.5 m, and appears to have comprised two adjoining cottages (Pl 99), with an attached building that probably functioned as a barn. The two cottages were at the western end of the range and together they occupied an area measuring approximately 11.5 m square. They were built in stone (walls *60*, *61*, and *69*), set in regular horizontal faced courses, with a rubble and sandy mortar core, showing some slight variation in constructional style. The northern wall (*60*), for example, was the most substantial and better-constructed, and formed the front elevation of the cottages. It was *c* 0.6 m thick and in the east had a well-dressed exterior, with some peck-marked stones. In contrast, the eastern (*69*), western (*61*), and southern (*61*) walls were more poorly dressed. The internal partition wall (*57*) was *c* 0.45 m thick and was also constructed of stone.

Both cottages had comparable ground plans, consisting of two identically sized rooms at ground-floor level (Rooms 1, 4, 8, and 9). Those at the front were the larger, each measuring *c* 7 x 5 m, and were probably the living rooms/kitchens. Each contained a fireplace (*154* and *155*) on the eastern wall. These fireplaces were defined by a *c* 1 m-square sunken hearth, with that in the eastern cottage (Room 1)

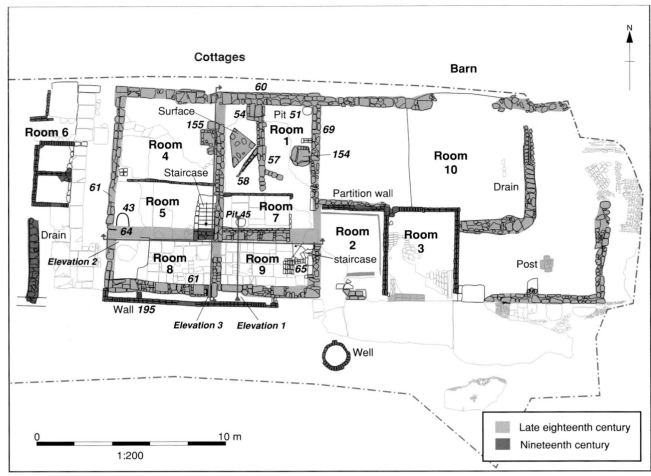

Figure 76: The late eighteenth- and nineteenth-century cottages and barn at Higher Moss Side Farm

being constructed of stone, whilst that to the west (Room 4) was of handmade brick. On either side of the hearths were the remains of the walls supporting the chimney breasts, constructed in both handmade brick and stone.

Several additional features and deposits were also present in the front room (Room 1) of the eastern cottage. These comprised the remnants of a surface composed of small stones, set in a matrix of silty sand, forming a bedding layer for a flagstone floor, and an arrangement of shallow stone-built drainage channels (*58*). These all fed into a square stone soak-away (*54*), which contained a reused stone roof tile at its base; this might conceivably have been derived from the earlier farmhouse.

This room also contained two slightly more unusual features, which appear to have been associated with the intentional placement of specific objects. One was a small shallow pit (*45*) close to the western wall, *c* 0.6 m from its south-western corner. This contained several objects, probably of late eighteenth-century date, including fragments of two near-complete ceramic vessels, a clay tobacco-pipe fragment, and a worn copper-alloy Georgian-era coin. The other

feature was also a pit (*51*), though this was larger in size and had been dug in the north-east corner of the room. This contained copper-alloy pins, a copper-alloy button, a bovine vertebra, two gunflints, and fragments of eighteenth-century pottery.

At the rear of each of the cottages was a smaller room, each measuring *c* 5 x 4.5 m, probably pantries, beneath which was a cellar (Rooms 8 and 9; Fig 77; Pl 100). The cellar associated with the western cottage was accessed via a stone-walled staircase from the living

Plate 98: Higher Moss Side Farm: pit 43 cut by wall 64, looking south

Plate 99: Higher Moss Side Farm: the late eighteenth-century cottages, looking east

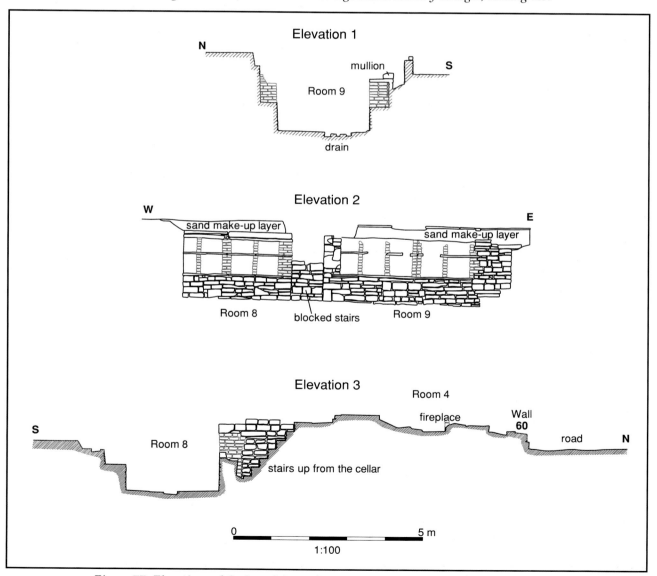

Figure 77: Elevations of the late eighteenth-century cottages at Higher Moss Side Farm

Plate 100: Higher Moss Side Farm: cellar Rooms 8 and 9, looking east

Plate 101: Higher Moss Side Farm: steps leading down into cellar Room 8, looking north

room/kitchen area (Room 4), containing stone stair treads supported by handmade brick (Pl 101). In contrast, access to the cellar in the eastern cottage was via a curving brick- and stone-built staircase directly from the pantry area (Pl 102).

Each cellar had a flagstone floor, interspersed with handmade brick, whilst the walls contained several recesses, which were presumably used for cold storage, all of comparable form. The northern wall within the western cottage (Room 8) contained four recesses, whilst that in the adjacent cellar (Room 9) contained five (Pl 103). In both instances, these were constructed of handmade brick, with stone lintels, and each recess contained a lower and upper stone shelf. In addition, the western and southern walls of both contained two brick-built recesses, although these only contained a lower stone shelf. A stone chute was also present between the alcoves on the southern wall of the eastern cellar (Room 9), though the precise function of this was not clear.

Each cellar was probably also provided with a cellar light on the southern external wall. Clear evidence for this was found in the eastern cellar, where the base of a stone-mullioned window was discovered *in situ* on top of the lintel of the westernmost of the alcoves (Pl 104). This was a chamfered mullion, typical of the seventeenth century (*cf* Miller 2002, 158), and almost certainly derived from the seventeenth-century farm that appears to have been present prior to the construction of the late eighteenth-century cottages (*Ch 4, p 70*).

A rectangular building (Room 10) was attached to the cottages, measuring *c* 20 x 11.5 m (Fig 76). This was probably the 'ruined barn' mentioned by Haynes and Tipper (1994, 49), which was extant in 1998 (Arrowsmith and Wilson 1998). The external wall was constructed of poorly coursed stone blocks and had an average width of 0.5 m. Breaks were noted in the northern and eastern walls, implying that access may have been through one or both of these walls. Further support for the presence of an entrance in the eastern wall was provided by a stone-sett surface, which spanned the break.

Several features which might have been original were identified, including a *c* 5 m-long, east/west-orientated stone wall, which created a 7 m-wide partitioned area at the south-western corner, an L-shaped sandstone drain, and a compacted layer of clinker, which probably formed a floor. In addition, a square-cut pit, with a square central void lined with stones, was present that probably secured a timber upright at the corner, presumably for a roof support. Immediately to the south, a flag and cobble surface was uncovered abutting its southern wall, seemingly a yard associated with the late eighteenth-century farm. A comparable surface was also present immediately to the west of the cottages.

Plate 102: Higher Moss Side Farm: steps leading down into cellar Room 9, looking east

Plate 103: Higher Moss Side Farm: the alcoves within cellar Rooms 8 and 9, looking north-west

Plate 104: Higher Moss Side Farm: the reused stone-mullioned window in the south wall of cellar Room 9, looking south

160

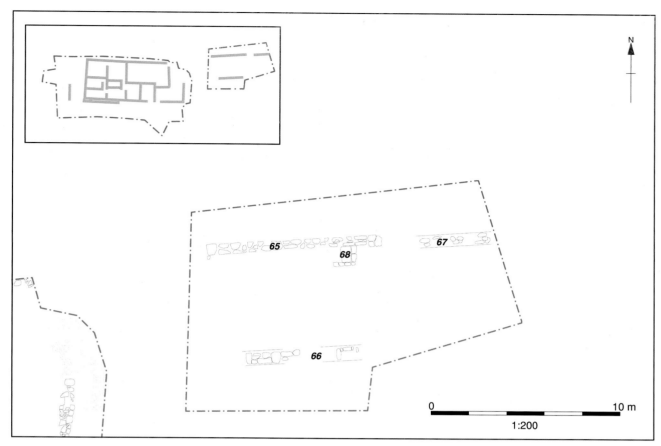

Figure 78: The late eighteenth-century weaver's cottage at Higher Moss Side Farm

It is likely that the cottage situated to the east of the farm (Fig 78) was constructed at a similar, late eighteenth-century date, particularly as there were close similarities in the materials used in, and the style of, its construction. It is also possible that this cottage formed a 'loom-weaving shed' mentioned by Haynes and Tipper (1994, 49) and was thus a small weaver's cottage. The surviving remains, although limited, indicated that it was 7 m wide, its external walls (**65** and **66**) being composed of stone, of a similar coarse construction to those associated with the farm. The only other feature was a doorstep (**68**) on its northern wall.

Nineteenth-century modifications

Several structures were identified during the excavation, which were clearly modifications of the two adjoining late eighteenth-century cottages (Fig 76). These included the insertion of single-skin brick-built partition walls to divide the former living room/kitchen at the front of each cottage. These additional rooms separated the front of the dwelling from the former pantry at its rear. The new room (Room 5) in the western cottage measured 4 x 2.5 m and was accessed through a doorway at the western end of the partition wall. The room (Room 7) in the eastern cottage was slightly smaller in size, measuring 3.05 x 1.8 m, and was defined by

both an east/west- and north/south partition wall, which created a short corridor to the east, which accessed Room 7 through a *c* 1 m-wide doorway. A stone flag floor within the new room was set upon a yellow sand bedding layer. Other minor nineteenth-century alterations included the slight remodelling of the fireplace (**155**) in the western cottage, and the insertion of a stone table in the cellar (Room 9) of the eastern cottage, which was supported by a brick pillar. It also seems that the stairs leading to the cellar in the western cottage were blocked with a stone wall during this period, indicating that this, and perhaps also the adjacent cellar, were no longer used. Further support for this was supplied by modifications to the external southern wall of the cellars. These comprised the construction of a two-course-thick brick wall (**195**), which effectively blocked the light wells.

Nineteenth-century modifications were also made to the presumed barn attached to the cottages. These were the construction of two right-angled lengths of walling in handmade brick, which created two adjacent rooms (Rooms 2 and 3) at the south-western corner. These replaced the earlier partitioned area (*p 159*) and both had near-identical dimensions, measuring some 4.8 x 3.8 m. Although their function(s) could not be ascertained, it is likely

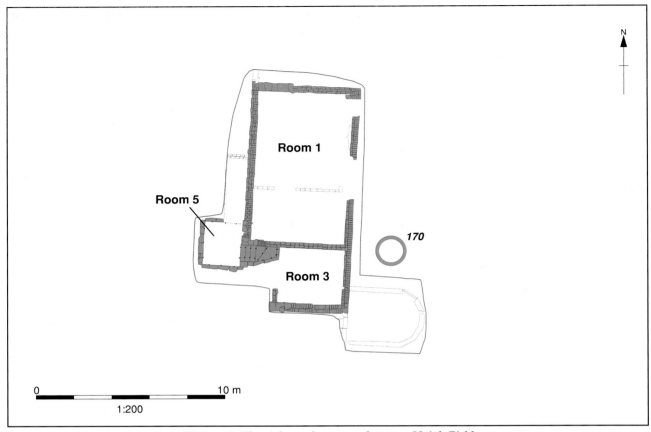

Figure 79: The eighteenth-century house at Haigh Field

that they were used for storage. A stone-sett floor in Room 3 incorporated a carved stone drain at the room's south-eastern corner.

Several structures were also identified in the surrounding area that may date to the nineteenth century. These included a brick-lined well to the south and a small rectangular outbuilding (Room 6). This was mainly constructed in brick, though its northern wall was of stone, and it was subdivided into two small, 1.6 m-wide, bays by a brick partition wall. Whilst it is possible that the outbuilding was for storage, it is perhaps more likely that it contained two nineteenth-century privies, serving the inhabitants of the cottages. Indeed, this may explain the presence of a stone-capped drain which extended in a north-south direction.

Archaeological excavation at Haigh Field

An area roughly L-shaped in plan, with maximum dimensions of 18 x 15 m north-east/south-west, was stripped during excavation, which revealed the partial footprint of the cottages at Haigh Field (Fig 79). The structural remains largely comprised stretches of drystone walling, acting as the foundations for handmade brick walls. Together, these defined the complete footprint of the northernmost of the two cottages, and the northern end of the adjoining cottage. The northernmost comprised, at ground-floor level, a single room (Room 1; Pl 105), *c* 8.5 x 5.5 m. Part of its original floor was also encountered, composed of flagstones. No other early features were present in this area.

In contrast, the southern cottage contained two rooms, the northernmost of which (Room 3) was within the excavation. This measured *c* 3 x 5.5 m and had a short handmade brick wall projecting northwards from its southern wall, perhaps the remains of a fireplace. The original design of the building also included a small stone-built cellar (Room 5), which could be accessed via a flight of stairs from the north-western corner of Room 3

Plate 105: Haigh Field: Room 1, looking east

162

Plate 106: Haigh Field: cellar Room 5, looking east

(Pl 106). The stairs had sandstone treads, mounted on stone bases, whilst the stone walls of the cellar enclosed a relatively small area, measuring a mere 2.2 x 2 m. There was evidence of sandstone slabs forming work surfaces 0.38 m above the floor, occupying all sides of the cellar apart from the south-east corner. Significantly, a single fragment of seventeenth-/eighteenth-century pottery was recovered from the backfill (**174**) of the construction cut for the southern wall, which provides both a *termimus post quem* for the construction of the cellar and also the other structural elements of the building (*Appendix 4*). Based on this sherd, and given the form and materials used in the construction, it is likely that the building was erected in the late eighteenth century. The only other feature which might have been contemporary with the early building was a circular stone-built well (**170**), immediately to the east.

The excavation also uncovered cursory evidence for late nineteenth-century activity, principally the backfilling of the small cellar (Room 5). The only post-eighteenth-century remains revealed were lengths of machine-made brick walling, which had been used to repair the eastern wall and to divide the ground-floor of the northern cottage into two rooms. It was also used to construct a conservatory on the rear of the property. These alterations undoubtedly date to the twentieth century.

7

LATE EIGHTEENTH- AND NINETEENTH-CENTURY LANDSCAPES 2: KINGSWAY BUSINESS PARK - LOWER LANE AND MOOR BANK LANE

Richard A Gregory, Ian Miller, and Michael Nevell

The late eighteenth- and nineteenth-century properties subjected to archaeological investigation along, or accessed from, Lower Lane and Moor Bank Lane (Fig 80) are considered below. As with the properties along Moss Side Lane (*Ch 6*), these included houses and agricultural buildings, and also several semi-domestic properties that functioned as weavers' cottages.

The Lower Lane Properties

Lower Lane Hamlet: Lower Lane Farm, Cherry Tree Farm, and Wychenley Cottage

Both Lower Lane Farm and Cherry Tree Farm, which had been established in the post-medieval period as the principal dwellings in the Lower Lane hamlet (*Ch 4, p 70*), were occupied continually throughout the late eighteenth and nineteenth centuries. At Lower Lane Farm, following the extensive rebuilding of the seventeenth-century house in the mid-eighteenth century (*Ch 4, p 74*), a cottage was built in 1793 (*p 169*), abutting the earlier building. During the nineteenth century, the post-medieval farmhouse and cottage were subjected to some minor modifications, and a shippon, or cow house, was built to the north, probably in the mid-nineteenth century (Fig 81). This building was extant in 2005 and a limited building survey was carried out, given its bad state of repair. Following its demolition, its footings were also exposed by an open-area excavation.

The cartographic sources indicate that during the nineteenth century several additions/modifications

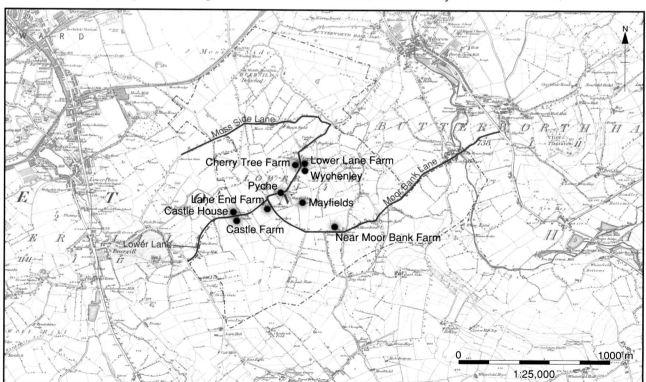

Figure 80: The southern sites within the Kingsway Business Park, occupied in the eighteenth and nineteenth centuries, superimposed on the OS first edition six-inch map (1850)

165

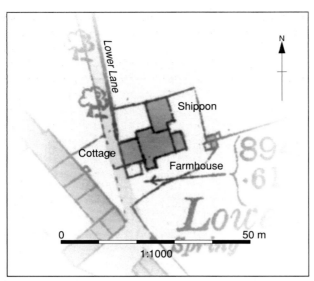

Figure 81: An extract from the OS first edition 1:2500 map (1893), showing Lower Lane Farm

were also made to the seventeenth- or eighteenth-century stone-built farmhouse and barn at Cherry Tree Farm (*Ch 4, p 77*). For instance, the first edition OS map (1850b) demonstrates that this linear complex was extended at both its south-eastern and north-western ends (Pl 107), and the documentary and archaeological investigations indicates that these functioned as two adjoining cottages at its south-eastern end, and a single cottage at its north-western end.

It is also likely, however, that the cottages to the south-east had formed a component of the earlier farmhouse (*Ch 4, p 81*), and that these were converted during the nineteenth century to create separate dwellings. This conversion probably involved rebuilding/modifying the former south-eastern extension to the farmhouse (*Ch 4, p 81*) and raising its height to two storeys through the construction of brick walls. Indeed, some support for this was provided in 1998, when a cursory examination of the then extant cottages was undertaken (Arrowsmith and Wilson 1998, 12). Whilst this noted that each was 'of a single bay with adjoining doorways, with square-cut surrounds', and a rendered front elevation, it was also observed that the side elevation of the easternmost cottage was 'of brick at first floor level, and sandstone on the ground-floor', suggesting that it incorporated elements of an earlier building (*ibid*). These cottages were demolished in 2004. One of them seems to have been associated with a datestone inscribed '1805 S M R' (Haynes and Tipper 1994, 46), and it is feasible that the cottages at both ends of the earlier farmhouse complex were constructed in this year. It is also reported that the earlier farmhouse was used for Methodist meetings during this period (*ibid*).

Cherry Tree Farm is shown on the Castleton township plan of 1844 (RLSL LA/Z/3/C) and the first edition OS

map (1850b) as a long rectangular range on the west side of Lower Lane. By the time of the publication of the first edition 1:2500 OS map (1893a), a further addition had been made, in the form of a large cottage, appended to the western wall of the more westerly of the cottages at the south-eastern end of the earlier building (Fig 82). This cottage was extant in 1998 and the archaeological assessment noted that it was 'of two bays, stone-built, with central doorway; square-cut mullions to fenestration on first floor', whilst the door and windows had 'square-cut surrounds' (Arrowsmith and Wilson 1998, 12). Furthermore, a photograph of this house taken in the early 1990s (*op cit*, fig 5.21) indicates that the window at first-floor level on the front elevation consisted of two rows of four-light mullioned windows. These would have provided the upper floor with good natural lighting, indicating that this part of the cottage probably contained a textile workshop.

During the nineteenth century, Wychenley Cottage formed another element of the Lower Lane hamlet, immediately to the south of Cherry Tree Farm and Lower Lane Farm (SD 9185 1189; Fig 80). Cartographic evidence indicates that it was constructed in the latter part of the nineteenth century as a pair of labourers' cottages. These are first depicted on the first edition 1:25,000 OS map (1893a) as a small range, fronting a short access off Lower Lane (Fig 83). An additional building is also depicted, which abutted the north-western side of the cottages, and probably represents another dwelling. Although the cartographic evidence indicates that this latter building was demolished in the later twentieth century, the original nineteenth-century labourers' cottages were extant in 2005 and were surveyed.

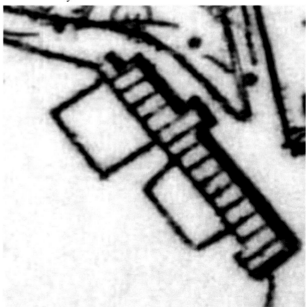

Plate 107: An extract from the OS first edition six-inch map (1850), showing Cherry Tree Farm

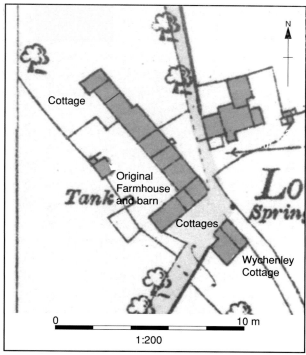

Figure 82: An extract from the OS first edition 1:2500 map (1893), showing Cherry Tree Farm

Documentary evidence

As is the case with much of the documentary evidence for Castleton, few historical records can be associated conclusively with individual properties. The late eighteenth-century Land Tax assessments, for instance, contain numerous references to households in Lower Lane, although neither Lower Lane Farm nor Cherry Tree Farm are mentioned specifically. Joseph Taylor, for instance, is listed as the occupier of a property at Lower Lane belonging to John Dixon in the Land Tax assessment for 1780 (LA QDL/S/24). The tax rating for this property was 9s 4½d, suggesting that it was a farm with associated land. Another property at Lower Lane, with a land tax rating of 4s 6½d, was occupied by 'Widow Taylor', whilst James Taylor occupied a cottage with a tax rating of 6d; John Oldham is recorded as the proprietor of both of these properties in 1780, although a George Taylor is listed as the proprietor and occupant of a new cottage at Lower Lane. Other properties in the hamlet in 1780 were occupied by John Dixon, although the comparatively low tax assessment suggests that they were cottages without land.

Robert Holt is named as proprietor of two properties on Lower Lane in the Land Tax assessment compiled in July 1790, one of which was occupied by 'Mrs Holt', with a tax assessment of 10s 10d (*ibid*), implying that this was the largest landholding in the hamlet. Holt's second property was occupied by J Haworth, with a tax assessment of 8s 3d, which again suggests that it was a reasonably sized

landholding. Interestingly, Robert Holt was also liable to 3s 3d tax 'for new erections at Lower Lane', whilst entries in the Land Tax assessment compiled in July 1792 levied 2s against James Standrin for a 'new erection at Lower Lane' (*ibid*). When coupled with the datestones of 1793 and 1805 noted in the fabric of Lower Lane Farm and its associated cottage (*below; p 166*), it is clear that the hamlet sustained considerable growth during this period. This is likely to have been in response to the local expansion of the handloom-weaving trade.

William Buckley is also listed in the Land Tax assessment for 1790 as the proprietor of two properties in Lower Lane, which were occupied by Ambrose Greenwood and Edmund Taylor (*ibid*). Several members of the Taylor family appear to have lived in the area during the late eighteenth century, whilst Daniel Greenwood is named as a farmer in the Lancashire Courts of Quarter Sessions for November 1780, together with Paul Greenwood, also of Lower Lane, and described as a cordwainer (LA QSB 1/1781/Jan/Pt3/39).

It is known that the farmhouse at Lower Lane Farm contained a datestone inscribed with 'R B T 1793', thought to refer to Robert and B Taylor of Butterworth (Haynes and Tipper 1994, 46). This was placed above a doorway on the southern elevation of the farmhouse, allowing access to a small adjoining cottage. In 1827, Robert and B Taylor of Butterworth sold the farm to John Brearley (*op cit*, 47).

Edmund Howarth was a resident of Lower Lane by the late 1830s, when he gave notice of 'making a first and final dividend of his estate' in 1838 (*Manchester Courier*, 3 November 1838), although it is unclear which property he occupied. Edmund had previously lived at Lane End, where he is

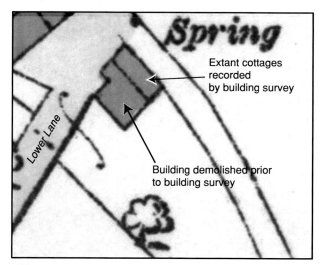

Figure 83: An extract from the OS first edition 1:2500 map (1893), showing Wychenley Cottage

listed as a flannel manufacturer in a directory of 1825; the same directory also lists J Butterworth as a flannel manufacturer at Lower Lane (Baines 1825, 691). Census records show that the Howarth family remained at Lower Lane until the 1870s (NA RG 10/4116).

Firm documentary evidence for the development of Cherry Tree Farm and Wychenley Cottage, other than the sequence of historical mapping, is scant, and none of the Census Returns differentiate these dwellings from Lower Lane Farm and the other cottages in the hamlet. It has been suggested that Cherry Tree Farm was established at an early date, and was also used as an inn (Haynes and Tipper 1994, 47). The Castleton township plan of 1844 (RLSL LA/Z/3/C) indicates that Cherry Tree Farm was the largest of the three properties in the hamlet, comprising a farmhouse with four cottages attached, then a barn, and another cottage at the north-western end. Wychenley Cottage is shown on this plan within Plot 2045, which the associated schedule describes as houses, occupation road, and garden, owned by John Gartside and occupied by John Brearley and others. Lower Lane Farm, situated on the east side of the public road, comprised a row of three domestic properties, with an agricultural building to the rear (RLSL LA/Z/3/C/2).

The Census Returns for 1841 record 14 separate households in the Lower Lane hamlet (NA HO 107/550). Amongst the residents were four separate Butterworth households, comprising two occupied by handloom weavers (John and James Butterworth, both aged 35), together with Jacob Butterworth, a farmer, and Joseph Butterworth, an agricultural labourer. Another five families at Lower Lane were engaged in handloom weaving, with the remaining residents being employed primarily as agricultural labourers.

Edward Howarth is listed as an agricultural labourer at Lower Lane in the Census Returns for 1851 (NA HO 107/2244), suggesting he lived in one of the smaller cottages. The farmhouse appeared to be occupied at that date by John Wild, a farmer with six acres of land. Wild shared the farmhouse with his nephews Edward and John Robinson (aged 28 and 26), who worked as a coal miner and a woollen weaver respectively, and a 31-year-old lodger, Daniel Wild, who was employed as an agricultural labourer. The 1851 Census Returns (*ibid*) also indicate that both James Butterworth and John Butterworth had seemingly taken up farming in preference to handloom weaving, being responsible for seven acres and four acres respectively. Other residents of the hamlet in 1851 included a bread baker, fustian cutters, a stone mason, a mule spinner, and several colliers and labourers. In total, 11 households are recorded at Lower Lane in 1851.

The Census Returns for 1861 list nine households living at Lower Lane (NA RG 9/3035). These include Ann Howarth, James Butterworth, and John Wild, who are all listed as farmers, although James Butterworth is cited as 'beer seller' as his secondary occupation. Most of the other residents were employed in local cotton and woollen mills, although there were also three coal miners and several agricultural labourers.

The data provided by the Census Returns for 1871 (NA RG 10/4116) indicate that 12 households lived at Lower Lane, and imply a slight expansion of the farming interests amongst the residents. These included Thomas Aspinall (19 acres), Samuel Sagar (ten acres), Joseph Lees (eight acres), and the 38-year-old Edward Howarth (three acres), who had married Mary Butterworth. Most of the other residents of the hamlet were employed in the local factory-based textile industry; the 36-year-old Robert Butterworth gave his occupation as 'woollen weaver', although it is unclear whether this refers to handloom or factory weaving. Nicodemius Woolfender is listed as a miner, although perhaps surprisingly, and in contrast to earlier census data, no-one appears to have been employed as an agricultural labourer.

In 1881, eight households are recorded at Lower Lane (NA RG 11/3819). Two of these families, those of Hargreaves Green and John Dixon, farmed seven acres and three acres of land respectively, with all the farmers listed in the 1871 Census Returns (NA RG 10/4116) having moved on. It has not been established which family occupied which farm, although it seems possible that the Dixon family was associated with Dixon Green Farm, situated just one field to the north of Lower Lane. In contrast to 1871, the heads of three of the other households in the hamlet were employed as farm labourers, hinting at a slight resurgence of farming locally. Nicodemius Woolfender is still listed as a miner, suggesting that coal was still being extracted at Dig Gate.

In *c* 1910, Richard Holt is known to have been farming at Lower Lane Farm (Haynes and Tipper 1994, 47). OS mapping of that year (1910a) shows the farm with the same footprint as on the first edition 1:2500 map (1893b), although a small outbuilding on the eastern side of the farmyard appears to have been remodelled. This building is shown to have been expanded further on the OS map of 1936, with a new structure erected in the north-eastern corner of the farmyard. Another two buildings had been erected by 1955, as Lower Lane Farm reached its maximum extent. Small outbuildings were also erected to the

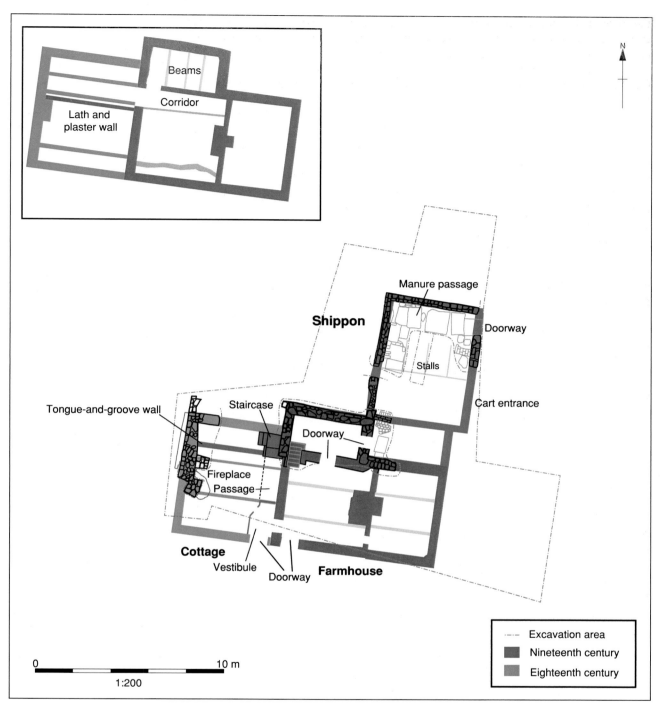

Figure 84: Late eighteenth- and nineteenth-century additions to Lower Lane Farm

rear of Cherry Tree Farm between 1910 and 1936, with further additions shown on the OS map of 1955, although this also marks the northern end of the farmhouse range as a 'ruin'.

Archaeological investigation at Lower Lane Farm: building survey and excavation

The late eighteenth-century cottage

A cottage was added to the mid-eighteenth-century farmhouse (*Ch 4, p 74*) in 1793 by Robert and B Taylor of Butterworth, as evidenced by the datestone above the doorway allowing access from the south (*p 167*).

This was a single-bayed, two-storeyed building, in stone, which was recorded during the building survey (Fig 84). Following demolition, its partial remains were also examined during the open-area excavation, which demonstrated that its footings had been cut through three sequential garden soils containing fragments of eighteenth-century pottery (*Appendix 4*). It was probably designed to house farm labourers, as its upper floor was too poorly lit to act as a workshop.

The building survey indicated that its northern wall was built of narrow, roughly dressed rubble blocks

Plate 108: Lower Lane Farm: the interior of the first-floor window, in the northern elevation of the late eighteenth-century cottage

Plate 109: Lower Lane Farm: the interior of the ground-floor window in the southern elevation of the late eighteenth-century cottage

laid in regular courses. A very small, possibly later, window was set in the centre of the ground-floor elevation, whilst close to the join with the western bay of the mid-eighteenth-century farmhouse, another two-light window with stone surrounds and a plain narrow square stone mullion was set immediately below the eaves; on its interior, this window was within a recess and had a projecting stone sill (Pl 108). The position of a doorway at ground-floor level, towards the western bay of the adjoining farmhouse, was marked by a line of handmade bricks.

The western and southern elevations were again stone-built, but were obscured by ivy. No features were visible in the western elevation, but original features within the southern elevation included the entrance to the cottage, although this was covered by a modern porch. This was immediately adjacent to the entrance into the mid-eighteenth-century farmhouse, directly opposite the doorway on its northern elevation (*above*). This was a plain square-headed opening with an apparently wooden frame that had been rendered over. To the west of the doorway was a wide window of two lights with a narrow, square-profiled stone mullion and stone surrounds (Pl 109), whilst on the floor above was a tall, wide window of originally four lights, with three thin stone mullions.

The ground and first floors of the cottage were originally single open rooms. There was a chimney breast on the western wall, and both rooms appear to have been heated by a fireplace. The excavation indicated that the chimney breast was constructed of a mixture of stone and brick, and the original fireplace on the ground floor was *c* 1.7 m wide. Other original features included two beams visible in the ceiling of the ground-floor room, which were square-profiled, saw-cut timber, aligned east/west across the room. The ceiling appeared to be of lath-and-plaster construction. Similarly, at first-floor level, two saw-cut beams were

aligned east-west across the room (Pl 110). These appeared to be the main purlins for the roof, and the space between them was covered with a lath-and-plaster ceiling.

Plate 110: Lower Lane Farm: the saw-cut beams in the first-floor ceiling of the late eighteenth-century cottage

Alterations to the late eighteenth-century cottage
The building survey detected several alterations to this cottage, dating to the late nineteenth or early twentieth century (Fig 84). For instance, the ground-floor room was divided internally with a tongue-and-grove panelled wall, to create a narrow room at the northern end of the cottage. As part of these alterations,

170

Plate 111: Lower Lane Farm: eastern elevation

the original northern doorway was blocked and the staircase moved into the narrow room. A vestibule was also constructed at the entrance at the front of the cottage and a passage may have led from this to either the staircase or the back room. A connecting door between the main farmhouse and the cottage may also have been added around this time, though it seems that the front doors on the southern elevation in both the farmhouse and the cottage were kept.

Similarly, the first-floor of the cottage was divided by the construction of a lath-and-plaster wall, to create a main bedroom at the front and a smaller room to its rear. Access between the rooms was via a doorway at the western end of the dividing wall. This contained a simple wooden door composed of six planks, with a very plain iron latch, which appeared to be late nineteenth- or early twentieth century in date. Nineteenth-century skirting boards were also added to the first-floor rooms, and the first-floor fireplace was blocked.

The mid-nineteenth-century shippon, and rebuilds to the mid-eighteenth-century farmhouse
The cartographic evidence (OS 1850b; 1893b) indicates that a stone-built shippon was constructed immediately to the north of the farmhouse, most

probably in the mid-nineteenth century. The building survey and excavation indicated that its exterior walls were constructed of stone blocks arranged in regular courses, employing a watershot technique, and it was evident that the western wall line had been partially set on foundations of river cobbles.

The northern gable end contained a small round owl hole at its apex. In addition, two small ventilation holes were set in this wall, on either side of a square recess with a wooden lintel.

The main elevation of the shippon was on the east. A rectangular doorway with a sliding wooden door at its north-eastern corner allowed access to the part of the barn that contained the manure passage (*p 172*). This entrance was protected by a wooden outbuilding. At the south-east corner was a tall, wide cart entrance, boarded over with a modern panel (Pl 111), with a large squared-sectioned saw-cut timber as a lintel, supported on stone jambs of ashlar blocks set in a long- and short-work pattern. Above the wooden lintel, the stone wall was badly cracked and failing structurally (Pl 112). The stonework of the southern jamb was set in a short section of the wall built in handmade brick. This joined the wall that connected the barn with the farmhouse.

171

Plate 112: Lower Lane Farm: eastern elevation of house and shippon (right)

The western elevation butted the projecting western bay of the farmhouse and continued as a change in build above the eastern wall of this bay, indicating that the farmhouse had been partly rebuilt to accommodate the barn. A small modern window was set opposite the main cart entrance and a blocked doorway at the northern end of the western elevation had a modern window inserted in its upper level (Pl 113); this had originally allowed access to the manure passage (*below*).

The northern wall of the eastern bay of the farmhouse was used as the southern end of the barn, though it is clear that this elevation was raised in height to accommodate the barn. This was achieved by adding additional courses of stone mixed with handmade brick to form the gable end of the barn, which extended above the roof of the eastern bay of the farmhouse.

The manure passage at the northern end of the barn originally had a door at either end, in the western and eastern elevations (*above*). To the south of the manure passage were four stalls, divided by simple wooden panels. Two of these still had vertical iron bars with chains to tether cattle (Pl 114). To the south was a wide

Plate 113: Lower Lane Farm: the blocked doorway at the western end of the manure passage

Plate 114: Lower Lane Farm: the cattle stalls in the northern end of the shippon

area (the feeding passage), from where fodder could be put into the stalls. This could be accessed via the wide cart entrance on the eastern elevation (*p 171*). To the south again, a narrow room directly adjacent to the farmhouse formed the southern end of the barn. The open-area excavation exposed flagstone and handmade brick surfaces within this area.

A raised loft area was above the narrow southern room, whilst another loft was present above the stalls and manure passage. It is likely that these two lofts were used to store fodder. The loft above the stalls was supported on a frame of roughly cut timbers, which, along with the stalls and the walls, had been washed with a white pigment. As far as could be seen, the roof had a central ridge purlin with two other main purlins on either side of the ridge. The covering was of graded stone tiles, with a ceramic louvre to ventilate the interior at the centre of the ridge.

Archaeological excavation at Cherry Tree Farm
The early nineteenth-century cottages
The open-area excavation exposed the remains of the early nineteenth-century cottages at Cherry Tree Farm, which had been added to both the south-eastern and north-western ends of the earlier farmhouse (Fig 85). The complete footprint of that at the north-western end was uncovered, which had been added to the extended barn (Room 3; *Ch 4, p 80*).

172

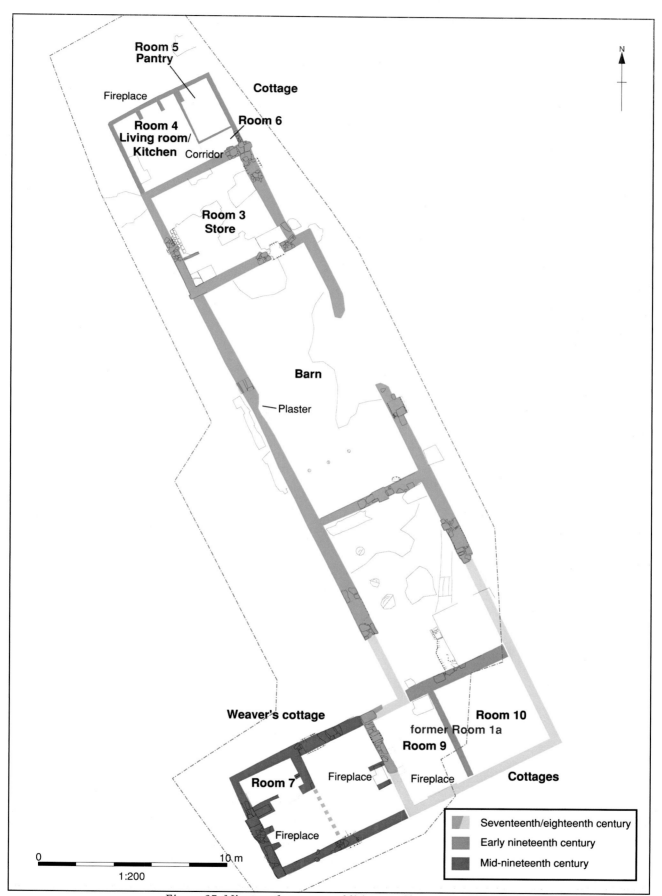

Room 5
Pantry

Cottage

Fireplace

Room 6

Room 4
Living room/
Kitchen

Corridor

Room 3
Store

Barn

Plaster

Weaver's cottage

Room 10
former Room 1a

Room 9

Room 7

Fireplace

Fireplace

Cottages

Fireplace

Fireplace

	Seventeenth/eighteenth century
	Early nineteenth century
	Mid-nineteenth century

N

0   10 m

1:200

Figure 85: Nineteenth-century additions to Cherry Tree Farm

173

The cottage measured *c* 6 x 4.2 m and its external walls were constructed of handmade bricks, two courses thick. Its interior was subdivided into several rooms by single-course-thick handmade brick walls, which defined a living room/kitchen and pantry. The living room/kitchen (Room 4) was the larger, measuring *c* 4.1 x 3.6 m, placed on the western side of the cottage. This had a floor composed of both flagstones and handmade bricks and contained a brick-built fireplace, on the cottage's northern gable. To the rear of the living room/kitchen was the pantry (Room 5), measuring *c* 2.9 x 1.8 m, which could be accessed via a short corridor (Room 6), 1.9 x 1.1 m. It is also possible that some minor modifications were made to the extended section of the barn (Room 3; *Ch 4, p 80*), concomitant with the construction of the cottage. These included replacing the original flagstone floor with a handmade brick surface, and building a handmade brick wall to create a small partitioned area at the south-western corner of this room.

The partial remains of the cottages at the south-eastern end of the earlier farmhouse were also uncovered. These two cottages (Rooms 9 and 10) were created by modifying or rebuilding an earlier element of the farmhouse (Room 1A; *Ch 4, p 81*), involving the division of the earlier building into two by the construction of a single-course-thick handmade brick wall. The near-complete footprint of the westernmost cottage (Room 9) was uncovered during the excavation. This indicated that it contained a single room at ground-floor level, measuring internally 5 x 3.1 m, with a brick-built fireplace on its south-western wall.

The mid-nineteenth-century weaver's cottage
In addition to the cottages, the entire footprint of the mid-nineteenth-century weaver's cottage, which had been appended to the south-eastern cottages, was uncovered during the excavation. Its external walls were constructed of irregular, but

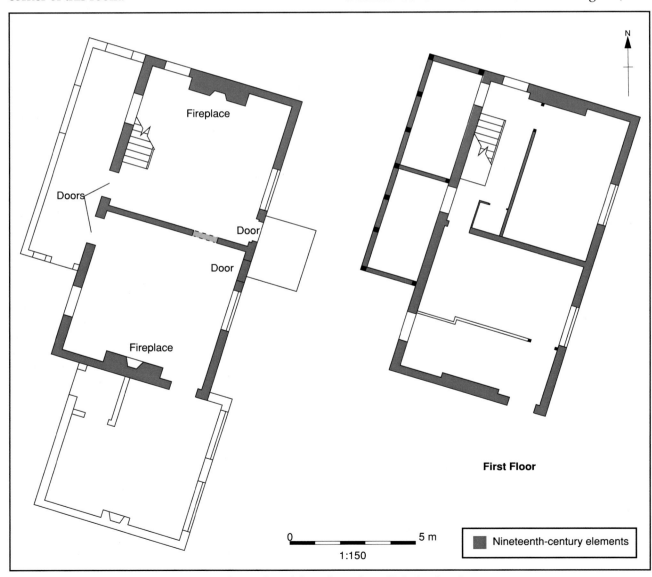

Figure 86: Ground- and first-floor plan of Wychenley Cottage

Plate 115: Mayfields: the cottages, looking north-west

well-coursed, drystone blocks, enclosing an area measuring 7 x 4.8 m. Opposing stone-built fireplaces were positioned on its south-western and north-eastern walls, within the two bays of the cottage. In addition, the western bay contained internal walls composed of stone and handmade brick, defining two rooms. Of these, a smaller room (Room 7) was the more clearly defined, at the rear of the cottage, measuring 2.2 x 3.5 m.

Building survey at Wychenley Cottage

The building survey indicated that the labourers' cottages at Wychenley had been constructed in handmade brick and, as such, probably dated to the mid-nineteenth century. Although these had been substantially modified and extended in the twentieth century, it is evident that they originally comprised a pair of small, one-up-one-down dwellings (Fig 86). The dwellings were identical in size, with internal areas of 5.8 x 5.4 m, and they were both accessed through opposing doorways, positioned on the north-western and south-eastern elevations, adjacent to the wall dividing the two dwellings. The façade of each (south-eastern elevation) contained single windows, at both ground-floor and first-floor levels, which had simple stone lintels and sills. Each of the dwellings also possessed gable-end fireplaces.

Mayfields

Mayfields was situated at the approximate centre of the Kingsway Business Park (SD 9185 1165;

Fig 80) at a height of 159 m aOD, and could originally be accessed from Lower Lane along a short track. Prior to the construction of the business park, the site was occupied by a row of terraced weavers' cottages (Pl 115), one of which contained a datestone inscribed with 'B B B 1787', almost certainly referring to Benjamin Butterworth. These cottages continued to be occupied during the early part of the nineteenth century, and several structures were added, all of which are depicted on the first edition OS map (1850b). In addition, a small warehouse and a stone outbuilding were added, probably prior to the construction of the nineteenth-century additions. This warehouse appears to have then been used as a barn from the mid-nineteenth century onwards. The first edition 1:2500 OS map (1893a) labels the site as 'Mayfields', and shows it to have comprised an L-shaped building at the western end, with another L-shaped range to the east, with a small building to the rear, and two rectangular cottages at the eastern end.

Both the late eighteenth-century cottages (Western Cottage and No 1 Mayfields) and the nineteenth-century cottages (Nos 2 and 3 Mayfields), along with the warehouse/barn and outbuilding, were extant in 2005 and were thus recorded as part of the building survey. Following demolition, the site was also examined by open-area excavation.

Documentary evidence

Mayfields is listed in the Land Tax assessment for 1780, which gives James Lord as the proprietor, and Thomas Whittles as the occupier, with a tax rating of 4s ½d (LA QDL/S/24). Thomas Whittles is also given as the occupant of Mayfields in the Land Tax assessment for 1782, although the proprietors at that date were the executors of James Lord. The tax at that date was at the slightly reduced rate of 3s 11d (*ibid*). However, the assessment compiled in June 1787 indicates that Mayfields had been purchased by Benjamin Butterworth (*ibid*), and it appears that John Butterworth, a woollen manufacturer, then occupied the first of the cottages, which contained a loom shop with two looms and two jennies (Haynes and Tipper 1994, 46). It also seems that this was connected with the adjacent cottage, which was used by handloom weavers employed by Butterworth.

Mayfields is mentioned in the Land Tax assessment of July 1790, which lists Benajmin Butterworth as the owner. The property was rated at 3s 8d, suggesting that there was only limited land with it (LA QDL/S/24). Benjamin Butterworth is similarly listed as the proprietor of Mayfields in the Land Tax assessment for 1797, when the property was rated as 3s 10d (*ibid*). It is likely that this is the same Benjamin Butterworth who invited architects 'and others who may wish to be concerned in the building of a cloth hall' in Rochdale in 1792. Printed in *The Leeds Intelligencer* (21 January 1793), this notice described the intended cloth hall as a 'spacious building…shortly to be erected in an eligible part of the town of Rochdale'.

John Butterworth was father-in-law to Abraham and James Milne, and died in 1810 at Moor Bank (LA WCW/Supra/C658B/54). The Milne family appears to have owned the two Moorbank farms, along Moor Bank Lane to the south-east of Mayfields, in the eighteenth century (*Ch 4, p 89*), and were also associated with the local textile industry; James and John Milne of Burnedge, for instance, are listed in a trade directory for 1825 as cotton spinners and fustian manufacturers (Baines 1825, 691).

Three families were weaving at Mayfields in 1831 and, at that date, the site is thought to have comprised the late eighteenth-century cottages, a barn, two other cottages, and a blacksmith's forge (Haynes and Tipper 1994, 46). The Census Returns for 1841 (NA HO 107/550), however, record five families at Mayfields, four of whom earned a livelihood from woollen weaving: John Butterworth; William Mills; Thomas Taylor; and Joseph Holroyd. The Mills family is listed in the Land Tax assessment for 1808, which gives Edward Mills as the occupant of two cottages at Lower Lane that were tax-rated at 2s (LA QDL/S/24). It seems possible, given the proximity of Lower Lane, that this actually refers to Mayfields. Similarly, John Butterworth is listed in the same Land Tax assessment as the occupant of a property on Lower Lane that may have been the farmhouse at Mayfields, with a tax rating of 5s.

James Butterworth, the head of the fifth family listed in the 1841 Census Returns (LA HO 107/550), is recorded as a farmer, sharing the farmhouse with his wife, two sons (James Jnr and Benjamin), and a 19-year-old farm labourer. It is interesting to note that James Butterworth was born at Mayfields, and it is likely that he rented the adjacent cottages to handloom weavers and controlled the distribution of woven cloth. A James Butterworth of Rochdale, described as a 'cotton spinner, dealer and chapman', was awarded a fiat of bankruptcy in 1834 (*London Gazette*, 11 February 1834), although it cannot be established confidently that this was the same Butterworth that lived at Mayfields in 1841.

Mayfields is shown on the Castleton township plan of 1844 (RLSL LA/Z/3/C; Pl 116) as a row of six buildings, comprising five domestic properties with an agricultural/commercial building in the centre. The property is described in the accompanying schedule as 'houses, buildings and yard', owned by James Butterworth and occupied by himself and others (RLSL LA/Z/3/C/2). Butterworth also owned and occupied the large field to the north (Plot 2092) and the access road (Plot 2091).

The Census Returns for 1851 show that James Butterworth continued to farm six acres, together with his wife, who also worked as a woollen spinner (NA HO 107/2244). James Butterworth Jnr appears to have moved into another of the Mayfields cottages with his wife and two

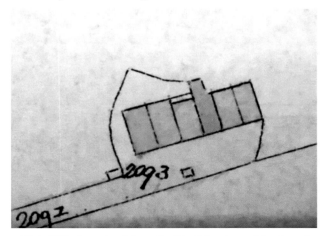

Plate 116: An extract from the Castleton township plan of 1844, showing Mayfields

176

young sons, and taken up woollen weaving. John Butterworth remained in another of the cottages as a woollen weaver, together with his wife, two daughters, and 14-year-old grand-daughter, who are all recorded as woollen spinners. The Mills and Taylor families appear to have left Mayfields by 1851, but whilst Joseph Holroyd had died in 1850 (LA WCW/ Supra/C1211B/3), his widow and grand-daughter continued to earn a living from woollen spinning, supplemented by 25-year-old James Holroyd's wages as an agricultural labourer. However, according to his last will and testament, Joseph Holroyd bequeathed to his wife the sum of £200, which equates to approximately £25,300 in modern terms, reflecting how lucrative handloom weaving was during the first half of the nineteenth century.

The Census Returns for 1861 show that James Butterworth was still working the farm, together with his wife, Mary, although there is no record of her continuing her secondary occupation of woollen spinning (NA RG 9/3035). John Butterworth had died by then, but his widow remained in the cottage and continued to earn a living by spinning wool. The adjacent cottage was occupied by Benjamin Robinson and his wife, both described as handloom woollen weavers, and their three daughters, who all worked in a nearby mill as power-loom weavers. The last cottage was occupied in 1861 by James and Alice Farrow, who are both described as woollen spinners.

James Butterworth had died by 1871, and the Census Returns (NA RG 10/4116) indicate that his widow had given up farming and taken up flannel making as an occupation, generating an income that was presumably supplemented by rents from the adjacent cottages, although it is of note that none of the occupants of these cottages earned a living from handloom weaving. The adjacent cottage was occupied by Robert Butterworth, a carter, together with his wife and their two young children, and three lodgers. James Farrow still lived in one of the cottages, and continued to earn a living from spinning woollen yarn, whilst the other cottage was occupied by Robert Turner, described as a farm labourer. The demise of handloom weaving at Mayfields is reinforced by the Census Returns for 1881, where three of the four families listed worked in a woollen mill; Mary Butterworth still lived at Mayfields, but is not accredited with an occupation in the Census Returns (NA RG 11/4103). Mary died during the 1880s and, after more than a century in the Butterworth family's occupation, Mayfields was taken over by John Dawson from Clitheroe.

The Census Returns for 1891 (NA RG 12/3329) show that John Dawson resided at Mayfields with his wife and eight children, and a 27-year-old male servant; Dawson is listed as a farmer in a trade directory for 1888-9 (Duncan 1889, 117). The adjacent cottage was occupied by Abraham Hall, a widower who was 'surviving on own means', together with his 56-year-old daughter. John Farrow occupied the next cottage, and is described as a retired woollen spinner. The last cottage was occupied by James Taylor, a cotton spinner, together with his wife and two young children. Again, none of the residents of Mayfields listed in the 1891 Census Returns were handloom weavers (NA RG 12/3329).

A trade directory for 1899-1900 contains an entry for William Uttley, a farmer at Mayfields, but does not list any of the residents in the adjacent cottages (Duncan 1900, 239). However, the Census Returns for 1901 provide a wealth of detail (NA RG 13/3833). William Uttley is not listed, although the 29-year-old Luke Uttley, born in the parish of Butterworth, is recorded at Mayfield Farm. He shared the farmhouse with his wife and infant son, and is described as a spinner. The adjacent cottage was uninhabited in 1901, whilst John Dawson appears to have moved into the second cottage, who shared it with his wife, four daughters, and son. His eldest two daughters were employed as woollen weavers, whilst his son worked as an iron turner. The third cottage was occupied by George Peel, a butcher from Rochdale, together with his wife, daughter, and three sons.

The OS map of 1910 (1910a) shows that Mayfields retained the same footprint as that shown on the second edition OS map (1893c), although the small building to the rear of the cottages appears to have been replaced by a narrow rectangular structure. On the next edition of OS mapping, published in 1936, this is shown to have been extended, with additional structures erected by the time the map issued in 1955 was produced.

Archaeological investigations: building survey and excavation

The 1787 weavers' cottages

One major aim of the archaeological investigation was to record the building at Mayfields dating to 1787 (p 175), and extant in 2005. The initial building survey indicated that this was once two adjoining, purpose-built, weavers' cottages (Western Cottage and No 1 Mayfields). These were both constructed of stone, two-bays deep and one-bay wide (Fig 87).

The southern elevation was built of coursed narrow rectangular blocks with hammer-dressed faces, and the open-area excavation indicated that this wall was c 0.6 m thick. The datestone, which read 'B B B 1787' (p 175), was in the centre of the two cottages, at the level of the upper windows. The doorway

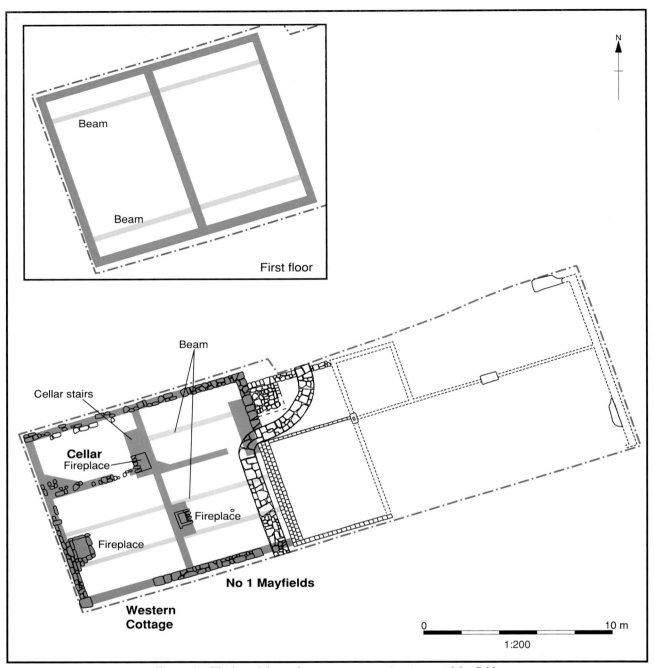

Beam

Beam

First floor

Beam

Cellar stairs

Cellar
Fireplace

Fireplace

Fireplace

No 1 Mayfields

**Western
Cottage**

0   10 m

1:200

Figure 87: The late eighteenth-century weavers' cottages at Mayfields

of the western cottage was at the eastern end of the southern bay and was square-headed, with narrow flat-faced stone jambs and a lintel (Pl 117). To the west, at ground-floor level, was a window with flat-faced stone mullions and surrounds, and three large lights. A long window on the upper floor, originally with six lights and stone mullions, was almost directly under the eaves. The central two lights had been filled with stone to create two windows of two lights.

The second cottage (No 1 Mayfields) probably originally had the same ground-floor window arrangement as the first, but the stone mullions

had been removed and the openings filled with modern window frames (Pl 118). Above this was a wooden lintel, internally supported on two stone corbels. The upper-floor window was similar to that in the western cottage, with two stone-blocked lights, originally the central pair of a long stone-mullioned window of six lights, now replaced with modern frames. The doorway was set to the east of the ground-floor window and was square-headed, with plain flat-faced stone jambs and a lintel.

The northern elevation was rendered, which obscured the stonework and masked details of the doors and windows. However, the excavation

Plate 117: Mayfields: the southern elevation of Western Cottage

indicated that the wall was again *c* 0.6 m thick and had been constructed of poorly coursed drystone blocks. The doorway to the western cottage was covered by a twentieth-century porch, though it was apparent that it was square-headed, with plain flat-faced stone jambs and a lintel. There were no visible window openings on the ground floor. The adjoining cottage (No 1 Mayfields) had a similar doorway set towards the eastern corner of the elevation, with a wide window, and a small window adjacent to the doorway on the ground floor. On the upper floor of the Western Cottage was a long mullioned window of four lights, with an additional single-light window; both were set close to the eaves. It is also possible that there was originally just one multi-light window facing north. The upper floor of No 1 Mayfields had modern windows of the same proportions and in the same locations as those on the upper floor of the Western Cottage.

The excavation indicated that the western wall was of unmortared stone, *c* 0.6 m thick. A window on the ground floor, of three lights with stone mullions, lit the rear bay of the Western Cottage (Pl 119). The

front bay of this cottage also had a stone-mullioned window of two lights. On the upper floor, a possibly later window of two lights without stone mullions lit the front bay, whilst the rear bay was lit by a stone-mullioned window of two lights. Each window had a plain flat-faced stone surround. A small stone chimney stack was also set to the north of the roof ridge.

The eastern elevation was obscured by the range of brick-built cottages that had been added to the east in the nineteenth century (*p 182*). However, some details relating to this elevation were uncovered during the excavation. It appears that, at ground-floor level at least, a large portion had been rebuilt in handmade brick during the construction of the adjoining cottage.

Relatively few original features were identified within these cottages. A wall dividing the northern and southern bays was in an identical position in both, and was probably an original feature, whilst two sets of original beams were visible, extending longitudinally across the southern bay of both cottages at ceiling height. These were hand cut and chamfered along the lower arris, with stops at the ends. It is likely that originally the upper floors in both were undivided and open to roof height. Two sets of beams were identified, one close to the southern elevation, the other close to the northern, which were probably original. These beams had narrow angled profiles and were roughly chamfered.

The excavation also confirmed that both cottages had similar ground-floor dimensions, each measuring *c* 8.6 x 4.6 m. Stone-built fireplaces, each *c* 0.9 x 0.8 m, were present in the southern bay of each of the cottages on their western walls (Pl 120), and a sherd of mid-nineteenth-century pottery was recovered from that in No 1 Mayfields. The

Plate 118: The southern elevation of No 1 Mayfields

Plate 119: Mayfields: the western gable end of Western Cottage

Plate 120: Stone-built fireplace in No 1 Mayfields, looking west

remains of another fireplace were also present in the rear room of the Western Cottage. This differed in construction, in that it was composed of handmade brick, with a flagstone hearth, placed on the eastern wall of this room.

A cellar was also found beneath the rear room of the Western Cottage. This measured *c* 4.1 x 2.6 m, extending to a depth of 1.9 m below the ground, and was constructed of walls, *c* 0.4 m thick, of poorly coursed drystone blocks. The northern, eastern, and southern walls contained alcoves, those to the north and south being 0.6 x 0.3 m, with a depth of 0.3 m, whilst the eastern alcove measured 0.25 x 0.3 m, and was 0.3 m deep. The north and south walls also retained stone springers indicative of a vaulted ceiling, although whether the vaulting was constructed of brick or stone is unknown. Its interior had a flagstone floor and was accessed via a dog-leg stone-built staircase at its eastern end (Pl 121).

Nineteenth-century features within the 1787 cottages
It appears that the southern façade of the 1787 cottages became structurally unsound in the nineteenth century, and began to bow outwards, creating a need for remedial works. These involved the insertion of iron braces and tie rods, anchored into the ceiling beams, which were designed to hold the façade in place.

The early nineteenth-century warehouse/barn
At the time of the building survey, a small, two-storeyed building was extant which, based on its architectural character, had been a small warehouse built in the early nineteenth century to serve the two weavers' cottages (Fig 88). However, the documentary evidence (*p 176*) indicates that

Plate 121: Mayfields: the cellar steps in Western Cottage, looking east

180

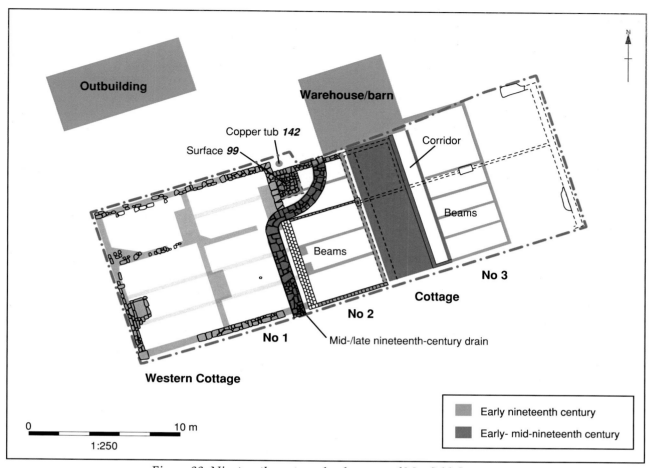

Figure 88: Nineteenth-century development of Mayfield Cottages

by 1831 it functioned as a barn. Although there were problems with access, which meant that this structure could only be recorded briefly, it was apparent, based on its position and the building materials used, that it was built prior to the creation of the nineteenth-century cottages (*p 182*), originally forming a separate building, and that its upper storey was modified and partially rebuilt in the late nineteenth century. Following this, in the early twentieth century, it became part of one of the adjacent cottages and provided additional living accommodation.

The early nineteenth-century elements were visible in its western elevation, where the stonework was typical of this period, being composed of small squared, possibly water-shot, blocks laid to course with brick appearing in the upper courses. It is also possible that a small blocked window on the ground floor of its northern elevation was an early nineteenth-century feature. Similarly, the eastern elevation had two small rectangular windows, one on the ground floor and the other above. Although the southern elevation was obscured, it is likely that it was originally accessed from the south, though this was later blocked by a nineteenth-century cottage (*p 183*).

The upper parts of the northern and western elevations were later rebuilds or repairs, being composed of machine-made brick covered with a whitewash or paint. The roof was a ridge with gable ends, not covered with graded stone. Internally, it had a king-post truss structure of machine-cut timbers.

The open-area excavation also uncovered a sandstone-capped drain, extending southwards from the building immediately north of the excavation trench (Fig 88). However, this drain clearly post-dated the construction of one of the nineteenth-century cottages (No 2 Mayfields), as it cut through its wall foundation. It also ran beneath the floor of one of the late eighteenth-century cottages (No 1 Mayfields).

The early nineteenth-century outbuilding
An outbuilding was also briefly recorded by the building survey. This stood to the rear of the late eighteenth-century cottages and was probably built to provide additional services.

It was a long stone-built range divided into two bays, with a modern corrugated roof. The western elevation had been repaired with handmade brick, with a later brick outbuilding added against this

181

Plate 122: Mayfields: the northern elevation of the stone outbuilding

façade. The eastern elevation was of handmade brick with stone quoins. The stonework of the northern (Pl 122) and southern elevations (Pl 123) was of small hammer-dressed squared blocks laid to course.

Each of the two bays had a square-headed door in the southern elevation, facing the back of the cottages, whilst a tall narrow window to the side of the western doorway had a projecting stone sill. This window was partially blocked and an inserted wooden sash frame was present, which appeared nineteenth-century in style. The rear northern elevation showed a blocked window with a projecting stone sill at the eastern end, and a later blocked doorway with a wooden frame at

Plate 123: Mayfields: the southern elevation of the stone outbuilding

the western end. Internally, the eastern bay had a partially raised and stepped floor with a wide, shallow channel. A connecting door led into the western bay, where the floor was at a lower level.

The early nineteenth-century cottages (Nos 2 and 3 Mayfields)

The building survey allowed the form and the sequence of construction of the later cottages to be discerned. These two additional cottages (Fig 88) were constructed during the early nineteenth century, both one-bay wide and two-bays deep. One (No 2 Mayfields), which was a purpose-built weaver's cottage, had been built against the eastern side of the late eighteenth-century cottages, whilst the other (No 3 Mayfields) initially formed a separate building a short distance to the east. A gap was retained between these two cottages to allow access to the warehouse to the north (*p 180*).

Only the southern elevation of No 2 Mayfields was visible, constructed in handmade brick and mimicking the southern elevations of the two adjacent late eighteenth-century stone cottages, with window openings in the same places and of the same proportions. On the ground floor, the window space held a modern wooden casement frame with three lights, whilst the upper window was the same width as the original six-light windows of the earlier cottages, but held modern window frames set between two mullions, probably of brick. This window was also set high, directly under the eaves. The doorway was square-headed, but render obscured the original surrounds; the door was a modern replacement.

The excavation provided details of the eastern and southern elevations. It was clear that the eastern elevation was also constructed of handmade brick, though its southern elevation was constructed in stone and had a width of *c* 0.6 m. The surviving remains also indicated that a large portion of the eastern stone wall of the 1787 cottages (*p 179*) had been repaired and replaced by a three-course-wide handmade brick wall during the construction of this cottage.

Its interior area measured *c* 7.8 x 4 m, and a one-course-thick handmade brick partition wall divided the ground floor into two rooms, with the larger room at the front of the house and a smaller room to the rear. A *c* 0.8 m-wide doorway was also present, its threshold defined by flagstones, on the northern wall of the smaller of these rooms, butting against the eastern wall of the earlier cottages.

Significantly, remains were identified which may relate to the blacksmith's forge documented in the

Plate 124: The southern elevation of No 3 Mayfields and the infilled space to the west

Plate 125: Mayfields: the beam with the number '4' carved into it

early nineteenth century (*p 176*). These include a fragmented flagstone surface (**99**), *c* 1.6 m square, within the north-western corner of the rear room, which was bounded by single skin of handmade bricks. This sealed a relatively clean sand deposit, which produced a number of fragments of metalworking debris. Further evidence for the forge was found to the north, immediately outside the cottage, in the form of a cylindrical copper-alloy tub (**142**). This had a diameter of 0.43 m and was 0.3 m deep, the sides being 5 mm thick, and it is possible that it formed a quenching tub.

Other internal features at ground-floor level included a single, very rough beam extending longitudinally across the ceiling of the rear room, and two similar very roughly cut beams in the front room. In addition, a recess on the western wall of this room may have housed a cupboard.

The first-floor of this cottage could not be accessed during the building survey. It is possible, however, that, as with the adjacent late eighteenth-century cottages, this originally formed a single open room, functioning as a loom shop.

In a similar fashion to the other cottages at Mayfields, No 3 was one-bay wide and two-bays deep, though there was less evidence for this cottage having a weaving function(s). Its southern façade was the most visible elevation (Pl 124). At ground-floor level, this contained a doorway, adjacent to the western end of the cottage. This was narrower than the doors at the other cottages and a later render obscured any details of the surround. To the east, a small window and a slightly larger one had modern window frames. The upper floor was lit by three small windows on the front; none of these appeared to have originated as the long multi-light mullioned windows typical of weavers' cottages; all had modern frames and glazing, while

the render obscured the surrounds. The northern elevation was largely obscured. However, on the upper floor, two windows were present close to the eaves.

The ground-floor of the cottage was divided into two rooms, similar in dimensions to the ground-floor rooms in No 2 Mayfields. Within the larger, front room, there were three black-stained beams, in their original form similar to the beams in the other cottages, but they had been modified to produce a scalloped effect. No beams were visible in the northern bay.

At the first-floor level, the original internal configuration had been much altered. The only original features noted were a beam within the southern bay, and another in the northern bay. Both were similar to those seen in the upper floors of the other cottages. The beam in the northern bay also had a large number 4 carved into it (Pl 125).

At some stage prior to the production of the first edition OS map (1850b), the gap separating Nos 2 and 3 Mayfields was filled by an additional cottage (Fig 88). This was two-bays deep, but was narrower than the other cottages at Mayfields. Although it was extant at the time of the building survey, it had been much altered during the twentieth century, when it had been converted into a garage, its ground-floor level being obliterated by this conversion (Pl 124). At first-floor level, its southern elevation, which was the only one visible, contained a window, with a modern frame. The form of this window suggested that this building did not function as a weaver's cottage. In its interior, at first-floor level, original features included a beam within the southern bay. As the construction of this cottage effectively blocked access to the warehouse/barn to its rear, a long corridor was created. This ran from the front door of this cottage to the south-eastern corner of the warehouse/barn.

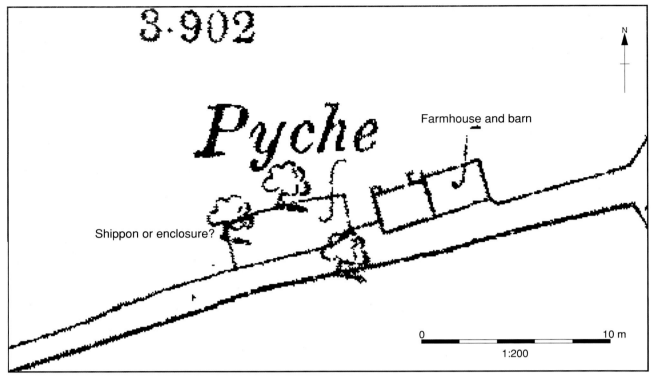

Figure 89: An extract from the OS first edition 1:2500 map (1893), showing Pyche farm

Pyche farm

Pyche farm (Fig 80) was continually occupied during the nineteenth century, though the first edition 1:2500 OS map (1893a) indicates that another linear building, or enclosure, had been constructed immediately to the west of the eighteenth-century building (Fig 89). This may have formed the cowshed (shippon) that may have existed at the site (Haynes and Tipper 1994, 46). This building had been demolished by the time of the publication of the revised OS map (1910b) and the farm had been enclosed by a wall, which had several small outbuildings attached to its northern side.

Documentary evidence

Pyche is shown on the Castleton township plan of 1844 (RLSL LA/Z/3/C) as a linear range comprising a cottage with an agricultural building attached to its western end. It is referred to in the accompanying schedule (RLSL LA/Z/3/C/2) as the 'Beehive public house, building and garden', owned by the Rector of Middleton and occupied by John Wild. However, none of the entries in the Census Returns for 1841 (NA HO 107/550) can be attributed to the building with any degree of confidence.

It is listed in the 1871 Census Returns as Pich Farm, occupied by James Holt, a 55-year-old 'outdoor labourer' from Todmorden (NA RG 10/4116). Holt was still occupying the cottage in 1891, together with his 22-year-old nephew and niece, John and Sarah Howarth (NA RG 12/3329). The building is there identified as 'Pyche', and is similarly annotated

as such on the first edition 1:2500 OS map (1893a) and its revision (1910b). A trade directory for 1899-1900 gives Pyche as the residence of Mary Aspinall (Duncan 1900, 239), although the Census Returns for 1901 indicate that 'Pyche House' was occupied by William Shepherd, a coal carter, his wife, two sons, and a nephew from Shropshire, who was employed as a 'farm servant' (NA RG 13/3833).

Archaeological excavation

During the excavation, several features were uncovered which appeared to relate to the nineteenth- and twentieth-century history of the farm (Fig 90). Two lengths of handmade brick walling were present in the interior, both parallel with the gable walls of the building. These walls were two-courses thick and were bonded with a sandy cement mortar, suggesting that they were constructed in the late nineteenth century. They were spaced *c* 2 m apart and defined a room (Room 1) which had been inserted at the western end of the eighteenth-century farmhouse. This room was filled by a deposit (*59*) providing further confirmation of its date, as it was associated with a wide array of early twentieth-century pottery.

To the west of the farm, a length of drystone wall was *c* 0.6 m wide, with a flagstone surface to its west. The position of the wall equates with a boundary, plotted on twentieth-century OS mapping (*eg* OS 1930), which enclosed the farm, though it is possible that the flagstones formed elements of a possible late nineteenth-century shippon, depicted on the first

184

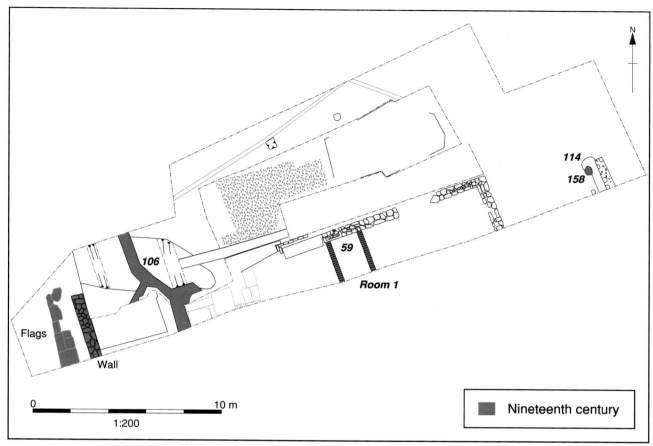

Figure 90: Nineteenth-century additions to Pyche farm

edition 1:2500 OS map (1893a; *p 184*). Other nineteenth-century features were identified immediately to the east, comprising a system of drains (**106**) that probably served the barn attached to the farmhouse (*Ch 4, p 81*), whilst to the east, a single posthole (**158**) had been inserted into an earlier gully (**114**; *Ch 4, p 82*).

Lane End Farm

The documentary evidence indicates that Lane End Farm (Fig 80), which was established in the post-medieval period (*Ch 4, p 82*), was continually occupied throughout the late eighteenth and nineteenth centuries (*below*). The nineteenth-century mapping and the evidence derived from the archaeological excavation suggest that, during the late eighteenth century, the seventeenth-century farm, which consisted of a dwelling and attached barn (*Ch 4, p 83*), was extended, represented by an L-shaped range depicted on the first edition six-inch OS map (1850b). Following its construction, the buildings were not substantially altered during the nineteenth century. In contrast, it appears that the seventeenth-century barn was substantially modified in the late nineteenth century, to convert it into a shippon.

Documentary evidence

Lane End appears to have been occupied in the early nineteenth century by John Butterworth, a carrier and farmer, being listed in a directory for 1825 (Baines 1825, 691). It is possible that this is the same J Butterworth that is listed in the same directory as a flannel manufacturer at Lower Lane (*p 168*), which may actually refer to Lane End (*ibid*); the hamlet is shown on the first edition OS map (1850b), for instance, as comprising two groups of buildings at the junction of Lower Lane with Moss Bank Lane, but this small settlement is annotated as Lower Lane. In 1834, Butterworth was declared an insolvent debtor, late of Lane End in Castleton (*London Gazette*, 11 February 1834; *Manchester Courier*

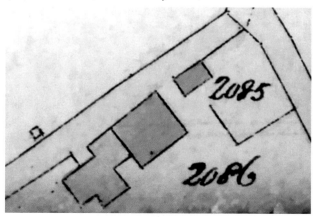

Plate 126: An extract from the 1844 township map of Castleton, showing Lane End Farm

185

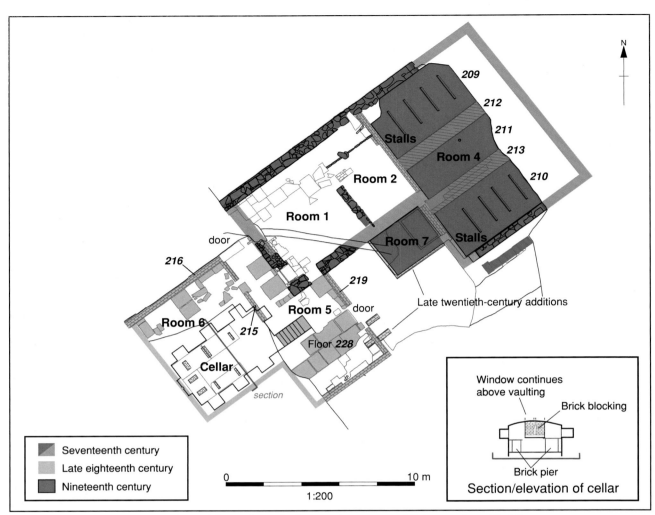

Figure 91: Late eighteenth- and nineteenth-century additions to Lane End Farm

and *Lancashire General Advertiser*, 22 November 1834). Whilst this suggests that he had recently vacated the farm, he is recorded at Lane End as a weaver in the Census Returns for 1841 (NA HO 107/550).

Lane End Farm is shown on the Castleton township plan of 1844 (RLSL LA/Z/3/C; Plot 2086) as comprising two cottages and an agricultural building at the southern end (Pl 126). It is described in the accompanying schedule as 'houses, buildings, garden and yard', owned by Thomas Wilson Hardwin and occupied by Richard Whittaker and others (RLSL LA/Z/3/C/2).

The Census Returns for 1851 record the occupants as John Lees, a 70-year-old agricultural labourer, with his wife Mary (aged 68) and 18-year-old daughter, Jane (NA HO 107/2244). It seems possible that the Lees occupied a cottage rather than the farmhouse, which may have been uninhabited in 1851. The Census Returns for 1861, however, record that Lane End was occupied by a James Lees, a farmer of 21 acres, who shared the farmhouse with his two sons and two daughters (NA RG 9/3035).

The Lees had evidently vacated Lane End Farm by the 1870s, as the Census Returns for 1871 indicate that three families were living there (NA RG 10/4116). These included James Ashworth, a 29-year-old farmer, although he only had nine acres, as opposed to the 21 acres that had been farmed by James Lees. The other two families were headed by Adam Smith, a collier from Rochdale, and Thomas Greenwood, an iron moulder, also from Rochdale. By 1881, however, Lane End Farm appears to have reverted to single-occupancy, providing accommodation for Thomas Aspinall, a farmer of 26 acres from Oldham. Thomas shared the farmhouse with his wife, three sons, and three daughters (NA RG 11/4103). The Aspinall family were still working Lane End Farm in the twentieth century, as recorded in the 1901 Census (NA RG 13/3833).

Archaeological excavation
The late eighteenth-century extension
The remains of a probable late eighteenth-century building, which had been added onto the southern corner of the seventeenth-century farm (*Ch 4, p 83*),

Plate 127: Lane End Farm: the interior of the vaulted cellar, looking north-east

Plate 129: Lane End Farm: the late nineteenth- and twentieth-century shippon, looking north

were present within the excavated area (Fig 91). It is likely to have been constructed to furnish the farm with additional living space, and this was confirmed, in some measure, as access from the adjacent dwelling was possible through its original gable-end doorway, and also via an additional doorway that had been inserted through the south-western wall of the seventeenth-century dwelling.

The external walls of the extension (*216* and *219*) were constructed of handmade brick, two courses thick, and two *c* 1.4 m-wide doorways were evident on the north-western and north-eastern elevations. The interior was divided into two principal ground-floor rooms (Rooms 5 and 6) by a two-course-thick handmade brick wall (*215*). One of these rooms (Room 5) had an L-shaped plan, with maximum dimensions of 9 x 3.7 m, and a floor composed of stone flags (*228*), some of which, against the southern wall, contained various slots and apertures. A doorway at its north-western end allowed access through wall *215* into Room 6. This probably measured *c* 6.2 x 5.4 m and also contained a flagstone floor.

An extant vaulted cellar beneath Room 6 was accessed via a flight of stairs from Room 5, composed of stone

Plate 128: Lane End Farm: the interior of the vaulted cellar, looking south-west

treads set on handmade brick supports. The cellar measured 5.37 x 2.7 m, with a maximum height of 1.72 m (Pl 127), and its walls were of handmade brick, whilst it had a shallow brick-vaulted ceiling. A cellar light at its western end had a flagstone sill and a saw-cut stone mullion, though this window had been blocked with brick at a later date. The walls of the cellar also incorporated seven alcoves, each 0.77 m wide and 0.43 m deep, which were probably used for cold storage. It also contained three large sandstone slabs, forming waist-high benches around three sides of the room, supported on brick pillars (Pl 128).

Late nineteenth-century alterations to the barn
The excavation indicated that, probably during the late nineteenth century, the seventeenth-century barn, attached to the dwelling, underwent major refurbishment (Fig 91). This involved the laying of a concrete floor (Pl 129) and its subdivision into three north-east/south-west-aligned bays (*209-11*), indicative of a cowshed (shippon). This arrangement included a central feeding passage (*211*), with drainage channels (*212* and *213*) on either side, covered by wooden planks, their position indicating that access was through a doorway on the north-eastern side of the shed. This passage was between the stalls (*209* and *210*), which were defined by upright stone slabs, forming two sets of five single stalls, each measuring *c* 1 m wide, on either side of the feeding passage.

Castle Hamlet: Castle House and Castle Farm
Castle Hamlet lay at the western end of Lower Lane, and settlement there appears to have first appeared in the mid-late seventeenth century, following the construction of a small house on the northern side of the lane (*Ch 4, p 85*). This was then followed by the construction of Castle Farm, on the southern side of Lower Lane, most probably in the mid-eighteenth century (*Ch 4, p 86*). Both properties were then occupied and modified throughout the late eighteenth and nineteenth centuries.

Plate 130: Castle House: the first-floor eighteenth-century window

Castle House

The building survey indicated that the seventeenth-century structure at Castle House (*Ch 4, p 85*; Fig 80) was modified during the late eighteenth century. Similarly, the cartographic evidence indicates that, during the early nineteenth century, an additional range had been added to the southern side of the seventeenth-/eighteenth-century house. This range was extant in 2007 and was also examined during the building survey.

Documentary evidence

Castle House appears to have been occupied in the early 1840s by Samuel Greenwood, who is recorded in the 1841 Census Returns as a farmer, together with his wife and two young children (NA HO 107/550). The adjacent cottage was occupied at that date by Robert Greaves, a 30-year-old weaver.

The Census Returns for 1851 record several households living at Castle House, including James Greenwood, who farmed three acres of land, whilst his 13-year-old daughter worked as a cotton weaver, and his ten-year-old son was a fustian cutter (NA HO 107/2244). The other families were those of David Ashworth, a coal miner, Joseph Taylor, and Joseph Wilkinson, both described as agricultural labourers.

The Census Returns for 1861 indicate that Castle House was occupied by James Lord and his wife Hannah, both described as power-loom cotton weavers, with Elizabeth Clarkson from Bury, a servant, residing at the

adjacent cottage (NA RG 9/3035). Samuel Greenwood, a farmer of six acres, is also recorded at Castle House, presumably the same Greenwood family recorded in the Census Returns for 1841 and 1851. Interestingly, two of his sons are recorded as fustian cutters, whilst his 25-year-old daughter was a throstle piecer in a cotton mill (NA HO 107/550).

Later references to Castle House may be drawn from trade directories, one of which lists Joseph Taylor as a farmer (Duncan 1889, 117). However, the only entry in the 1901 Census is for John Wild, a carter, and his family (NA RG 13/3833).

Building survey

The building survey indicated that the seventeenth-century house was raised to two storeys in the late eighteenth century. Again, this was evident from the fabric of, and architectural details within, the north-eastern and south-eastern elevations of the building, a break between the lower seventeenth-century elements and raised eighteenth-century walling being evident at the south-western end of the north-western elevation, whilst similarly, a later building phase was evident in the south-eastern gable. In this instance, the later raising of the roof entailed building a new gable apex, using small-coursed stone rubble.

The two first-floor windows within the north-eastern elevation were also clearly late eighteenth-century in date. These were placed above the seventeenth-century ground-floor windows (*Ch 4, p 86*), both of which had

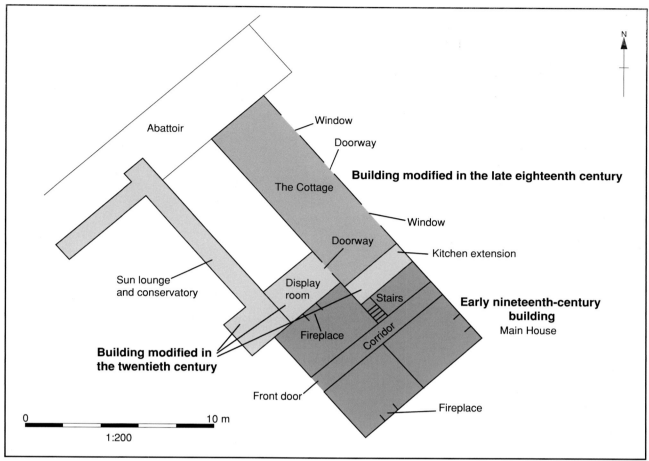

Figure 92: The Castle House buildings modified in the late eighteenth century, and the ground-floor plan of the early nineteenth-century building

two saw-cut stone mullions (Pl 130). Significantly, these were identical to the saw-cut stone mullions in the seventeenth-century ground-floor windows (*Ch 4, p 86*), indicating that these had been inserted into the earlier window surrounds as part of the late eighteenth-century modifications.

The nineteenth-century range formed a two-storey building with a squat L-shaped footprint (Fig 92). It was built of roughly dressed coursed rubble, with quoins at all the corners. The south-western elevation formed the main façade of the building (Pl 131), and at ground-floor level there was a centrally placed door, which had a plain stone surround with a plain stone drip hood over the door lintel. The door was a late twentieth-century replacement, as was a single-light fan above the door. The fenestration consisted of a single double-light window at the north-western end of the elevation, and a six-light window with timber mullions at the southern end. At the first-floor level there were three double-light windows, equally spaced. All the windows were late twentieth-century replacements.

The north-eastern elevation at the rear was built in the same manner as the principal elevation, and

contained a dog-legged section at its western end (Pl 132). The fenestration consisted of three small double-light windows, two in the ground floor and a single window on the first floor of the western dog-leg.

The south-eastern gable was in the same building style as the others, with three windows, two equally spaced in the first floor, and a single window in the

Plate 131: Castle House: the south-western elevation of the nineteenth-century range

Plate 132: Castle House: the north-eastern elevation of the nineteenth-century range

ground floor, at the southern end of the elevation. All the windows had single-piece stone surrounds and late twentieth-century replacement windows. The north-western gable had no fenestration.

The ground-floor plan of the house consisted of a central main corridor running from the front door through the building, with two rooms on either side. A surviving original feature within the corridor was a continuous timber ornamental display shelf with supporting brackets. The two rooms on the northern side of the corridor were smaller than those to the south, and one of these, at the front of the house, had a central, twentieth-century, fireplace against the gable wall. The two larger rooms on the southern side of the corridor were of equal size, and, again, that at the front of the house had a central fireplace on the house's gable wall. There was also slight evidence to suggest that this room may have originally functioned as the kitchen, as the floor was of large, square semi-glazed tiles. The room to its rear had a fireplace on its north-eastern wall. The stairs leading to the first-floor landing could be accessed via a doorway leading from the central corridor. Beyond the first-floor landing were three square rooms, two at the front of the house, and a single room to the rear. Two of these rooms, the back room and the front room in the south-west portion of the house, had similar fireplaces with glazed tiles in the Art Deco style.

Castle Farm
A standing building at Castle Farm (Fig 80) was subjected to survey, which indicated that it was late eighteenth-century in date and was a weaver's

cottage, which had been added to the southern end of the mid-eighteenth-century farmhouse (*Ch 4, p 86*). Following the demolition of the building, its footprint was excavated.

The cartographic and documentary evidence (*p 191*) indicate that the eighteenth-century farmhouse and later weaver's cottage were still occupied during the nineteenth century, and that an outbuilding to the north, constructed in the early eighteenth century (*Ch 4, p 87*), also remained. All of these buildings are depicted on nineteenth-century mapping (*eg* 1850b; Fig 93), which suggests that several additions had been made to the weaver's cottage and outbuilding by the mid-nineteenth century. Both the building

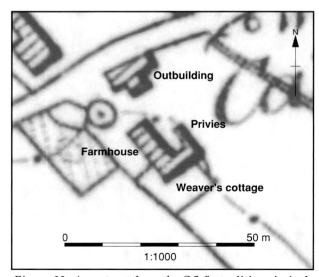

Figure 93: An extract from the OS first edition six-inch map (1850), showing Castle Farm

survey and excavation produced evidence for these additions, and the building survey also identified nineteenth-century elements within the weaver's cottage that indicated its interior had been modified during this period.

Documentary evidence
The 1861 Census Returns record John Lord from Castleton, a farmer of 13 acres, as the occupant of Castle Farm (NA RG 9/3035). John was assisted on the farm by his wife, Susan Lord, and their 14-year-old son, whilst their four daughters worked as power-loom operators. The adjacent cottage was occupied at this date by Richard Heardman, together with his wife and 16-year-old daughter, all from Castleton and all described as 'power-loom cotton weavers'.

John Lord is similarly listed as a farmer at Castle Farm in the Census Returns for 1871 (NA RG 10/4116), although he tended the slightly reduced area of ten acres. He was assisted on the farm by his wife and 20-year-old son, described as an agricultural labourer. There is no entry in the Census for the adjacent cottage, suggesting that it may have been empty. By 1881, however, three families were residing at Castle Farm (NA RG 11/4103). James Clegg and

his wife Jane had taken over the farm, whilst their 18-year-old daughter worked as a weaver and their 16-year-old daughter as a 'cotton operative'. James Clegg is listed as a farmer in a trade directory for 1888-9 (Duncan 1889, 117). The other households listed in the 1881 Census (NA RG 11/4103) were John Howarth, an unemployed mechanic, and Robert Brierley, who is described as a woollen weaver; it is unclear whether Brierley was a handloom weaver, although it seems more likely that he worked at a local weaving shed. By the early twentieth century, Castle Farm was occupied by J Houldsworth, who was one of small number of farmers listed in a trade directory for Castleton township (Clegg 1907, 126).

Archaeological investigation: building survey and excavation
The weaver's cottage, added to the southern side of the earlier farmhouse (*Ch 4, p 86*) in the late eighteenth century, was of two-and-a-half storeys (including a loft floor), with a two-bay rectangular footprint orientated on a south-western/north-eastern alignment (Fig 94). It was constructed entirely of handmade brick.

The external elevations and interior of this building were recorded, but only one surviving

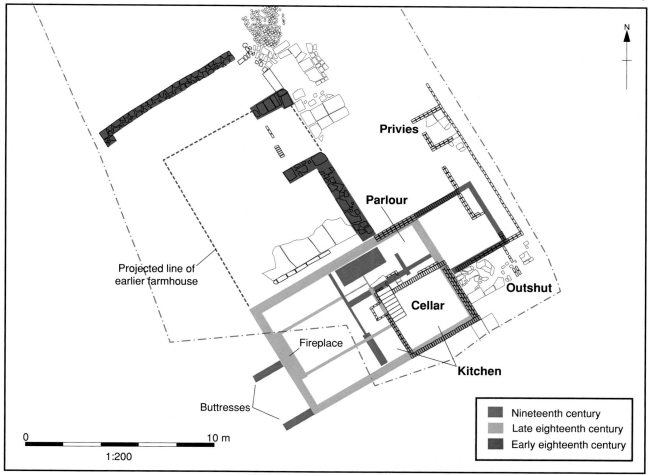

Figure 94: The late eighteenth-century weaver's cottage at Castle Farm and the nineteenth-century additions

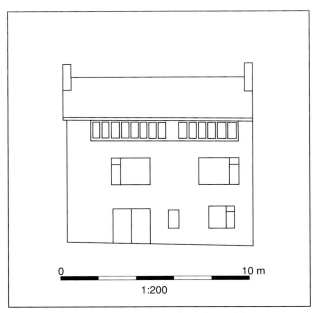

Figure 95: The south-eastern elevation of the weaver's cottage at Castle Farm

late eighteenth-century element was present, in the south-eastern elevation, at loft-floor level (Fig 95). This was a continuous multi-light window, running along the entire length of the elevation, which had 15 lights and 14 stone mullions, although most of the lights had been blocked and only two remained open at the time of the survey

(Pl 133); it clearly indicates that weaving occurred within the loft area. All of the other windows were twentieth-century replacements, and it is unclear which marked the positions of the original late eighteenth-century windows. Similarly, modern doorways had been inserted into the fabric of the building. However, it is likely that the original doorway into the cottage was on the south-eastern elevation, close to the south-eastern corner of the building, although this had been converted into a window in the mid-nineteenth century. The only other late eighteenth-century feature external to the building was a double-pot chimney stack, with original late eighteenth-century-style pots, at the apex of the south-western gable (Pl 134).

Similarly, only a handful of original features were identified inside, but it appears that there may originally have been a single room. The south-western part of this contained a wide late eighteenth-century fireplace (Fig 94), with a stone surround, which had been reduced in size during the mid-nineteenth century and completely blocked in the late twentieth century (Pl 135). Original ceiling beams, that retained their arris, were visible along the length of the room on either side of the fireplace (Pl 136). In addition, a bressumer beam was present which spanned the width of the room (Pl 137).

Plate 133: Castle Farm: the south-eastern elevation of the weaver's cottage, showing the blocked multi-light windows at loft level

Plate 134: Castle Farm: the late eighteenth-century chimney pots on the south-western gable of the weaver's cottage

Plate 135: Castle Farm: the ground-floor fireplace in the weaver's cottage

Plate 136: Castle Farm: the ground-floor ceiling beams in the weaver's cottage

Plate 137: Castle Farm: the bressumer beam in the weaver's cottage

The excavation provided few further details, but did uncover a small cellar at the north-eastern corner of the building (Pl 138). This was constructed almost entirely from handmade bricks, with stone used to provide steps for the stairs, the sills for a probable window in the north-eastern elevation, and the alcoves which formed part of the other three elevations. The alcoves were supplemented by a cupboard space on the north-eastern side at the top of the stair access. The surviving remnants of the ceiling were also constructed of handmade brick, and appeared to form the edges of a barrel-vault. The floor had not survived, although a fragment of what appeared to be a stone flag was evident in the south-western corner of the cellar, bonded into the base of the brick wall.

The building survey also suggested that the first-floor level originally formed a single open room. Again, original features were scarce but they did include ceiling-bridging-beams, which spanned the shorter width of the building. Significantly, in the south-west of the first floor (Pl 139), two of the ceiling beams had four crude-cut mortises inserted into their under-sides (Pl 140). The position of the centres of the four mortises, which formed a rectangle measuring 2 x 2.7 m, probably indicates the position of the corner uprights for a broad loom.

Several walls were identified, which had been inserted into the cottage (Fig 94). One divided the ground-floor into two rooms, the southernmost of which contained the late eighteenth-century fireplace, and may have functioned as the kitchen, whilst that to the north may have been a parlour. It was also evident that a single brick-built dividing wall had been inserted at first-floor level, on the same alignment as the ground-floor wall. No walls were inserted in the second-floor loft area. It was perhaps during this period that a staircase was also added, allowing easier access between the ground and first floors.

In addition to the modifications made to the interior of the cottage, it is evident from historical mapping that an outshut had been appended to the north-east corner during the earlier part of the nineteenth century. This was extant at the time of the building survey and proved to be a single storey constructed in handmade brick, 4.5 m square, with a modern window and door. The footprint indicated that, internally, its north-eastern corner contained a small brick-built partition, and based on its size and arrangement, the outshut may have functioned either as a dairy or a washhouse. The excavation also uncovered the remains of two brick-built privies on the north-western side of the outshut. The positions of these, like the outshut, are plotted on the first edition OS map (1850b; Fig 93).

Evidence for another brick-built extension to the cottage was also identified by the building survey, on the south-western gable, probably originally two-

Plate 138: Castle Farm: the cellar at the north-eastern corner of the weaver's cottage

Plate 139: Castle Farm: the south-western gable wall of the weaver's cottage, showing one of the ceiling beams with two crude-cut mortices

Plate 140: Castle Farm: one of the crude-cut mortices in the ceiling-bridging beams at the weaver's cottage

storeyed. It had been demolished in the twentieth century and was evident only as two side-by-side sloping brick 'buttresses', which abutted the gable wall (Pl 133).

The excavation, and cartographic evidence, indicated that the eighteenth-century outbuilding to the north of the farmhouse was also extended during the early part of the nineteenth century (Fig 96). This involved

the construction of an additional room, with external walls of handmade brick and stone, which was separated from the eighteenth-century outbuilding by a covered passageway.

The Moor Bank Lane Property

Near Moor Bank Farm

The building survey indicated that the original seventeenth-century farmhouse at Near Moor Bank Farm (*Ch 4, p 89*; Fig 80) was partly rebuilt and extended in the late eighteenth century. This also involved the construction of a barn attached to the modified farmhouse.

It is perhaps surprising that this farm is not shown on the earliest maps, including those produced by Yates in 1786 and Greenwood in 1818. In the light of the compelling archaeological evidence for an earlier building, however, their absence from the mapping may be attributed to an omission by the surveyors. Later cartographic evidence does, however, indicate that by the mid-nineteenth century an additional range had been built on the northern side of the farmhouse (Fig 97). This replaced a late eighteenth-century outshut, and was extant in 2004, so was

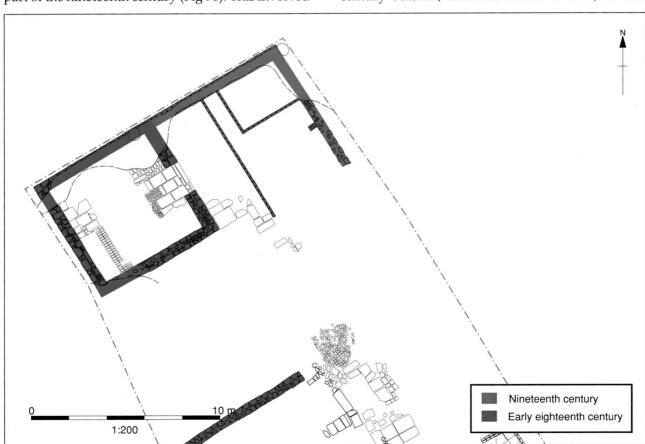

■	Nineteenth century
■	Early eighteenth century

0   10 m

1:200

Figure 96: Nineteenth-century additions to the outbuilding at Castle Farm

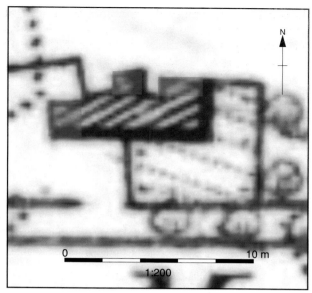

Figure 97: An extract from the OS first edition six-inch map (1850), showing Near Moor Bank Farm, with the nineteenth-century additions highlighted

recorded during the building survey. In addition, the first edition OS map (1850b) indicates that by this date a small room had been appended to the northern side of the barn, though this had been demolished by the time of the publication of the first edition 1:2500 OS map (1893c). It is also evident from the first edition OS map that a larger building had been added to the western gable of the barn. However, later OS mapping (*ie* OS 1893c; 1910a) indicates that this building had been reconstructed in the late nineteenth or early twentieth century. It was also extant in 2004, functioning as a stable and hayloft, and its exterior was recorded during the building survey.

Documentary evidence
There are several references to Moor Bank in the documentary sources, although these rarely differentiate between the three different farms, and it is thus difficult to associate individuals firmly with the separate buildings. Land Tax assessments for Castleton provide two entries for Moor Bank in 1782, and indicate that Edmund Grindrod occupied a property owned by John Greenwood, whilst 'widow Mills' occupied that owned by Benjamin Gartside (LA QDL/S/24). Edmund Grindrod again appears at Moor Bank in a Land Tax assessment compiled in June 1787, whilst the other property appears to have been occupied at that date by the owner, Benjamin Gartside (*ibid*). However, the Land Tax assessment compiled in July 1790 lists Edmund Grindrod as the occupier of both properties at Moor Bank and identifies Elija Dickinson as the proprietor. The tax assessment for one of the properties in 1790 was 6s, whilst the second was just 1s 3d (*ibid*). It would seem likely that this assessment referred to

Near Moor Bank Farm, as the nearby farms of Moor Bank and Further Moor Bank lay in the adjacent township of Butterworth, and were thus omitted from the Land Tax assessment for Castleton. The assessment for the following year, calculated in June 1791, however, lists Edmund Grindrod as the sole occupier of Moor Bank, and gives Benjamin Gartside as the proprietor (*ibid*).

The Castleton Land Tax assessment for 1808 lists Thomas Whittles at Moor Bank, at a tax rate of 5s 3d (*ibid*). The assessment for 1809 again lists Thomas Whittles, but also gives Ambrose Greenwood as the occupier of a second property (and also of Silver Lane), which was owned at that date by Benjamin Gartside (*ibid*). By 1817, the two properties were occupied by Robert Whittles and the widow of Ambrose Greenwood, with the tax rated at 5s 8d and 9d respectively. The comparatively low rate levied against Ambrose Greenwood suggests that the family lived in a small cottage with little, or no, associated land.

Notwithstanding the probable seventeenth-century origins of the site, the first cartographic source to show a building in the position of Near Moor Bank Farm is Hennet's survey of 1830. 'Near Moorbank' is named on the first edition OS map (1850b), which shows an east/west-aligned range of buildings, with a narrower extension to the west. This map also shows a Moor Bank Farm a short distance to the east, on the southern side of Moor Bank Lane. It seems that John Brearley, who had bought Lower Lane Farm in 1827, was living at Moor Bank Farm in 1848, as stated in a will of that year (LA WCW/ Supra/C1190/29).

Near Moor Bank Farm was occupied at this date by Edmund Fitton. He is described in the 1841 Census Returns as a 60-year-old farmer, who resided with his wife, Sarah, and their son, John (NA HO 107/550). The 1851 Census Returns record that Edmund farmed 11 acres of land at Moor Bank, and was assisted by his 25-year old son (NA HO 107/2244). Other family members living at Near Moor Bank Farm by 1851 included Edmund's 29-year-old daughter, who had moved from Manchester with her two young sons. Another agricultural labourer, the 36-year-old Thomas Sutcliffe from Castleton, also lived at the farm, together with his wife and two young children. There is no indication from the Census Returns of any textile-manufacturing being undertaken at Near Moor Bank at this date.

The only entry for Moor Bank Farm in the 1861 Census Returns is for Benjamin Clegg, from Butterworth, who is described as a farmer of 11½ acres. Benjamin was assisted on the farm by his wife (NA RG 9/3035).

The Census Returns for 1871 (NA RG 10/4116) record Stephan Wildman at 'Moor Bank', and it seems likely that this entry refers to Near Moor Bank Farm. Originally from Ireby in Yorkshire, Wildman farmed nine acres, and lived with his wife and a 19-year-old male servant from Oldham. By 1881, Moor Bank was being farmed by the 42-year-old William Wildman (NA RG 11/4103), from Keighley in Yorkshire and probably a relative of Stephan Wildman. William's family consisted of his 40-year-old wife, his three daughters, son, and a 70-year-old aunt. In addition, a 16-year-old 'farm servant' is recorded at the farm in the Census Returns. The records imply that William's wife worked on the farm, and one of his daughters was employed as a dairy maid, although his eldest daughter appears to have worked in a cotton mill. The Wildman family appear to have remained at Near Moor Bank Farm into the twentieth century, and are listed there as farmers in a trade directory for 1916 (Clegg 1916, 232).

The Census Returns for 1891 also record Edward Chadwick as a farmer at Moor Bank, together with his sister (NA RG 12/3329). The farmhouse was occupied by Edmund Chadwick, presumably Edward's younger brother, together with his wife and two sons. Edmund is described as a farm labourer, and his wife as a domestic housemaid.

The 1893 OS first edition 1:2500 map of the area (1893c) shows Near Moor Bank Farm with a similar plan form to that depicted on earlier mapping, except that there was now a large square addition to the north-eastern corner of the farmhouse. The Census Returns for 1901 record that the Wildman family were still farmers at Near Moor Bank Farm (NA RG 13/3833). The complex in its most developed form is shown on the 1955 OS 1:2500 map for the area, this north-eastern addition having been demolished, and a range of farm buildings surrounded the yard on the northern side of the farmhouse.

The last owners of Near Moor Bank Farm were Mr and Mrs Leach, who farmed 60 acres mainly for beef, including land previously held by Dig Gate Farm and Moorbank Farm (formerly Further Moorbank; *Ch 4, p 88*; Haynes and Tipper 1994, 44). At the end of the twentieth century, the farm had been reduced to horse stabling only. A serious fire gutted the cart shed which adjoined the western gable of the farmhouse in 2002, and no repairs or rebuilding was undertaken. All of these buildings were demolished in 2005.

Archaeological investigation: building survey and excavation
Rebuilding the farmhouse
The building survey indicated that the rear (northern) elevation of the seventeenth-century farmhouse was demolished and rebuilt during the late eighteenth century, as part of a scheme designed to widen the building (Fig 98), probably to insert a new staircase. A short stub of seventeenth-century masonry extended from the western gable wall (*Ch 4, p 89*), forming the remains of the northern elevation of the seventeenth-century farmhouse, but now within the interior of the extended building.

As with other parts of the farmhouse, this elevation had been rendered and painted. It also contained three twentieth-century windows, which probably denote the position of the original late eighteenth-century windows. One was at ground-floor level to the east of the door, and had yellow sandstone jambs, sill, and lintel, whilst the other two were at first-floor level. One of these was positioned at the centre of the elevation, whilst the other was close to the western gable wall. The elevation also contained a centrally positioned doorway, which was probably inserted in the nineteenth century (*p 201*).

Further details relating to the late eighteenth-century rebuilding of the northern side of the farmhouse were provided by the excavation. Whilst this indicated that the rebuilt northern wall was of drystone construction, it also uncovered a drystone-walled cellar that had probably been beneath an outshut, to the rear of the western bay of the building. It was clear, therefore, that this outshut formed an additional element of the late eighteenth-century scheme of rebuilding, though, based on historical mapping, its life was comparatively short, as it is not depicted on the first edition OS map (1850b).

The outshut was probably single storeyed, as this would explain the absence of a ground-floor window in the western section of the extant northern elevation of the farmhouse, and it is quite possible that it functioned as a pantry. The cellar could be accessed from the interior of the farmhouse via a right-angled flight of stairs composed of flagstone treads, which were carried by handmade brick supports, apart from the lower step, which was supported by flagstones (Pl 141). The cellar was 3 m square, with a depth of 2 m below the ground surface (Pl 142), and was defined by 0.55 m-thick drystone walls, and a handmade brick barrel-vaulted ceiling. Stone-lined alcoves were also present in all four walls, which were probably used for cold storage (Pl 143), and it also had a cellar light at the centre of its western wall. It had a flagstone floor, and at its centre, two handmade brick piers supported a large sandstone slab acting as a table top (Pl 142), measuring 1.4 m square. The sandstone slab had been snapped in half and lay amongst the backfill, resting only on the southern of the two brick piers. The size of the slab suggested that it had been

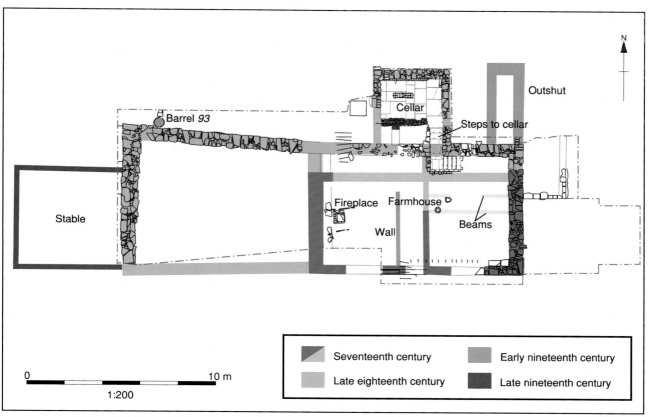

Figure 98: Late eighteenth- and nineteenth-century modifications to Near Moor Bank barn

Within the figure the following labels appear:

N

Outshut

Cellar

Barrel 93

Steps to cellar

Fireplace

Farmhouse

Stable

Wall

Beams

0   10 m

1:200

Seventeenth century   Early nineteenth century

Late eighteenth century   Late nineteenth century

Plate 141: Near Moor Bank Farm: steps leading into the cellar, looking north

Plate 142: Near Moor Bank Farm: the cellar, looking west

Plate 143: Near Moor Bank Farm: the stone-lined alcoves and cellar light in the west wall of the cellar, looking west

Plate 144: Near Moor Bank Farm: the southern elevation of the farmhouse, barn, and stables

installed during the original build of the cellar, as it was too large to fit through the entrance.

Other late eighteenth-century features were recorded in the eastern bay inside the seventeenth-century farmhouse. These included two composite timber ceiling beams that had been rendered with plaster.

The barn

It is highly probable that, as part of the building works that extended the farmhouse, a single-storeyed stone-built barn was also constructed, which was abutted onto the western end of the dwelling (Fig 98; Pl 144). Although this building was extant at the time of the survey, only its exterior could be recorded due to its unsafe condition (*p 197*). However, it was evident from this and an earlier photograph of this building (Haynes and Tipper 1994, fig 5.15) that the barn had been substantially modified at some stage in the late twentieth century. These modifications entailed raising the roof of the structure to the same

Plate 145: Near Moor Bank Farm: the northern elevation of the farmhouse, barn, and stables

level as the farmhouse, and inserting a series of new windows into the elevations of the barn, as well as constructing a brick-built chimney on its rear elevation (Pl 145), which housed a coal-fired domestic boiler. Indeed, the only original feature that was recorded by the building survey was a central cart entrance on its southern elevation. The excavation indicated that the exterior walls of the barn were of drystone construction.

Nineteenth-century additions and features

At some stage during the early nineteenth century, an additional range was added to the northern side of the farmhouse, which abutted that elevation rebuilt in the late eighteenth century. This range formed a narrow, single-storey outhouse with a single small square single-light window at the northern end of its western elevation. The excavation also exposed the footings for its eastern wall, indicating that it had been constructed in handmade brick.

Within the farmhouse, the building survey also indicated that a nineteenth-century wall had been inserted at ground-floor level into the western bay. This created a central passageway from the front door to a rear door, which had probably been inserted following the demolition of the late eighteenth-century outshut (*p 198*). It is quite likely that the creation of this passage also entailed the removal of the original seventeenth-century fireplace within the property, opposite the original entrance. The removal of this fireplace therefore necessitated the construction of a 'new' fireplace, which abutted the western gable wall, and the excavation indicated that it was constructed in stone and handmade brick (Pl 146).

A sunken wooden barrel (*93*; Pl 147) was also found on the northern side of the barn. Two of the composite staves had been shortened on its northern side to connect it with a 0.09 m-wide channel, made from handmade half-bricks with a lime mortar bond, covered by and mounted on stone slabs, which sloped away to the north. The barrel had a diameter of 0.5 m at the top, and 0.6 m in the centre, and it had been filled entirely with concrete.

A small stable was added to the western end of the late eighteenth-century barn (*above*) at the close of the nineteenth century, which the cartographic evidence indicates replaced an earlier building (*p 197*). This stable was recorded during the building survey, as of two storeys, constructed of machine-made brick. It had stable doors on its northern and western elevations, and a tall, six-light window, cutting through both the storeys, on its northern elevation (Pl 145). Within its interior, at ground-floor level, were timber boxes for three or four horses, whilst its upper floor formed an open hay loft.

Plate 146: Near Moor Bank Farm: the stone and handmade brick fireplace, looking west

*Plate 147: Near Moor Bank Farm: barrel **93**, looking west*

8

LATE EIGHTEENTH-AND NINETEENTH-CENTURY LANDSCAPES 3: CUTACRE

Richard A Gregory and Peter Arrowsmith

During the late eighteenth and early nineteenth centuries, Cutacre was an agricultural landscape, dominated by enclosed fields and farmsteads (Fig 99), the origins of which were largely early post-medieval (*Ch 5*), although there was also a scattering of coal-mining sites. Indeed, mining formed the major nineteenth-century industry in this and the wider area and, by the 1840s, coal was locally mined through a number of small collieries. In the north-east of the Cutacre area, these included Bank House

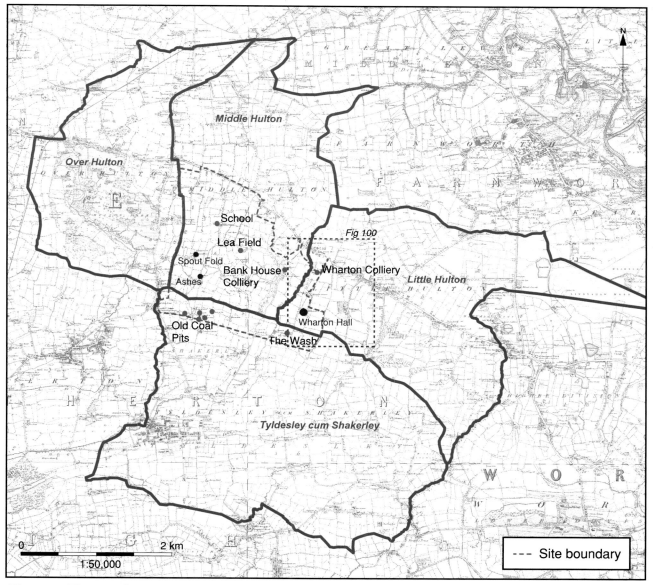

Figure 99: The area of the Cutacre development, superimposed on the OS first edition six-inch maps (1849; 1850), with sites mentioned in the text

Colliery in Middle Hulton and Wharton Colliery, to the north of Wharton Hall. Both were operated by Francis Charlton (BA ZJA 752; OA North 2006a, 15). In the south-west of the development area, a group of 'old coal pits' is labelled on the first edition six-inch OS map (1849), which may indicate mining in the eighteenth or early nineteenth century.

The scale of the industry increased dramatically in the late nineteenth century, when large collieries were established, which are depicted on the first edition 1:2500 OS map (1893d; Fig 100). In the south-east of the Cutacre area, these included Wharton Hall Colliery, to the south of the hall, which was established in *c* 1870, when the Wharton Hall estate was sold to Gerald Potter and others, who formed the Wharton Hall Colliery Company. In August 1881, the company in turn sold the estate to the Bridgewater Trustees (Farrer and Brownbill 1911a, 30 n62; SCA BW/T 7/14). The founding of this colliery led to the loss of one of the farmsteads within the Cutacre area, known as The Wash. Once

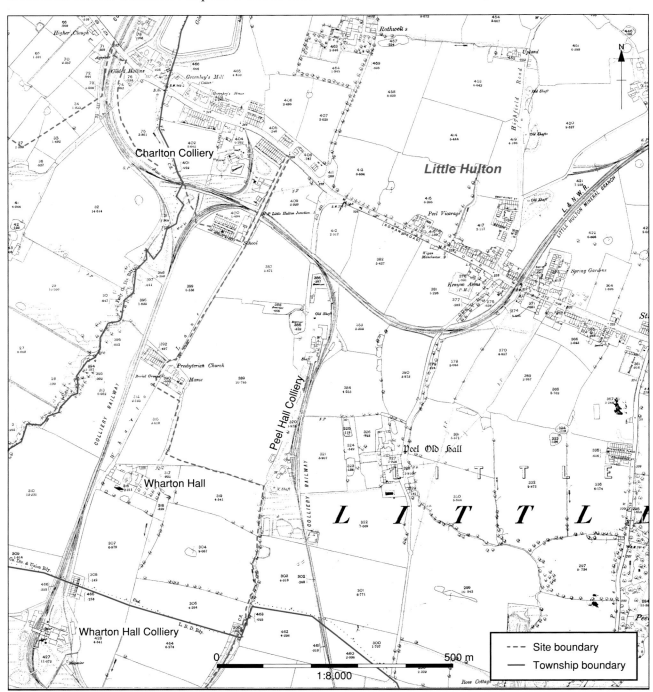

Figure 100: Late nineteenth-century collieries in the vicinity of Wharton Hall, depicted on the OS first edition 1:2500 map (1893)

established, the colliery was served by a railway link to the L&YR's Pendleton and Hindley line, a short distance to the south, the colliery railway continuing to the north, alongside Wharton Lane, to join with the LNWR's Little Hulton Mineral Branch.

Several other large collieries were also established just beyond the boundary of the Cutacre site, with the Peel Hall Colliery to the east, and Charlton Colliery to the north, which were likewise linked to the railway network. The transformation of the local landscape was noted in the early twentieth century by John Partington, who described Wharton Hall as 'buried amidst coal-pit heaps' (Partington c 1910, 151).

The nineteenth century also witnessed the construction of a limited number of new buildings within the Cutacre area, which included Middle Hulton's first school (Fig 99). This was on the Bagot estate land and was built in the 1830s, or early 1840s, by the vicar of Deane (Partington 1909b, 64). By 1841, there was also a row of four workers' houses at Lea Field on Leadbeaters farm. This was possibly converted from a building which is shown on this site on the c 1764 Bridgewater estate plans (SCA BW/E/1), and which is identified in an early nineteenth-century survey of Middle Hulton as a barn (Arrowsmith 2013, 9-11; Partington 1909b, 55).

Evolving Late Eighteenth- and Nineteenth-century Farmsteads

Ashes

Although the excavation at Ashes uncovered evidence for an early post-medieval farmhouse, which was expanded on two separate occasions during the late seventeenth and eighteenth centuries (Ch 5, p 97), it also provided insights into the development of this farmstead during the nineteenth century. The site contained a series of late eighteenth- and nineteenth-century structural remains, indicating additions and modifications to the farmstead during this period, which probably typify the processes of rebuilding and modification that occurred at some of the other farmsteads within the Cutacre area. Significantly, much of this evidence could be related directly to historical OS mapping, specifically that dating to the mid- and late nineteenth century, and the early part of the twentieth century (ie OS 1849; 1893b; 1908).

Documentary evidence
During the late eighteenth century, John Mort, who had held the tenancy of Ashes since 1728 (Ch 5, p 96), bequeathed to his eldest son Robert 'this my estate

which I now live upon during the term of my lease' (LA WCW/Supra/C517B/59). Robert Mort continued to occupy the farm until c 1802, after which time the tenancy passed to the Ashcroft family, and the annual rent was raised from £8 to £30 (SCA BW/M 2/5/1/10).

John Ashcroft (LA QDL/S56) was the first of at least four generations of his family who worked the farm for over a century, and during this tenancy, the Middle Hulton survey of the early nineteenth century describes the farmstead as comprising a 'messuage with barn' (Partington 1909b, 54). Another John Ashcroft was the tenant when the Census Returns of 1841-71 (NA HO 107/541; HO 107/2206; RG 9/2810; RG 10/3921) were taken, and after his death, the farm was first run by his widow Kezia and then by their son, James Ashcroft, who died in 1921 (Bolton and District Family History Society 1983, no 13). James Ashcroft, who was presumably his son of that name, worked the farm in the 1930s, as evidenced from a 1932 trade directory (Tillotsons Newspapers Ltd 1932, 637).

Archaeological investigation: excavation
During the open-area excavation, the principal modifications evident related to the pre-existing early post-medieval farmhouse, which appears to have been subjected to extensive rebuilding during this period. The evidence for this was primarily in the form of sections of handmade brick walling, which had been laid directly on top of the stone foundations that defined the early post-medieval farmhouse's northern and eastern sides. Within the cellar, which formed an element of the seventeenth-century farmhouse (Ch 5, p 97), it was clear that additional internal skins of brickwork had been added to its walls. These suggest that the early farmhouse was extensively rebuilt in the late eighteenth or early nineteenth century. Infilling of the cellar's cupboard and window also took place, and the basement was subdivided into three smaller cellars, through the insertion of two north/south-aligned brick walls (Rooms 2-4; Fig 101; Pl 148). The central room (Room 4) contained a doorway and stone-shelved cupboard, flanking a thicker portion of what appears to have been the base of a chimney breast. Also, as part of the modifications, the steps into the basement were probably moved and a brick barrel-vaulted ceiling was added, as was a floor of slates.

Other modifications were evident in the southern rooms of the early post-medieval farmhouse (Ch 5, p 100). Each of these was provided with a brick-built fireplace (Pl 149), which had been inserted into the western wall of each room. Two pits (616 and 618), identified within Room 1, probably date to a similar

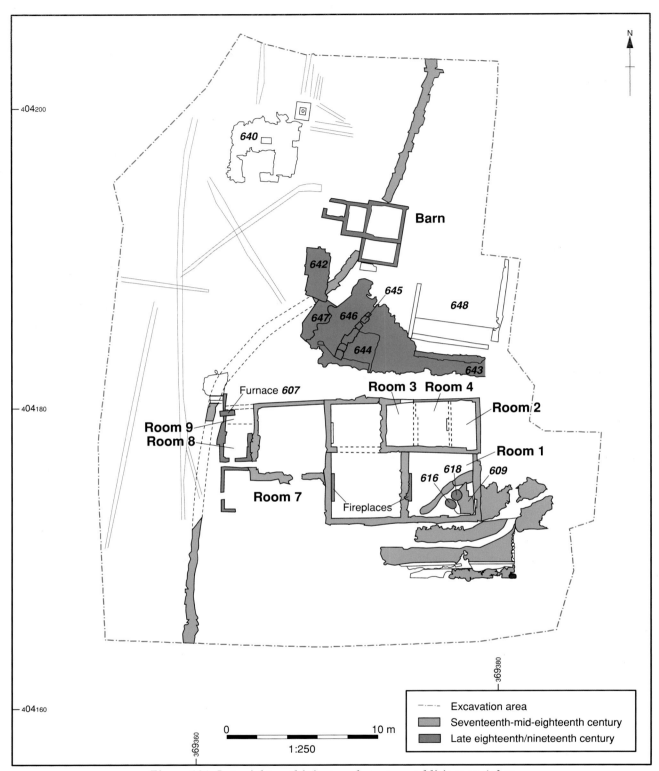

Figure 101: Late eighteenth/nineteenth-century additions to Ashes

period. Both of these cut an earlier cobble surface (*609*; *Ch 5, p 100*), and they contained finds which ranged in date from the seventeenth to nineteenth centuries.

In addition to these modifications, several small rooms were added to the western end of the farmhouse. Initially, two small brick-built rooms (Rooms 8 and 9) were constructed, which abutted

the western wall of the eighteenth-century extension to the original building (*Ch 5, p 101*). These appear to be depicted on the first edition six-inch OS map (1849; Pl 150) and hence they probably date to the early nineteenth century. Room 8 was 2.5 m north/south by 2.15 m east/west and had an entrance, defined by a stone threshold, in its southern wall. To the north, and adjoining this room, was Room 9,

Plate 148: Ashes: the nineteenth-century north/south dividing wall within the seventeenth-century cellar, creating Rooms 3 and 4, looking south

Plate 149: Ashes: fireplace in Room 1, looking west

207

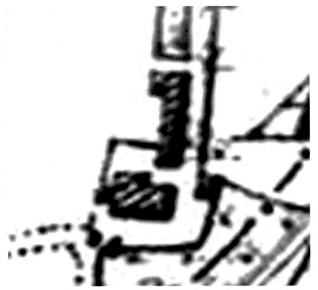

Plate 150: Extract from the OS first edition six-inch map (1849), showing the western extension to Ashes

external wall. This feature was filled with a deposit of slag and charcoal, or clinker, and coal ash (*607*) that appeared to be *in situ*, and probably indicates metal processing there. It seems most likely that it was a small furnace, possibly part of a blacksmith's hearth, with the area outside the room, to the west, being the point from which fuel was fed into it or ash removed. This area had been backfilled with a deposit (*601*) that contained pottery broadly dating from the eighteenth to early twentieth centuries, along with a nineteenth-century clay tobacco pipe (*Appendix 4*). It is also apparent from the first edition six-inch OS map (1849; Pl 150) that a projecting room existed on the northern side of the farmhouse during the mid-nineteenth century. This might represent another early nineteenth-century extension; however, no evidence for this was recognised during the excavation.

which was 1.35 m north/south by 2 m east/west. An east/west-aligned linear brick-built feature was identified in its north-western corner, with a curved eastern end (Pl 151), and to the west of this was an opening which had been built into the room's

In the late nineteenth century, a further brick-built room (Room 7; Fig 101) was attached to the western end of the farmhouse, to the south of Room 8. This is depicted on the OS map of 1908, and was separated from Room 8 by a narrow, 0.35 m-wide, passage. It measured 3.05 m north/south by 2.15 m east/west and may have been used as a store or coal bunker.

*Plate 151: Ashes: probable furnace **607**, looking north*

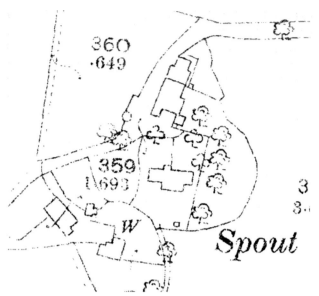

Plate 152: Extract from the OS first edition 1:2500 map (1893), showing Spout Fold

Apart from the farmhouse, the nineteenth-century mapping depicts the position of a large barn to the north, which had been constructed prior to 1800 (*Ch 5, p 97*). The historical mapping (*eg* OS 1908) also indicates that during the late nineteenth century several additions were made to the barn, including the construction of two extensions on its western side. It appears that it was comprehensively demolished in the late twentieth century and replaced by a garage, the footings (*648*) of which were uncovered within the open-area excavation. Indeed, the only surviving remains relating to the barn were part of one of its later nineteenth-century additions. This took the form of a roughly L-shaped extension, comprising four distinct rooms, each with brick walls and a combination of brick and concrete floors. Its maximum dimensions were 5.5 x 4.2 m and it seems likely that it was used to house livestock.

Associated with the main range of farm buildings were several external surfaces (*640, 642, 643, 644, 645, 646,* and *647*), which might also date to the nineteenth century. However, it was evident that there were subtle differences within the form of these surfaces, and in the building materials employed, which suggests that they relate to different episodes of resurfacing during that century. It is perhaps worth noting that one of the surfaces (*646*) contained a stone with a possible socket for a gate-post, which may have been associated with a line of edged flags (*645*); these presumably formed a path at some stage.

Spout Fold

Spout Fold (Fig 99) was continuously occupied during the nineteenth century, its form being depicted on historical OS mapping (*eg* OS 1893b;

Pl 152). These sources indicate that by the mid-nineteenth century additions and modifications had been made to the farm. Some of these were extant in 2016 and were thus recorded as part of the building survey at the site.

Documentary evidence
In 1800 Spout Fold was still occupied by Richard Seddon, who had been resident at the farm since 1776 (*Ch 5, p 113*), and the lease of the property was then renewed, at which time the annual rent was raised from £1 1s to £14 (SCA BW/M 2/5/1/10). Richard died in 1816, leaving the farm to his wife Elizabeth, and bequeathing to his daughters Sarah, Ann, and Mary, 'ten pounds a piece and each of them their own loom' (LA WCW/Supra/C716A/9; BA PMH 7/13). Elizabeth died in March 1831 at the age of eighty-two (MA L 85/1/4/4), and for the last ten years or so of her life, she may have sublet the farm to a James Shaw (LA QDL/S56). In the Middle Hulton survey of the early nineteenth century, the farmstead was described as a 'messuage with barn' (Partington 1909b, 44).

There were four households living at Spout Fold at the time of the 1841 Census (NA HO 107/541). One was headed by the farmer Robert Eckersley, possibly the person of that name who was given a lease of the Bagot farm at Spout Fold in 1799 (MA L 5/2/6/2). That farmstead was probably also the home in 1841 and 1851 of the household of Thomas Boardman, a cotton handloom weaver (NA HO 107/541; HO 107/2206). He presumably lived in the cottage which was listed at the farm along with the house in a Bagot survey of *c* 1860 (MA L 5/4/1/3).

The other two households listed at Spout Fold in 1841 can be identified as the occupants of the Bridgewater-owned farm. One comprised Sarah Seddon, Elizabeth's eldest daughter, who now held the farm, and Alice Harper, a 14-year-old weaver. The other household comprised an agricultural labourer, William Harper, and his family. Harper was the brother-in-law of Sarah Seddon, having married her sister Mary in April 1819 (MA L 85/1/3/4). After Sarah's death, he took over the farm, and died in 1871, being buried alongside his wife in the same grave as Giles and Sarah Edge in Deane churchyard (Bolton and District Family History Society 1983, no 277).

Archaeological investigation: building survey
Andy Phelps and Chris Wild
During the nineteenth century, an extension was added to the eighteenth-century farmhouse (*Ch 5, p 114*); this projected northwards from the eastern end of its northern elevation, and was extant at the time of the building survey (Fig 102; Pl 153). It is evident that this extension was constructed in the

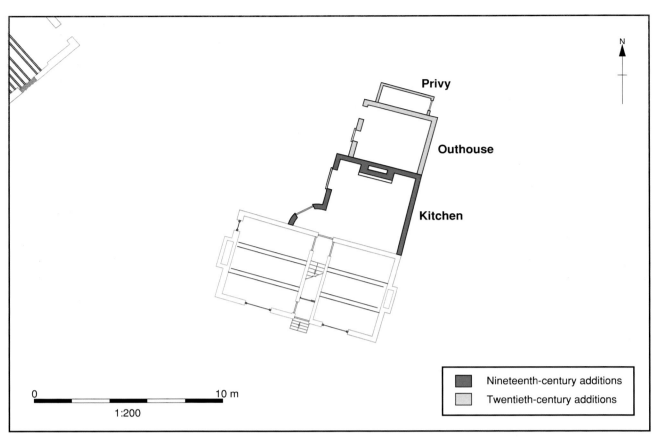

Figure 102: Nineteenth- and twentieth-century additions to Spout Fold

Plate 153: Spout Fold: the farmhouse from the rear, with both nineteenth- and twentieth-century extensions

Plate 154: Spout Fold: cast-iron cooking range in the kitchen extension of the farmhouse

early part of the nineteenth century, as its position is plotted on the first edition six-inch OS map (1849).

Externally, the extension had a shuttered rectangular window in the centre of the east wall and another towards the northern end of the west wall. A curved entrance porch had been added into the corner, between this wall and the northern wall of the farmhouse, to create a doorway into the rear of the house. It is evident that this extension was built as a kitchen for the farmhouse, thus freeing up one of the rooms (the western ground-floor room?) in the main body that would have originally housed the kitchen during the eighteenth century (*Ch 5, p 117*). Although its poor condition prevented access and detailed investigation, one feature of historical interest was a cast-iron cooking range set against the northern wall (Pl 154). During the early twentieth century, a small machine-made brick single-storey extension was added to the northern elevation of the kitchen, along with an external privy. These elements, along with the early nineteenth-century kitchen, were then covered by a roof composed of Welsh slate laid in diminishing courses, below ceramic V-shaped interlocking ridge tiles.

The Nineteenth-century Development of Wharton Hall

Documentary evidence

During the nineteenth century, Wharton Hall continued to be tenanted as a farm. In the early 1890s, Rev Nightingale wrote that it 'is a good sized farmhouse, and has been tenanted by a family of the name of Green for at least four generations' (Nightingale 1892, 109). The name of John Green repeatedly occurs in the Land Tax assessments of 1780-1831 as the occupant of the farm (LA QDL/S/55). In the censuses of 1841-71, William Green is listed, farming 56 acres in 1851 (NA HO 107/2206), and 130 acres in 1861 (NA RG 9/2810). In 1881 the family was headed by William's widow Frances, who was farming 105 acres, and the household also included her eldest son John, who farmed 75 acres in neighbouring Middle Hulton (NA RG 11/3819). At the time of the 1891 Census, Wharton Hall was occupied by her second son, Edward (NA RG 12/3099). His tenure ended in *c* 1900, when Thomas Wharmby took over the farm (SCA P 6/2/8-9), and in the 1920s and

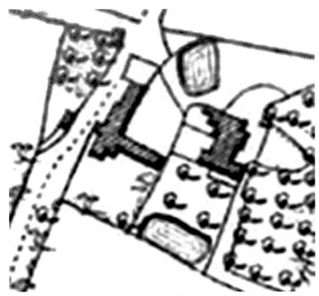

Plate 155: Extract from the OS first edition six-inch map (1850), showing Wharton Hall

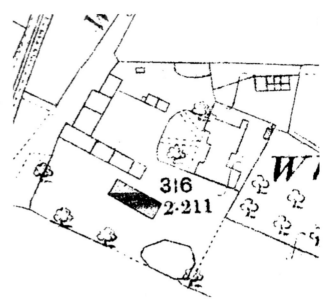

Plate 156: Extract from the OS first edition 1:2500 map (1893), showing Wharton Hall

1930s, trade directories indicate that the tenant was his son Moses Wharmby (Tillotson and Son 1922, 871; Tillotsons Newspapers Ltd 1932, 1002).

By the mid-nineteenth century through to the early twentieth, in addition to the Greens and their successors, it appears that there were other households living at the site. The Census Returns from 1851 to 1911 list two or three families, with the address being variously given as Wharton Fold, Wharton (Hall) Cottages, and Wharton Hall Yard (NA HO 107/2206; RG 9/2810; RG 10/3921; RG 11/3819; RG 12/3099; RG 13/3605; RG 14/23278). These occupants were typically farm labourers or coal miners.

Archaeological investigation: excavation

Wharton Hall underwent various modifications during the nineteenth century, when it was tenanted as a farm (*p 211*). These were revealed during the open-area excavation and could be divided into two broad phases of construction (Phases 4 and 5). Although some of these modifications could be related to both the first edition six-inch (1850a; Pl 155) and 1:2500 OS maps (1893d; Pl 156), significantly, the archaeological evidence allows a more nuanced understanding of the additions and rebuilds of this century.

Phase 4: early/mid-nineteenth-century modifications

The structural remains indicated that a fairly extensive programme of building work occurred during the early and mid-nineteenth century. Within the hall, this appears to have included the insertion of several internal brick walls, some of which seemed to have functioned in a damp-proofing capacity, including a brick wall (*1195*) constructed along the internal face of the northern wall of the stone-built hall (Pl 157). A similar wall was observed butting the eastern wall of the cellar (*1191;* Fig 103) for a distance of 1.7 m. Other features within the hall included a brick-lined chamber

*Plate 157: Wharton Hall: brick wall **1195**, lining the internal face of stone wall **1120**, looking west*

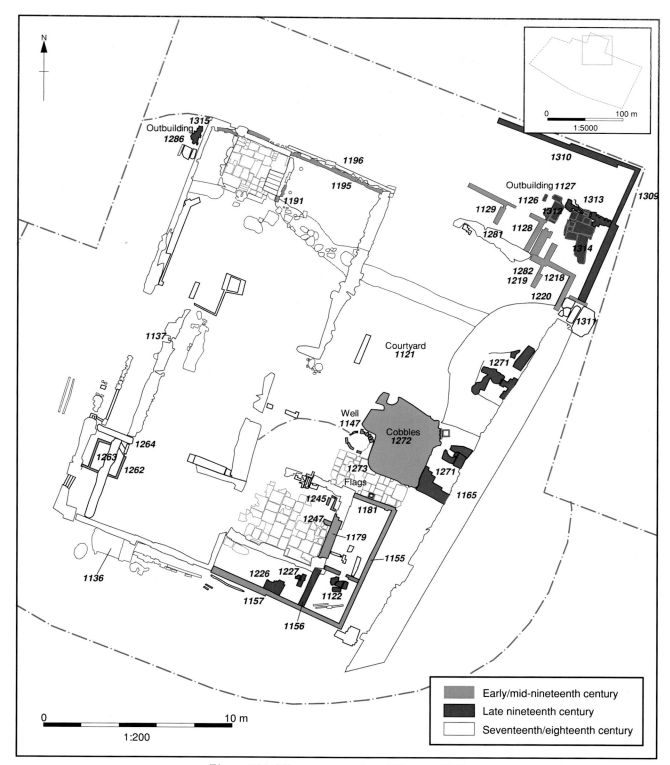

Figure 103: Nineteenth-century Wharton Hall

(*1262*; Pl 158) within the southern cross-wing, which also contained an inner brick-built chamber. The inner chamber was filled with coal and fuel waste (*1265*), to a depth of 1 m, and also quantities of fragmented pottery, glass bottles, and clay pipe, dating from the eighteenth and nineteenth centuries (*Appendix 4*). This may once have been a coal store, although latterly it had been abandoned

and filled with rubbish. Another feature inserted into this area during this period was a brick drain (*1264*), whilst a flag surface (*1136*) was probably laid at this time, abutting the external wall of the southern cross-wing.

This period also witnessed substantial rebuilding and expansion of the extension that had been added

*Plate 158: Wharton Hall: chamber **1262** and drain **1264**, looking north-east*

*Plate 159: Wharton Hall: brick wall **1179**, built above earlier wall **1180**, looking north-east*

to the south-eastern side of the hall's southern cross-wing during the late seventeenth century (Phase 2; *Ch 5, p 132*). The work involved its enlargement through the construction of an additional handmade brick wall (***1181/1155/1157***), two bricks thick, and surviving to a height of six courses. This U-shaped wall clasped the south-eastern corner of the seventeenth-century hall and the north-eastern corner of its eighteenth-century extension, and its position is depicted on the first edition six-inch OS map (1850a; Pl 155). Several partition walls had also been inserted into the eastern and southern parts of the structure, creating rectangular rooms around the original building, whilst the external walls of the earlier extension were also partially rebuilt in brick (***1179***), with some of the lower stone foundations being retained (***1180***; Pl 159).

The nineteenth-century extension also contained the remains of a flagstone floor (***1122***), which had been laid on a compacted coal-rich levelling layer. Few other internal features were extant, although a fragmentary brick wall, aligned north/south, bordered by a flagstone, was possibly part of a former fireplace (***1227***) in the southernmost room of the extension. A possible fireplace had also been inserted into the eighteenth-century extension (***1247***), along with brick drains (***1245***), suggesting that this element performed a domestic role during the nineteenth century.

Immediately to the north of the extended southern wing, and between the late seventeenth-century garden wall (***1165***; *Ch 5, p 135*) and the early seventeenth-century hall, a surface was also laid, probably during the earlier part of the nineteenth century, to create a courtyard (***1121***; Pl 160). This surface was composed of cobbles (***1272***), which had been laid on sequential bedding deposits (***1151/1161***, ***1152***, and ***1153***). Significantly, the finds recovered from these underlying deposits included sherds of nineteenth-century pottery, attesting to the date of the surface, and other fragments of pottery dating from the sixteenth to nineteenth centuries.

Another feature within the courtyard, and one that was probably contemporary with the cobbled surface, was a brick-lined well (***1147***; Pl 161). This was 1 m in diameter, and survived to a depth of more than 4 m, cutting through naturally deposited clay ***1255***. The lower 13 courses were constructed from handmade brick, and the upper three of machine-cut brick, indicating a later modification. The base of the well was lined on its eastern side by a row of three wooden planks, positioned vertically in the naturally deposited clay. These were probably installed as a revetment during its construction, and associated pottery sherds (fill ***1148***) provided a nineteenth-century date for the construction. In addition, two burnt bricks were recovered, suggesting the possibility of a fire at the hall during the eighteenth or nineteenth century.

214

*Plate 160: Wharton Hall: cobbled surface **1272** and well **1147**, looking south-east*

*Plate 161: Wharton Hall: well **1147**, looking south-east*

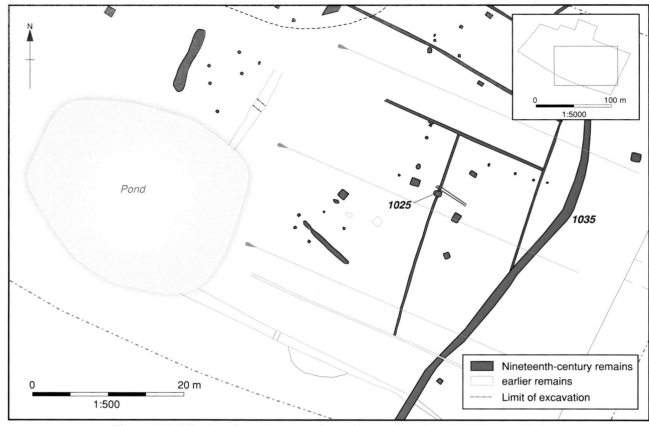

Figure 104: Nineteenth-century remains to the south and east of Wharton Hall

A small outbuilding (*1127*) had also been constructed at the northern end of the courtyard, in the early part of the nineteenth century. This was evident as a series of fragmentary brick walls (*1126, 1128, and 1129, 1218, 1219, 1220*, and *1282*), generally aligned north/south or east/west, that probably once created animal stalls. Two of the walls (*1128* and *1282*) abutted Phase 2 stone wall *1281* (*Ch 5, p 135*), seemingly the remains of an older building. A flagstone floor (*1312*) survived in the north-east of the structure.

Features possibly associated with this earlier nineteenth-century phase of activity were also identified in the southern and eastern parts of the site (Fig 104). These included land drains, clusters of postholes, and pits of various sizes and shapes. Although little dating evidence was recovered from these features, they seem to date from the nineteenth century. Indeed, many of the postholes probably defined fencelines associated with the development of an orchard, shown on the first edition OS map (1850a; Pl 155).

With the exception of one pit containing an animal burial (*1025*), their functions were largely unclear. All were also bordered on the east by a shallow curvilinear ditch (*1035*), extending approximately north/south; this perhaps formed the eastern boundary of the hall at this time, although it does not correspond to any of the boundaries shown on the first edition OS map (1850a).

Phase 5: late nineteenth-century modifications
Several minor modifications were made to the hall during the later nineteenth century (Fig 103). These included the construction of an outshut (*1286*) attached to the building's north-western elevation, which is visible on an early twentieth-century photograph of the hall (*Ch 5, p 125*). It measured 2.8 x 1.3 m, consisting of a flagstone floor within a single-skin brick wall, which had been constructed above cobbled surface *1315* and soil *1109*.

Other modifications occurred within the southern cross-wing, specifically in that part that had been extended in the early nineteenth century (*p 213*). In this area, a 2 m-long north/south brick partition wall (*1156*) was added. This was attached to the southern end of Phase 4 wall *1179* (*p 214*), subdividing the room in the southern part of the extension. This new room was 5 m long and retained evidence for a brick floor (*1226*) attached to southern wall *1157*.

Other activity also occurred within the environs of the hall. This included the construction of a right-angled section of walling (*1310/1309*), appended to an earlier garden wall (*1165*; *Ch 5, p 135*), which was composed of handmade and machine-cut brick. A 1.5 m-wide entrance (**1311**) was created through the remodelled boundary wall, leading into the orchard to the east. During this remodelling, the outbuilding (**1127**) to the north-east of the hall was also modified. This entailed the construction of an additional brick wall (**1313**), aligned east/west, across its northern range. A surface of flagstones (**1314**), butting the internal foundation of wall **1313**, provided evidence for a floor, although it is probable that some of the flagstones were retained to form a footpath from entrance **1311**.

Some resurfacing also occurred within the courtyard area (**1121**; *p 214*) on the eastern side of the hall. This involved the laying of a flagstone surface (**1271/1273**), which abutted, and presumably repaired, the earlier cobbled surface (**1272**). This new surface was also partly laid above the earlier well (**1147**), which itself was modified, by adding the three courses of machine-cut brick to the upper part of the well shaft (*p 214*); it is possible that the superstructure was elaborated or a pump installed. Several pet burials were also uncovered within the former garden, south of the hall, which probably date to this period.

9

SYNTHESIS

Richard A Gregory

Within Greater Manchester, it is comparatively rare that an opportunity arises to examine archaeologically a large and coherent block of landscape, which contains multiple strands of evidence for its use and evolution. Fortunately, both the Kingsway and Cutacre projects presented such opportunities and both areas, which together form the largest archaeological landscape study in Greater Manchester, have produced extremely valuable evidence, in the form of buried archaeological remains and upstanding buildings. This evidence provides excellent insights into aspects of both prehistoric and historic activity in two distinct landscape areas, that at Kingway relating to the use and exploitation of the Pennine fringe, and that at Cutacre being associated with the use of an area on the Lancashire Coal Measures.

Earlier Prehistoric Activity

Significantly, both Kingsway and Cutacre produced complementary evidence relating to the earlier prehistoric landscape. That from Kingsway took the form of pollen data, which allow some insights into the character of this landscape during the late Mesolithic and Neolithic periods, and, accordingly, the transition from a lifestyle dominated by hunter-gathering to one which was increasingly focused on farming. Although this palaeoenvironmental evidence specifically relates to the earlier prehistoric landscape that existed within, and immediately surrounding, Kingsway, it is quite likely, based on previous palaeoecological work centred on the mosses of Greater Manchester (Hall *et al* 1995), that other parts the metropolitan area, including the Cutacre landscape, contained comparable sequences of vegetation, which were also subjected to similar episodes of disturbance by the fledgling communities that roamed and settled the region.

The Kingsway data provide a fairly detailed picture of the vegetation during this period (*Ch 2, p 19*). For instance, it indicates that, prior to *c* 5600 cal

BC, the landscape was predominantly covered by hazel-type scrub, which was interspersed with boggy areas. Significantly, it also appears that during this time late Mesolithic communities were possibly using fire to create small openings, which allowed herbs to flourish and that, in turn, might have provided sources of wild food and attracted animals, presumably resulting in them being more easily hunted.

By the mid-sixth millennium cal BC, alder had replaced hazel as the dominant vegetation, though possible anthropogenic disturbance to the natural vegetation cover, perhaps through fire setting, continued and may well have been partly responsible for the decrease in hazel. During the late fifth millennium cal BC, oak woodland briefly regenerated, though anthropogenic disturbance seemingly continued and was, once more, associated with burning.

This was then followed, during the fourth millennium cal BC, by a decrease in oak and an expansion in birch, with some limited evidence for the Elm Decline, which may have occurred at a similar time as the adoption of a Neolithic lifestyle, as this early decline in elm is an event seen throughout Britain and north-west Europe during the mid-Holocene, *c* 3900-3700 cal BC (*c* 5000 BP) (Parker *et al* 2002), and seems to have been the first major decline in woodland following the post-glacial forest maximum (Bridgland *et al* 2011). However, clearer evidence for Neolithic activity, in the form of farming, dates to the early part of the third millennium cal BC, based on the evidence for more sustained clearance, associated with a rise in grass pollen, together with cereal-type pollen, suggesting small-scale arable cultivation, and pollen indicative of pastoral farming.

It is therefore apparent from the Kingsway pollen data that, during the late Mesolithic period, communities were engaged in limited clearance, followed by more substantial episodes, associated with the adoption of pastoral farming and small-scale cereal cultivation, indicating the beginning of the Neolithic period (*cf* Thomas 2013). At Cutacre, clear evidence for these early communities was found in the form of a small collection of worked-stone artefacts (*Ch 2, p 24*), which, although difficult to interpret, might date to the late Mesolithic period (Pl 162). Many of these items were recovered from tree throws, and it is possible that they were either placed into these naturally created 'pits', as part of early ritual acts and/or were a residue of activity that included the deliberate uprooting of trees. Indeed, if the latter was the case, this perhaps formed one direct example of an early disturbance/clearance event, similar to those that were detected in the Kingsway pollen data.

Bronze Age Settlement

During the excavation at Cinder Hill, in Cutacre (*Ch 2*), the remains of a small prehistoric settlement were unexpectedly uncovered. This proved particularly surprising, as at the start of the project it was considered that the area had only a slight potential to contain evidence for prehistoric settlement. This assumption was largely based on the locational traits of later prehistoric settlement in the region (*cf* Collens 1999), which suggested that early settlement would be confined to those landscape areas that geologically contained free-draining deposits (*ie* sands and gravels). These topographically lay adjacent to watercourses, or wetlands. Indeed, these topographical and geological locations were commonly assumed within Greater Manchester, and effectively discounted many areas of poorly drained glacial till as unsuitable for prehistoric settlement (*pers obs*).

However, it is now clear that such assumptions may at least be partly unfounded for those settlements dating from the Bronze Age onwards. For instance, although the Cutacre settlement was adjacent to a watercourse, it was established on deposits of glacial till, and also lay within a wider landscape composed of heavy clays, which would have been more difficult to work and cultivate than superficial deposits composed

Plate 162: Two microliths, a side-and-end scraper, and a hammer or grinding stone from Cutacre, with microliths hafted to form composite tools (Yaroshevich 2012)

220

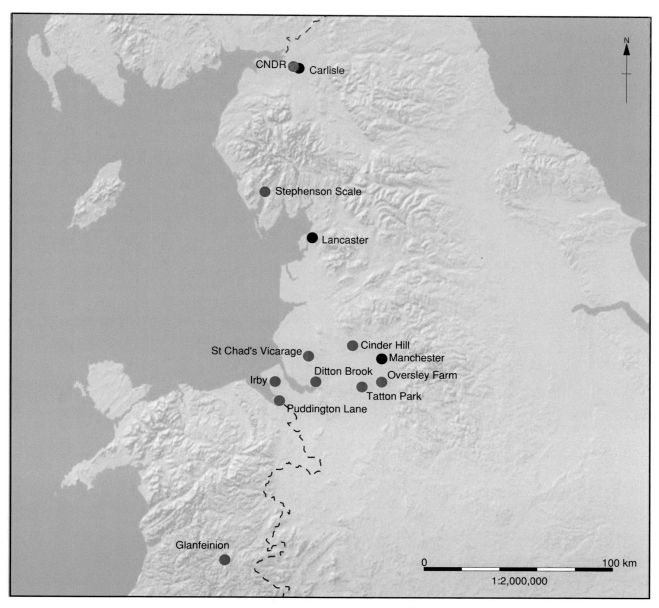

Figure 105: Bronze Age sites mentioned in the text

of sands and gravels. Given this, within Greater Manchester/south-east Lancashire, it may well be that topographical considerations were the more important factor in the siting of prehistoric settlement, and, perhaps, the presence of a watercourse, or standing body of water, was a major locational factor.

Based on the modelling of the radiocarbon dates, the settlement was probably established at *1480-1260 cal BC (95% probability)*, or *1420-1300 cal BC (68% probability)*, and was occupied until *1380-1080 cal BC (95% probability)*, or *1290-1170 cal BC (68% probability)*. Therefore, it clearly dates to the Middle Bronze Age (*c* 1500-1100 cal BC; *cf* Bradley 2007, 183). In terms of the British chronological schemes, its occupation also equates with the Taunton and Penard bronze-metalworking traditions, and the use of Deverel-Rimbury pottery (Needham 1996; 2017; Needham *et al* 1997).

Although a multitude of Middle Bronze Age settlements are known from southern Britain (*cf* Bradley 2007, 187-96), regionally the discovery of this settlement is highly significant, as it is currently the only Middle Bronze Age settlement known from Greater Manchester, and also the earliest dated house within the metropolitan county. In addition, it is only the second definitive Middle Bronze Age settlement (*ie* that associated with a dwelling) to have been identified within the Mersey Basin (Fig 105), with the other being at Irby on the Wirral (Philpott and Adams 2010; *p 224*). Indeed, the only other evidence from the region for dated Middle Bronze Age occupation derives from Oversley Farm, Cheshire, now covered by Manchester Airport's second runway, Puddington Lane, on the Wirral peninsula, and Ditton Brook I, Ditton, and St Chad's Vicarage, Kirkby, both in Merseyside.

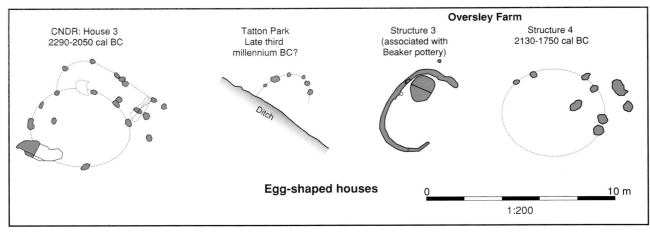

Figure 106: Egg-shaped houses from north-west England

At Oversley Farm (Garner 2007), two isolated Middle Bronze Age pits were discovered, whilst, similarly, at Ditton Brook (Cowell 2000, 13), two pits were found, one of which was dated to the Early/Middle Bronze Age. The Middle Bronze Age remains at Puddington Lane consisted of a hearth, adjacent to two postholes (Gregory and Adams 2019). Although in all three cases these might relate to settlement of this period in the vicinity of the sites, no clear evidence for such settlements, in the form of domestic structures, was recovered by excavation. The evidence from St Chad's Vicarage did, however, include two slightly arcing gullies, which may have formed elements of structures, probably securing windbreaks, again suggesting the presence of nearby settlement. One of these gullies was dated to the Early/Middle Bronze Age (1940-1420 cal BC; 3360±110 BP; Beta-94193) and also contained fragments from a Collared Urn (Adams in prep).

The settlement at Cinder Hill contained a single roundhouse, built using oak and ash timbers, which had been repaired on at least one occasion, and was eventually abandoned and left to rot. The roundhouse had a diameter of *c* 7 m and was post built, whereby the post-ring probably supported the roof as well as acting as the outer wall of the house. The posts within the post-ring were widely spaced, and these gaps may have been filled by wattle and daub, or perhaps prefabricated panels (Pope 2015, 171). Two posts were also present in the interior, one of which was at the dead centre; however, it is likely that these were not load-bearing elements of the roundhouse *per se*, but were instead used as supports during its initial construction (*ibid*).

The entrance was orientated in a south-easterly direction, which is a common trait for prehistoric roundhouses, although this is particularly noted in the Iron Age and Roman period (Oswald 1997). The precise reasons for this orientation are unclear, though it has been postulated, at least for those dating to the later prehistoric period, that entrance position may

have been conditioned by cosmological concerns, particularly relating to the position of the rising sun, especially at the equinoxes and the mid-winter solstice (Parker Pearson 1999). However, this aside, at a more prosaic level, a south-easterly doorway would provide shelter from the prevailing wind and maximise the amount of daylight entering the dwelling (*cf* Pope 2007, 212). A final feature associated with the Cinder Hill roundhouse was a drip-gully, the position of which indicates that the eaves of the structure overhung the outer wall line by some 2 m.

This roundhouse adds to the growing corpus of timber houses from the North West dating to the second millennium BC, which also complement the few known examples that date to the latter part of the third millennium cal BC. Taken together, these allow the form and evolution of early house types to be considered. In this respect, as far as can be ascertained, it appears that, at the very beginning of metal use in the North West, an architectural tradition of egg-shaped post-built houses existed (Fig 106), based on the evidence from Tatton Park (Higham and Crane 1999), Oversley Farm (Garner 2007, 35-40), and the Carlisle Northern Development Route (CNDR; Brown *et al* in prep).

Seemingly, this tradition of egg-shaped houses was followed by a change to post-built roundhouses, including those within either single or double post-rings. These formed part of a widespread Bronze Age tradition, identified across northern Britain, and on current dating evidence, these appeared around 1800 cal BC and continued into the Late Bronze Age (Pope 2015; Gregory in prep). The roundhouse from Cinder Hill is therefore part of this architectural tradition, of which several other examples dating to the second millennium BC are known from north-west England (Fig 107). The earliest of these, discovered near Carlisle, Cumbria, was a small, single post-ring roundhouse (House 1), with a diameter of *c* 4.7 m, which dates to 1900-

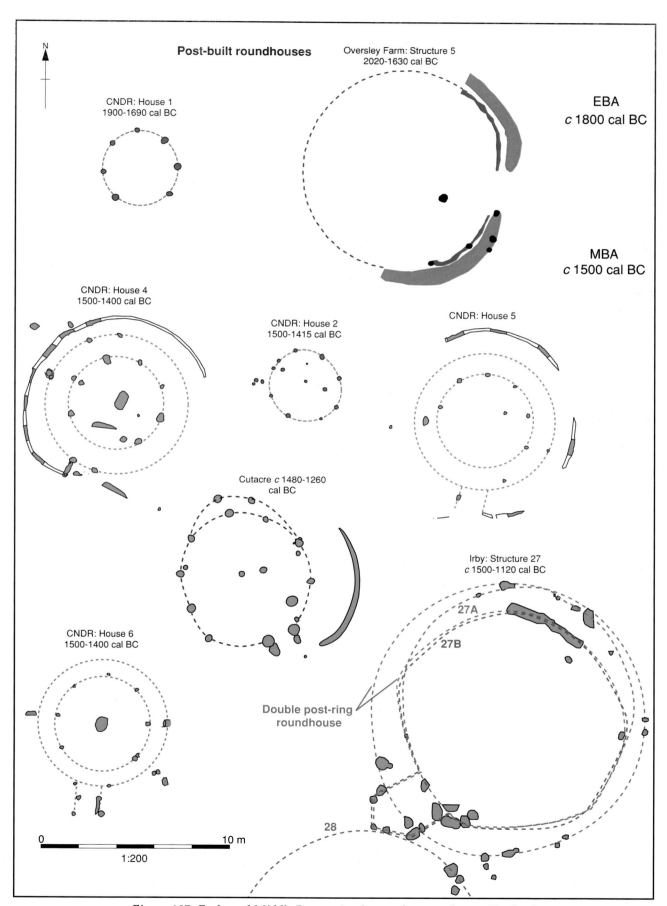

Figure 107: Early and Middle Bronze Age houses from north-west England

223

1690 cal BC (3485±35 BP; SUERC-32724; Gregory in prep). Another comparable Early Bronze Age post-built house has been recorded, also in Cumbria, at Stephenson Scale, which had a diameter of *c* 4 m (*cf* Hodgson and Brennand 2006, 34).

Four of the other known post-built roundhouses were also found in Cumbria. These were again in the vicinity of Carlisle (at CNDR; *p 222*), and, like that from Cinder Hill, dated to the Middle Bronze Age. One of these (House 2) was a small, single post-ring structure, with a diameter of *c* 4.6 m, radiocarbon dates placing its establishment/use at 1500-1415 cal BC (Gregory in prep). The other three known post-built roundhouses (Houses 4-6) relate to a discrete Middle Bronze Age settlement. All were large double post-ring structures, with internal diameters in the range of 8.4-9.4 m (*ibid*), and, in a similar fashion to the Cinder Hill roundhouse, these had porches. This settlement initially contained a single post-built roundhouse (House 5), which was replaced by two contemporary post-built houses (Houses 4 and 6), that, based on the radiocarbon evidence, date to 1500-1400 cal BC (*ibid*).

The other second millennium BC post-built roundhouses known in the North West are, like that from Cinder Hill, from the Mersey Basin. One was discovered at Oversley Farm (Fig 107; Structure 5), dating to the Early Bronze Age, radiocarbon-dated to 2020-1630 cal BC (3490±70 BP; Beta-133371). It may, therefore, date to the period (*c* 1800 cal BC) when the tradition of post-built roundhouses is thought to emerge in the North West (*p 222*). Only approximately half of this house was excavated, but it may have been defined by an arcing 'construction trench', inside which was a curvilinear trench containing stakeholes, interrupted by larger post-settings at 2.2 m intervals (Garner 2007, 42).

It seems more likely, however, that the 'construction trench' was actually an enclosing ring-ditch, comparable to that around the Middle Bronze Age roundhouse at Glanfeinion, near Llandinam, Powys (Fig 105; Britnell *et al* 1997), or even an enlarged drip-gully, rather than explicitly functioning as a structural feature. Therefore, it can be postulated that a single post-ring, defined by the larger posts, formed the outer wall line of the house, and also supported the roof within this feature; the gaps between these posts would have been filled by wattle and daub, secured by the stakeholes. Apart from these features, a floor and a posthole were discovered within the interior of the house. Its diameter would have been in the region of 10 m, indicating a fairly substantial structure, which might have housed more than one family unit.

In contrast, the post-built roundhouses at Irby have been radiocarbon dated to the Middle Bronze Age,

dating to the period *c* 1500-1120 cal BC (Philpott and Adams 2010), and in this respect they are chronologically comparable to the house at Cinder Hill. These structures were defined by a scattering of disparate postholes, which are difficult to interpret. They might relate either to a single large roundhouse (Structure 27), with a diameter of *c* 15 m, defined by a double post-ring, or, alternatively, three structures might have been represented (Structures 27A, 27B, and 28): two consecutive single post-ring houses (Structures 27A and 27B), with a diameter of *c* 14 m and a porch arrangement, built in the same position, with another house with a similar diameter (Structure 28) positioned immediately to the south-west (Fig 107). The latter hypothesis was favoured by the excavators, though it was noted that this would mean they all had unusually large diameters (Cowell 2010, 168). It was therefore suggested that these 'houses' might, in fact, have formed communal buildings, which served several family groups (*ibid*).

The Cinder Hill settlement also contained two sequential four-post structures, the earlier of which had probably been destroyed by fire. Such structures are often interpreted as raised granaries (*cf* Brück 2001; Pl 163), but at Cinder Hill the associated charred plant remains proved particularly informative, indicating that they might have been raised malting floors. Although such structures were a fairly common element of Middle Bronze Age and Iron Age settlements in southern Britain (*ibid*; Cunliffe 2005), they are only just beginning to be identified within the North West, as a feature of Chalcolithic/Bronze Age settlement, such as the two excavated near Carlisle (Gregory in prep). Although both are undated, it is likely that one was built in the late third or early second millennium cal BC, whilst the other was part of a settlement dating to the twelfth to tenth century cal BC. Given this, and the Middle Bronze Age dates for the structures at Cinder Hill, this type of feature appears to have been used in the North West during the second millennium BC.

Closer to Cinder Hill, four-post structures were also present at Oversley Farm, which, although undated, are presumed to be of the Early Bronze Age (Garner 2007). Two structures (Structures 6 and 7) were identified there, which were interpreted as either raised granaries or frames used in hide working, or textile manufacture. However, one of the posts in Structure 7 contained a fragment from a saddle quern, which may suggest that this, at least, was used as a granary. It is also worth noting that, at Oversley Farm, another larger rectangular structure was discovered apart from the four-post structures, which might also date to the Early Bronze Age, as it was sealed by 'abandonment' deposits radiocarbon dated to 2010-1660 cal BC (3500±60 BP; Beta-133369)

Plate 163: A reconstructed later prehistoric raised structure, interpreted as a granary, at Castell Henllys, Pembrokeshire, based on excavated evidence

and 1890-1660 cal BC (3640±40 BP; Beta-133368; *ibid*). It was suggested that this structure may have had a domestic function, as it contained an internal floor and a possible storage pit, which perhaps suggests that rectangular post-built structures also formed a component of Early Bronze Age domestic architecture.

The Cinder Hill settlement produced ecofacts and artefacts which allow further insights into what was, perhaps, a typical Middle Bronze Age settlement in the North West. The ecofacts suggested that the inhabitants grew both naked barley and wheat, and perhaps used the barley to make beer and/or sweet malt. These crops were also grown at the Middle Bronze Age settlement at Irby, where there appears to have been an emphasis on the cultivation of naked barley, though hulled barley was also recorded (Huntley 2010a). Though the types of wheat at Cinder Hill could not be determined, at Irby, emmer wheat (*Triticum dicoccum*) was favoured, although the cultivation of spelt wheat (*Triticum spelta*) also occurred.

The artefacts from Cinder Hill included fragments of pottery from locally produced barrel/bucket-shaped urns, which closely resemble northern Deverel-Rimbury pottery (Allen 2007a, 223). Significantly, Deverel-Rimbury pottery was also recovered

from an Early Bronze Age midden and a Middle Bronze Age pit at Oversley Farm (Allen 2007b, 65-70; 2007c, 108), indicating that this tradition, and perhaps other cultural traits associated with its use, had been adopted by those Middle Bronze Age communities that occupied the Mersey Basin. Interestingly, however, other Middle Bronze Age domestic-pottery traditions also appear to have existed in the Mersey Basin. This is evidenced by the assemblage of pottery recovered from the settlement at Irby (*p 224*). It was noted that the vessels in this assemblage differed from the Deverel-Rimbury types from Oversley Farm in that they had internally bevelled, as opposed to rounded, rims, and their profiles had more in common with Cordoned and Biconical Urns from the Pennines and Midlands (Woodward 2010).

Medieval Clearance, Agriculture, and Iron Production

The work at both Cutacre and Kingsway produced evidence for medieval activity, though that from Kingsway was the more limited, being confined to the identification of two possible medieval routeways and an early boundary/enclosure (*Ch 3, p 56*). Although none of these features could be dated, the routeways, which functioned as such into post-medieval and modern times, might have been on either side of, or ran through, an area of common land, known as Buersill Moor, that was gradually encroached upon during the late medieval period (*Ch 3, p 56*). It is also possible that the boundary, which lay between these routeways, relates to one of the earliest acts of enclosure in this area by Sir John Byron, in 1519 (*Ch 3, p 56*).

The Cutacre site contained more substantive evidence for medieval activity, including both palaeobotanical and archaeological remains. The palaeoenvironmental evidence (*Ch 3, p 38*) consisted of a fragment of dated charcoal and pollen signatures, which were both suggestive of woodland clearance in the early medieval period. In addition, the pollen profile produced evidence for cereal cultivation and pastoral farming close to Wharton Hall, during the same timeframe. Together, this evidence indicates that there must have been early medieval settlement somewhere comparatively close to this site, perhaps within the township of Little Hulton. Indeed, it is possible that this settlement is that 'farmstead/estate', which is referenced by the *tun* element within the place-name Hulton (*Ch 3, p 37*).

Significantly, it was also evident from the pollen evidence (*Ch 3, p 42*) that, close to Wharton Hall, arable farming predominated, between the mid-twelfth and mid-fourteenth centuries, with a decrease in pastoral farming, which might relate to the warmer climate that existed during this period (the 'medieval climatic optimum'; Mann 2002). However, this pattern was reversed from the mid-fourteenth century onwards, when cereal cultivation dramatically decreased, with the landscape seemingly given over to pastoral farming.

Cutacre also contained the most direct evidence for medieval activity, in the form of artefacts from Wharton Hall (*Ch 3, p 43*) and a selection of remains relating to a bloomery at Cinder Hill, producing iron (*Ch 3, p 44*). The medieval artefacts from Wharton Hall include pottery and glass from the twelfth to fifteenth centuries (Pl 164). These were, however, either residual or unstratified, and are therefore difficult to interpret with any precision. They presumably derived from domestic occupation, occurring within a medieval hall recorded in documentary sources (*Ch 3, p 42*), that had been comprehensively destroyed and replaced in the post-medieval period.

The remains associated with the bloomery were more 'complete', relating to a broad period of late medieval iron production between the twelfth and fourteenth centuries. It appears, however, that the site was revisited on several occasions and that these

Plate 164: Degraded fragments of medieval window glass from Wharton Hall

periodic episodes of production might relate to the time when oak was available for charcoal production within the nearby woodland areas (*Ch 3, p 52*), which appear to have been largely unmanaged.

The site contained evidence for many of the processes connected with iron production, including a charcoal clamp, which produced the fuel required for smelting, and several small cylindrical clay-walled, open-top smelting furnaces, resembling a clay stack (*Ch 3*, Pl 14), where the wrought-iron blooms were produced. These furnaces were heated by charcoal and used forced draughts produced by bellows to attain the required temperatures, with air being blown into the furnace through a blow hole, via a pipe (*tuyère*). It also seems that some of the furnaces were associated with timber structures, acting as windbreaks/shelters. Once the smelting process had begun, slag could leave the furnace through its mouth, or tapping arch, and would travel along a channel into a slag-tapping pit.

Apart from the furnaces, a possible reheating hearth was present, where the wrought-iron blooms could be reheated and hammered into iron billets. Indeed, one such billet was recovered from the site. Following smelting, the slag would have been collected and dumped into spoil heaps, which probably littered the site, and would have led to

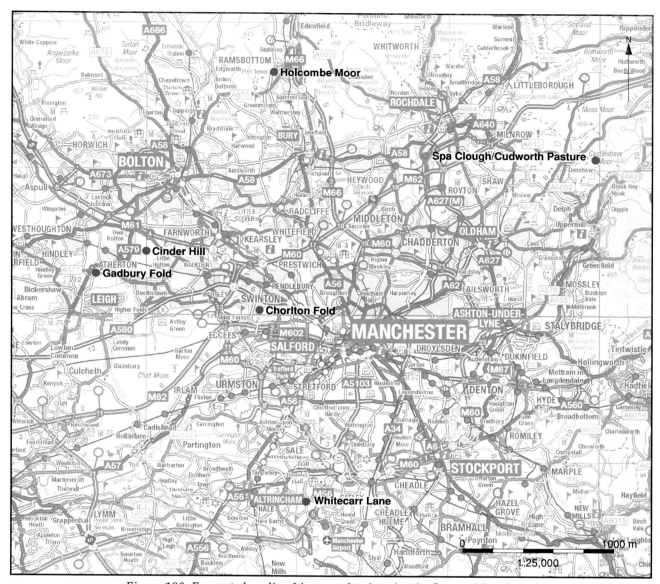

Figure 108: Excavated medieval iron-production sites in Greater Manchester

the field being named 'Cinder Hill', probably in the post-medieval period.

The remains at Cinder Hill therefore represent an excellent example of a late medieval bloomery, holding clear regional importance, and also adding to the growing evidence for medieval iron production in Greater Manchester (Fig 108). To date, several sites have been excavated, producing evidence for iron production, although in contrast to Cinder Hill, many of these sites did not contain direct evidence for smelting furnaces, iron production instead being indicated by industrial residues and other associated features. For instance, at Whitecarr Lane, Wythenshawe, a slag-tapping pit was identified, which also contained medieval pottery, whilst other features at the site included slag-filled channels, and postholes and slots for timber structures (Redhead 2004). At Gadbury Fold, near Atherton (*ibid*), and Chorlton Fold, near Monton (Bell 2007; OA North

2011), iron production was merely indicated by the presence of industrial residues. At the former, this comprised slag associated with late medieval and sixteenth-century pottery, and related to the smelting of the local Carboniferous claystone ironstone. In contrast, at the latter site, industrial residues deriving from both smelting and smithing were identified, which appear to have occurred within a late medieval enclosure. In this instance, it was suspected that these residues may have related to a furnace and smithy, perhaps forming one element of a late thirteenth- and fourteenth-century monastic grange at Monton (OA North 2011).

Another medieval iron production site in Greater Manchester has been located on Holcombe Moor, at a site that also has the field-name 'Cinder Hill'. This has been the subject of ongoing excavation by the Holcombe Moor Heritage Group, which uncovered a well-preserved bloomery furnace in 2018. Although this has been radiocarbon dated to cal AD 780-1020 (1113±28 BP; SUERC-81873), fragments of medieval gritty-ware pottery suggest that it more probably dates to the twelfth-fourteenth centuries (B Smith *pers comm*).

Two adjacent sites in the Castleshaw Valley have, however, produced more detailed evidence for early iron production that is largely comparable to that from Cinder Hill (Redhead 1992; 1993; 1996). These sites, known as Spa Clough and Cudworth Pasture, are some 200 m apart and, as with the evidence from Cinder Hill, appear to reflect later medieval iron production, performed by 'itinerant, seasonal smelters exploiting the local fuel and ore resources' (Redhead 1996, 12).

Excavation at Spa Clough revealed the bases of two iron-smelting furnaces that were probably comparable to those at Cinder Hill; these were small cylindrical shaft-type furnaces with associated tapping pits (Pl 165). The surviving walls of the furnaces indicated that they had internal diameters

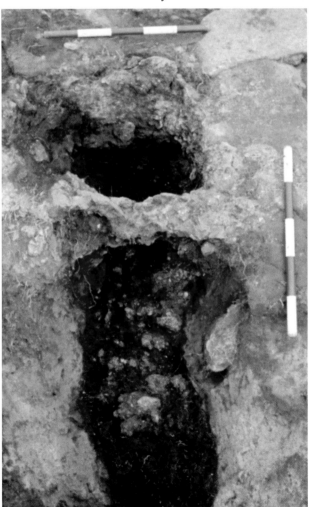

Plate 165: A furnace base, with tapping arch and channel, excavated at Spa Clough, Castleshaw

of 0.38-0.4 m (Fig 109). In addition, in one, a thick deposit of slag indicated the position of a *tuyère*, demonstrating that the furnaces also utilised forced draughts, produced by hand bellows. There, the furnaces also pointed to separated phases of iron production, as the later furnace was partly built across the site of the earlier (Redhead 1993). Radiocarbon and archaeomagnetic dating place their use in the late twelfth/thirteenth century (*ibid*), the same general period as those at Cinder Hill. In addition, in a comparable manner to Cinder Hill, this site produced evidence for associated structures, in the form of a revetting wall and post-pad (*ibid*), and the remains of a possible charcoal clamp (Redhead 1992).

At Cudworth Pasture, to the north-east of Spa Clough, an iron-smelting furnace was excavated by the antiquarian Ammon Wrigley in 1907 (Wrigley 1912). It appears that a furnace of seemingly comparable design to those at Spa Clough was present, which had an upright circular shaft, tapping hole/arch, and blow hole. This site was re-excavated in 1994 and scientific dating indicated that iron production was broadly contemporary with the furnaces at Spa Clough, probably dating to the late twelfth or thirteenth century (Redhead 1996). Although the furnace excavated in 1907 only survived as patches of baked clay, other features relating to early iron production were evident within the 1994 excavation area, some of which have parallels with those at Cinder Hill. Specifically, these included a tapping pit that was linked to the furnace, and an adjacent ore-roasting area. Another feature was a platform from which hot slag may have been raked to form a large slag spoil heap, which was estimated to comprise 29 tonnes of material (*ibid*).

Apart from the structural remains, the Spa Clough/ Cudworth Pasture sites also had other similarities with Cinder Hill. It is apparent, for example, that Carboniferous claystone ironstone was also the ore type selected, as opposed to bog iron (Redhead 1993). Another striking similarity was the use of mature oak (*ibid*). Again, this suggests that there was an absence of managed (coppiced) woodlands in the vicinity of Spa Clough/Cudworth Pasture and that, perhaps, iron smelting was only feasible once adequate stands of oak woodland had regrown. One notable difference between Cinder Hill and Spa Clough/Cudworth Pasture, however, was that, at Cinder Hill, some evidence existed for smithing, whereby the blooms were reheated and hammered into billets (*p 226*). No such evidence was present at Spa Clough/Cudworth Pasture, either in the form of reheating hearths or industrial residues, and it was suggested that, in this instance, the blooms may have been taken to a local smith for treatment.

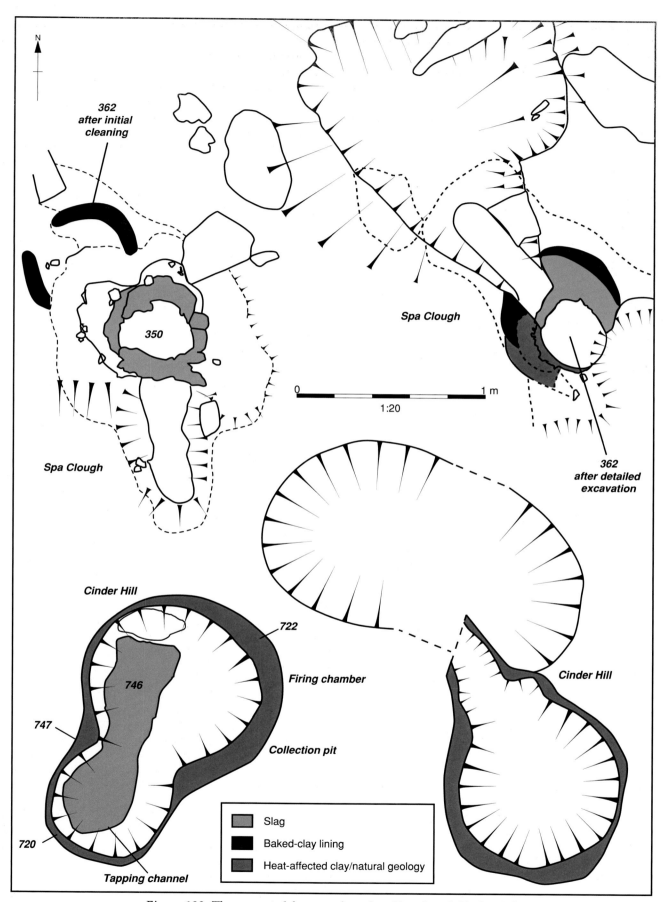

Figure 109: The excavated furnaces from Spa Clough and Cinder Hill

Post-medieval Rural Houses: *c* 1600-1780

The combined programme of building survey and archaeological excavation at both Cutacre and Kingsway produced valuable evidence relating to the different types of post-medieval rural houses and farm buildings that probably existed across a wider swathe of northern Greater Manchester. It is clear from this work that the houses in the two different landscapes, dating between the early seventeenth and late eighteenth centuries, relate to similar post-medieval building traditions; these extended across a fairly wide geographical area encompassing both the Lancashire Pennines and much of southern Lancashire, with parts of northern Cheshire, including those now within Greater Manchester. Therefore, many similarities exist between the rural houses discussed here, and other published examples in Greater Manchester and adjacent areas (*inter alia*; Pearson 1985; Arrowsmith 1997; Burke and Nevell 1996; Nevell 1997; Miller 2002; Nevell *et al* 2015). As such, the accumulated evidence from Cutacre and Kingsway allows some further insights into the types, chronology, and distribution of particular post-medieval building types within the wider region.

Social structure and rural houses

Unsurprisingly, the post-medieval rural houses of the region are a reflection of their inhabitants' social status and, in turn, the class-based social system, which had emerged within rural Lancashire in the sixteenth century (Miller 2002, 25). At a gross level, a major social division within rural Lancashire throughout the post-medieval period related to tenure, specifically between those who directly owned land and those who leased land (Nevell and Walker 1998, 33-4).

Land-owning classes

Throughout the seventeenth and eighteenth centuries, the land-owning classes of southern Lancashire and northern Cheshire consisted of different groups of varying social status, who owned and occupied a range of properties. At their apex were the aristocracy, the ruling elite, which in hierarchical terms were directly below the Crown and held extensive landholdings both in the region and beyond (Phillips and Smith 1994, 12). Within southern Lancashire and northern Cheshire, these included families such as the Stanleys, Earls of Derby (Coward 1983), the Booths, Earls of Warrington (Eastwood 2004), and the Egertons, the Earls and later Dukes of Bridgewater (Malet 1977), the latter owning all, and later parts, of the township of Middle Hulton, which covered much of the Cutacre area (*Ch 5, p 93*). These aristocratic families inhabited the largest dwellings in the region, with floor spaces of and above 1000 m² (Nevell and Walker 2002, 4), such as Lathom House and Knowsley Hall, in south-west Lancashire, the successive seats of the

Plate 166: The south range and main entrance to Dunham Hall in 1794

THE OLD HALL, WOODFORD.

Plate 167: A typical post-medieval hall built for the gentry/lesser gentry, here Woodford Old Hall, in Stockport, in 1880, but mainly constructed in the late sixteenth century

Stanley family (Miller 2002, 26, 30), and Dunham Massey, home of the Booths (Eastwood 2004; Pl 166). Although these houses differed in layout, they were generally monumental in character and were also the most architecturally elaborate.

Beneath these was a collection of less wealthy families, broadly comprising the gentry (*ie* those that did not labour with their hands; Phillips and Smith 1994, 19). These included traditional feudal lords, such as the Byron family, who, within the Kingsway area, were first stewards and then the owners of the manor of Rochdale, during the late medieval and post-medieval periods (*Ch 3, p 56; Ch 4, p 65*), and also those wealthy landowners who emerged in the seventeenth century, when they gained manorial rights through acquisition. These included men such as Adam Mort and his heir, Thomas, who owned estates in south Lancashire and Cheshire during the early seventeenth century, including Wharton Hall and the adjacent manor of Astley (*Ch 5, p 122*). The gentry formed a relatively small group in Lancashire, and it has been estimated that in 1642 they comprised only 2-3% of the population (Blackwood 1978).

Another set of landowners were situated beneath the substantial gentry families, which formed a fairly ill-defined group, sometimes referred to as the minor/lesser gentry (*cf* Phillips and Smith 1994, 19; Walton 1987, 14). These were smaller landowners, comprising those families who merely owned portions of a subdivided manor, and may not have had tenants on their land; in terms of

wealth, they merged with the upper ranks of the class immediately below, known as the yeomanry (Phillips and Smith 1994, 19; Walton 1987, 14; Miller 2002, 26; *below*).

The gentry and lesser gentry built, owned, and inhabited the post-medieval halls of the region (Pl 167), which were of varying size and differed in layout, depending on the individual family's wealth (*below*). These were, however, smaller in size than the great halls occupied by the aristocracy (*p 230*), with floor areas, in Greater Manchester at least, ranging between 800 m^2 and 200 m^2 (Nevell and Walker 2002, 4).

Beneath the gentry were the yeomanry, who worked the land directly but also utilised hired labour. In Lancashire, they had become an important element of rural society by the late sixteenth century, and continued to act as such throughout the seventeenth and most of the eighteenth century, prior to the Industrial Revolution (Miller 2002, 28, 120-1). As with the gentry, the yeomanry can also be divided into various sub-classes, based on land tenure. The elite yeoman farmers were freeholders ('free' tenants) and, as with the gentry, held their land directly, were exempt from giving agricultural service to the lord of the manor, and, importantly, had the right to pass their land to their heirs (*op cit*, 28). This 'class' of yeoman farmer was particularly numerous in the Lancashire Pennines (*cf* Pearson 1985), and included those farmers who acquired land, as freeholders, in the area of the Kingsway Business Park. This class of yeoman farmer became established in this area, following the selling of land in Castleton and Butterworth townships by Sir John Byron in the early 1600s (*Ch 4, p 65*). As is apparent from the work in Kingsway, the freehold yeomanry was responsible for constructing fairly substantial and distinctive rural houses and buildings (*p 238*).

Tenant farmers
Much of the rural populus rented land through various tenure agreements, which varied according to where in the North West these were. In general terms, tenant-right existed in northern Lancashire, copyhold in east Lancashire, and customary leases in south Lancashire (Phillips and Smith 1994, 26). Although there were differences between each of these forms of tenure (*cf* Miller 2002, 28-9), they did share some common characteristics. For instance, in all cases, the tenants paid a nominal and fixed annual rent to the lord of the manor (*in lieu* of agriculture service). Normally, this was kept at reasonable levels, as tenants contributed to the improvement of the landlord's estate (*ibid*). However, on the uptake of the lease, an entry fee (a fine) was paid, which presented the landowner with an opportunity to increase his income (Phillips and Smith 1994, 26). The tenure was often held for a number of lives (usually three) or even by inheritance, which allowed land and properties to remain within particular families (Miller 2002, 29). In addition, some forms of tenure allowed the tenants to sell materials (*eg* coal) found within their holding (*ibid*).

There were several different types of tenant farmers in southern and Pennine Lancashire, the most privileged being yeoman farmers, which held their land by copyhold, a term that specifically references the title deed received by the tenant, being a *copy* of the manorial court roll (Miller 2002, 28-9). Beneath these were a lower class of farmer, who were normally leaseholders. Within this group were those individuals, explicitly referred to as husbandmen, within the seventeenth- and eighteenth-century documentary evidence relating to the Cutacre area. These include Giles Halliwell, who leased the southern farmstead at Spout Fold in the earlier part of the seventeenth century (*Ch 5, p 113*), and Edward Aldred, who leased Mills Brow farm at some date prior to 1722 (*Ch 5, p 104*). The other husbandmen referred to in documents were at Wharton Hall, and may thus have commanded greater wealth. These were William Warton, who probably leased the property in the early seventeenth century, and James Boardman, who leased the hall in the mid-seventeenth century, along with another tenant, James Grundy (*Ch 5, p 122*).

Tenant farmers, like the freehold yeoman farmers, would have constructed houses and farm buildings (which have also been termed as 'yeoman houses' in the archaeological literature; *cf* Nevell and Walker 2002). In terms of size and form, these buildings appear to have included some comparable to the yeoman houses held by freeholders (*p 231*), though others appear to have been smaller in size. Indeed, this has been confirmed, in some measure, by analysis of floor areas from 50 farmhouses surveyed in Greater Manchester (*op cit*, 4). From this data, it appears that those houses owned by freeholders were larger, with floor areas within the range of 200-400 m^2; in contrast, the tenanted properties occupied by the leasehold farmers had floor sizes ranging between 50 m^2 and 400 m^2, with the majority below 200 m^2 (*ibid*).

Labourers/cottagers
The lowest classes within post-medieval rural society were those individuals who were dependent on external employment from either the gentry or freehold and tenant farmers (yeoman and husbandmen). These were labourers, housed within cottages often associated with a small amount of land, or more flimsy hovels, which were situated within or adjacent to farms (Burke and Nevell 1996, 44; Nevell and Walker 1998, 79-84). These labourers included farm workers, craftsmen, textile workers, and tradesmen, and they

> plied their trade as circumstances allowed but who might take advantage of grazing rights on the common land when seasonal or cyclical fluctuations meant the loss of their main employment (Brunskill 1997, 86).

'The Great Rebuilding' and the chronology of house building
One noteworthy feature of the post-medieval period, which holds particular relevance to the rural houses of historic Lancashire and Cheshire, is a concerted and widespread phase of building activity by the gentry, yeomanry, and more affluent husbandmen (*above*). In essence, this involved the creation of box timber-framed, as well as stone and brick-built, buildings, which were often much more substantial and durable than those that were built during the medieval period. This could involve the construction of a new dwelling on the site of a demolished medieval predecessor, the conversion of a standing medieval building, or, in many instances, the construction of a new post-medieval building on another part of the site, or even a virgin site. Many of these buildings were 'improved' in several stages, which might extend over several generations, when money became available.

In all instances, these 'new' post-medieval houses embodied different notions of domestic space, when compared with the layout of medieval dwellings. Specifically, there was a shift towards the segregation of activities into specialised rooms (*ie* the living room or kitchen, parlour, bedroom/chamber), allowing greater levels of comfort and privacy, and, as such, they are the precursors of the layout of present-day houses (Burke and Nevell 1996; Nevell and Walker 2002; Miller 2002). This post-medieval activity also entailed the construction of more durable outbuildings, such as barns and shippons. Likewise, cottages housing the agricultural workforce also became more substantial and durable from the seventeenth century onwards (Burke and Nevell 1996, 44).

Effectively, in terms of domestic architecture, this process of conversion and building represents a conceptual architectural shift, from 'open' house types, which contained a single open room used as the principal domestic space (*ie* medieval halls and longhouses; *cf* Genville 1997), to a 'closed' house type, containing fireplaces and individual rooms with differing functions (*cf* Johnson 1993). This process appears initially to have involved the conversion of the more substantial pre-existing medieval properties, specifically medieval halls, to create fully formed and novel closed house types, such as two- or three-cell houses, often with an internal chimney stack and lobby entrance (*ibid*). The precise reasons why these changes came about when they did are difficult to discern, though it has been argued that the preoccupation with closure and privacy related to more general concepts of closure, which also extended to the enclosure of farmland during this period, partly a result of an underlying need to impose social and political order, as well as being associated with changing ethics and world views that were linked to the wider rise of Protestant belief (*op cit*, 164, 179).

This phase of building activity is often referred to as 'The Great Rebuilding' in the literature, a term coined by the landscape historian, William George Hoskins, who identified a broader national trend of post-medieval rebuilding, which he suggested dated to between 1570 and 1640 (Hoskins 1953). It is now clear, however, that this concentrated phase of post-medieval building/rebuilding was much more drawn out and complex and, in fact, occurred at different times in different regions.

At a gross level, in the North West rebuilding by the more affluent members of society appears to have started in the late sixteenth century and then continued at different rates, by different social classes, throughout the remainder of the post-medieval period (Miller 2002). It has been suggested, on the basis of datestones and inscribed lintels from the surviving gentry and yeoman houses in Cheshire, Greater Manchester, and Lancashire, that two concerted phases of building

activity occurred, during the late sixteenth and seventeenth centuries. One was in the period 1580-1620, and was associated with 'flamboyant external timber-framing', whilst the other covered the period 1660-1700 and entailed the construction of 'brick and stone structures with plainer exteriors' (Nevell and Walker 2002, 16).

However, these estimates and assumptions, whilst valuable, mask very local trends and nuances, which are exemplified by two areas in the North West that have been subjected to detailed analysis and are, in many ways, comparable to Cutacre and Kingsway. One is the Douglas Valley (Miller 2002), which is a similar landscape to Cutacre, whilst the other is the landscape surrounding Burnley and Colne, in the Lancashire Pennines, which has some similarities with Kingsway (Pearson 1985).

Within the Douglas Valley, detailed building analysis suggests that an initial phase of rebuilding began in the 1570s, which was confined to members of the gentry, whilst the wealthiest members of the yeomanry began to build or rebuild properties in *c* 1600 (Miller 2002, 31). Following this, there was an increase in the construction of yeoman properties in the latter half of the seventeenth century, which had petered out by 1720 (*ibid*). Significantly, several large yeoman farmhouses also appeared during this period that were purposefully built in a double-pile plan (*op cit*, 131). There was then a renewed phase of rebuilding by the gentry in the mid-eighteenth century to replace or modify the by then outdated sixteenth- and seventeenth-century buildings (*op cit*, 135).

A similar pattern of building/rebuilding appears to have occurred in the area surrounding Burnley and Colne. There, it appears that the gentry and the wealthiest yeoman farmers were initially engaged in the construction of large, substantial stone houses during the period 1560-1610, which were similar in design (Pearson 1985). This was then followed during the seventeenth century by the construction of more readily discernible gentry and yeoman houses. Most of the former in this area date to *c* 1600 to *c* 1675, and many were also rebuilt and refurbished in the eighteenth century (*op cit*, 56-7).

It appears that there was also a distinct phase of building yeoman houses in the early part of the seventeenth century, which led to the emergence of dwellings of broadly similar design (*op cit*, 84). In contrast, the latter part of the seventeenth century is characterised by the appearance of stone-built yeoman houses of different designs and sizes (*ibid*). These comprised large elongated houses with uncoordinated plans, medium-sized houses, including those with double-pile plans, and small houses that merely consisted of two cells (*ibid*).

During the early eighteenth century, many of the gentry houses were remodelled and updated, whilst some new gentry houses were also constructed in the middle part of this century (*op cit*, 120). The smaller farmhouses built during the eighteenth century were largely of the double-pile type (*op cit*, 122).

In the lowland township of Warburton, where the tenant farmer predominated, the pattern of rebuilding was also similar to that in the Douglas Valley (Nevell *et al* 2015). Late medieval farmsteads were expanded and rebuilt in timber in the sixteenth to mid-seventeenth century, with many containing inglenook fireplaces. There was then a lull until the beginning of the eighteenth century, when the houses of both the larger yeoman farmers and the lesser tenants were rebuilt in brick. Double-pile houses were introduced on several sites, but mostly the existing two- and three-unit properties were expanded, either by the addition of extra ground-floor rooms or an upper storey.

As far as the data from the investigated sites permit, Wharton Hall (Pl 168) may have been rebuilt in 1629 (*p 235*). It is also possible that a late medieval farmstead at Hulton Heys was demolished or

modified in the early seventeenth century, and a 'new' post-medieval farm built, which in 1666 had two hearths (*Ch 5, p 102*). The farmhouse at Ashes might also have been built during the earlier part of the seventeenth century, as it was possibly occupied as early as 1639 (*Ch 5, p 95*).

This evidence would therefore suggest that, in the Cutacre area, 'The Great Rebuilding' was a comparatively late development, occurring just after the first phase of concerted post-medieval building activity postulated for the North West (*p 233*), and also well beyond the initial phases of modernisation of gentry and yeoman houses in the Douglas Valley (*p 233*). It is also clear that, once established, these post-medieval properties were progressively modified and improved througout the late seventeenth and eighteenth centuries. In the mid-eighteenth century, it also appears that several of the farms that had been occupied in the seventeenth century, such as Spout Fold (*Ch 5, p 113*), were demolished and replaced by more 'modern' farmhouses, whilst other properties, such as Mills Brow (*Ch 5, p 104*), were enlarged by the construction of additional dwellings, as circumstances required.

At Kingsway, all of the buildings investigated had been established on virgin sites, which is unsurprising considering that, up until the post-medieval period,

Plate 168: The exterior of the post-medieval Wharton Hall had been refaced in brick by the time of this undated photograph, and probably prior to the 1830s, then covered with a wash and painted in parts to resemble timber framing

most of the Kingsway area was common land, known as Buersill Moor (*Ch 3, p 56*). Indeed, the initial stimulus for house building within this area was the financial difficulties of Sir John Byron, which led to him selling off parts of the Moor, in the early 1600s, as freeholds, to a series of yeoman farmers, in effect small entrepreneurial landowners, who are listed in a survey of Rochdale commissioned in 1626 (*Ch 4, p 65*). This spurt of early seventeenth-century building equates with a similar period of yeoman housebuilding identified further north in the Burnley/Colne area, which led to the construction of houses of broadly similar design (*p 233*). It is quite likely that at least some of the seventeenth-century buildings investigated at Kingsway relate to this episode (*eg* Lane End and possibly Higher Moss Side Farm; *Ch 4, p 82, p 68*).

It is also clear, however, that at Kingsway this process of yeoman building continued into the mid- and late seventeenth century, also seen further north in the Burnley/Colne area, where it was associated with the appearance of houses of differing design and sizes (*p 233*). For instance, of the seventeenth-century houses investigated at Kingsway, it is evident from a datestone that Near Moor Bank Farm was built in 1632, which corresponds to the time when the area had been mortgaged to Sir John Byron's eldest son (also John Byron; *Ch 4, p 65*). Presumably, again, financial difficulties were the driving force behind the sale of land during this period.

In addition, it is possible that Lower Lane Farm, another of those subjected to archaeological investigation, dates to 1694 (*Ch 4, p 72*). It is also evident from datestones that other properties, which did not form part of the archaeological investigation, were constructed on land that was seemingly sold

off by the Byron family. These include Broad Shaw farm, which has a datestone of 1651 (Arrowsmith and Wilson 1998; this has also been read as '1631' by Haynes and Tipper 1994, 149), and Dixon Green, which has a datestone of 1685 (*ibid*).

As at Cutacre (*p 234*), some post-medieval housebuilding at Kingsway clearly dates to the eighteenth century, probably, on balance, from the middle of the century. 'New' farmhouses were constructed on, or immediately adjacent to, the sites of demolished seventeenth-century houses (*eg* Pyche farm; *Ch 4, p 81*), and standing seventeenth-century buildings (*eg* Lower Lane Farm; *Ch 4, p 72*) were comprehensively rebuilt, representing mid-eighteenth-century 'modernisation'. In addition, houses were constructed on sites which contained no clear evidence for earlier buildings (*eg* Castle Farm; *Ch 6, p 86*).

Post-medieval halls: Wharton Hall

The development of the Cutacre area presented an opportunity to examine a post-medieval gentry house in some detail, by means of excavation (*Ch 5, pp 126-35*). A beam from the hall, purportedly inscribed with the date 1629, clearly points to building work at that time, and it has been postulated, on the basis of the documentary evidence, that this might actually confirm the point at which the hall was constructed. It is known that Adam Mort acquired the property in 1628 (*Ch 5, p 122*), and it is quite possible that this fairly wealthy landowner decided to demolish the putative existing and presumably outdated medieval hall, and build a 'new' and more 'modern' dwelling.

This new house was *c* 19 m long, and comprised a central range (the hall), with projecting cross-

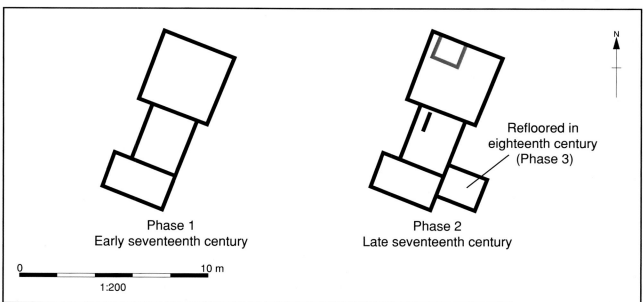

Phase 1
Early seventeenth century

Phase 2
Late seventeenth century

Refloored in
eighteenth century
(Phase 3)

0   10 m

1:200

Figure 110: The post-medieval development of Wharton Hall

wings at either end (Fig 110). It is possible that the northern cross-wing contained two parlours, and the southern two service rooms. Documentary sources also indicate that this was a timber-framed structure and had two storeys, with a first-floor at least above the central range, which was perhaps the 'chamber' mentioned in a probate inventory of 1631 (*Ch 5, p 126*).

The size and H-shaped plan of Wharton Hall is not particularly unusual, having been adopted by many other late sixteenth- and seventeenth-century gentry house-builders in Lancashire and Cheshire (*cf* Nevell and Walker 2002). This type of post-medieval gentry house followed a tradition of H-shaped, or double-ended halls, which had developed in the late medieval period and similarly comprised a central range flanked by cross-wings (Brunskill 1997, 38). The later development of this house plan, as at Wharton Hall, involved the provision of one or more upper storeys above the central range, allowing the creation of private chambers, and also a fireplace/chimney stack, in contrast to the medieval tradition, whereby the central hall was open to the roof and contained a centrally positioned hearth (*op cit*, 42).

In a survey of 64 gentry and yeoman houses in Greater Manchester, 22 H-shaped halls dating to the period 1500-1700 were identified (Nevell and Walker 2002). These were complemented by another type of similar-sized gentry house, consisting of a main range with a single cross-wing, creating a structure with an L- or T-shaped ground plan. Many of these houses were adaptations of pre-existing medieval

halls, by flooring over the open hall, with the construction of additional wings, or the extension of pre-existing wings. 'New' halls were also built adjacent to an older medieval hall (38 examples in the Greater Manchester sample), whilst a limited number (eight examples in the Greater Manchester sample), perhaps in a similar fashion to Wharton Hall, were constructed on the sites of demolished medieval halls (*ibid*).

At Wharton Hall, it was also apparent that it had seen a phase of seventeenth-century rebuilding and extension. The Hearth Tax returns show an increase in the number of hearths at the property, probably between 1662 and 1664, increasing from four to seven (*Ch 5, p 126*). Such a number is commensurate with a house of this size. This rebuilding was the work of Robert Mort, who appears to have been the first of the family to have occupied the house, until 1692, and therefore may have wished to improve the property when he first became resident. The archaeological evidence indicates that these improvements involved the insertion of a fireplace with a stone stack in the central range, along with the rebuilding and extending of the northern cross-wing, where a small cellar was also constructed, and the building of a small extension abutting the southern cross-wing, which perhaps functioned as a kitchen. Indeed, from the late seventeenth century onwards, such dedicated rooms became incorporated into the main block, rather than being separate buildings as was common in earlier centuries, which also allowed cooking to be moved out of the main living room (Brunskill 1997,

Plate 169: Dam House, a seventeenth-century building owned by the Mort family

236

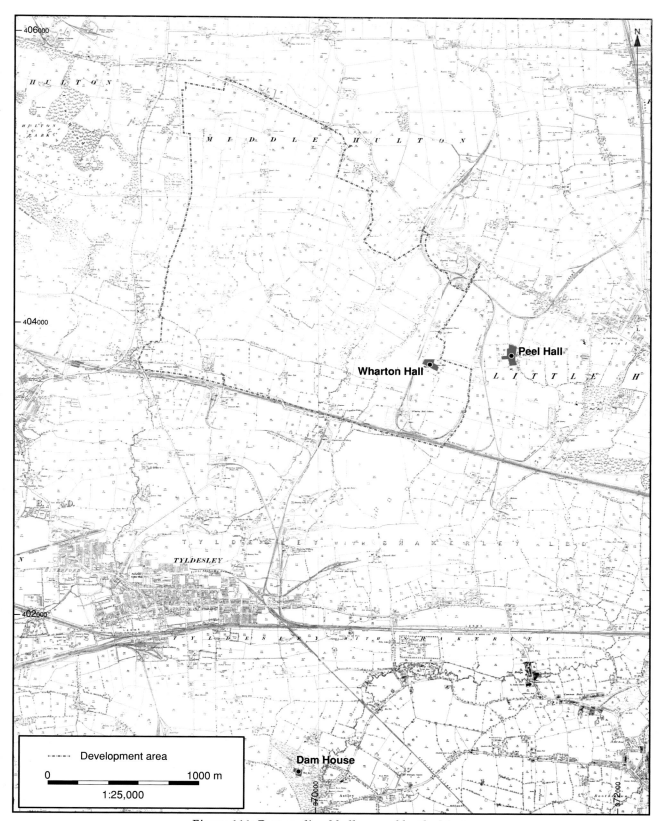

Figure 111: Post-medieval halls owned by the Morts

201). The Wharton Hall kitchen was refloored in the eighteenth century (*Ch 5, p 135*).

It is also worth noting that, as well as Wharton Hall, during the seventeenth century the Mort family occupied two other gentry houses close to Cutacre, at Dam House (Pl 169), also known as Astley Hall, and Peel Hall, or Wicheves (Fig 111). Compared with Wharton Hall, these properties were more architecturally distinct, which is probably because they successively formed the principal residences of the Mort family. Dam House was Adam Mort's main home in the early seventeenth century (Arrowsmith 1998), whilst Peel Hall was purchased by Adam's son, Thomas Mort, following his father's death in 1631, after which it formed his main residence until his death in 1638 (LA WCW/Supra/C122C/37). Dam House is the only one of the three Mort properties to be still standing (Pl 169), possibly having been constructed in about 1600, by Adam Mort, and substantially remodelled, or even mostly rebuilt, in 1650 by his grandson, the second Adam Mort (*ibid*; Nevell *et al* 2000; Howard *et al* 2001).

Farms of the yeomanry and husbandmen

The majority of the post-medieval buildings investigated at Kingsway and Cutacre were constructed and occupied by farmers. In the case of Kingsway, these were freehold yeoman farmers, whilst those at Cutacre consisted of tenant farmers, or husbandmen. The buildings themselves comprised a dwelling and sometimes other agricultural buildings, such as barns and outhouses, which in form appear to mirror those found across other parts of Lancashire and Greater Manchester (*p 230*).

Yeoman farms at Kingsway

Several yeoman farmhouses were investigated at Kingsway, constructed during the seventeenth and also the eighteenth century, with many of the latter probably dating to the middle decades of that century (*p 235*). Significantly, many of these were of broadly similar design and also had similarities to those yeoman farmhouses recorded in the Lancashire Pennines to the north, around Burnley and Colne (*cf* Pearson 1985), and also to the east and south, in the Pennine areas of Milnrow, Littleborough, and Mossley (Hartwell *et al* 2004, 41). Those houses that survive today, or were recorded at Kingway prior to demolition, are 'of strong character, low-set, with stone walls and roofs, long ranges of mullioned windows, and stony paths, yards and boundary walls' (*ibid*).

Two-cell houses

Where house plans are discernible, the most common form recorded was a small, single-depth (or single-room deep) house, containing two cells. These all date to the seventeenth century and include those properties investigated at Lower Lane Farm, Lane End, Near Moor Bank Farm, and Castle House (Fig 112).

In all cases, and in a comparable way to the small yeoman houses in other Pennine areas (*cf* Pearson 1985), one of the cells formed the housbody, which acted as the principal living room and cooking area (Brunskill 1997, 200). Accordingly, this room would have been heated either by an inglenook fireplace (common up until the mid-seventeenth century), or a fireplace built with a stone stack (utilised from

the mid-seventeenth century onwards; Pearson 1985, 128). The direct evidence for fireplaces in these buildings was limited, though it appears that, at Lower Lane Farm, probably built in the late seventeenth century (*Ch 4, p 73*), there was a stone stack. Castle House dated to the mid-/late seventeenth century (*Ch 4, p 85*) and as such may originally have contained a stone stack, whilst Near Moor Bank Farm and Lane End dated to the early/mid-seventeenth century (*Ch 4, pp 89, 83*), and are more likely to have contained inglenook fireplaces.

These fireplaces formed a distinct area within the post-medieval house, which was principally used for cooking, with a timber and plaster firehood, carried on a timber beam or bressumer (Pearson 1985, 128). The bressumer, in turn, was supported by an external wall and an internal stone or timber heck (partition wall) next to the entrance. The inglenook was also usually lit by a small external window (a fire window) and its back wall often contained recesses, which functioned as boxes to keep salt dry (Burke and Nevell 1996, 39).

The other cell in these small seventeenth-century houses functioned as the parlour. During this time, in single-storeyed buildings this acted as an unheated bedroom; however, when the house had an upper storey with bedrooms, it functioned as a private sitting room, which was often heated by a fireplace (Brunskill 1997, 200-1). The seventeenth-century houses at Lower Lane and Near Moor Bank Farm had a first floor, which may have contained one or more bedrooms; however, it is interesting to note that during the seventeenth century both of their parlours were unheated by permanent hearths, and it is quite possible that they performed other functions, though of course they might have been heated by a portable heat source in the form of a brazier. Eventually, however, in the mid-eighteenth century, the parlour associated with Lower Lane was rebuilt with a fireplace (*Ch 4, p 77*).

That at Lane End was also originally unheated, though it is unclear whether this building possessed a first floor. Castle House, in its original plan, was single storeyed and hence the parlour probably functioned as a bedroom. However, during the late eighteenth century, a first floor was added to this house, which presumably provided bedroom space and hence the parlour might then have functioned as a private sitting room (*Ch 4, p 188*). It is also apparent at Lane End that the cell containing the parlour was subdivided, to create another small room (*Ch 4, p 84*). This probably functioned either as a pantry, where dry foodstuffs were stored, or as a buttery/milkhouse, which would have contained milk, butter, and other liquids stored in wooden and/

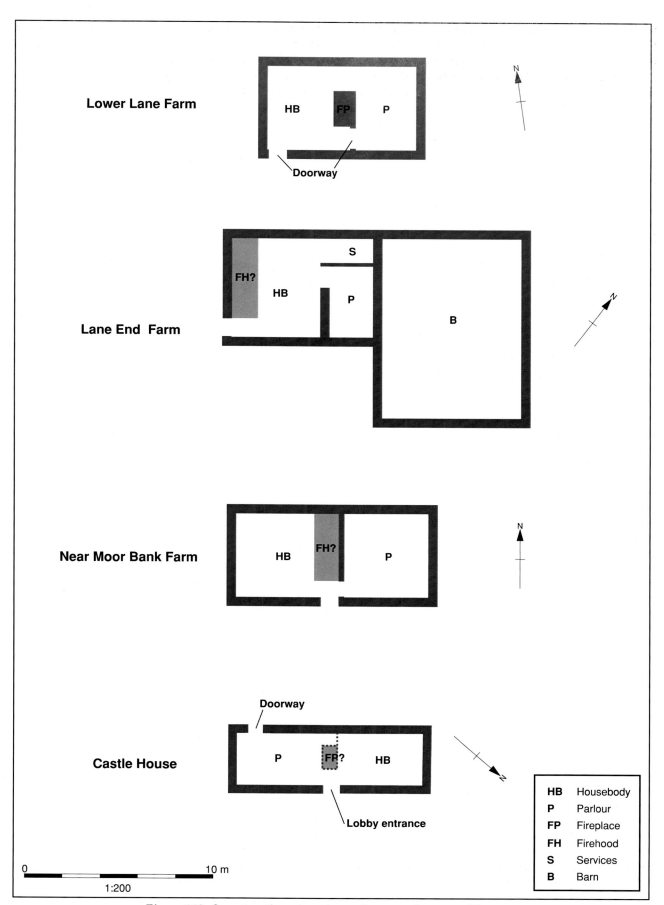

Figure 112: Seventeenth-century two-cell yeoman houses at Kingsway

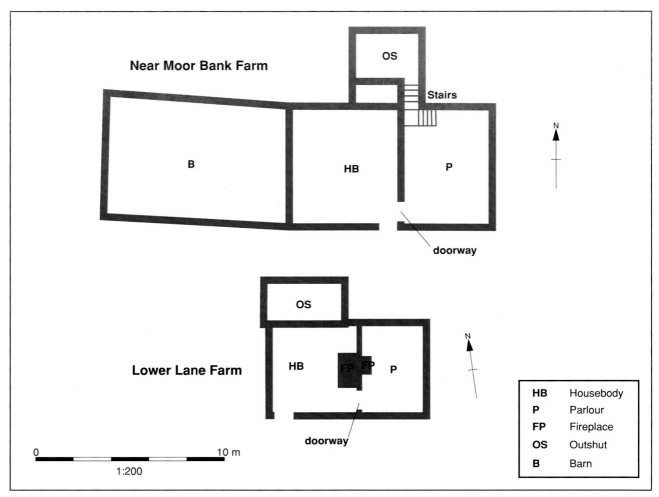

Figure 113: Eighteenth-century additions to two-cell yeoman houses at Kingsway

or earthenware vessels (Pearson 1985, 94; Brunskill 1997, 201).

Several different arrangements of entrance existed within the seventeenth-century Kingsway houses, which largely conform to the more general arrangements that existed in yeoman houses of that date in the wider region. For instance, within Pennine Lancashire and Greater Manchester, three main entrance arrangements are apparent (*inter alia* Pearson 1985; Brunskill 1997; Burke and Nevell 1996). These have been classified as cross-passage, gable end, and lobby entrances.

With the cross-passage entrance, the house contained a corridor, with doorways at either end, and the resulting cross-passage might either be positioned at the end of the house, or within it, between two of its cells. Although such an arrangement was certainly used in those houses within the Pennine areas and the upland parts of Greater Manchester, this entrance type was not apparent at Kingsway.

A doorway positioned on the gable wall of the building allowed access directly into the housebody,

and therefore was to the side of the inglenook or fireplace stack. This arrangement may have been employed at Lane End.

Lobby entrances allowed access through the façade of the house into the housebody, and were either positioned at one end of the house, or at its centre. The lobby (or baffle) entrance was created by the heck wall of the inglenook or the stone stack of the fireplace, and meant that those entering the house had to turn either left or right to access its rooms. In the seventeenth century, Near Moor Bank Farm appears to have had a central lobby entrance (Fig 113), and it is also likely that Castle House (Fig 114) had a similar arrangement.

The entrance at Lower Lane Farm appears slightly eccentric, however, in that it did not conform to these main types. In this instance, the housebody was entered directly from the end of the façade and there was seemingly no lobby, as the fireplace was not positioned on the gable wall, but instead was on the opposing internal wall. Castle House was also unusual in that it contained an additional entrance on its rear elevation, close to the gable end

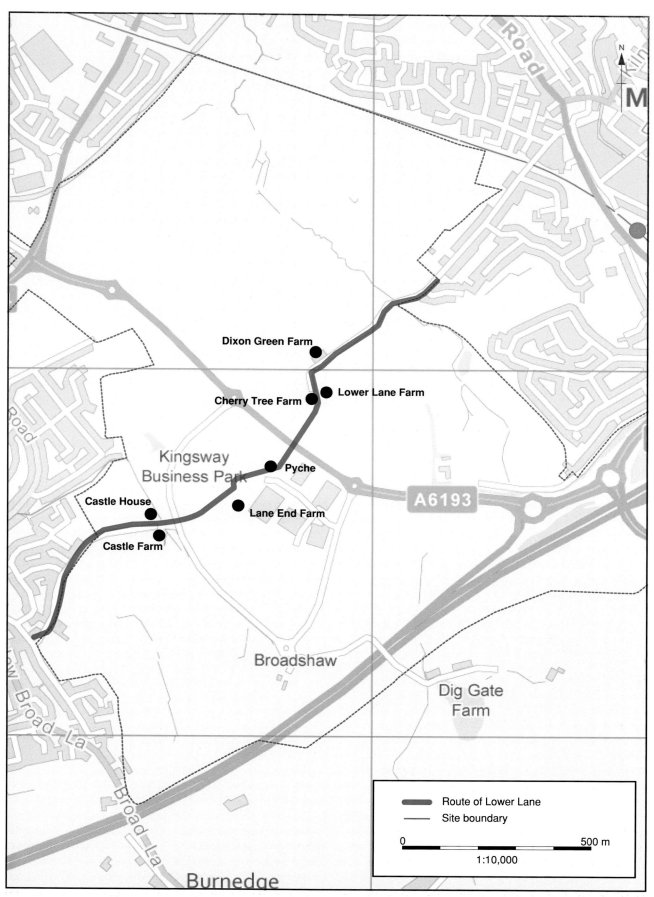

Figure 114: Surveyed and/or excavated seventeenth-century farms on Lower Lane

of the building. Additional entrances associated with seventeenth-century houses, although rare, usually allowed access to the parlour (Pearson 1985, 87), which may have been the case at Castle House.

Perhaps significantly, small cellared outshuts were added to both Lower Lane Farm and Near Moor Bank Farm during eighteenth-century remodelling (Fig 113). At Lower Lane Farm, this remodelling dated to the middle of the century, and comprised the rebuilding of the bay containing the parlour and the rear section of the house. In this remodelling, the outshut, built against the seventeenth-century housebody, may have been a pantry, with the cellar perhaps functioning as a cold store. At Near Moor Bank Farm, the remodelling and the construction of the cellared outshut dated to the late eighteenth century and again entailed the rebuilding and extending of the rear wall of the property, to insert a staircase, along with the construction of a cellared outshut.

An extant seventeenth-century two-cell house still exists in the Kingsway area, though not part of the project. This is Dixon Green Farm, which is protected as a Grade II Listed Building (NHLE 1162546), and was surveyed in 2005. This farmhouse is another property on Lower Lane (Fig 114), and a datestone on its south-west elevation, that reads 'I W M: 1685' (Pl 170), indicates that it was built late in the century, probably by the Whitworth family (M Nevell *pers comm*). It closely follows the design of the other two-cell houses at Kingsway, suggesting that these formed a standard seventeenth-century building type for the region, being stone built, with the typical housebody and parlour arrangement, and a lobby entrance allowing access into the housebody.

A three-cell house
Another seventeenth- or eighteenth-century two-cell house probably once stood at Cherry Tree Farm, and had an attached barn. The evidence is not particularly clear but, based on its length, this single-depth dwelling was probably divided into two bays, again forming a housebody and parlour. An additional stone-built room was subsequently added to its southern end, to create a three-cell yeoman house (Fig 115). It appears that this extension was single storeyed and may have been an additional parlour. This type of three-cell house, although rare at Kingsway, is often encountered in other parts of Lancashire and Greater Manchester (*cf* Pearson 1985, 66; Burke and Nevell 1996, 38).

A T-shaped house
Another house type, again dating to the seventeenth century, was at Lower Moss Side Farm (*Ch 4, p 65*), which appears to have been a slightly larger

Plate 170: The datestone at Dixon Green Farm

property than the other yeoman houses recorded at Kingsway, perhaps reflecting the greater wealth of those responsible for its construction. This appears to have had a T-shaped plan, consisting of a north-south range, comprising a housebody and parlour, with an additional cellared room to the rear. The function of this rear room may have been as an additional parlour, though in the few recorded early seventeenth-century T-shaped houses in the Lancashire Pennines, rear rooms, such as that at Lower Moss Side Farm, contained a kitchen (*cf* Pearson 1985, 62), which could presumably, therefore, also have been the case at Lower Moss Side Farm.

Small double-pile houses?
Excavation at Castle Farm exposed the footprint of a building, two rooms deep, that appeared to date to the mid-eighteenth century. From a 'ghost' roofline detected during the building survey, on an adjacent and later cottage, it is also apparent that it had two storeys. It is thus quite likely that this was an example of a purpose-built small double-pile farmhouse, of a type that became fairly widespread in rural areas between the mid-eighteenth and late nineteenth centuries, being found in all parts of England (Brunskill 1997, 84); in Lancashire, the first experiments in constructing larger double-depth

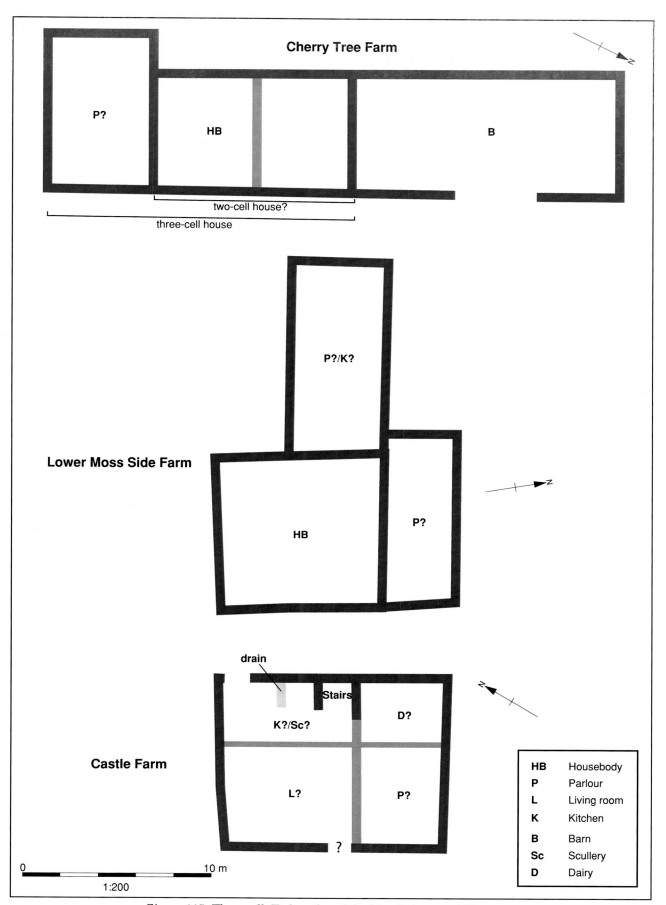

Figure 115: Three-cell, T-shaped, and double-pile houses at Kingsway

houses date to the mid-/late seventeenth century (Pearson 1985, 71-3). Within Greater Manchester, the adoption of the double-pile house plan amongst the eighteenth-century yeoman class also mirrored its adoption by the gentry at a similar time (Burke and Nevell 1996, 41). In addition, as with the larger houses, some of the eighteenth-century yeoman-style double-pile houses were embellished with classical detailing (*op cit*, 42; Brunskill 1997, 84).

This compact house type contained four rooms at ground-floor level, the front rooms comprising a living room and parlour, whilst at the rear were a scullery/kitchen and dairy. These pairs of rooms were generally separated by a staircase, leading to a first floor, containing four bedrooms (Brunskill 1997, 84). The main access to the house was through an off-centre doorway, which might lead either into a lobby, or directly into the living room. Some examples also had a secondary entrance at the rear of the property (*ibid*). Based on the very piecemeal evidence from Castle Farm, it seems possible that the partition wall identified in this building denoted the position of a staircase at the rear of the house (*Ch 4, p 87*). This would probably have been to the north of this wall, which would have meant that the smaller of the rear rooms to the south may have functioned as the dairy, with the scullery/kitchen being in the larger room to the north of the stairs, which also tellingly contained a drain. Access to this putative scullery/kitchen would also have been possible through a secondary entrance close to the northern gable wall of the building. Given this, the façade, the living room, and parlour, and main entrance would have been on the western side of the house.

Another double-pile house of similar date might also have existed at Pyche, replacing a seventeenth-century property (*Ch 4, p 81*). This assumption is based on a photograph of the later house (Haynes and Tipper 1994, 46, fig 5.18), which clearly indicates that it was two-storeyed, possessed a centrally positioned entrance, and also chimney stacks on the two gable walls. Excavation at the site, however, only uncovered the rear portions of this property, and thus provided few additional details.

Agricultural buildings
Several of the yeoman farms investigated were also associated with agricultural buildings, that at Castle Farm forming a separate structure. Its function is not entirely clear, but its size suggested that it was a store. The other agricultural buildings recorded were clearly barns and/or shippons, appended directly onto the yeoman house in a linear arrangement; however, there was no direct access between the barn/shippon and dwelling, so these were not traditional longhouses (Brunskill 1987, 106). This arrangement was apparent at Lane End Farm and Cherry Tree Farm, where the barn/shippons were contemporary with the two-celled houses. At the latter site, however, this linear arrangement was extended further in the eighteenth century by the construction of an additional room on the southern end of the dwelling, and also an additional store room on the northern end of the barn/shippon. A linear arrangement also existed at Near Moor Bank Farm (Fig 113), where a barn had been added to the dwelling as part of a phase of late eighteenth-century remodelling, whilst a barn was attached to the double-pile house at Pyche, though under a separate roof. Such an arrangement also occurred at Dixon Green Farm (*p 241*), where a stone barn was added to the late seventeenth-century two-cell house at some stage in the eighteenth century (M Nevell *pers comm*).

Significantly, this linear arrangement of separate dwelling and barn/shippon exhibits similarities with a particular type of special-purpose rural building, known as the laithe house. This style of building was prevalent in the Pennine areas of Lancashire and Yorkshire, and dates to between 1650 and 1880, though the period 1780-1820 was its constructional *floruit* (Brunskill 1987, 110). True laithe houses were a double-depth dwelling (one or two bays wide), with the farm building under the same roof (*cf* Brunskill 1997, 98), and hence they are slightly different from the Kingsway examples. It is likely, however, that the Pennine laithe houses and the linear arrangement of dwelling and farm buildings at Kingsway may have had a similar genesis and *raison d'être*, in that they probably both reflect 'a society which enjoyed the profitable combination of hand-powered textile work and part-time farming' (Brunskill 1987, 110).

The influence of the early textile industry
Although it is difficult, based on the evidence derived from archaeological investigations, to determine the presence of additional activities at the yeoman farmhouses of Kingsway, some limited evidence was present. For instance, at Lower Moss Side Farm, a pit in one of the rooms of the house contained degraded felt (*Ch 4, p 68*). Similarly, at Lower Lane Farm, a comparable pit containing organic-rich material was identified to the west of the seventeenth-century house (*Ch 4, p 74*). In both instances, these pits might have contained detritus derived from textile working (the spinning and/or weaving of wool) and therefore they create a direct link between these houses and the local textile industry. The seventeenth-century house at Lower Moss Side Farm also had a fairly large cellar, which could have been used to store raw materials used in textile working, or finished products. Although

244

direct archaeological evidence for the early textile industry is slim, it is quite likely that at Kingsway, during the seventeenth and earlier part of the eighteenth century, part-time textile working was an essential, and at times an extremely profitable, element of the rural economy.

The documentary evidence indicates that in 1656 one of the farms at Moor Bank (either Moor Bank Farm or Further Moor Bank; *Ch 4, p 89*) was occupied by James Buckley, a weaver. Similarly, the Butterworths of Moss Side were listed as cloth-makers in 1656 (*Ch 4, p 69*). Slightly later in the seventeenth century, John Milne, who died in 1679, probably occupied Near Moor Bank Farm (which was possibly built by his father, John Milne senior; *Ch 4, p 89*), is documented as an important woollen clothier, and in 1664 (following his father's death) he also became a woollen merchant, in partnership with James Whitworth of Buersill (Haynes and Tipper 1994, 23). Samuel Dewhurst, who in 1673 was resident at one of the farms at Moss Side, was also a local woollen merchant, who sold raw materials to local cloth-makers, who would then produce cloth and sell this on for a profit (*op cit*, 48).

At Kingsway and across the wider region, this post-medieval 'industry' could have been organised in several ways. During much of the period, textile manufacture would have been undertaken by small independent manufacturers (Walton 1987, 61), who normally comprised a single-family unit, headed by a 'clothier', engaged in all elements of textile manufacture (*cf* Wild 1971). Indeed, in some parts of the Pennines, such as the Castleshaw and Piethorne valleys, 'clothiers' formed the dominant textile manufacturers, although they 'rarely employed any persons outside of their own family' (*op cit*, 223).

In the latter part of the seventeenth century, however, the putting-out system emerged in the Rochdale woollen industry (Walton 1987, 62). Following its establishment, small independent clothiers continued to produce textiles, but this new system allowed for the emergence of large merchant capitalists, who distributed the work through middlemen (*ibid*). Within this system, the middlemen received yarn from, and returned the cloth to, a manufacturer who controlled the distribution of both raw material and finished cloth (Nevell 2008, 33-8).

Indeed, in the Kingsway area, one of these early capitalist manufacturers may have been John Milne of Near Moor Bank Farm (*above*), as, in partnership with James Whitworth of Buersill, he is known to have purchased wool from Ireland, which was sent via Liverpool to Rochdale (Haynes and Tipper 1994, 23). Milne and Whitworth then used local weavers to produce the cloth, some of which was bleached at Buersill Fold. Presumably the finished cloth was then returned to Milne and Whitworth for distribution. Significantly, this enterprise appears to have been fairly profitable, as on John Milne's death in 1679, his textile business 'had a joint stock of wool and capital worth £1000, a considerable sum of money in those days' (*ibid*).

Husbandmen's houses at Cutacre
Significantly, in much of the Cutacre area, particularly that in the township of Middle Hulton, property was held by leasehold, whereby small farms were occupied by husbandmen, who had also built the dwellings (*p 232*). It therefore offers a valuable comparison with the building types and agricultural buildings used by the freehold yeoman farmers at Kingsway.

Ashes: an expanding farmhouse
The first farmhouse built at Ashes, in the mid-seventeenth century, was a stone-built two-cell structure, largely comparable to those investigated at Kingsway (*p 238*). It had a single-depth plan and contained the main housebody and a smaller parlour, both of which were heated rooms (Fig 116). Indeed, cursory remains of a fireplace were evident in the parlour, on the gable wall, probably with a stone stack. The presence of a heated parlour would indicate that this dwelling had a first-floor containing bedrooms.

In contrast to the yeoman farms at Kingsway, Ashes was fairly dramatically expanded in the late seventeenth century, into a medium-sized house, which was larger than most of the yeoman houses recorded at Kingsway. This expansion entailed the construction of two additional stone-built rooms, which may have functioned as parlours, as this fits with documentary evidence that indicates that by 1691 the house possessed three such rooms (*Ch 5, p 96*). The documentary evidence also refers to a buttery at this time, though no physical remains could be identified. The addition of these parlours converted the property to double-depth, comparable to the purpose-built double-pile houses (*p 241*). This created four compactly arranged ground-floor rooms, though it is unclear whether this extension had an upper storey, allowing four first-floor chambers, which is a defining feature of the double-pile house (Brunskill 1997, 84).

The expansion of Ashes, with its double-depth ground-floor plan, coincided with the period when double-pile houses emerged, and the builders may have been inspired by these new designs (*ibid*). In Lancashire,

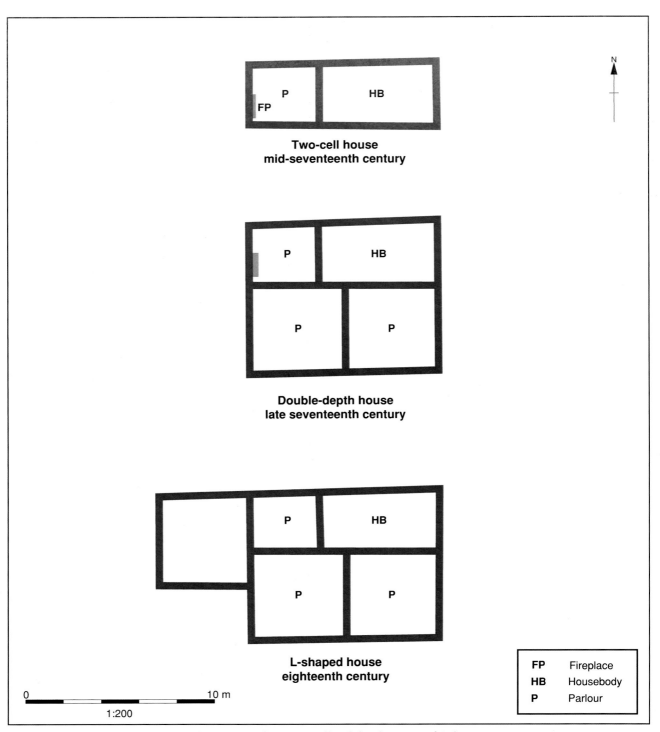

N

FP	Fireplace
HB	Housebody
P	Parlour

Two-cell house
mid-seventeenth century

Double-depth house
late seventeenth century

L-shaped house
eighteenth century

0   10 m

1:200

Figure 116: The post-medieval development of Ashes

purpose-built double-depth farmhouses, with a doorway on the gable end of the building, first appeared in the middle of the seventeenth century (*cf* Pearson 1985, 71); during the late seventeenth century, medium-sized double-depth houses were built that had a centred entrance on the main façade, and these were the forerunners of the smaller double-depth houses which became a dominant house type from the mid-eighteenth century onwards (*op cit*, 72-3). Ashes is somewhat unusual, however, in that the two additional rooms were larger in size than those in the original house, which might suggest that there was a more radical reorganisation of space within the late seventeenth-century farmhouse. Indeed, it could be that the main living area was transferred to one of the larger rooms in the extension. A further expansion of this farmhouse occurred in the early/mid-eighteenth century, when another room was constructed to the west, creating a house with an L-shaped ground plan (*Ch 5, p 101*).

This progressive expansion suggests that the Mort family of Middle Hulton, who built, expanded, and occupied this property, were comparatively wealthy. Indeed, this level of wealth probably explains why John Mort, the occupier of the farm in the mid-eighteenth century, described himself as a 'yeoman' in a lease dating to 1758, as opposed to a 'husbandmen' (NRO E(B) 1218). Although John Mort was a leaseholder, it therefore appears that he considered himself slightly higher in social rank than many of his rural contemporaries. The documentary evidence indicates that the Mort family's wealth was not solely generated by farming (*Ch 5, pp 96-7*) but also by additional activities, that may in fact have generated higher sources of income. These initially comprised tanning, and by the mid-eighteenth century included bleaching, indicating a connection with the domestic-textile industry of this area.

A double-pile house
The farmhouse at Mills Brow was a classic example of an eighteenth-century double-pile farmhouse. At ground-floor level, it possessed a central entrance and lobby, which also contained the staircase leading to the first floor, with a set of two rooms on either side (Fig 117). The larger rooms at the front would have functioned as the living room and parlour, whilst those to the rear acted as the kitchen and dairy/pantry. Above these, at first-floor level, were four bedrooms, whilst there was a cellar beneath one of the rooms at the front of the house. It was probably constructed by John Aldred in the mid-eighteenth century, adopting a design which was becoming increasingly commonplace during this period, witnessed by the construction of similar style houses in the Kingsway area (*p 241*). This type of house plan was also employed on the Dunham estate on the Cheshire border in the eighteenth century, when many of the tenant farmhouses were rebuilt in this style (Gregory and Miller 2013, 28-30).

A two-cell house
The farmhouse at Spout Fold was possibly built by Richard Seddon, perhaps as a home for himself and his new wife Elizabeth in *c* 1776 (*Ch 5, p 113*), and was a late example of a two-cell house. In common with such houses, the ground floor contained a housebody and a slightly smaller parlour, both of which were heated (Fig 118). Entry into the house was through a centrally positioned doorway, which led into a small baffle-style lobby that accessed the housebody. The baffle entry was created by the southern wall of a centrally positioned staircase, which could be accessed from both the housebody and parlour. The stairs in turn led to the two first-floor bedrooms.

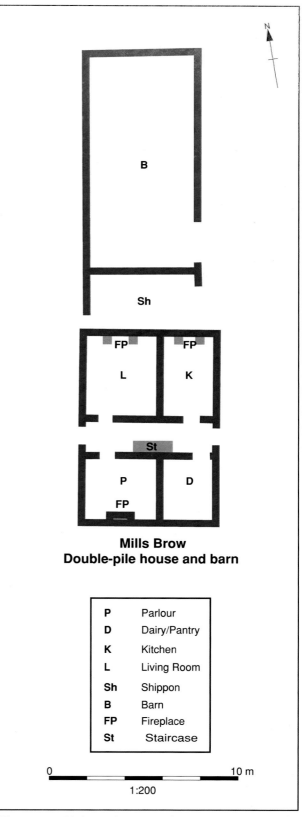

Mills Brow
Double-pile house and barn

P	Parlour
D	Dairy/Pantry
K	Kitchen
L	Living Room
Sh	Shippon
B	Barn
FP	Fireplace
St	Staircase

0   10 m
1:200

Figure 117: Eighteenth-century farmhouse at Mills Brow

Agricultural buildings
Both Spout Fold and Mills Brow were associated with agricultural buildings of mid-eighteenth-century date. It was evident from their layouts that these were

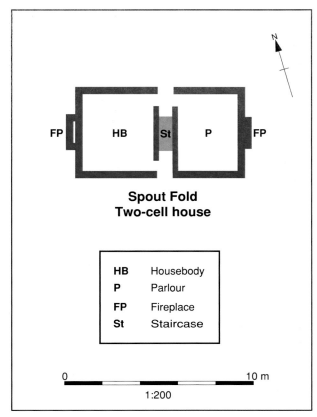

Spout Fold
Two-cell house

HB	Housebody
P	Parlour
FP	Fireplace
St	Staircase

0   10 m
1:200

Figure 118: Eighteenth-century farmhouse at Spout Fold

a specific type of building, known as a Lancashire or combination barn, which contained both a threshing area and shippon. These, as the name indicates, were a common type of building in Lancashire, dating to the period 1750-1850 (Brunskill 1987, 111-13). The similar Lancashire barns at Spout Fold and Mills Brow therefore represent comparatively early examples of this type of agricultural building.

At Spout Fold, the barn was a separate building, some distance from the farmhouse. In contrast, that at Mills Brow was appended to the house, to create a linear range, which, in a similar way to some of the Kingsway houses with barns/shippons, mimics a Pennine laithe house (*p 243*). However, although the arrangement of buildings at Mills Brow was akin to this distinctive type of rural building, it did not create this in the strictest sense, in that the combination barn and farmhouse were not under the same roof.

The Industrial Era

In both the Kingsway and Cutacre development areas, the period between the late eighteenth and the close of the nineteenth century is broadly characterised as a phase when rebuilding and extension took place. Many of the yeoman and husbandmen farms were either rebuilt, modified,

or extended, and, in the Kingsway area, the earlier part of this period can also be characterised by the appearance of cottages designed to house agricultural labourers, which in addition acted as semi-domestic workshops.

Cutacre
Late eighteenth/nineteenth-century modifications and expansion

In Cutacre, it appears that during the late eighteenth and nineteenth centuries, although there was not a substantial rise in 'new' buildings, the existing building stock was rebuilt, or modified and expanded. These modified buildings included some of the tenanted farms, such as Ashes and Spout Fold, and Wharton Hall, which by the nineteenth century was also a tenanted farm occupied by members of the Green family (*Ch 8, p 211*).

Ashes appears to have undergone fairly substantial modification in the late eighteenth/early nineteenth century, which was either the work of the Mort family, who were resident at the farm during the late eighteenth century (*Ch 8, p 205*), or the Ashcrofts, who occupied it in the nineteenth century. This modification involved rebuilding fairly large parts of the earlier farmhouse in brick, probably to modernise what, by then, may have been a fairly dilapidated and outdated building. This 'modernisation' also involved remodelling the seventeenth-century cellar and adding brick-built fireplaces to some of the rooms within the farmhouse. Several additional rooms were also added to its western end, one of which contained a furnace, and several other small rooms were added to both the farmhouse and an eighteenth-century barn to the north in the late nineteenth century. Similarly, Spout Fold was also 'modernised' in the early nineteenth century, either by members of the Seddon or Harper family (*Ch 8, p 209*). This entailed the construction of an extension to the existing farmhouse, which functioned as a kitchen.

At Wharton Hall, two phases of modification were completed during this period (*Ch 8, p 212*). The first dates to the early/mid-nineteenth century and was fairly extensive in nature, comprising the rebuilding and expansion of an extension that had been added to the south-eastern side of the hall's southern cross-wing during the eighteenth century; the construction of a well; and the construction of an outbuilding. During the late nineteenth century, the hall was subjected to more minor modifications, which included the construction of an outshut and a partition wall within that part of the hall that had been extended in the early nineteenth century. All of these modifications relate to the declining status of this former gentry dwelling, which was now effectively converted into a humbler, tenanted farmhouse.

Kingsway

Late eighteenth- to mid-nineteenth century: a booming farming and textile economy

Significantly, the data generated during the archaeological investigations at Kingsway imply that there was a fairly concerted phase of rebuilding/adaption of pre-existing yeoman farms during the late eighteenth century and the first decade of the nineteenth century in this area (Fig 119). For instance, on Moss Side Lane, the seventeenth-century farmhouse at Higher Moss Side Farm was probably demolished in the late eighteenth century (*Ch 6, p 155*) and replaced by two terraced double-pile single-fronted cottages (Brunskill 1997, 92). A barn was also constructed that was attached to the eastern end of the cottages, and together these elements formed a linear range, reminiscent of the Pennine laithe house (*p 243*). Other terraced labourers' cottages were also constructed at Haigh Field in the late eighteenth century on a virgin site, and it is quite possible that this range began life as a small row of single-unit cottages (*op cit*, 88), which were, by the 1840s, knocked through to create two adjoining, larger, cottages (*Ch 6, p 150*).

On Lower Lane, at Lower Lane Farm, although the earlier, albeit modified, yeoman house was retained, an additional single-unit cottage was constructed in 1793, which abutted the western side of the earlier building (*Ch 7, p 169*). Similarly, the seventeenth-century farmhouse at Lane End Farm was also extended in the late eighteenth century (*Ch 7, p 186*). This L-shaped extension could be accessed from the earlier farmhouse, its construction more than doubling the available space within the farm. Given this increase in floor size, it is tempting to speculate that at least some was given over to house farm labourers, or perhaps for semi-domestic textile production (*below*). At Castle House, another seventeenth-century farmhouse was expanded in the late eighteenth century, though in this case it involved raising the height of the building to create a first floor. An L-shaped extension was also tagged onto the corner of the seventeenth-century building, which was comparable to the L-shaped extension added to Lane End Farm.

Again, this may suggest that this extension allowed parts of the farm to be used for housing farm labourers or for textile production. Indeed, this is confirmed, in some measure, by the documentary evidence, which indicates that, in 1851, agricultural labourers were resident at Castle House (*Ch 7, p 188*). A reference to fustian cutting is also made at that time, suggesting the existence of supplementary activities. Of the other properties on Lower Lane, the existing house at Cherry Tree Farm was substantially modified in the first decade of the nineteenth century, probably in 1805 (*Ch 7, p 166*). This entailed the conversion of the south-eastern end of the seventeenth/eighteenth-century farmhouse into two adjoining, single-unit cottages, with another one-and-a-half-unit cottage (Brunskill 1997, 88) added to the north-western end of the earlier farm complex (Pl 171).

Properties on Moor Bank Lane also seem to have been subjected to modification during this period. This is evident at Near Moor Bank Farm, where the seventeenth-century farmhouse was substantially modified in the late eighteenth century (Fig 113). In addition, a barn was added to the farmhouse, in a laithe-house-style arrangement (*p 243*).

Overall, therefore, the sites investigated provide clear evidence for modification, in the form of extensions to existing farmhouses, and the construction of cottages probably designed to house farm labourers Together, this evidence suggests that agricultural productivity may have been increasing in this area and this was, perhaps, linked to the growing demand for foodstuffs from the emerging industrial towns of Greater Manchester and Lancashire.

Late eighteenth- and early nineteenth-century weavers' cottages

In addition to the construction of cottages for farm labourers, a particular type of building emerged in Pennines, and the Kingsway area, during the late eighteenth century, which was intimately linked to textile production. These buildings are termed weavers' cottages and have been identified across fairly wide swathes of rural Lancashire and Yorkshire, and also parts of Greater Manchester (*Ch 6, p 137*).

These were usually associated with handloom weaving (Pl 172) and could be either two- or three-storey buildings, which functioned both as houses and workshops (Giles 2004). The presence of the workshop element is normally visible as a row of long mullioned windows, which provided good daylight for textile working. Spatially, there was no set pattern to the placement of the workshop and domestic areas, and the former might occur on any floor of the property. Workshops could also be situated within cellars, which provided humid conditions that were advantageous for weaving (Timmins 1977; 2004). One common arrangement, however, in rural Lancashire and Yorkshire, and one that certainly applied to some of the Kingsway examples, was 'a two-storeyed dwelling with one or two living rooms on the ground floor and, on the first floor, chambers for sleeping and weaving, the loom or looms being set up against the window' (Giles 2004, 81).

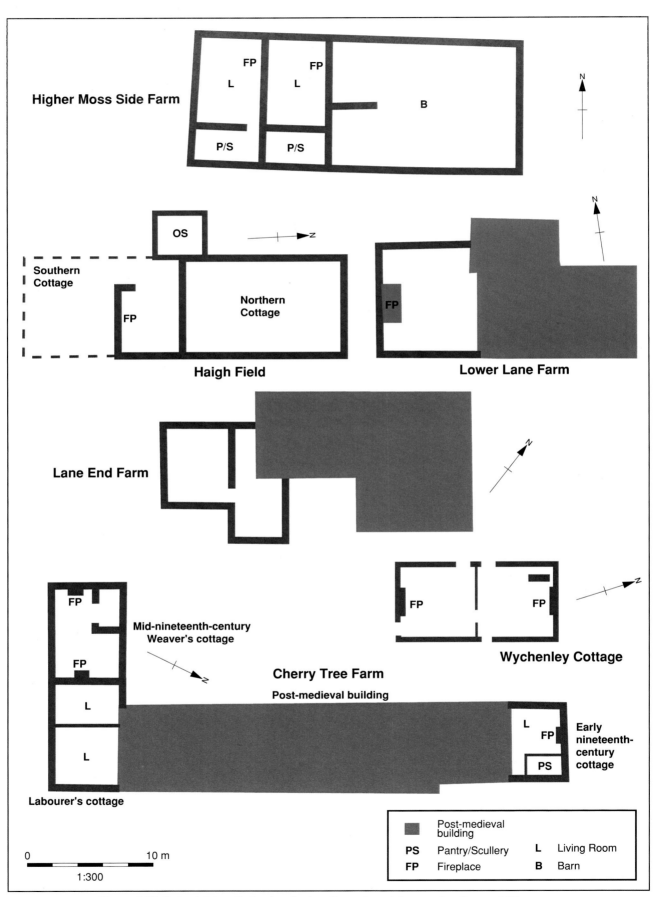

Figure 119: Late eighteenth-/early nineteenth-century labourers' cottages at Kingsway

Plate 171: The excavation of the early nineteenth-century cottage added to the barn at Cherry Tree Farm

Plate 172: A depiction of handloom weavers in a domestic loomshop

Plate 173: Typical three-storey Lancashire weavers' cottages, with loomshops in the first and second storeys

Another common arrangement was a cottage with three storeys, in which often 'the ground floor was used for living, the first floor for sleeping and weaving, and the top floor entirely for weaving' (*ibid*; Pl 173). Although some examples in Yorkshire and Lancashire might date to before 1770 (such as that at South View in Cheadle, to which a *c* 1720 date has been attributed; M Nevell *pers comm*), the majority were built in the late eighteenth and early nineteenth centuries (Giles 2004, 80). During this period, their appearance in the woollen-producing districts of Lancashire and Yorkshire was a result of the abundance of raw yarn then available, as a consequence of technological advances, and the absence, prior to the 1820s, of automated power-looms, which ultimately led to the full mechanisation of weaving and the emergence within historic Lancashire of the factory system, characterised by both integrated mills, in which both spinning and weaving took place, and dedicated weaving mills (Phelps *et al* 2017).

During the archaeological investigations in the Kingsway area, four sites with weavers' cottages were identified that date to the main period of such buildings. Those late eighteenth-century examples at Higher Moss Side and Castle House were constructed adjacent to pre-existing farmhouses, highlighting the importance of both farming and weaving to the economies of these settlements, and the late eighteenth-/early nineteenth-century examples at Mayfields and Moss Side Farm formed elements of stand-alone textile complexes that, at this time, were not associated with any farm buildings.

Little remained of the weaver's cottage at Higher Moss Side Farm, but the other three sites were extant at the time of the initial investigations (Fig 120). That at Castle Farm was a two-and-half-storeyed single-depth building, with a domestic area at ground-floor level, and an associated small cellar. The first floor acted as a workshop, and was probably also used for sleeping, whilst the loft area was entirely given over to weaving and was lit by a continuous window, situated on the principal elevation, that had once had 15 lights separated by 14 stone mullions. Evidence of the type of loom used in this cottage was identified at first-floor level, in the form of four crudely cut mortises on the underside of two ceiling bridging beams (*Ch 7, p 194*). The spacing of these indicated that a broad loom had been in use. These were employed in the specialised weaving of textiles over 36 inches wide (914 mm), and could be operated by a single weaver, being twice as fast as earlier looms (Nevell 2008, 33-4). The combined documentary and archaeological evidence suggests that handloom weaving was occurring at this site between the late eighteenth century and the 1840s.

At Moss Side Farm, a three-bay, single-depth cottage was built in the late eighteenth century. Although few original features survived, it is evident that it was built in stone and was two storeyed, and the upper floor was associated with windows sited directly below the eaves, which probably once formed a continuous mullioned window. This implies that a loomshop existed on the first floor, with domestic accommodation below. An ancillary building immediately to the south-east of the cottage was probably built in 1831 and may have been a small warehouse/workshop to serve this textile-manufacturing site (*Ch 6, p 153*).

The weavers' cottages at Mayfields clearly demonstrate the significance of textile manufacture in the Kingsway area, and provide an excellent example of a semi-domestic textile site. The earliest elements date to 1787, and comprise two adjoining purpose-built weavers' cottages constructed in stone by a local woollen manufacturer, who was a member of the Butterworth family (possibly John Butterworth; *Ch 7, p 175*). These two-storeyed cottages had double-depth plans, at ground-floor level both being divided into two rooms. These formed the domestic parts of the cottages, being a living room/kitchen at the front of the house with a pantry to the rear. One of the cottages also had a small cellar beneath the pantry. Similarly, in both cottages, the first-floor formed the workshop and sleeping area, both being lit by a long mullioned window, originally with six lights.

During the early nineteenth century, this semi-domestic complex was expanded, probably as a result of the increasing demand for handloom weaving during this period (Timmins 1993, 24). Initially, this involved the construction of a small building immediately to the rear of the cottages,

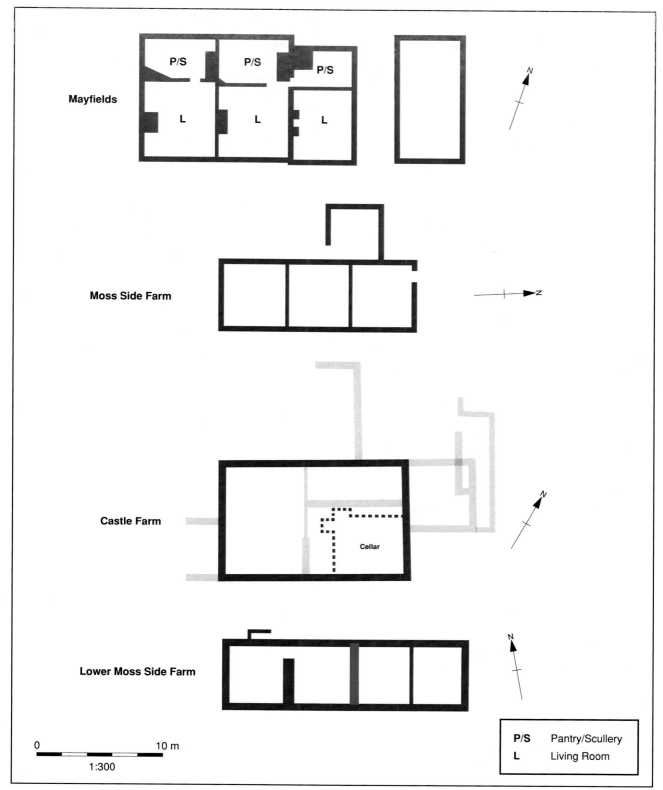

Figure 120: Weavers' cottages at Kingsway

which may have functioned as a warehouse, and then later a barn, along with another outbuilding. This was then followed by the construction of an additional adjoining cottage, which seems to have been not only used for weaving but was also associated with a blacksmith's forge, present at the site in 1831 (*Ch 7, p 176*); by implication, the cottage must, therefore, have been constructed prior to this date. Although it was constructed in brick, it was of comparable design to the earlier buildings, in that it was a single-bay wide, with two rooms at ground-floor level and a loomshop above, lit by a six-light window. Another detached, double-depth cottage, a single-bay wide, was also constructed immediately to the east. It is unclear, however, whether this was used for weaving or whether it was only a dwelling; but taken as a whole, the complex suggests that a thriving textile business existed at Mayfields in the early to mid-nineteenth century.

At Dixon Green Farm (*p 241*), two brick-built weavers' cottages were appended to the northern and southern ends of an earlier farmstead in the late eighteenth or early nineteenth century (M Nevell *pers comm*). This again appears to point to the presence of both farming and weaving at this site.

Mid-nineteenth-century buildings
Several buildings were identified at Lower Moss Side Farm, Cherry Tree Farm, Lower Lane Farm, and Wychenley Cottage in Kingsway that clearly date to the mid-nineteenth century (*Ch 7*). These comprised both agricultural buildings and labourers' and weavers' cottages (*p 249*). The presence of these latter buildings indicates that handloom weaving continued to form an element of the rural economy into the mid-nineteenth century, even though by this date the factory-based system of weaving was well established (*p 251*). The presence of handloom weavers at this period is, therefore, akin to the situation in central Lancashire, where 'handloom weavers still plied their trade... even in the early 1850s' (Walton 1987, 104). However, at Kingsway, it appears that handloom weaving continued even later as, at Mayfields (*above*), documentary evidence indicates that both it and wool spinning continued to form a feature of these dwellings into the 1860s (*Ch 7, p 177*). Indeed, this seems to validate the suggestion that in the woollen trade 'the main period of transition to power-looms was as late as the 1850s or 1860s' (Timmins 1993, 24).

At Wychenley Cottage, two adjoining single-unit labourers' cottages of standard design were built in the mid-nineteenth-century, whilst at Cherry Tree Farm, a two-bay, single-depth weaver's cottage was added to the farm complex in the mid-nineteenth century (Fig 118). Although this latter cottage had been demolished prior to the archaeological investigations, a photograph indicates that loomshops were present in both bays at first-floor level (Haynes and Tipper 1994, 47, fig 5.21). The domestic area of the properties was at ground-floor level, and one of the bays had been subdivided into a living room and pantry, mimicking the plan of a one-and-a-half-unit cottage (Brunskill 1997, 88).

At Lower Moss Side Farm, a seventeenth-century yeoman farmhouse was demolished in the mid-nineteenth century and replaced by two adjoining, two-bay cottages (*Ch 6, p 140*; Fig 120). Both were two-storeyed buildings, though the western bay of the westernmost cottage was slightly elevated; part of the cellar below the western bay of the seventeenth-century farmhouse was also incorporated into the design of this cottage. The ground-floor rooms formed domestic areas, along with the first-floor in the western bay of the westernmost cottage. In contrast, the first floor of the eastern bay of this cottage and also the first-floor of the adjoining cottage were lit by multi-light windows, demonstrating that they functioned as loomshops and, probably, also sleeping areas. The evidence points therefore to the presence of a dedicated semi-domestic textile-manufacturing site, that might conceivably date to the 1850s.

It appears, however, that the life of these weavers' cottages was comparatively short, based on the evidence of an adjacent barn, as timbers within its construction were from wooden loom frames which probably derived from the nearby cottages (*Ch 6, p 145*), suggesting that weaving had become a redundant activity by the time the barn was constructed. Indeed, the construction of the barn probably signalled the shift from a reliance on weaving and farming, to solely farming, and might also have entailed the functional conversion of the cottages into a farmhouse and labourer's cottage. A datestone associated with the barn indicates that it was built in either the 1860s or 1880s (*Ch 6, p 145*); however, given that it was perhaps built to facilitate this economic shift, the earlier date is probably more applicable, as it is unlikely that handloom weaving occurred in the area during the 1880s.

A mid-nineteenth-century agricultural building was also constructed at Lower Lane Farm, suggestive of an expansion in agricultural productivity at this time, associated with dairy farming, most probably to supply foodstuffs to the rapidly expanding urban populations of the region (*cf* Phillips and Smith 1994). This building functioned as a shippon and its interior possessed the classic threefold arrangement of manure passage, stalls, and feeding passage, above which was a raised loft (*cf* Brunskill 1987, 63).

Late nineteenth-century modifications
During the late nineteenth century, several modifications were made to the earlier buildings at Kingsway. At Haigh Field (Pl 174), Lower Lane Farm, Mayfields, and Pyche, these comprised fairly minor works, though at other sites the modifications were more substantial, such as those at Moss Side Farm (*Ch 6, p 152*). These included the addition of a cellared extension and the insertion of a sunken room into the interior of one of the late eighteenth-century cottages, perhaps as part of the conversion of the cottages into a farmhouse. Other associated modifications included the construction of a yard and the conversion of an

early nineteenth-century warehouse/workshop into a shippon.

Similarly, at Mayfields, the early nineteenth-century warehouse/barn was rebuilt late in the century, and major modifications were also made to the seventeenth-century barn at Lane End Farm, to convert it into a shippon (*Ch 7, p 187*). This evidence appears to suggest that during this period dairy farming remained important economically, following on from the apparent refocusing on pastoral farming in the mid-nineteenth century (*above*). Again, the stimulus for this undoubtedly lay in supplying dairy products to the region's urban centres.

Ritual and Magic: Foundation Deposits and Charms?

Intriguingly, during the excavations at Kingsway, evidence was also collected for activity that was seemingly 'ritual' in character. Specifically, this comprised the burying of complete pottery vessels or other objects beneath the floor of a building. One instance of this was at Cherry Tree Farm, where a complete earthenware vessel (Pl 175) had been buried beneath the floor of its seventeenth-/eighteenth-century barn/shippon, adjacent to a doorway leading out of the northern gable of this building. Although this style of vessel has a long chronological currency

(*Appendix 4, p 340*), given the date of this building, it is possible that it dated to either the seventeenth-/or early/mid-eighteenth century.

This practice of burying complete vessels continued, however, considerably longer, as evidenced by the burial of a compete kitchenware storage jar beneath the floor of an extension to the late eighteenth-century cottages at Moss Side Farm (*Ch 6, p 152*), shortly after this had been built. Collections of late eighteenth-century objects were also deliberately buried inside a late eighteenth-century cottage at Higher Moss Side Farm. Two pits were discovered within this, one containing two near-complete ceramic vessels, a fragment of clay tobacco-pipe, and a worn copper-alloy Georgian-era coin, whilst the other contained copper-alloy pins, a copper-alloy button, a bovine vertebra, two gunflints, and fragments of eighteenth-century pottery (*Ch 6, p 156*).

Although the exact reasons for the burial of these objects is unclear, it is likely that they relate to one of two practices. In the case of the burial of the complete yet empty vessels, it is quite possible that these were foundation deposits, with the pots being buried during the construction of the buildings/extensions, perhaps designed to bestow good luck/fortune on the structure. Indeed, this depositional practice has been noted within other post-medieval domestic buildings in England, though it appears to have been particularly commonplace in other parts of

Plate 174: Excavating Haigh Field cottages

Plate 175: The complete earthenware vessel from the barn at Cherry Tree Farm

Europe, such as the Netherlands, where complete earthenware pots were often buried beneath thresholds or fireplaces within post-medieval buildings (Merrifield 1987, 120).

At Higher Moss Side Farm (*p 255*), the collection of objects contained within the pit, and also those objects buried within the complete vessels, might represent charms, which provided 'luck' and would also have guarded against witchcraft. As such. these items might have been part of a wider tradition involving the use of charms to protect against witches; this was particularly prevalent in seventeenth-century England, but continued within certain rural areas up until the twentieth century (*op cit*, 162). Coins were often used to protect against witchcraft, especially in dairies, where difficulties in butter-making were often attributed to witchcraft (*ibid*). Similarly, metal pins were used as charms against witchcraft during the seventeenth and eighteenth centuries, often to pierce a cloth heart that was then placed within a stoneware 'witch-bottle' (*op cit*, 163; Pl 176). This practice had 'the purpose of saving the victim by throwing back the evil spell on the witch who cast it' (*op cit*, 167-8) and, perhaps, a similar reasoning lay behind the deposition of the charms at Higher Moss Side Farm.

Conclusion: Success and Significance

When reflecting on the outcomes of the two landscape projects at the Kingsway Business Park and Cutacre, it is apparent that both have produced valuable sets of archaeological and palaeoenvironmental evidence. This is, in many respects, complementary and allows insights into the patterns and types of rural settlement, and associated activities that, perhaps, typified those

taking place across a swathe of northern Greater Manchester, an area which, historically, was within south-east Lancashire. Both contained evidence for prehistoric activity, clearly indicating that the two respective landscapes were utilised by the region's earliest communities. The more archaeologically tangible evidence from Cutacre (*Ch 2*) can be directly compared with those prehistoric remains known in the Mersey Basin, and also from the wider North West. Indeed, some of the prehistoric remains from Cutacre, specifically those relating to the Middle Bronze Age settlement (*Ch 2, p 25*), hold great significance, in that they are currently unique in Greater Manchester and also represent a rare example of settlement dating to this period in the wider region (*cf* Hodgson and Brennand 2006).

Similarly, although both landscapes provided evidence for medieval activity, that demonstrating late medieval iron production at Cutacre is important (*Ch 3, p 44*). Such activity, although probably once fairly commonplace, has only occasionally been examined archaeologically within northern Greater Manchester/south-east Lancashire (*cf* C Newman 2006, 132-3). Therefore, these remains are extremely significant, in that they provided a rare example of an excavated medieval bloomery site, which, in turn, is an important addition to the small regional corpus of comparable sites that currently exists.

In many respects, the greatest contribution of these projects was the information provided on the form and character of habitation during the last 400 years. Both development areas, through a combination of documentary research, building survey, and open-area excavation, have produced valuable data on the range of house types that existed within northern Greater Manchester, as well as their chronologies and evolution. In some cases, evidence was also uncovered for some of the activities that were practised within them. Naturally, many of these activities related to farming, though others demonstrated cottage-based industries, such as textile manufacturing, that formed a significant feature of the post-medieval rural economy, and also led to the creation of architecturally distinctive types of rural buildings.

Whilst these building types are not in themselves unusual, they do provide further valuable detail relating to the development of yeoman and tenanted farms, and workers' cottages within Greater Manchester. Those from the Kingsway Business Park also represent one of the densest groups of post-medieval/industrial-era rural buildings that have yet been subjected to

Plate 176: A typical collection of items (stoneware bottle, pins, cloth heart, and hair), used as charms against witchcraft in the post-medieval period

archaeological investigation within the boundaries of the metropolitan county (N Redhead *pers comm*). Additionally, the sites highlight the clear benefits that can be achieved by combining building survey and excavation at sites that are earmarked for demolition and redevelopment. At Wharton Hall in Cutacre, a more affluent form of rural house was recorded, when compared with the other dwellings examined by the two projects. Therefore, its excavation forms an important addition to the growing body of knowledge about seventeenth-century gentry houses in Greater Manchester, and also the later decline of this distinct class of dwelling into humbler tenanted farms.

BIBLIOGRAPHY

Cartographic Sources

Greenwood, C, 1818 *Map of the County Palatine of Lancaster*

Hennet, G, 1830 *Map of the County Palatine of Lancaster*

Ordnance Survey (OS), 1849 6":1 mile First Edition Lancashire sheet 94, surveyed 1845-6

Ordnance Survey (OS), 1850a 6":1 mile First Edition Lancashire sheet 95, surveyed 1844-6

Ordnance Survey (OS), 1850b 6":1 mile First Edition Lancashire sheet 89, surveyed 1844-7

Ordnance Survey (OS), 1893a 1:2500 Lancashire sheet LXXXIX.5, surveyed 1889-91

Ordnance Survey (OS), 1893b 1:2500 Lancashire sheet LXXXIX.6, surveyed 1891

Ordnance Survey (OS), 1893c 1:2500 Lancashire sheet XCV.9, surveyed 1891

Ordnance Survey (OS), 1893d 1:2500 Lancashire sheet XCIV.12, surveyed 1888-92

Ordnance Survey (OS), 1908 1:2500 Lancashire sheet XCIV.12, revised 1907

Ordnance Survey (OS), 1910a 1:2500 Lancashire sheet LXXXIX.6, revised 1907

Ordnance Survey (OS), 1910b 1:2500 Lancashire sheet LXXXIX.5, revised 1908

Ordnance Survey (OS), 1930 1:2500 Lancashire sheet LXXXIX.5, revised 1928

Ordnance Survey (OS), 1936 1:2500 Lancashire sheet LXXXIX.6, revised 1936

Ordnance Survey (OS), 1955 1:2500 Lancashire sheet LXXXIX.6, revised 1955

Yates, W, 1786 *Survey of the County Palatine of Lancaster*

Primary Sources

Bolton Archives (BA)
PMH 7/4 Window Tax assessment for Middle Hulton, 1760

PMH 7/13 Survey and valuation of Middle Hulton township, 1818

PMH 14/1 Middle Hulton township account book, 1679-1805

ZFL 5/2-6 Mortgage of part of Leadbetter Fold, Little Lever, 1701-9

ZJA 752 Plans of Wharton Hall Colliery and Wharton Hall estate, 1838-77

ZZ 640/1-2 Deane parish tithe account books, 1776-89

Chetham's Library (CL)
Booth 2/1/1/1 Deed of grant by Humphrey Booth of Salford to Adam Byrom and others, 1631

GB418/2 Raines collection

Lancashire Archives (LA)
DDHu 10/6 Letter to Henry Hulton, 1709

DDHu 19/30 Lease from William Hilton of Hilton [Hulton] to John Thomasson, 1654

DDKe 2/16/10 Hearth Tax for Little Hulton, 1664

DDKe 2/16/11 Hearth Tax for Middle Hulton, 1664

DDKe 29/6 Copy of the will of Adam Mort of Tyldesley, 1630

DDX 75/17 Marriage settlement of Sir William Egerton and Honora Leigh, 1674

DDX 349/29 Assignment of mortgage from Nathan Mort of Atherton, gent, to Mary Mort, spinster, 1709

DDX 409/30 Lease for 999 years at 1s rent: for £4, 1759

DDX 643/1 Draft marriage settlement by lease and release, 1674

DRM 1/27 Tithe award for Butterworth, 1846

DRM 1/58 Tithe award for Little Hulton, 1844

DRM 1/59 Tithe award for Middle Hulton, 1844

DRM/1/100 Tithe award for Tyldesley cum Shakerley, 1847

Mf 27-29 Hearth Tax returns, 1663-73

QDD 43/F3 Bargain and sale by Humphrey Booth of Salford to his son Humphrey Booth and others, 1635

QDL/S/24 Land Tax assessments for Castleton, 1780-1832

QDL/S/55 Land Tax assessments for Little Hulton, 1780-1831

QDL/S/56 Land Tax assessments for Middle Hulton, 1780-1831

QDV 4 Dissenting meeting house register, 1689-1852

QSB 1/1781/Jan/Pt3/39 Recognizance, 21 November 1780

QSP 985/7 Registration of Wharton Hall as dissenters' meeting place, 1709

WCW/Infra/C1363/71 Archdeaconry of Chester Probate Records, John Mort of Middle Hulton, 1691

WCW/Infra/C1392/31 Archdeaconry of Chester Probate Records, John Holt of Lower Lane, Castleton, yeoman, 1719

WCW/Infra/C1392/47 Archdeaconry of Chester Probate Records, James Smith, Butterworth, collier, 1719

WCW/Supra/C98C/29 Archdeaconry of Chester Probate Records, Robert Smith of Little Hulton, nailer, 1628

WCW/Supra/C104C/37 Archdeaconry of Chester Probate Records, William Warton of Little Hulton, husbandman, 1631

WCW/Supra/C118A/22 Archdeaconry of Chester Probate Records, James Boardman, Little Hulton, husbandman, 1637

WCW/Supra/C122C/37 Archdeaconry of Chester Probate Records, Thomas Mort of Little Hulton, gent, 1638

WCW/Supra/C203/53 Archdeaconry of Chester Probate Records, John Mather of Middle Hulton, 1675

WCW/Supra/C203/66 Archdeaconry of Chester Probate Records, Margaret Mort of the Peel, widow, 1675

WCW/Supra/C259B/37 Archdeaconry of Chester Probate Records, Robert Mort of Wharton Hall, gent, 1691

WCW/Supra/C262A/36 Archdeaconry of Chester Probate Records, Thomas Mort of Little Hulton, gent, 1692

WCW/Supra/C281B/17 Archdeaconry of Chester Probate Records, Richard Edge of the Moss in Middle Hulton, yeoman, 1705

WCW/Supra/C345A/30 Archdeaconry of Chester Probate Records, Robert Mort of Middle Hulton, tanner, 1728

WCW/Supra/C365A/54 Archdeaconry of Chester Probate Records, Adam Mort of Atherton, gent, 1734

WCW/Supra/C416A/11 Archdeaconry of Chester Probate Records, Giles Edge of Middle Hulton, yeoman, 1753

WCW/Supra/C433A/7 Archdeaconry of Chester Probate Records, Edward Aldred of Atherton the elder, 1759

WCW/Supra/C460B/41 Archdeaconry of Chester Probate Records, Margaret Mather of Middle Hulton, widow, 1767

WCW/Supra/C489A/41 Archdeaconry of Chester Probate Records, Ralph Seddon of Middle Hulton, yeoman, 1775

WCW/Supra/C517B/59 Archdeaconry of Chester Probate Records, John Mort of Middle Hulton, yeoman, 1784

WCW/Supra/C658B/54 Archdeaconry of Chester Probate Records, John Butterworth of Moor Bank within Butterworth, yeoman, 1810

WCW/Supra/C716A/9 Archdeaconry of Chester Probate Records, Richard Seddon of Middle Hulton, 1816

WCW/Supra/C1190/29 Archdeaconry of Chester Probate Records, Charles Turner of Lower Lane, woollen weaver, 1848

WCW/Supra/C1211B/3 Archdeaconry of Chester Probate Records, Joseph Holroyd of Mayfields, Castleton, woollen weaver, 1850

Manchester Archives (MA)
L 5/1/1/8 Marriage settlement of Honora Egerton and Thomas Arden Bagot, 1711

L 5/2/1/2 Lease of Bankhouse and Greenhalghs, 1795

L 5/2/4/1-2 Leases of Hulton Heys, 1734-92

L 5/2/6/1-2 Leases of Morris's Farm or the Spout, 1792-9

L 5/4/1/1 A plan of the estate belonging to Egerton Bagot Esqr in the Townships of Worsley, Middle Hulton and Kersley in the County Palatine of Lancaster, by R Cassan, c 1772

L 5/4/1/3 Volume of plans of estate in Middle Hulton, Worsley, Kearsley and Little Hulton, with survey book, c 1860

L 85/1/3 Church of St Mary, Deane, marriage registers 1754-1890

L 85/1/4 Church of St Mary, Deane, burial registers 1781-1887

National Archives (NA)
HO 107/541 Census Returns, 1841. Lancashire, Hundred of Salford, Parish: Deane; Township: Farnworth; Halliwell; Heaton; Horwich; Little Hulton or Peel; Middle Hulton; Over Hulton; Kersley or Kearsley; Rumworth; West Houghton

HO 107/550 Census Returns, 1841. Lancashire, Hundred of Salford, Parish: Rochdale (part); Township: Blatchinworth and Calderbrook; Butterworth; Castleton. Hamlet: Littleborough; Buershill; Marland

HO 107/2206 Census Returns, 1851. Lancashire, Registration District: 468, Bolton. Registration sub-district: 2, Hulton. Parish: Deane; Hamlet: Little Hulton; Middle Hulton; Over Hulton; Rumworth

HO 107/2244 Census Returns, 1851. Lancashire, Registration district: 476, Rochdale. Registration sub-district: 3, Castleton Without. Parish: Rochdale (part);

Hamlet: Castleton with Buersill; Lowerplace Newbold; Marland; Lower-lane; Broadlane; Back-lanes; Roeacre; Captain-fold; Castleton-moor and Bluepits

RG 9/2810 Census Returns, 1861. Lancashire, Registration District: 468, Bolton. Registration sub-district: 2, Hulton. Parish: Deane; Hamlet: Little Hulton; Middle Hulton; Over Hulton; Rumworth

RG 9/3035 Census Returns, 1861. Lancashire, Registration district: 476, Rochdale. Registration sub-district: 3, Castleton Without. Parish: Rochdale (part); Hamlet: Castleton with Buersill; Lowerplace Newbold; Marland; Lower-lane; Broadlane; Back-lanes; Roeacre; Captain-fold; Castleton-moor and Bluepits

RG 10/3921 Census Returns, 1871. Lancashire, Registration District: 462, Bolton. Registration sub-district: 2B, Hulton. Civil parish, township or place: Middle Hulton; Over Hulton; Rumworth

RG 10/4116 Census Returns, 1871. Lancashire, Registration district: 470, Rochdale. Registration sub-district: 3C, Castleton Further. Civil parish, township or place: Castleton

RG 11/3819 Census Returns, 1881. Lancashire, Registration district: 461, Bolton. Registration sub-district: 2B, Hulton. Civil parish, township or place: Little Hulton; Middle Hulton; Over Hulton

RG 11/4103 Census Returns, 1881. Lancashire, Registration district: 470, Rochdale. Registration sub-district: 3C, Castleton Further. Civil parish, township or place: Castleton

RG 12/3099 Census Returns, 1891. Lancashire, Registration district: 461, Bolton. Registration sub-district: 2B, Hulton. Civil parish, township or place: Little Hulton; Middle Hulton; Edge Fold; Over Hulton; Rumworth (part); Dean

RG 12/3329 Census Returns, 1891. Lancashire, Registration district: 470, Rochdale. Registration sub-district: 3C, Castleton Further. Civil parish, township or place: Castleton

RG 13/3605 Census Returns, 1901. Lancashire, Registration district: Bolton. Registration sub-district: Hulton. Civil Parish, township or place: Little Hulton (part)

RG 13/3833 Census Returns, 1901. Lancashire, Registration district: Rochdale. Registration sub-district: Castleton Further. Civil parish, township or place: Burnedge; Milnrow (part); Rochdale (CB) (part)

RG 14/23278 Census Returns, 1911. Lancashire,

Registration district: Bolton. Registration sub-district: Farnworth. Civil parish, township or place: Little Hulton (part)

National Museums Liverpool: Maritime Archives and Library (NML)
D/EARLE 9/7 Marriage settlement of Thomas Earle and Mary Mort, 1754

D/EARLE 10/5 Will of Mrs Mary Earle, 1787

Northamptonshire Record Office (NRO)
E(B) 916 A survey, extract of the leases, and rental of His Grace the Duke of Bridgewater's Lancashire Estate, 1722

E(B) 980 & 981 Lease and counterpart lease by the Duke of Bridgewater to Edward Alread, 1722

E(B) 1199 Lease by the Duke to Bridgewater to Sarah Edge, 1758

E(B) 1218 Lease by the Duke to Bridgewater to John Mort, 1758

Rochdale Local Studies Library (RLSL)
LA/Z/1/C/1-4 Poor rate books for Castleton, 1750-1800

LA/Z/3/C Castleton Township survey of 1844

LA/Z/3/C/1 Castleton household survey of 1831

LA/Z/3/C/2 Schedule for the Castleton Township survey of 1844

Salford City Archives (SCA)
BW/E/1 Old estate plans - Bridgewater

BW/M 2/5/1/5 Bridgewater estate rentals, 1757-62

BW/M 2/5/1/10 Bridgewater estate rental, 1796-1802

BW/T 6/22 Deeds relating to property at Little Hulton, 1754-1840

BW/T 7/1 Wharton Hall deeds, 1582-1639

BW/T 7/14 Conveyance of Wharton Hall estate to Bridgewater trustees, 1881

BW/T 7/19 Sale of Bagot estate to Bridgewater trustees, 1895-6

P 6/2/8-9 Little Hulton poor rate books, 1899-1900

Trade directories
Baines, E, 1825 *History, directory and gazetteer of the County Palatine of Lancaster*, London

Clegg, J, 1907 *Commercial directory of Rochdale*, Rochdale

Clegg, J, 1916 *Commercial directory of Rochdale*, Rochdale

Duncan, J G, 1889 *Rochdale and district commercial directory for 1888-9*, Rochdale

Duncan, J G, 1900 *Rochdale and district commercial and postal directory for 1899-1900*, Rochdale

Tillotson and Son, 1922 *PO Bolton directory*, Bolton

Tillotsons Newspapers Ltd, 1932 *Tillotsons' Bolton directory*, Bolton

Newspapers
Blackburn Standard, 8 October 1851

Lancaster Gazette, 4 October 1851

London Gazette, 11 February 1834

Manchester Courier, 3 November 1838

Manchester Courier, 27 June 1840

Manchester Courier and Lancashire General Advertiser, 22 November 1834

Manchester Mercury, 13 May 1823

Morning Chronicle, 5 May 1815

The Leeds Intelligencer, 17 April 1764

The Leeds Intelligencer, 21 January 1793

The Leeds Times, 13 August 1859

Secondary Sources

Adams, M H, in prep An Early-Middle Bronze Age settlement site at St Chad's Vicarage, Kirkby, Merseyside, *J Merseyside Archaeol Soc*

Allen, C, 2007a The other Early Bronze Age and Middle Bronze Age pottery, in F Brown, C Howard-Davis, M Brennand, A Boyle, T Evans, S O'Connor, A Spence, R Heawood, and A Lupton, *The archaeology of the A1 (M) Darrington to Dishforth DBFO road scheme*, Lancaster Imprints, **12**, Lancaster, 219-22

Allen, C, 2007b The Early Bronze Age pottery, in Garner 2007, 53-75

Allen, C, 2007c The later prehistoric pottery, in Garner 2007, 108

Allen, C, Harman, M, and Wheeler, H, 1987 Bronze Age cremation cemeteries in the East Midlands, *Proc Prehist Soc*, **53**, 187-221

Allen, R C, 1992 *Enclosure and the yeoman*, Oxford

Amery, A, and Davey, P J, 1979 Post-medieval pottery from Brookhill, Buckley, Clywd (Site 1), *Medieval and later pottery in Wales*, **2**, Bull Welsh Medieval Pottery Res Grp, Clwyd, 49-85

Andersen, S Th, 1979 Identification of wild grass and cereal pollen, *Danmarks Geologiske Undersogelse*, 1978, 69-92

Archaeological Surveys, 2005 *Cutacre Surface Mining and Reclamation Facility, Greater Manchester: magnetometer survey*, Unpubl rep

Archaeological Surveys, 2006 *Cutacre Surface Mining and Reclamation Facility, Greater Manchester*, Unpubl rep

Arrowsmith, P, 1997 *Stockport: a history*, Stockport

Arrowsmith, P, 1998 *Astley Hospital, Wigan: an archaeological assessment*, Unpubl rep

Arrowsmith, P, 2013 *Logistics North, Bolton and Salford, Greater Manchester: an archaeological desk-based assessment*, Unpubl rep

Arrowsmith, P, and Wilson, P, 1998 *Kingsway Business Park development, Rochdale: an archaeological assessment*, Unpubl rep

Ashmore, P J, 1999 Radiocarbon dating: avoiding errors by avoiding mixed samples, *Antiquity*, **73**, 124-30

Atkinson, G, 1998 *The Canal Duke's collieries: Worsley 1760-1900*, Manchester

Atkinson, M D, 1992 *Betula pendula* Roth and *B pubescens* Ehrh, *J Ecol*, **80**, 837-70

Baines, E, 1836 *History of the County Palatine and Duchy of Lancaster*, **3**, London

Barker, D, 1986 North Staffordshire post-medieval ceramics - a type series, Part One: Cistercian ware, *Staffordshire Archaeol Studies Mus Archaeol Soc Rep*, **3**, 58-75

Barker, D, 1993 *Slipware*, Princes Risborough

Barnes, B, 1982 *Man and the changing landscape: a study of occupation and palaeo-environment in the central Pennines*, Liverpool

Bayley, J, Crossley, D, and Ponting, M (eds), 2008 *Metals and metalworking: a research framework for archaeometallurgy*, Hist Metall Soc Occ Pap, **6**, London

Bayliss, A, 2007 Bayesian buildings: an introduction for the numerically challenged, *Vernacular Architect*, **38**, 75-86

Bayliss, A, Bronk Ramsey, C, van der Plicht, J, and Whittle, A, 2007 Bradshaw and Bayes: towards a timetable for the Neolithic, *Cambridge Archaeol J*, 17, 1-28

Behre, K E, 1981 The interpretation of anthropogenic indicators in pollen diagrams, *Pollen et Spores*, **23**, 225-45

Bell, S, 2007 *Chorlton Fold, Monton, Eccles, archaeological excavation*, Unpubl rep

Benson, A P, 1983 *Textile machines*, Princes Risborough

Berglund, B E, and Ralska-Jasiewiczowa, M, 1986 Pollen analysis and pollen diagrams, in B E Berglund (ed), *Handbook of Holocene palaeoecology and palaeohydrology*, Chichester, 455-84

Birley, A R (ed), 2009 *Tacitus: Agricola and Germany*, Oxford

Bishop, B J, 2008 A microlithic industry from Woodbridge Road, Guildford, Surrey, *Archaeol Collect*, **94**, 125-57

Blackford, J J, Innes, J B, Hatton, J J, and Caseldine, C J, 2006 Mid-Holocene environmental change at Black Ridge Brook, Dartmoor, SW England: a new appraisal based on fungal spore analysis, *Rev Palaeobot Palynol*, **141**, 189-201

Blackwood, B G, 1978 *The Lancashire gentry and the Great Rebellion, 1640-60*, Manchester

Bolton and District Family History Society, 1983 *St Mary's Deane Parish Church*, Bolton

Bowden, M (ed), 2000 *Furness iron: the physical remains of the iron industry and related woodland industries of Furness and southern Lakeland*, London

Bradley, R, 2007 *The prehistory of Britain and Ireland*, Cambridge

Brears, P C D, 1971 *English country pottery: its history and techniques*, Newton Abbot

Bridgland, D, Innes, J, Long, A, and Mitchell, W, 2011 *Late Quaternary landscape evolution of the Swale-Ure Washlands, North Yorkshire*, Oxford

Brierley, H, 1909 *The registers of the parish church of Prestwich: baptisms, burials and weddings 1603-1668*, Lancashire Parish Reg Soc, **34**, Preston

Britnell, W J, Silvester, R J, Gibson, A, Caseldine, A E, Hunter, L, Johnson, S, Hamilton-Dyer, S, and Vince, A, 1997 A Middle Bronze Age round-house at Glanfeinion, near Llandinam, Powys, *Proc Prehist Soc*, **63**, 179-97

Bronk Ramsey, C, 1995 Radiocarbon calibration and analysis of stratigraphy: the OxCal program, *Radiocarbon*, **37**, 425-30

Bronk Ramsey, C, 1998 Probability and dating, *Radiocarbon*, **40**, 461-74

Bronk Ramsey, C, 2001 Development of the radiocarbon calibration program OxCal, *Radiocarbon*, **43**, 355-63

Bronk Ramsey, C, 2009 Bayesian analysis of radiocarbon dates, *Radiocarbon*, **51**, 337-60

Brown, F, Clark, P, Dickson, A, Gregory, R A, and Zant, J, in prep *From an ancient Eden to a new frontier: an archaeological journey along the Carlisle Northern Development Route*, Lancaster Imprints, Lancaster

Brück, J, 2001 Body metaphors and technologies of transformation in the English Middle and Late Bronze Age, in J Brück (ed), *Bronze Age landscapes: tradition and transformation*, Oxford, 149-60

Brunskill, R W, 1987 *Traditional farm buildings of Britain*, 2nd edn, London

Brunskill, R W, 1997 *Houses and cottages of Britain: origins and development of traditional buildings*, London

Bryant S, Morris, M, and Walker, J S F, 1986 *Roman Manchester: a frontier settlement*, Archaeol Greater Manchester, **3**, Manchester

Buck, C E, Cavanagh, W G, and Litton, C D, 1996 *Bayesian approach to interpreting archaeological data*, Chichester

Burke, T, and Nevell, M, 1996 *Buildings of Tameside*, Tameside

Cappers, R T J, Bekker, R M, and Jans, J E A, 2006 *Digitalezadenatlas van Nederland, digital seed atlas of the Netherlands*, Groningen

Challis, K, 2002 A medieval iron smelting site at Stanley Grange, Derbyshire, *Hist Metall*, **36**(1), 33-42

Chartered Institute for Archaeologists (CIfA), 2014 *Standard and guidance for the creation, compilation, transfer and deposition of archaeological archives*, Reading

Collens, J, 1999 Flying on the edge: aerial photography and settlement patterns in Cheshire and Merseyside, in M Nevell (ed), *Living on the edge of empire: models, methodology and marginality*, Archaeol North West, **3**, Manchester, 36-41

Colley-March, H, 1883 The road over Blackstone Edge, *Trans Lancashire Cheshire Antiq Soc*, **1**, 73-86

Connelly, P, 2006 *Archaeological works, Gibfield Park, Atherton, Wigan, Greater Manchester: archaeological investigations in a medieval and post-medieval mining landscape*, Unpubl rep

Cotter, J, 2000 *Post-Roman pottery from excavations in Colchester, 1971-85*, Colchester Archaeol Rep, **7**, Colchester

Countryside Commission, 1998 *The character of England, 2: North West*, Cheltenham

Coward, B, 1983 *The Stanleys, Lord Stanley and Earls of Derby, 1385-1672*, Manchester

Cowell, R W, 2000 Ditton Brook, Ditton, in R W Cowell and R A Philpott, *Prehistoric, Romano-British and medieval settlement in lowland North West England*, Liverpool, 7-26

Cowell, R W, 2010 The Bronze Age, in Philpott and Adams 2010, 167-9

Crew, P, 2013 Twenty-five years of bloomery experiments: perspectives and prospects, in D Dungworth and R C P Doonan (eds), *Accidental and experimental archaeometallurgy*, London, 25-50

Crew, P, and Crew, S, 2001 Excavations at Llwyn Du, Coed y Brenin, Merioneth, 2001: woodland management and charcoal processing at a late 14th-century ironworks, *Archaeol Wales*, **41**, 83-7

Crewe, S, 1987 *Stained glass in England 1180-1540*, London

Crofton, H T, 1889 Lancashire and Cheshire coalmining records, *Trans Lancashire Cheshire Antiq Soc*, **7**, 26-73

Crofts, R G, Hough, E, Humpage, A J, and Reeves, H J, 2012 *Geology of the Manchester district: a brief explanation of the geological map. Sheet explanation of British Geological Survey, 1:50,000 Sheet 85 Rochdale (England and Wales)*, Keyworth

Crofts, R G, Hough, E, and Northmore, K J, 2010 *Geology of the Rochdale district: a brief explanation of the* geological map. Sheet explanation of British Geological Survey, 1:50,000 Sheet 76 Rochdale (England and Wales), Keyworth

Crossley, D W, 1981 Medieval iron smelting, in D W Crossley (ed), Medieval industry, CBA Res Rep, 40, London, 29-41

Cunliffe, B W, 2005 Iron Age communities in Britain, 4th edn, London

Curtis, C D, and Coleman, M L, 1986a Controls on the precipitation of early diagenetic calcite, dolomite and siderite concretions in complex depositional sequences, in D L Gautier (ed), Roles of organic matter in sediment diagenesis, Soc Econ Palaeontol Mineral Spec Publ, 38, Tulsa, 23-33

Curtis, C D, Coleman, M L, and Lover, L G, 1986b Pore water evolution during sediment burial from isotopic and mineral chemistry of calcite, dolomite and siderite concretions, Geochimica et Cosmochimica Acta, 50, 2321-34

Curtis, C D, Pearson, M J, and Somogyi, V A, 1975 Mineralogy, chemistry and origin of a concretionary siderite sheet (clay-ironstone band) in the Westphalian of Yorkshire, Mineral Mag, 40, 385-93

Curtis, C D, and Spears, D A, 1968 The formation of sedimentary iron minerals, Econ Geol, 63, 257-70

Davey, P J, 1985 Clay pipes from Norton Priory, in P J Davey (ed), The archaeology of the clay tobacco pipe IX, BAR Brit Ser, 146, Oxford, 157-236

Davey, P J, 1989 Pottery production in Prescot, J Merseyside Archaeol Soc, 5 (for 1982-3), 103-6

Davey, P J, and Forster, E, 1975 Bronze Age metalwork from Lancashire and Cheshire, Liverpool

Davey, P J, and Morgan, D E M, 1978 Some examples of coarse earthenware from Rainford, J Merseyside Archaeol Soc, 2, 75-80

Dickin, E, Steele, K, and Wright, D, 2010 Hulless barley for functional food, HGCA Project Rep, 472, Kenilworth

Dineley, M, and Dineley, G, 2000 Neolithic ale: barley as a source of malt sugars for fermentation, in S Fairbairn (ed), Plants in Neolithic Britain and beyond, Oxford, 137-53

Draper, J, 1984 Post-medieval pottery, 1650–1800, Princes Risborough

Dungworth, D, 2015 Archaeometallurgy: guidelines for best practice, London

Earle, T A, 1890 Earle of Allerton Tower, Trans Hist Soc Lancashire Cheshire, n ser, 6, 15-76

Eastwood, D, 2004 The Booths: builders of Dunham Massey, Leek

Edlin, H L, 1949 Woodland crafts in Britain, London

Ekwall, E, 1922 The place-names of Lancashire, Manchester

English Heritage, 1991 Management of archaeological projects, 2nd edn, London

English Heritage, 1995 Geophysical survey in archaeological field evaluation, Swindon

English Heritage, 2006 Understanding historic buildings: a guide to good recording practice, London

Evans, C, Pollard, J, and Knight, M, 1999 Life in the woods: tree-throws, 'settlement' and forest cognition, Oxford J Archaeol, 18(3), 241-54

Faegri, K, Kaland, P E, and Krzywinski, K, 1989 Textbook of pollen analysis, Chichester

Farrer, W, and Brownbill, J, 1907 Victoria history of the county of Lancaster, 3, London

Farrer, W, and Brownbill, J, 1911a Victoria history of the county of Lancaster, 5, London

Farrer, W, and Brownbill, J, 1911b Victoria history of the county of Lancaster, 4, London

Fishwick, H, 1889 The history of the parish of Rochdale, Rochdale

Fishwick, H, 1913 The survey of the manor of Rochdale, 1626, Chetham Soc, n ser, 71, Manchester

Fletcher, J S, 1880 The correspondence of Nathan Walworth and Peter Seddon of Outwood, Chetham Soc, 109, Manchester

Fletcher, M, and Arrowsmith, P, 1995 The south chapel vault, Eccles Parish Church, Salford, Unpubl rep

Gaillard, M J, 2007 Pollen methods and studies: archaeological applications, in S Elias (ed), Encyclopaedia of Quaternary science, Amsterdam, 2570-95

Garner, D J, 2007 The Neolithic and Bronze Age settlement at Oversley Farm, Styal, Cheshire, Gifford Archaeol Monog, 1, Oxford

Gelling, M, and Cole, A, 2003 *The landscape of place-names*, Donington

Gent, H, 1983 Centralized storage in later prehistoric Britain, *Proc Prehist Soc*, **49**, 243-67

Gibson, A, and Woods, A, 1990 *Prehistoric pottery for the archaeologist*, Leicester

Giles, C, 2004 The Yorkshire textile loomshop: from weaver's cottage to the factory, in P S Barnwell, M Palmer, and M Airs (eds), *The vernacular workshop: from craft to industry, 1400-1900*, CBA Res Rep, **140**, York, 75-89

Giles, C, and Goodall, I H, 1992 *Yorkshire textile mills*, London

Godwin, H, 1994 *History of the British flora*, Cambridge

Gowlett, J A J, and Hedges, R E M (eds), 1986 *Archaeological results from accelerator dating*, Oxford

Greater Manchester Archaeological Unit (GMAU), 1991 *Cutacre reclamation and open cast coal project: an archaeological assessment*, Unpubl rep

Gregory, R A, 2007 *Roman Manchester: the University of Manchester's excavations within the vicus 2001-5*, Oxford

Gregory, R A, 2014 *Windermere reflections. Reflections on history: exploring the industrial archaeology of the Windermere area*, Lancaster

Gregory, R A, 2015 Excavation at Millfield Lane, Merseyside, *Merseyside Archaeol J*, **15**, 95-116

Gregory, R A, in prep The Chalcolithic and Bronze Age landscape: burnt mounds and settlement, in Brown *et al* in prep

Gregory, R A, and Adams, M, 2019 Excavation at two cropmark enclosures at Puddington Lane, Burton, Wirral, 2010–2015, *J Chester Archaeol Soc*, n ser, **89**, 1-69

Gregory, R A, and Miller, I, 2013 *Uncovering the estate: the archaeology of Dunham Massey*, Greater Manchester's Past Revealed, **10**, Lancaster

Gregory, R A, and Miller, I, 2015 *Greengate: the archaeology of Salford's historic core*, Greater Manchester's Past Revealed, **13**, Lancaster

Gregory, R A, Raynor, C, Adams, M, Philpott, R, Howard-Davis, C, Johnson, N, Hughes, V, and Higgins, D A, 2014 *Archaeology at the waterfront 1: investigating Liverpool's historic docks*, Lancaster Imprints, **23**, Lancaster

Grenville, J, 1997 *Medieval housing*, London and Washington

Grimm, E C, 1991-2011 *Tilia, TiliaGraph and TG-View*, Illinois

Hall, A R, and Huntley, J P, 2007 *A review of the evidence for macrofossil plant remains from archaeological deposits in Northern England*, Engl Heritage Res Rep Ser, **87**, London

Hall, D, Wells, C E, and Huckerby, E, 1995 *The wetlands of Greater Manchester*, Lancaster Imprints, **3**, Lancaster

Hartley, B R, and Fitts, R L, 1988 *The Brigantes*, Gloucester

Hartwell, C, Hyde, M, and Pevsner, N, 2004 *Lancashire: Manchester and the South-East*, Pevsner Architectural Guides: Buildings of England, New Haven and London

Haselgrove, C, Armit, I, Champion, T, Creighton, J, Gwilt, A, Hill, J D, Hunter, F, and Woodward, A, 2001 *Understanding the British Iron Age: an agenda for action*, Salisbury

Hastie, M, 2010 Charred plant remains, in R White and P Richardson, *The excavation of Bronze Age roundhouses at Oldmeldrum, Aberdeenshire*, Scot Archaeol Internet Rep, **43**, 19-21 [Online] Available at: http://archaeologydataservice.ac.uk/archives/view/sair/contents.cfm?vol=43 (accessed 20 June 2015)

Hather, J G, 2000 *The identification of the northern European woods: a guide for archaeologists and conservators*, London

Hayes, G, 2004 *Collieries and their railways in the Manchester coalfields*, Ashbourne

Haynes, H, and Tipper, D A, 1994 *De Balderston II*, Rochdale

Higham, N J, and Crane, T, 1999 The Tatton Park Project, part 1: prehistoric to sub-Roman settlement and land use, *J Chester Archaeol Soc*, **74** (for 1996-7), 1-62

Hildyard, R, 2005 *English pottery 1620-1840*, London

Hillman, G, 1981 Reconstructing crop husbandry practices from charred remains of crops, in R Mercer (ed), *Farming practice in British prehistory*, Edinburgh, 123-62

Hodgson, J, and Brennand, M, 2006 The prehistoric period resource assessment, in M Brennand (ed), *The archaeology of North West England: an archaeological research framework for North West England: volume 1, resource assessment,* Archaeol North West, **8,** Manchester, 23-58

Hodgson, J, and Brennand, M, 2007 The prehistoric period research agenda, in M Brennand (ed), *Research and archaeology in North West England: an archaeological research framework for North West England: volume 2, research agenda and strategy,* Archaeol North West, **9,** Manchester, 31-54

Hoskins, W G, 1953 The rebuilding of rural England, 1570-1640, *Past Present,* **4**(1), 44-59

Howard, R E, Laxton, R R, and Litton, C D, 2001 *Tree-ring analysis of timbers from Astley Hospital, Church Road, Astley, Manchester,* Centre Archaeol Rep, **66/2001,** Swindon

Howard-Davis, C L E, 2004 Pottery, in R Heawood and C L E Howard-Davis, *Old Abbey Farm Risley: building survey and excavation at a medieval moated site,* Lancaster Imprints, **11,** Lancaster, 109-21

Howells, M F, 2007 *Wales: British regional geology,* London

Hradil, I, Grimsditch, B, and Nevell, M, 2007 *Castle Farm, Kingsway, Rochdale: an archaeological building survey report for the Kingsway redevelopment,* Unpubl rep

Hradil, I, and Nevell, M, 2004 *Near Moor Bank Farm, Rochdale: an archaeological building survey report for the Kingsway redevelopment, part 1,* Unpubl rep

Hradil, I, and Nevell, M, 2005 *Wychenley Cottage: an archaeological building survey report for the Kingsway redevelopment, part 3,* Unpubl rep

Hradil, I, and Nevell, M, 2007 *Castle House, Kingsway, Rochdale: an archaeological building survey of an 18th and 19th century farm complex,* Unpubl rep

Huntley, J P, 2010a *Northern England: a review of wood and charcoal recovered from archaeological excavations in northern England,* Engl Heritage Res Dep Rep Ser, **68-2010,** Portsmouth

Huntley, J P, 2010b Charred plant remains, in Philpott and Adams 2010, 78-92

Huntley, J P, and Stallibrass, S, 1995 *Plant and vertebrate remains from archaeological sites in northern England: data reviews and future directions,* Architect Archaeol Soc Durham Northumberland Res Rep, **4,** Durham

Hurst, J D, and Wright, S M, 2011 Midlands purple and Cistercian wares in the West Midlands in the 15th-16th centuries, *Medieval Ceram,* **32,** 55-66

Hurst Vose, R, 1980 *Glass,* London

Innes, J B, and Blackford, J J, 2003 The ecology of Late Mesolithic woodland disturbances: model testing with fungal spore assemblage data, *J Archaeol Sci,* **30,** 185-94

Innes, J, Blackford, J, and Chambers, F, 2006 *Kretzschmaria deusta* and the Northwest European Mid-Holocene *Ulmus* decline at Moel Y Gerddi, North Wales, United Kingdom, *Palynol,* **30,** 121-32

Innes, J B, Blackford, J J, and Simmons, I G, 2004 Testing the integrity of fine spatial resolution palaeoecological records: microcharcoal data from near-duplicate peat profiles from the North York Moors, UK, *Palaeogeog Palaeoecol,* **214,** 295-307

Innes, J B, Blackford, J J, and Simmons, I G, 2011 Mesolithic environments at Star Carr, the eastern vale of Pickering and environs: local and regional contexts, *J Wetland Archaeol,* **11,** 85-108

Jacomet, S, 2006 *Identification of cereal remains from archaeological sites,* 2nd edn, Basel

Johnson, M, 1993 *Housing culture: traditional architecture in an English landscape,* London

Joly, C, Barille, L, Barreau, M, Mancheron, A, and Visset, L, 2007 Grain and annulus diameter as criteria for distinguishing pollen grains of cereals from wild grasses, *Rev Palaeobot Palynol,* **146,** 221-33

Kenyon, D, 1991 *The origins of Lancashire,* Manchester

King, C, and Nevell, M, 2005a *Mayfields Farm and cottage: an archaeological building survey report for the Kingsway redevelopment, part 2,* Unpubl rep

King, C, and Nevell, M, 2005b *Lower Moss Side Farm: an archaeological building survey report for the Kingsway redevelopment, part 4,* Unpubl rep

King, C, and Nevell, M, 2005c *Moss Side Farm: an archaeological building survey report for the Kingsway redevelopment, part 5,* Unpubl rep

King, C, and Nevell, M, 2006 *Lower Lane Farm, Rochdale: an archaeological building survey report for the Kingsway redevelopment, part 6,* Unpubl rep

Knight, S, and Pagani, L, 1990 *Cosmography: maps from Ptolemy's Geography,* Leicester

Lewis, J M, Heawood, R, and Howard-Davis, C, 2011 *Bewsey Old Hall, Warrington, Cheshire: excavations 1977-81 and 1983-5,* Lancaster Imprints, **17,** Lancaster

267

Lindley, D V, 1985 *Making decisions*, 2ⁿᵈ edn, London

Lunn, J, 1953 *A short history of the township of Tyldesley*, Tyldesley

Lunn, J, 1968 *A short history of the township of Astley*, Privately publ

Lunn, J, 1971 *History of Atherton*, Atherton

McCarthy, M R, and Brooks, C M, 1988 *Medieval pottery in Britain AD 900-1600*, Leicester

Malet, H, 1977 *Bridgewater: the Canal Duke 1736-1803*, Manchester

Mann, M E, 2002 Medieval climatic optimum, in M C MacCracken and J S Perry (eds), *Encyclopedia of global environmental change. Volume 1, the earth system: physical and chemical dimensions of global environmental change*, Chichester, 514-16

Margary, I D, 1967 *Roman roads in Britain*, 3ʳᵈ edn, London

Marshall, J, 1969 *The Lancashire and Yorkshire Railway*, **1**, Newton Abbot

Martin, A, and Allen, C, 2001 Two prehistoric ring ditches and an associated Bronze Age cremation cemetery at Tucklesholme Farm, Barton-under-Needwood, Staffordshire, *Trans Staffordshire Archaeol Hist Soc*, **39**, 1-15

Mathias, P, 1967 *The first industrial nation*, London

Mellor, M, 1994 *Medieval ceramic studies in England: a review for English Heritage*, London

Merrifield, R, 1987 *The archaeology of ritual and magic*, London

Miller, G, 2002 *Historic houses in Lancashire: the Douglas Valley 1300-1770*, Nelson

Miller, I, and Gregory, R A, 2010 *The Rock Triangle, Bury: the archaeology of an industrial suburb*, Greater Manchester's Past Revealed, **2**, Lancaster

Miller, I, and Plummer, A, 2016 *Gin Pit: the archaeology of an historic coal-mining settlement*, Greater Manchester's Past Revealed, **15**, Lancaster

Miller, I, and White, A J, forthcoming The post-Roman pottery, in I Miller, C L E Howard-Davis, N J Hair, and R M Newman, *Excavations at 39, Church Street and Mitchell's Brewery, Lancaster 1988-2000*

Mills, D, 1976 *The place-names of Lancashire*, London

Mook, W G, 1986 Business meeting: recommendations/resolutions adopted by the twelfth International Radiocarbon Conference, *Radiocarbon*, **28**, 799

Moore, J, 2001 Can't see the wood for the trees: interpreting woodland fire history from microscopic charcoal, in U Albarella (ed), *Environmental archaeology: meaning and purpose*, Dordrecht, Boston, and London, 211-27

Moore, P D, Webb, J A, and Collinson, M E, 1991 *Pollen analysis*, 2ⁿᵈ edn, Oxford

Moorhouse, S, and Roberts, I, 1992 *Wrenthorpe potteries*, Yorkshire Archaeol, **2**, Wakefield

Morgan, P (ed), 1978 *Cheshire*, in J Morris (ed), Domesday Book, **26**, Chichester

Mullineux, C E, 1964 *Mast and pannage: a history of Swinton to 1765*, Pendlebury

Museum of London, 2007 *Online catalogue of post-medieval ceramics* [Online] Available at: http://www.museumoflondon.org.uk/ceramics/pages/object (accessed 20 October 2019)

Needham, S, 1996 Chronology and periodisation in the British Bronze Age, *Acta Archaeologica*, **67**, 121-40

Needham, S, 2017 Assemblage, structure and meaning in bronze metalwork studies: an analysis of the British Penard assemblage, *Oxford J Archaeol*, **32**(2), 111-56

Needham, S, Bronk Ramsey, C, Coombs, D, Cartwright, C, and Pettitt, P, 1997 An independent chronology for British Bronze Age metalwork: the results of the Oxford radiocarbon accelerator programme, *Archaeol J*, **154**, 55-107

Nevell, M, 1992 *Settlement and society in the Mersey Basin, c 2000 BC to AD 400*, Unpubl PhD thesis, Univ Manchester

Nevell, M, 1997 *The archaeology of Trafford: a study of the origins of community on north-west England before 1900*, Trafford

Nevell, M, 2008 The archaeology of industrialisation and the textile industry: the example of Manchester and the south-western Pennine uplands during the 18th century (Part 1), *Ind Archaeol Rev*, **30**(1), 33-48

Nevell, M, Burke, T, and Hradil, I, 2000 *Dam House, Astley, Wigan: an archaeological building survey of an early brick gentry house*, Unpubl rep

Nevell, N, Carney, M, Cracknell, J, Haworth, J, Hill, C, and Jubb, D, 2015 *Warburton. Glimpses of rural life: the archaeology and history of a Cheshire village*, Univ Salford Archaeol Monog, **4**, Salford

Nevell, M, and Walker, J, 1998 *A history and archaeology of Tameside, 6. Lands and lordship in Tameside: Tameside in transition 1348-1642*, Tameside

Nevell, M, and Walker, J, 2002 *Denton and Dukinfield Halls and the archaeology of the gentry and yeoman house in north-west England 1500 to 1700*, Tameside

Newman, C, 2006 The medieval period resource assessment, in M Brennand (ed), *The archaeology of North West England: an archaeological research framework for North West England, Volume 1: resource assessment*, Archaeol North West, **8**, Manchester, 115-44

Newman, C, and Newman, R, 2007 The medieval period research agenda, in M Brennand (ed), *Research and archaeology in North West England: an archaeological research framework for North West England: volume 2, research agenda and strategy*, Archaeol North West, **9**, Manchester, 95-114

Newman, R, and, McNeil, R, 2007a The post-medieval period research agenda, in M Brennand (ed), *Research and archaeology in North West England: an archaeological research framework for North West England: volume 2, research agenda and strategy*, Archaeol North West, **9**, Manchester, 115-32

Newman, R, and, McNeil, R, 2007b The industrial and modern period research agenda, in M Brennand (ed), *Research and archaeology in North West England: an archaeological research framework for North West England: volume 2, research agenda and strategy*, Archaeol North West, **9**, Manchester, 133-58

Newman, RM, 2006 The early medieval period resource assessment, in M Brennand (ed), *The archaeology of North West England: an archaeological research framework for North West England: volume 1, resource assessment*, Archaeol North West, **8**, Manchester, 91-114

Newman, R M, and Brennand, M, 2007 The early medieval period research agenda, in M Brennand (ed), *Research and archaeology in North West England: an archaeological research framework for North West England: volume 2, research agenda and strategy*, Archaeol North West, **9**, Manchester, 73-94

Nicholls, H G, 1866 *Iron making in the olden times: as instanced in the ancient mines, forges, and furnaces of the Forest of Dean*, 1981 facsimile reprod, Coleford

Nightingale, Rev B, 1892 *Lancashire nonconformity: the churches of Wigan, Warrington, St Helens, &c*, Manchester

Noel Hume, I, 2001 *If these pots could talk*, New England

North West Archaeological Surveys, 1992 *Castle Steads, Bury: archaeological evaluation report*, Unpubl rep

Oswald, A, 1975 *Clay pipes for archaeologists*, BAR Brit Ser, **14**, Oxford

Oswald, A, 1997 A doorway on the past: practical and mystic concerns in the orientation of roundhouse doorways, in A Gwilt and C Haselgrove (eds), *Reconstructing Iron Age societies: new approaches to the British Iron Age*, Oxford, 87-95

Oxford Archaeology North (OA North), 2005 *Kingsway Business Park, Rochdale, Greater Manchester: archaeological investigations interim report*, Unpubl rep

Oxford Archaeology North (OA North), 2006a *Surface mining and reclamation facility, Cutacre, Wigan, Greater Manchester*, Unpubl rep

Oxford Archaeology North (OA North), 2006b *Kingsway Business Park, Rochdale, Greater Manchester: archaeological survey and excavation*, Unpubl rep

Oxford Archaeology North (OA North), 2008a *Surface mining and reclamation facility, Cutacre, Wigan, Greater Manchester: post-excavation assessment*, Unpubl rep

Oxford Archaeology North (OA North), 2008b *Rock Triangle, Bury, Greater Manchester: post-excavation assessment report*, Unpubl rep

Oxford Archaeology North (OA North), 2008c *The Grand Arcade, Millgate, Wigan: final excavation report*, Unpubl rep

Oxford Archaeology North (OA North), 2010 *Surface mining and reclamation facility, Cutacre, Salford, Greater Manchester: post-excavation assessment*, Unpubl rep

Oxford Archaeology North (OA North), 2011 *Chorlton Fold, Monton, Eccles, Greater Manchester: final excavation report*, Unpubl rep

Oxford Archaeology North (OA North), 2012 *Lower Lane, Kingsway, Rochdale, Greater Manchester: archaeological evaluation*, Unpubl rep

Oxford Archaeology North (OA North), 2014a *Logistics North Employment Site, Cutacre, Little Hulton, Bolton: archaeological evaluation*, Unpubl rep

Oxford Archaeology North (OA North), 2014b *Hulton Heys, Cutacre, Little Hulton, Greater Manchester: archaeological evaluation*, Unpubl rep

Oxford Archaeology North (OA North), 2016 *Spout Fold and Mills Brow Farms, Cutacre, Greater Manchester: building recording*, Unpubl rep

Paget-Tomlinson, E W, 1993 *The illustrated history of canal and river navigations*, Sheffield

Parker, A G, Goudie, A S, Anderson, D E, Robinson, M A, and Bonsall, C, 2002 A review of the mid-Holocene elm decline in the British Isles, *Progr Phys Geog*, **26**(1), 1-45

Parker Pearson, M, 1999 Food, sex and death: cosmologies in the British Iron Age with particular reference to East Yorkshire, *Cambridge Archaeol J*, **91**(1), 43-69

Parnell, H, 1835 *Fifteenth report of the Commissioners of Inquiry into the excise establishment and into the management and collection of the excise revenue throughout the United Kingdom: malt*, London

Partington, J H, 1909a *A short history of Middle Hulton and some of its inhabitants*, Unpubl doc, Chetham's Library, Manchester

Partington, J H, 1909b *Little Hulton, manor of Worsley*, Unpubl doc, Chetham's Library, Manchester

Partington, J H, *c* 1910, *Manor of Barton, Westhoughton and Hulton*, Unpubl doc, Chetham's Library, Manchester

Paynter, S, 2011 *Introduction to Heritage Assets: pre-industrial ironworks*, London

Pearson, B, Price, J, Tanner, V, and Walker, J, 1985 The Rochdale Borough survey, *Greater Manchester Archaeol J*, **1**, 103-31

Pearson, S, 1985 *Rural houses of the Lancashire Pennines 1560 to 1760*, RCHME Suppl Ser, **10**, London

Peglar, S M, 1993 The mid-Holocene *Ulmus* decline at Diss Mere, Norfolk, UK: a year-by-year pollen stratigraphy from annual laminations, *Holocene*, **3**(1), 1-13

Phelps, A, Gregory, R, Miller, I, and Wild, C, 2017 *The textile mills of Lancashire: the legacy*, Lancaster

Phillips, C B, and Smith, J H, 1994 *Lancashire and Cheshire from AD 1540*, London

Philpott, R A, 2006 The Romano-British period resource assessment, in M Brennand (ed), *The archaeology of North West England: an archaeological research framework for North West England: volume 1, resource assessment*, Archaeol North West, **8**, Manchester, 59-90

Philpott, R A, and Adams, M H, 2010 *Irby, Wirral: excavations on a late prehistoric, Romano-British and medieval site, 1987-96*, Liverpool

Piccope, Rev G J (ed), 1861 *Lancashire wills and inventories: the third portion*, Chetham Soc, **54**, Manchester

Platt, S S, 1900 Stone axe hammer found at Low House Farm, near Milnrow, *Trans Rochdale Lit Sci Soc* (for 1899-1900), **7**, 95-7

Pollard, J, 2000 Ancestral places in the Mesolithic landscape, *Archaeol Rev Cambridge*, **17**, 123-88

Pollard, R, and Pevsner, N, 2006 *The buildings of England, Lancashire: Liverpool and the South-West*, Yale

Pope, R, 2007 Ritual and the roundhouse: a critique of recent ideas on the use of domestic space in later British prehistory, in C Haselgrove and R Pope (eds), *The earlier Iron Age in Britain and the near Continent*, Oxford, 204-28

Pope, R, 2015 Bronze Age architectural traditions: dates and landscapes, in F Hunter and I B M Ralston (eds), *Scotland in later prehistoric Europe*, Edinburgh, 159-84

Pounds, N J G, 2000 *A history of the English parish: the culture of religion from Augustine to Victoria*, Cambridge

Rackham, O, 2003 *Ancient woodland: its history, vegetation and uses in England*, Kirkcudbright

Raines, F R, 1872 *The visitation of the County Palatine of Lancaster, made in the year 1664-5, by Sir William Dugdale, Knight, Part II*, Chetham Soc, **85**, Manchester

Redhead, N, 1992 *An iron furnace complex at Spa Clough, Castleshaw: interim report*, Unpubl rep

Redhead, N, 1993 *Spa Clough, Castleshaw: second interim excavation report*, Unpubl rep

Redhead, N, 1996 *Cudworth Pasture, Castleshaw: excavation report*, Unpubl rep

Redhead, N, 2003 The Castleshaw and Piethorne valleys: the industrial exploitation of a Pennine landscape, in M Nevell (ed), *From farmer to factory owner: models, methodology and industrialisation*, Archaeol North West, **6**, Manchester, 69-78

Redhead, N, 2004 A good summer for iron smelting archaeology in Greater Manchester!, *Hist Metall Soc News* (for 2003-4), **55**, 1

Reimer, P J, Bard, E, Bayliss, A, Beck, J W, Blackwell, P G, Bronk Ramsey, C, Buck, C E, Cheng, H, Edwards, R L, Friedrich, M, Grootes, P M, Guilderson, T P, Haflidason, H, Hajdas, I, Hatté, C, Heaton, T J, Hoffmann, D L, Hogg, A G, Hughen, K A, Kaiser, K F, Kromer, B, Manning, S W, Niu, M, Reimer, R W, Richards, D A, Scott, E M, Southon, J R, Staff, R A, Turney, C S M, and van der Plicht, J, 2013 IntCal13 and Marine13 radiocarbon age calibration curves, 0-50,000 years cal BP, *Radiocarbon*, **55**, 1869-87

Richmond, I A, 1925 The Roman road across Blackstone Edge, *Trans Rochdale Lit Sci Soc* (for 1923-5), **15**, 41-63

Rickard, J, 2006 *Mocha and related dipped wares, 1770-1939*, New York

Rives, J B (ed), 2009 *Agricola and Germania*, London

Robertson, W, 1881 *Rochdale past and present: a history and guide*, Rochdale

Rowe, P, 1998 *Flint report Nosterfield 1991, 1994-1996* [Online] Available at: http://www.archaeologicalplanningconsultancy.co.uk/mga/projects/noster/speciali/rowe98.html (Accessed 25 June 2017)

Royal Commission for the Historic Monuments of England (RCHME), 1996 *Recording historic buildings: a descriptive specification*, Swindon

RPS Planning, Transport and Environment (RPS), 2005 *Archaeological written scheme of investigation: surface mining and reclamation facility, Cutacre, Wigan, Greater Manchester*, Unpubl doc

RPS Planning, Transport and Environment (RPS), 2006 *Written scheme of investigation (WSI) for a programme of archaeological investigation (Stage 2) at the surface mining and reclamation facility, Cutacre, Salford, Greater Manchester*, Unpubl doc

Rylands, J P, 1887 *Lancashire inquisitions, Stuart period, Part II*, Lancashire Cheshire Rec Soc, **31**, Preston

Sabin, D, and Donaldson, K, 2005 *Cutacre Surface Mining and Reclamation Facility, Greater Manchester: a magnetometer survey for Oxford Archaeology North*, Unpubl rep

Sauder, L, and Williams, S, 2002 A practical treatise on the smelting and smithing of bloomery iron, *Hist Metall*, **36**, 122-31

Schairer, J F, and Yagi, K, 1952 The system $FeO-Al_2O_3-SiO_2$, *Amer J Sci*, **Bowen vol**, 471-512

Schweingruber, F H, 1990 *Microscopic wood anatomy*, 3rd edn, Birmensdorf

Simmons, I G, and Innes, J B, 1996 The ecology of an episode of prehistoric cereal cultivation on the North York Moors, England, *J Archaeol Sci*, **23**, 613-18

Smith, A G, and Cloutman, E W, 1988 Reconstruction of vegetation history in three dimensions at Waun–Fignen–Felen, an upland site in South Wales, *Phil Trans Royal Soc London B*, **322**, 159-219

Smith, J H, 1973 *The great human exploit: historic industries of the North West*, Chichester

Smith, K E S, 1995 Iron-working in north-west Wales in the late fourteenth century, *Archaeol J*, **152**, 246-90

Sparke, A (ed), 1916 *The registers of the parish church of Deane, volume I, part I*, Lancashire Parish Reg Soc, **53**, Preston

Sparke, A (ed), 1917 *The registers of the parish church of Deane, volume I, part II*, Lancashire Parish Reg Soc, **54**, Preston

Sparke, A (ed), 1940 *The registers of the parish church of Deane, part III*, Lancashire Parish Reg Soc, **79**, Preston

Spavold, J, and Brown, S, 2005 *Ticknall pots and potters from the late fifteenth century to 1888*, Ashbourne

Spencer, A, 1950 Preliminary report on archaeological investigations near Radcliffe, Manchester, *Trans Lancashire Cheshire Antiq Soc*, **62**, 196-203

Stace, C, 2010 *New flora of the British Isles*, 3rd edn, Cambridge

Stockmarr, J, 1971 Tablets with spores used in absolute pollen analysis, *Pollen et Spores*, **13**, 615-21

Stone, P, 2010 *Northern England: British regional geology*, 5th edn, London

Stuiver, M, and Kra, R S, 1986 Editorial comment, *Radiocarbon*, **28**(2B), ii

Stuiver, M, and Polach, H A, 1977 Reporting of ^{14}C data, *Radiocarbon*, **19**, 355-63

Stuiver, M, and Reimer, P J, 1986 A computer program for radiocarbon age calculation, *Radiocarbon*, **28**, 1022-30

Stuiver, M, and Reimer, P J, 1993 Extended ^{14}C data base and revised CALIB 3.0 14C age calibration program, *Radiocarbon*, **35**, 215-30

Tait, J, 1924 *Taxation in Salford Hundred 1524-1802*, Chetham Soc, n ser, **83**, Manchester

Talbot, O, 1974 The evolution of glass bottles for carbonated drinks, *Post-medieval Archaeol*, **8**, 29-62

Thomas, G R, and Young, T P, 1999a Bloomery furnace mass balance and efficiency, in A M Pollard (ed), *Geoarchaeology: exploration, environments, resources*, Geol Soc London, Spec Publ, **165**, London, 155-64

Thomas, G R, and Young, T P, 1999b A graphical method to determine furnace efficiency and lining contribution to Romano-British bloomery iron-making slags (Bristol Channel Orefield, UK), in S M M Young, P D Budd, R A Ixer, and A M Pollard (eds), *Metals in antiquity*, BAR Int Ser, **792**, Oxford, 223-6

Thomas, J S, 2013 *The birth of Neolithic Britain: an interpretative account*, Oxford

Timmins, J G, 1977 *Handloom weavers' cottages in Central Lancashire*, Centre North-West Reg Stud Univ Lancaster Occ Pap, **3**, Lancaster

Timmins, J G, 1993 *The last shift: the decline of handloom weaving in nineteenth-century Lancashire*, Manchester

Timmins, J G, 2004 Domestic weaving premises in Lancashire: a contextual analysis, in P S Barnwell, M Palmer, and M Airs (eds), *The vernacular workshop: from craft to industry, 1400-1900*, CBA Res Rep, **140**, York, 90-100

Tipping, R, 2002 Climatic variability and 'marginal' settlement in upland British landscapes: a re-evaluation, *Landscapes*, **3**(2), 10-28

Tweddle, J C, Edwards, K J, and Fieller, N R J, 2005 Multivariate statistical and other approaches for the separation of cereal from wild Poaceae pollen using a large Holocene dataset, *Veg Hist Archaeobot*, **14**, 15-30

Tyson, N, 1985 Excavations at Radcliffe Tower, 1979-80, *Greater Manchester Archaeol J*, **1**, 39-53

United Kingdom Institute for Conservation (UKIC), 1984 *Environmental standards for the permanent storage of excavated material from archaeological sites*, UKIC Conservation Guidelines, **3**, London

University of Manchester Archaeological Unit (UMAU), 1996 *Cutacre reclamation and open cast project: an archaeological assessment*, Unpubl rep

van der Veen, M, 1992 *Crop husbandry regimes: an archaeobotanical study of farming in northern England 1000 BC-AD 500*, Sheffield Archaeol Monog, **3**, Sheffield

van Geel, B, 1978 A palaeoecological study of Holocene peat bog sections in Germany and the Netherlands based on the analysis of pollen, spores and macro- and microscopic remains of fungi, algae, cormophytes and animals, *Rev Palaeobot Palynol*, **25**, 1-120

van Geel, B, and Aptroot, A, 2006 Fossil ascomycetes in Quaternary deposits, *Nova Hedwigia*, **82**(3-4), 313-29

Vaughan, J, 2008 The post-medieval and later pottery, in F Brown and C Howard-Davis, *Norton Priory: monastery to museum. Excavations 1970-87*, Lancaster Imprints, **16**, Lancaster, 344-58

Wadsworth, A P, and Mann, J, 1931 *The cotton trade and industrial Lancashire 1600-1780*, Manchester

Walker, J S F, and Tindall, A S, 1985 *The country houses of Greater Manchester*, Archaeol Greater Manchester, **2**, Manchester

Walker, K, 1990 *Guidelines for the preparation of excavation archives for long-term storage*, London

Walton, J K, 1987 *Lancashire: a social history 1558-1939*, Manchester

Ward, G K, and Wilson, S R, 1978 Procedures for comparing and combining radiocarbon age determinations: a critique, *Archaeometry*, **20**, 19-31

Watkin, W T, 1883 *Roman Lancashire*, Liverpool

Webster, J, 1995 Sanctuaries and sacred places, in M J Green (ed), *The Celtic world*, London and New York, 445-64

Whitaker, J, 1773 *The history of Manchester*, Manchester

Wild, M T, 1971 The Saddleworth parish registers, *Textile Hist*, **1**, 214-32

Williams, C T, 1985 *Mesolithic exploitation patterns in the Central Pennines: a palynological study of Soyland Moor*, BAR Brit Ser, **139**, Oxford

Williams, M, with Farnie, D A, 1992 *Cotton mills in Greater Manchester*, Preston

Wilson, P, and Nevell, M, 2004 *Kingsway, Rochdale: a revision of the 1998 archaeological desk-based assessment*, Unpubl rep

Wood, P N, Bradley, J, and Miller, I, 2008 A pottery production site at Samlesbury, near Preston, Lancashire, *Medieval Ceram*, **30**, 21-47

Woodward, A, 2010 Prehistoric pottery, in Philpott and Adams 2010, 117-20

Wrigley, A, 1912 *Songs of a moorland parish,* Saddleworth

Yaroshevich, A, 2012 Experimentally obtained examples of projectile damage: cases of similar fracture types on microlithic tips and side elements, *Bulgarian e-Journal Archaeol*, **2**(1), 1-13 [Online] Available at: http://be-ja.org/index-php/Be-JA/article/view/32 (accessed 20 October 2019)

Young, R, 1987 *Lithics and subsistence in North Eastern England,* BAR Brit Ser, **161**, Oxford

Young, T P, 1993 Sedimentary ironstones, in R A D Pattrick and D A Polya (eds), *Mineralization in Britain,* London, 446-89

Young, T P, 2007 *Evaluation of archaeometallurgical residues from Cinderhill* (sic), *Cutacre, Salford, Greater Manchester,* Unpubl rep

Young, T P, 2012 *Archaeometallurgical residues from the Brecon to Tirley gas pipeline,* Unpubl rep

Young, T P, 2014a *Report on archaeometallurgical residues from Torr Quarry, Leighton, Wanstrow, Somerset,* Unpubl rep

Young, T P, 2014b *Archaeometallurgical residues from Ynysfach Ironworks, Merthyr Tydfil,* Unpubl rep

Young, T P, 2014c *Archaeometallurgical residues from Dwr-y-Felin School, Neath (GGAT 677 & 716),* Unpubl rep

Young, T P, 2015 *Archaeometallurgical residues from Churchills Farm, Hemyock, Devon,* Unpubl rep

Young, T P, and Poyner, D, 2014 Two medieval bloomery sites in Shropshire: the adoption of water-power for iron smelting, *Hist Metall,* **46**, 78-97

INDEX

Abattoir 86, *see also* Castle House
Agricultural
  activity 31, 39, 43, 93
  buildings 153, 165, 168, 186, 238, 244-5, 247-8,
      254
  labourer 140, 147, 149-50, 168, 177, 186, 188,
      191, 197, 209, 248-9, *see also* Farmer;
      Husbandmen
Alcoves *see* Castle Farm; Lane End Farm; Mayfields;
      Moor Side Farm; Moss Side Farm
Alder House (formerly Alder Fold), Atherton 123,
    126
Aldred
  Edward 104, 232
  John 105, 247
Anglo-Saxon, settlement 53
Animal
  bone 156, 255
  pasturing 21
Archaeometallurgical residues 14, 48-51, 53
Architrave *see* Castle House; Lower Lane Farm
Arris *see* Castle Farm; Mayfields; Moor Bank Farm
Ashes 10, 94-102, 104, 205, 207-8, 234, 245-6, 248
  barn 97, 205-6, 209, 248
  brick wall 205
  ceiling (barrel-vaulted) 205
  cellar 97-9, 205, 207, 248
  cobbled surface 100, 102
  cupboard 99, 205
  culvert 99
  doorway 100, 205, 246
  drain 99
  expansion 100, 245-6, 248
  façade 246
  fireplace 98, 205, 207, 248
  foundation 10, 99, 205
  gable walls 245
  garage 209
  gully 100
  hearth 97-8, 208
  housebody 96-7, 100, 245
  kitchen 248
  lintel 99
  messuage 205
  parlour 97, 100, 245
  rebuilding/rebuilt 102, 205, 248
  tenancy 205
  tenements 95
  window 97-9, 205
Ashton, Ralph 121-2
Aspinall, Thomas 168, 186
Astley 37, 122-3, 140, 231, 237
Atherton 1, 21, 35, 104, 123, 126, 227

Axe
  bronze 17
  stone (Neolithic) 21

Bagot
  estate 9, 13, 93-5, 102, 104, 113, 205
    plan 102, 104, 113
    tenements 93, 95
  family 93, 102, 113
Bank House Colliery 6, 203, *see also* Coal mining
Barley 31-3, 39, 225, *see also* Cereals
  naked 32-3, 225
Barn 93, 233, 238, 244 *see also* Ashes; Cherry Tree Farm;
      Hulton Heys; Lane End Farm; Lower Lane Farm;
      Mayfields; Mills Brow; Moor Bank Lane Farm;
      Moss Side Farm, Higher; Moss Side Farm, Lower;
      Pyche; Shippon; Spout Fold; Wharton Hall
  Lancashire 110-12, 117, 119-21, 248, *see also* Mills
      Brow; Spout Fold
Barrow/barrow cemetery 17, 21
Beam *see* Castle Farm; Castle House; Cinder Hill;
      Lower Lane Farm; Mayfields; Mills Brow;
      Moor Bank Farm; Moss Side Farm; Moss Side
      Farm, Lower; Wharton Hall
Belfield Hall, near Rochdale 54-6
Bellows 37, 46, 52, 226, 228, *see also* Furnace
Bewsey Hall, near Warrington 124
Billet 49, 51, 53, 226, 228, *see also* Furnace
Blackrod 33
Blacksmith's forge 176, 182, 253
Bleach Croft field 94
Bleaching pit 68
Bloomery 13-14, 37, 44, 46, 49-53, 95, 226-7, 256, *see*
    also Furnace
Bolton 1, 37, 121, 123, 138, 140, 148
Booths
  Bank Farm 35
  family 35, 230-1
Boundary wall 101, 129, 135, 217, 238
Brackley Colliery 3, *see also* Coal mining
Brazier 238
Brewing 32
Brick
  handmade 67, 74, 76, 84, 87, 106, 142-3, 156, 159,
      162, 170-2, 174-5, 179-84, 187, 194, 198,
      201, 205, 217
  making 95
  wall *see* Ashes; Castle Farm; Cherry Tree Farm;
      English Garden Wall; Haigh Field; Lane End
      Farm; Mayfields; Mills Brow; Moss Side Farm;
      Moss Side Farm, Higher; Moss Side Farm,
      Lower; Pyche; Spout Fold; Wharton Hall

Gable *see* Castle Farm; Cherry Tree Farm; Lower Lane
     Farm; Moor Bank Farm, barn; Moor Bank Farm;
     Spout Fold
  ghost outline *see* Castle Farm
  walls *see* Ashes; Castle Farm; Lane End Farm; Moor
     Bank Farm; Pyche
Gadbury Fold 21, 227
Garage *see* Ashes; Mayfields; Mills Brow
Garden *see* Lane End Farm; Moss Side Farm; Pyche;
     Wharton Hall; Wychenley Cottage
Garrett (hall, Tyldesley) 41
Gentry 231-4, 236, 244
  houses 234, 237
Glass
  medieval window 44, 226
  post-medieval 49-50, 213
Granary *see* Castell Henllys; Cinder Hill
Grazing activity 1, 19, 41, 232
Great Lever Hall 121-2
Great Rebuilding 232-4
Great Wickenshaw 72
Green family 124, 248
  John 124, 211
  Hargreaves 168
Green Lane 21, 58
Greenwood, Ambrose 167, 197
Grundy family 122
Gudgeon 86 (Castle House)
Guest family 93
Gully *see* Ashes; Cherry Tree Farm; Cinder Hill;
     Moss Side Farm, Higher; Pyche; Wharton
     Hall
  drip *see* Cinder Hill
Gunflint 156, 255

Haigh Field 12, 58, 146-50, 162-3, 249, 254-5
  brick wall 162-3
  cellar 162-3
  cottages 162
  drain 162
  flagstones 162
  foundation 162, 255
  hollow-way 55, 58
  Land Tax 150
  outbuilding 162
  privies 162
  window 146
Half Acre Gate 83
Halliwell family 149
Halliwells Tenement 104
Hammer (stone) 21, *see also* Prehistoric, tools
Hammer/grinding stone 24-5, 220
Handloom
  weavers 137-8, 168, 176-7, 191, 209, 251, 254
  weaving 65, 94, 168, 177, 249, 252, 254
Harrison, Ralph 147, 150
Hearth 17, 32-3, 238, *see also* Ashes; Cinder Hill;

     Hulton Heys; Mayfields; Mills Brow; Moss
     Side Farm, Higher; Wharton Hall
  reheating *see* Cinder Hill
  Tax 13, 95, 97-8, 102, 104, 123, 126, 236
Heath, Sir Robert 65
Hemyock 53
Holcombe Moor 227
Hollingworth Lake 17
Hollow-way *see* Haigh Field; Moss Side Lane
Holroyd, Joseph 176-7
Hospitaller Order of monastic knights 54, 56
House (type)
  bark 96-7
  closed 233
  double-pile 106, 234, 242-5, 247
  egg-shaped 222
  laithe 244, 248-9
  T-shaped 242
  three-cell 233, 242
  two-cell 74, 84, 97, 238, 242, 244, 247
Housebody *see* Ashes; Dixon Green Farm; Lane End
               Farm; Lower Lane Farm; Moor Bank
               Farm; Moss Side Farm, Lower; Spout
               Fold; Wharton Hall
Huddersfield 35
Huguenots 63
Hulton 1, 3, 15, 21, 33, 35, 37-8, 41-3, 95-6, 122-3, 126,
     203, 226
Hulton Heys 10, 42, 95-6, 102-3, 234
  barn 102-4
  cartshed 10, 102-3
  enclosure 102
  fence/windbreak 103
  foundation 103
  hearth 102
  outshut 102
  pond 102-3
  stable 102
  tenancy 102
Hunter-gatherer 17
Hurst family 93
Husbandmen 232, 238, 245, 247, *see also* Farmers

Industrial, residues 44, 227-8
Industrialisation 13, 137
Industry 1, 3, 63-4, 94-5, 138, 149, 204, 245
Inventory, probate 94-6, 102, 122, 126, 236
Irby 33, 221, 224-5
Iron 50-3
  bar 49, 51, 172
  blooms 48-9, 51-3, 228
  brace 180
  furnace 52, *see also* Furnace
  latch 77, 171
  ore 44, 51, 53, 228
  production 37, 50-3, 225-8, 256
  smelting 44, 50, 52, 228

shippon 165, 171-2, 254
  staircase 76, 171
  stone blocks 171
  window 73-6, 166, 170, 172
hamlet 70, 165-6, 168
Mill 9, 137
Lowhouse 54-5

Malting floor *see* Cinder Hill
Manchester 1, 2, 13, 33-5, 63, 93, 123, 139, 150, 197
Manor *see* Rochdale, manor of
Marsden 17
Massey family 41-2
Mather family 102
Mayfields 7, 12, 138, 175-83, 252, 254-5
  alcoves 180
  arris 179
  barn 175-6, 180-1, 183, 253, 255-6
    rebuilt 255
  beam 179-80, 183
  brick wall 182
  cellar 180, 252
  channel 182
  cottages 175-83, 252
    rebuilt 179, 181
  cupboards 183
  datestone 175, 177
  doorway 175, 177-9, 182-3
  drain 181
  eaves 178-9, 182-3
  façade 180, 182-3
  Farm 177
  fireplace 180
  flagstones 180, 183
  foundation 181
  garage 183
  hearth 180
  Land Tax 176
  lintel 178-9
  mullion (stone) 178-9
  outbuilding 175, 181-2, 253
  pantry 252
  porch 179
  quenching tub 183
  roof 179, 181
  staircase 180
  stone blocks 175, 179-80
  warehouse 175, 180, 182-3, 255; *see also* Mayfields,
      barn
  window 177-9, 181-3, 252, 254
  workshop 252
Meadowland 21
Medieval
  activity 37, 43, 121, 225-6, 256
  hall 43-4, 121, 226, 233, 236
  landscapes 14, 37, 53
  pottery *see* Pottery, medieval

settlement 10, 13, 38, 42, 53, 56, 66, 137, 226
  townships 38, 54-7
Mersey Basin 221, 224-5, 256
Mesolithic
  late 19, 21, 219
  microliths 17, 24-5, 220
  tools 17
Messuage *see* Ashes; Spout Fold; Wharton Hall
Metalworking, *see also* Iron-working
  at Cinder Hill 21, 32
  bronze metalworking traditions 221
  post-medieval 21, 100
  Roman 33
  slag *see* Slag
Microliths *see* Mesolithic
Middle Hulton 13, 21, 37-8, 41-3, 51, 93-6, 102, 104-5,
         113, 123, 203-5, 209, 211, 230, 245, 247
  leasehold 245, 247, *see also* Farmers; Leasehold
  tenements 42, 93
Mills Brow 8, 42, 95-7, 104-12, 232, 234, 247-8
  barn 105-6, 108
    Lancashire 110-13
      roof 111
    threshing 106, 108, 110-11, 248
  beam 113
  brick wall 113
  cellar 106, 109-11, 247
  copyhold 232
  cow house 110, 112-13
  cupboard 108
  dairy 108, 247
  doorway 106, 108, 111-13
  drain 110
  eaves 111
  fireplace 108-9
  garage 106
  hay loft 113
  hearth 104
  kitchen 108, 247
  lobby 108, 247
  mortar 106, 111
  pantry 108-9, 247
  parlour 109-10, 247
  porch 106
  roof (barrel-vaulted) 110
  shippon 105
  staircase 109-10, 247
  tenements 104
  window 105-6, 112-13
Milne family 89, 176, 245
Milnrow 1, 2, 17, 54-5, 58, 139, 150, 238
Mining 1, 3, 6, 95, 138-9, 150, 203-4, *see also* Coal mining
Moor Bank Farm 7, 12, 55, 58, 65, 88-91, 176, 196-202,
         235, 238, 240, 242, 244-5, 249
  alcoves 198, 200
  arris 91
  barn 88-9, 196-7, 199, 201, 249
    gable 197

Western Cottage 140-2, 156, 159, 161, 175, 177-80
  datestone 144, 254
  doorway 141, 143, 144, 145
  drain 67
  eaves 141, 143
  feeding passage 254
  fireplace 142
  flagstones 67, 76
  foundation 142
  housebody 68, 242
  kitchen 68, 242
  lintel 144-5
  mortar 142, 144
  outbuilding 144-5
  parlour 68, 242
  pillars 142
  porch 141
  rebuilding 140, 142, 254
  staircase 142, 145
  window 141, 143-4, 254
  workshop 141, 143-4
Moss Side Lane 9, 12, 55, 58-9, 65-6, 68, 70, 137, 146-8, 150, 165, 249
  hollow-way 66
  sunken lane/trackway 58-9, 61
Mossland 1, 19
Mossley 238
Motte-and-bailey castle *see* Castle Hill
Mowroad 19
Mullion *see also* Window
  chamfered *see* Lower Lane Farm; Moss Side Farm, Higher
  double stone *see* Castle House
  stone *see* Castle Farm; Mayfields
    slab *see* Moor Bank Farm
  saw-cut *see* Castle House; Lane End Farm

Nail (handmade) 77, *see also* Lower Lane Farm
Near Kiln Field 9
Neolithic 17-19, 21, 25, 32, 219
New Nook 17
Newbold hamlet 54-6
Niche *see* Lower Lane Farm
Norman castle 54, *see also* Castle Hill

Old English 37, 53
Oliver Fold 93-4
Orchard *see* Wharton Hall
Outbuilding *see* Castle Farm; Haigh Field; Lower Lane Farm; Mayfields; Moss Side Farm, Higher; Moss Side Farm, Lower; Moss Side Farm; Wharton Hall
Outshut *see* Castle Farm; Hulton Heys; Lower Lane Farm; Moor Bank Farm; Wharton Hall
  cellared *see* Moor Bank Farm
Oven (general) 8, 32-3
Oversley Farm 221-2, 224-5

Owl hole *see* Lower Lane Farm; Moss Side Farm; Spout Fold

Palaeochannel
  Cinder Hill 22, 24-5, 28, 32, *see also* Cinder Hill
  Wharton Hall 12, 14, 38-9, 41-2, 126, *see also* Wharton Hall
Palstave 17, *see also* Bronze Age
Pantry *see* Cherry Tree Farm; Lane End Farm; Lower Lane Farm; Mayfields; Mills Brow; Moor Bank Farm; Moss Side Farm, Higher
Parlour 233, 238, 244, *see also* Ashes; Castle Farm; Castle House; Cherry Tree Farm; Lane End Farm; Lower Lane Farm; Mills Brow; Moor Bank Farm; Moss Side Farm, Lower; Spout Fold; Wharton Hall
Partition wall *see* Castle Farm; Castle House; Mayfields; Mills Brow; Moss Side Farm, Higher; Spout Fold, barn; Wharton Hall
Peat 2, 12, 19
Peel
  Church 35
  Hall 6, 42, 95, 122-3, 126, 205, 237-8
    rebuilding 126
  Hall Colliery 205, *see also* Coal mining
Pennines
  landscape of 1
  prehistory 17, 19, 21
  post-medieval building traditions in 230
Pillars
  brick *see* Lane End Farm; Moss Side Farm, Higher; Moss Side Farm, Lower
  timber *see* Moss Side Farm
Pits
  charcoal-burning (clamp) 49, *see also* Furnace
  slag-tapping 50, 52, 226-7, *see also* Furnace
Polisher 21, *see also* Neolithic
Pollen 12, 21, 38, 41, 43, 219
Pond *see* Hulton Heys; Wharton Hall
Porch *see* Lower Lane Farm; Mayfields; Mills Brow; Moss Side Farm, Lower; Roundhouse; Spout Fold
Post *see* Roundhouse; Structure, four-post
Post-pipe *see* Roundhouse; Structure, four-post
Post-ring *see* Roundhouse
Pottery 29, 31, 33, 68, 70, 75, 100, 132, 153, 208, 225-6
  Bronze Age 28-31
  Medieval 44, 50-1, 127, 130, 227
    Northern Gritty 44, 50, 228
  Prehistoric
    Collared Urn 222
    Deverel-Rimbury type 31, 221, 225
  Post-medieval 48, 50, 100, 126, 128-9
    Blackware 69, 100, 128-9, 131
    Cistercian-ware 100, 129-30
    coarse brown-glazed red ware 128
    creamware 76, 128

sunken *see* Moss Side Farm
Roundhouse 24-8, 31-3, 222, 224, *see also* Cinder Hill
   eaves 28, 222
   porch 27-8, 224
   post 26-8, 222, 224
   post-pipe 26-8
   post-ring 26-8, 32, 222, 224
   roof 26, 28, 222, 224
Route/routeway 1, 2, 9, 35-6, 58, 65, 72, 102, 137, 139, 226, *see also* Roads; Turnpike

Saddleworth 17
Salford 1, 3, 53
Sandhole (Bridgewater) Colliery 3
Scraper 24-5, 220, *see also* Prehistoric
Seddon, Richard 113-14, 209, 247
Shakerley 1, 3, 9, 37-8, 41-3, 93-4, 96, 203
Shippon 233, 244, 248 *see also* Barn; Cherry Tree Farm; Cowshed; Lane End Farm; Lower Lane Farm; Mills Brow; Moss Side Farm; Pyche; Wharton Hall
Sir Isaac Newton Way 2, 9
Slag 44, 46, 49-53, 79, 100, 208, 226-8, *see also* Furnace; Iron-working
   bowls 51-3, 81
   cakes 51, 53
   smithing 48, 50-1
Slag-tapping process 46, *see also* Furnace; Iron-working
   channel *see* Channel, slag-tapping
Smelting 51-3, 226-7, *see also* Furnace; Iron-working
   furnaces 37, 226-8
   process 52, 226
Soak-away *see* Moss Side Farm, Higher
Soil, relict *see* Wharton Hall
Spa Clough 228-9
Spinners 176-7
   woollen 149, 176-7
Spinning 64, 137, 177, 244, 252, 254
Spotland township 55
Spout Fold 8, 95, 97, 104, 113-21, 209-11, 232, 234, 247-8
   barn 113, 209
      Lancashire 117-21, 248
      threshing 113, 117, 121, 248
   brick wall 119, 209
   cart entrance 117, 121
   copyhold 232
   cow house 117
   doorway 114, 119, 211, 247
   eaves 119
   expansion 248
   farm 114-21
   fireplace 117
   gable 119
   hay loft 119
   housebody 117, 247
   kitchen 211
   later additions to farmhouse 209-10

lobby (baffle-style) 117, 247
messuage 209
mortar 114, 117
owl hole 119
parlour 247
porch 211
roof 117, 119, 211
staircase 114, 117, 247
tenements 113
window 114, 117, 211
Statue, silver 35
St George's Foundry 140, 150
Stables *see* Hulton Heys; Moor Bank Farm
Stainton West 25
Staircase *see* Castle Farm; Lower Lane Farm; Mayfields; Mills Brow; Moor Bank Farm; Moss Side Farm, Higher; Moss Side Farm, Lower; Spout Fold
Stanlaw Abbey 56
Stanley
   family 230
   Grange 48
Stanney
   Brook 1, 9, 54-5, 58, 61, 65-6, 68
   Street 33
Stephenson Scale 224
Stone
   blocks *see* Castle House; Cherry Tree Farm; Lower Lane Farm; Mayfields; Moss Side Farm, Higher;
   dressed *see* Moss Side Farm; Pyche
   sandstone *see* Wharton Hall
   burnt 29
   carved head 19, 21
   mason-dressed 86
   slabs 98-9, 201
   stack 236, 238, 240, 245
Street Gate 33
Structure, four-post *see* Bronze Age
Sunken lane/trackway *see* Moss Side Lane
Survey
   geophysical 8, 21, 25
   photographic 7-9, 58
   standing building 13-14

Tan Pit Croft 97
Tanning 96-7, 247
Tapping, *see also* Furnace
   arch 226, 228
   channel 48
   pit 44, 46, 48, 50, 52, 226-8
Tatton Park 222
Taylor family 147-8, 167, 177
   Edmund 147-8, 167
   James 73, 148, 167, 177
   Joseph 167, 188
   Thomas 176
Tenancy *see* Ashes; Hulton Heys